FEDERAL WHEAT COMMODITY PROGRAMS

FEDERAL WHEAT COMMODITY PROGRAMS

Don F. Hadwiger

THE IOWA STATE UNIVERSITY PRESS / AMES

DON F. HADWIGER, professor of political science at Iowa State University, has been on leave as coordinator of the Washington, D.C., policy studies for Atlanta University Center for the 1969–70 year. He formerly taught at Southwest Missouri State College and was a Congressional Fellow with the American Political Science Association and a USDA outside scholar. He received degrees from University of Oklahoma (B.A., 1953), University of Nebraska (M.A., 1954), and University of Iowa (Ph.D., 1956). Hadwiger is coauthor with Ross Talbot of *Pressures and Protests: The Kennedy Farm Program and the Wheat Referendum of 1963* and *The Policy Process in American Agriculture.*

© 1970 The Iowa State University Press, Ames, Iowa 50010. All rights reserved. Composed and printed by The Iowa State University Press. First edition, 1970. Standard Book Number: 8138–0630–5. Library of Congress Catalog Number: 72–92693.

TABLE OF CONTENTS

PREFACE

THIS HISTORY of federal policy dealing with the production and use of wheat in general seeks to answer three questions. Where did the policy come from? What was the policy? What was its effect?

Existing farm policy studies have examined a particular time period, a particular program, an organization or individual, or the economic aspects of a series of decisions. This study is less ambitious than most in being confined to a single commodity. It is more ambitious in seeking to discuss both the political and economic aspects of commodity policy during half a century.

The plan has been to integrate political and economic analyses by following the thread of policy for a particular commodity. In interpreting economics data, I have relied on available analyses by economists, trying to reconcile those economic analyses where possible. I have tried equally to respect and to rely on applicable studies by historians, political scientists, and natural scientists. It has seemed logical to treat more briefly those subjects on which comprehensive analyses are available and to analyze somewhat more extensively those subjects (such as the Benson policies) requiring original treatment.

The theory or basis for organization is not rigorous or complicated. It is stated below as a number of assumptions.

❖ The integrity or uniqueness of "wheat policies" (in the sense of patterns of rules) may derive from the search for a particular objective,
from a historical period, from an administration, or from some other
source. These policies have been delineated by other authors in different ways.[1]

As outlined here, each policy is the subject matter for a chapter:

Reserve levels of wheat. A survey of policies with respect to the
level of reserve stocks of wheat, such as the ever-normal granary, is an
appropriate context in which to present the entire chronology of domestic policy (Chapter 2). At the same time the policy during periods
of domestic wheat scarcity will be discussed.

Export policies. Efforts to expand and stabilize wheat exports will
be seen in overview (Chapter 3).

The two-price plans, particularly the McNary-Haugen Plan of the
1920's (Chapter 4).

Cooperative marketing, as embodied in the Agricultural Marketing Act of 1929 (Chapter 5).

The domestic allotment plan, included in the Agricultural Adjustment Act of 1933 (Chapter 6).

Price supports and mandatory controls as authorized in the Agricultural Adjustment Act of 1938 (Chapter 7).

Flexible price support proposals since 1933, particularly as enacted
and implemented under the Agricultural Act of 1954 (Chapter 8).

The soil bank or conservation-oriented measures passed in 1936
and in 1956 (Chapter 9).

The Freeman measures, concentrating upon the marketing certificate program (Chapter 10).

The management of government stocks (Chapter 11). Like Chapters 2 and 3, Chapters 11, 12, and 13 follow a dimensional rather than
a chronological delineation.

The distribution of producer benefits (Chapter 12).

Food aid programs designed to dispose of wheat surpluses (Chapter 13).

❖ Policy is in response to a situation. Within each of the policy chapters is a discussion of the unique aspects of the situation in which the
policy was enacted and implemented. The situation in general is dis-

---

1. Compare, for example, Don Paarlberg, *American Farm Policy* (New York:
Wiley, 1964), and Dale E. Hathaway, *Government and Agriculture* (New York:
Macmillan, 1963).

cussed in Chapter 1, which deals with wheat culture and organization of the wheat economy.

❖ Policy is usually initiated by an agency, group, or coalition of groups, the objectives of which can be stated. The objective may be enactment of legislation or some other end which involves a legislative decision.

❖ The initiating group has a plan of action either in the form of a grand strategy or more likely several strategies for achieving the objectives. It has seemed appropriate sometimes to distinguish between types of strategies designed basically to capitalize on a situation in contrast to those designed as strategics to gain policy leadership, and between strategies designed to pass legislation contrasted to the legislative mechanisms designed to achieve policy goals.

❖ One process of decision making culminates in legislation. This process is described, and the policy is outlined. Some technical provisions in the policy may be treated separately, as for example provisions for increasing farm income or provisions for production control. Chapter 12 is devoted to the consideration of the complex and technical provisions which affect the distribution of benefits under wheat programs.

❖ The policy has a number of significant results or effects, including cost to government, effect upon wheat producers' incomes, and effect upon the supply of wheat.

❖ A number of involved groups took positions with respect to policy proposals and exercised some influence upon the decision. Their positions and influence are described.

The final chapter summarizes, and provides further interpretation of, the policies outlined in the book.

This publication has been written for several audiences. It is intended for policy makers, particularly for those who have not "lived through it all." It is clear that frequently there has been a partial repetition of situations and policies and furthermore that a knowledge of the history and details of wheat policy has been almost a prerequisite for those who would influence it.

It is hoped the publication will be of interest to the "old hands" as well, since it is from the perspective of a nonparticipant.

The publication is also intended for fellow social scientists, both as descriptive of policy and illustrative of policy making. In the hope of increasing its usefulness as a reference book, considerable effort has been devoted to references and index.

The publication is offered to everyone interested in federal farm policy.

ACKNOWLEDGMENTS

IN 1965 I was invited to spend a year as a research scholar in the U.S. Department of Agriculture to write a history of federal wheat commodity policy. I gladly accepted this invitation, which was extended with the understanding that I alone was responsible for the accuracy, objectivity, and quality of the work.

This project, I believe, is in the tradition of the USDA's broad-ranging search for knowledge. In past eras our farmers' department has been a pacesetter among government agencies in its efforts to deepen self-awareness of bureaucratic processes, and to seek better ways of relating to its clients. Philosopher, social reformer, pioneer of new techniques for data gathering and analysis, the Department of Agriculture generates lively intellectual pursuits even though these occasionally suffer severe curtailment.

The USDA's Economic Research Service and some of its other agencies develop capable and imaginative research teams, and in virtually every USDA administration a few top-ranking social scientists have proved their versatility as policy makers. Economist John Schnittker, undersecretary from 1965 to 1968, exemplified the component qualities of professional scholar, humanist, and successful political negotiator. Schnittker's earlier survey of wheat commodity policy may have given rise to the decision to undertake a comprehensive history. No doubt it was hoped such a history would capture much useful information for the record and that it could serve to broaden the perspective of current and future policy makers. It is hoped the example of this history of wheat policy will encourage the writing of histories of other public policies.

I found a friendly and stimulating environment in the USDA, and my colleagues were generous and indeed forbearing in their response to many requests for assistance. I am especially indebted to William Askew, Victor Vaughn, Lyle Schertz, George Robbins, Reed Phillips, and Frank Gomme, and also to my associates in the USDA's Agriculture History Branch, particularly Wayne Rasmussen, Gladys Baker, and Jane Porter, who were obliged to respond every day to my requests for advice and direction. Dr. Baker, who read the entire manuscript, discovered and corrected numerous errors. Other persons read individual chapters and were helpful in the same manner. To all these admirable people I express appreciation.

Information on which this study is based was obtained in large part from sources in the National Agriculture Library, USDA. The expert and dedicated staff of the library lent me much assistance and also provided space for me to study.

I am also appreciative of the support of the Iowa Agricultural Experiment Station, which permitted me the necessary research time in which to perfect a final draft, and which also paid the costs of typing the manuscript. The typing was beautifully done by Mrs. Edna Henry, Mrs. Carolyn Robinson, and Mrs. Carol Hansen.

Published material from several sources has been made available by copyright holders and reproduced with their kind permission: Houghton Mifflin Company, page 6; Wiley Publishing Co., page 173; Doubleday and Company, Inc., pages 172, 178; Oxford University Press, pages 3, 329; Cornell University Press, page 337; The Eagleton Institute of Politics, Rutgers University, page 353; University of Oklahoma Press, page 96; and the Stanford Food Research Institute.

TO   ELLEN

FEDERAL WHEAT COMMODITY PROGRAMS

1 / THE WHEAT CULTURE

WHEAT, and its product bread, is the Western metaphor for food—that which sustains human life. Wheat, the staff of life, is also a determinant of culture now as in the past.

Wheat became and remained the staple food in the diets of Europeans despite centuries of competition with potatoes, rye, and other cereal grains. It became part of the traditional diet in North America, India, China, and in its apparent birthplace—the Middle Eastern countries of North Africa, Persia, and Turkey.

Wheat can be produced on almost any land fit for cultivation. As Paul de Hevesy said, "Wheat and men have it in common that they can endure almost every climate."[1] Mainly during the first two decades of the present century wheat acreage expanded into the semiarid areas of the world: into the American and Canadian plains, the Argentine Pampas, the continental peripheries of Australia, and the drylands of Asia. The twentieth-century pattern of world wheat production is

---

1. *World Wheat Planning and Economic Planning in General* (London: Oxford Univ. Press, 1940), p. 33.

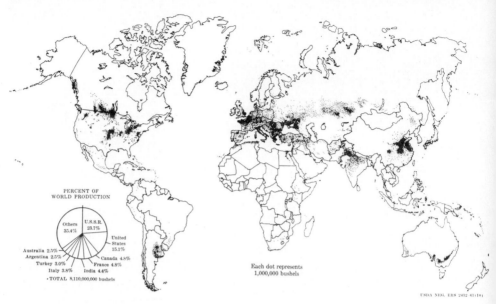

FIG. 1.1. World wheat production, average 1957–61.
Source: ERS-USDA.

portrayed in Figure 1.1. As a food, wheat made inroads on the "rice crescent" of Southeast Asia, where a majority of the world's population has always lived.

In the United States wheat had always followed the frontier as the easy-to-raise, easily transportable, principal income crop of the pioneers. This adaptable crop was as helpful as the river and railroad in facilitating settlement of the continent. The pursuit of wheat as the frontier crop became the excuse used by the restless pioneers who could not resist the impulse to skip westward from one frontier claim to another. Author Hamlin Garland, whose father moved the family from Wisconsin to Iowa and then to the Dakotas, described the frontier fever as it had infected an Iowa community in the midst of drought:

> The movement of settlers toward Dakota had now become an exodus, a stampede. Hardly anything else was talked about as neighbors met one another on the road or at the Burr Oak schoolhouse on Sundays. Every man who could sell out had gone west or was going. In vain did the county papers and Farmer's Institute lecturers advise cattle raising and plead for diversified tillage, predicting wealth for those who held on; farmer after farmer joined the march to Kansas,

Nebraska, and Dakota. "We are wheat raisers," they said, "and we intend to keep in the wheat belt."[2]

Wheat, the basic crop, was indeed a center of attention in those frontier communities. Garland reminisced:

> As I look back over my life on that Iowa farm the song of the reaper fills a large place in my mind. We were all worshippers of wheat in those days. The men thought and talked of little else between seeding and harvest, and you will not wonder at this if you have known and bowed down before such abundance as we then enjoyed.
>
> Deep as the breast of a man, wide as the sea, heavy-headed, supple-stocked, many-voiced, full of multitudinous, secret, whispered colloquies —a meeting place of winds and of sunlight—our fields ran to the world's end.[3]

Supporting the frontier spirit, as generators of westward movement, were pressures of massive European immigration and industrial unemployment during depressions and the incentive of inexpensive or free land granted both to the enterprising railroads and to the settlers.[4] "Golden periods" of good weather on the Plains which produced successive abundant crops created an environment of optimism about the soil and the area. At such times "increased cultivation was an almost inevitable consequence."[5]

THE FRONTIER CROP

Indeed little else but wheat could be cropped on the arid frontier, so wheat was produced even though it was a bargain-counter item on the world market throughout the main period of migration.[6]

The Plains culture was in some respects a harsh one. Frontier farmers had never suffered anything more traumatic than the physical and climatic extremes—and the sense of physical isolation from other

---

2. *A Son of the Middle Border* (New York: Macmillan, 1917, 1962), p. 197.
3. Ibid., p. 125.
4. Wilfred Malenbaum found that the periods of rapid wheat acreage expansion in Canada, Argentina, the United States, and Australia followed in the wake of railway development, peaks in immigration, and waves of internal migration. See Malenbaum, *The World Wheat Economy, 1885 1939* (Cambridge, Mass.: Harvard Univ. Press, 1953), p. 129.
5. John A. Schnittker, *Wheat Problems and Programs in the United States*, North Central Reg. Publ. 118, Univ. of Missouri (1960), p. 23.
6. Robert Post, retired USDA wheat specialist, suggested to the author in 1965 that there remains a large area in the United States in which producers will choose to grow wheat with almost no regard for the economic circumstances.

humans—to which they were exposed on the Plains. Presented to them, however, were many scenes of overwhelming grandeur—the expansive seas of wheat or grass, the ominous cloud horizons, and skies full of storm or full of blue. Garland observed one such striking scene as he first approached his family's Dakota homestead:

> For the first time I set foot upon a landscape without a tree to break its sere expanse. . . . There was beauty in this plain, delicate beauty and a weird charm, despite its lack of undulation. Its lonely unplowed sweep gave me the satisfying sensation of being at last among the men who held the outposts—sentinels for the marching millions who were approaching from the east.[7]

This land of extremes had an enormous capacity to frustrate human aspirations. Even the able and industrious father in Willa Cather's novel *O Pioneers!* had to admit failure at the end of his Nebraska sojourn:

> In eleven long years John Bergson had made but little impression upon the wild land he had come to tame. It was still a wild thing that had its ugly moods; and no one knew when they were likely to come, or why. Mischance hung over it. Its Genius was unfriendly to man. . . . There it lay outside his door, the same land, the same lead-colored miles. He knew every ridge and draw and gully between him and the horizon. To the south, his plowed fields; to the east, the sod stables, the cattle corral, the pond—and then the grass.
>
> Bergson went over in his mind the things that had held him back. One winter his cattle perished in a blizzard. The next summer one of his plow horses broke its leg in a prairie-dog hole and had to be shot. Another summer he lost his hogs from cholera, and a valuable stallion died from a rattlesnake bite. Time and again his crops had failed. He had lost two children, boys, that came between Lou and Emil, and there had been the cost of sickness and death. Now, when he had at last struggled out of debt, he was going to die himself. He was only forty-six, and had, of course, counted upon more time.[8]

"The Great Plain drinks the blood of Christian men and is satisfied," wrote O. E. Rolvaag in his novel *Giants in the Earth.* Women rather than men, however, were the more pitiful victims of the Plains. "Out here nobody pays attention to our tears . . . it's too open and wild,"[9] said Rolvaag's tragic Beret, who suffered insanity in a Dakota sod house.

Garland concluded in "The Farmer's Wife":

---

7. *A Son of the Middle Border,* p. 207.
8. (Boston: Houghton Mifflin, 1913 and 1941), pp. 10–11.
9. Perennial Classic ed. (New York: Harper, 1927 and 1955), p. 413.

> Born an' scrubbed, suffered and died.
> That's all you need to say, elder
>   Never mind sayin' "made a bride,"
> Nor when her hair got gray.
>   Jes' say, "Born 'n worked t' death":
> That fits it—save y'r breath.[10]

In the life style of the Plains, youth was but a brief moment, according to a few great writers who emerged from the region.[11] Descendants of the pioneers ultimately suffered the same dreary lives as their fathers but without the redeeming heroics of the frontier.

> Evening and the flat land,
> Rich and sombre and always silent;
> The miles of fresh-plowed soil,
> Heavy and black, full of strength and harshness;
> The growing wheat, the growing weeds,
> The toiling horses, the tired men;
> The long empty roads,
> Sullen first of sunset fading,
> The eternal, unresponsive sky.
> Against all this, Youth.
> Flaming like the wild roses,
> Singing like the larks over the plowed fields,
> Flashing like a star out of the twilight;
> Youth with its unsupportable sweetness,
> Its fierce necessity,
> Its sharp desire,
> Singing and singing,
> Out of the lips of silence,
> Out of the earthy dusk.[12]

Hamlin Garland tried to rescue his sister from the "sterile environment" of a "barren farm" so that she might not have to "live and die the wife of some Dakota farmer."[13] Miss Cather bemoaned the fate of those who chose to stay in the avaricious small-town communities of the Plains.[14] But life on the Plains, whatever its quality, became comfortable—and even luxurious during the good years—for those farmers who took full advantage of the opportunity to mechanize and to specialize in wheat production.

---

10. Life on the Argentine wheat ranchos was equally grim, as described by James R. Scobie, *Revolution on the Pampas* (Austin: Univ. of Texas Press, 1964), ch. 4.
11. "Literature of the Great Plains," in Walter Prescott Webb, *The Great Plains* (Boston: Ginn and Company, 1931).
12. "Prairie Spring," introduction to *O Pioneers!*
13. *A Son of the Middle Border*, p. 339.
14. "The Sculptor's Funeral," in Scully Bradley, Richard Croom Beatty, and E. Hudson Long, eds., *The American Tradition in Literature, Revised* (New York: W. W. Norton, 1962), pp. 1330–32.

TABLE 1.1. Ten leading wheat-producing states in 1879 and 1965

State	Percent of U.S. wheat production in 1879	State	Percent of U.S. wheat production (avg. 1960–65)
Illinois	11.1	Kansas	19.3
Indiana	10.3	North Dakota	10.99
Ohio	10.0	Oklahoma	6.18
Michigan	7.7	Montana	5.88
Minnesota	7.5	Washington	5.85
Iowa	6.8	Nebraska	5.58
California	6.3	Texas	5.2
Missouri	5.4	Illinois	4.77
Wisconsin	5.4	Indiana	3.67
Pennsylvania	4.2	Ohio	3.67

Source: Percentages for 1879 were obtained from Louis Bernard Schmidt, "The Westward Movement of the Wheat Growing Industry in the United States," *Iowa Journal of History and Politics* (July 1920), pp. 396–412.

THE PLAINS ECONOMY

Wheat found its home on this last frontier of the United States. It became the basis of a one-crop culture in the Great Plains and in the rolling Palouse area of Oregon and Washington.

In the United States the desire for greater farm efficiency led to publicly supported production research activities, results of which raised yields and increased the area where wheat could be efficiently grown. Wheat expanded permanently onto the Plains (Table 1.1), aided by the development of new seed varieties for arid climates and the development of techniques and machinery for dryland farming.[15] In 1930 Alonzo E. Taylor explained that the increase of U.S. wheat acres in the previous decade was a result primarily of the development and use of the motorized tractor.[16]

Today the bulk of wheat production (in 1956, 60 percent of total U.S. production and 73 percent of the wheat acreage) is found in a region covering much of western Texas, Oklahoma and Nebraska, most of Kansas and North Dakota, and eastern Colorado (Fig. 1.2).

A second smaller wheat belt is located in the rolling Palouse and the Columbia Basin in eastern Washington and stretches into Idaho and Oregon; it contained 8 percent of the acreage and 16 percent of the production in 1956. Of the remaining production (24 percent in 1956), most is scattered through the midwestern and eastern states. While wheat was capturing the drylands it was losing out to corn in the subhumid areas where precipitation was adequate to raise corn,

15. Malenbaum, *World Wheat Economy*, pp. 39–43.
16. "The Contractility of Wheat Acreage in the United States," *Wheat Studies of the Stanford Food Research Institute*, 6(February 1930):171–76.

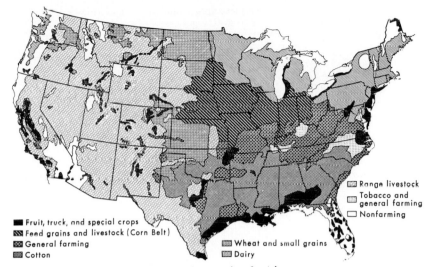

FIG. 1.2.   The Wheat Belt and other major farming areas.
Source: *1959 U.S. Census of Agriculture.*

and it was usually replaced by alternative crops on drylands developed
for irrigation. Cotton was usually preferred over wheat in southern
Plains areas where the summer season is adequately long.

Some alternative or complementary farm products have inter-
penetrated the Plains wheat areas. Beef cattle have been raised on the
intermittent range lands on the arid western edge of the Plains, and
cattle have typically been grazed on the winter wheat during its winter
and early spring growth. Feedlots have grown up in the Wheat Belt
to supply the huge markets for meat both in eastern and western
population centers. There has been some truck farming on irrigated
tracts.

Communities in the arid Plains have recently manifested much
interest in industrialization. In a few large cities such as Wichita,
Kansas, considerable industrial growth has taken place. The increase
in total expenditures for plant and equipment in Kansas during the
1950s was proportionately greater than for the United States as a
whole.[17] Yet opportunities for diversification have been less eagerly
sought than were opportunities for fortifying the one-crop specialization. Wheat has remained a principal export from the region and a
major generator of income (Table 1.2). As a result of this specialization in wheat, however, the Wheat Belt economy has been extremely
unstable.

---

17. *1958 U.S. Census of Manufactures,* vol. 1, sec. 5, table 4, p. 14.

TABLE 1.2. Percentage of total cash receipts from farm marketings of wheat, by selected states, 1959

State	Percentage
North Dakota	36.6
Kansas	33.7
Montana	33.4
Oklahoma	24.7
Washington	22.8
Colorado	14.4
Idaho	16.2
Oregon	12.4
Nebraska	10.5

Source: *Wheat and the National Economy,* USDA (September 1960); reprinted in *Congressional Record* (bound), Aug. 29, 1960, p. 18119.

The wheat farms and towns have experienced severe stress under the whip-cracking swings of yield and price. Formerly wheat prices were the most variable of any major national commodity, and wheat yields have continued to be the least certain (Figs. 1.3–1.4). The farm and town economy of the Plains has collapsed periodically as a result

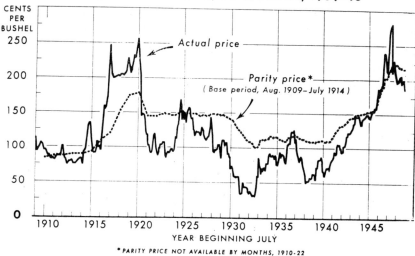

WHEAT: PRICE RECEIVED BY FARMERS AND PARITY PRICE, UNITED STATES, BY MONTHS, 1909-48

* PARITY PRICE NOT AVAILABLE BY MONTHS, 1910-22

FIG. 1.3. Income instability in the wheat economy. The Plains economy, as a one-crop economy, has often been depressed by severe and persisting declines in the price of wheat. As shown in the graph, the market price (solid line) remained below parity from 1921 to 1924 and for almost a decade after 1925.

Source: *Wheat Situation,* USDA (July 1949).

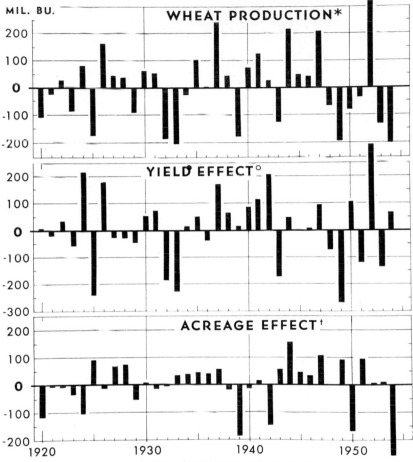

ACREAGE AND YIELD EFFECTS ON WHEAT PRODUCTION

WHEAT PRODUCTION*

YIELD EFFECT°

ACREAGE EFFECT†

*CHANGE FROM PRECEDING YEAR.   °CHANGE IN YIELD TIMES ACREAGE IN PRECEDING YEAR
†CHANGE IN ACREAGE TIMES YIELD IN PRECEDING YEAR.

U. S. DEPARTMENT OF AGRICULTURE   NEG. 1352–55 (1)   AGRICULTURAL MARKETING SERVICE

FIG. 1.4. Variability of wheat production. Fig. 1.3 suggested the effect of price instability upon the wheat economy. Wheat farm income is also affected by the amount of production, which has been similarly unstable. In 1932, for example, when market prices would not cover costs of production even assuming a normal yield, the yield was in fact far below normal. In such periods of low prices and low production, the Plains economy collapsed. Many Plains residents were not able to endure this type of double-barreled catastrophe.
Source: S. E. Crumb, *The Larvae of the Phalaenidae*, USDA Tech. Bull. 1136, fig. 8.

of falling prices and/or failing crops. Recurrent economic distress, along with physical isolation, ethnic attachments, and other factors, have made the Plains a seasonal home of American radicalism. The Populist Party, America's unique response to the evils of industrialism, was largely a Wheat Belt phenomenon, as was the Nonpartisan League which socialized the Dakotas. Kansas provided the U.S. Socialist Party with its largest presidential vote (in 1912), and Kansas has also been a stronghold of radical right-wing groups. The "radical" farm organization, National Farmers Union, is largely a wheat organization, and the Plains units of the American Farm Bureau Federation have been among the radical-conservative elements within that organization.

Specialization in wheat has presumably been of direct benefit to producers and landowners (who together constitute a fairly large segment of the Kansas population). Other groups share in the distribution of these benefits indirectly, and the resulting distribution of income among occupations is about the same as in the United States (Table 1.3). The wage for hired labor, however, seems extremely low. One reason for the low average wage is that employment was seasonal, and work seasons have been getting shorter.

Wheat specialization, along with the automobile and hard-surfaced roads, has contributed to the demise of small towns. Wheat

TABLE 1.3. Median earnings in 1959 of selected occupation groups (male) in the United States and in the Wheat Belt

Occupation groups	United States	North Dakota	Kansas	Four Washington wheat counties[a]
	(dollars)			
Professional, managerial, and kindred	6,640	5,611	6,175	5,911
Farmers, farm managers	2,136	2,762	2,594	6,163
Craftsmen, foremen, kindred	5,240	4,208	4,953	5,039
Operatives, kindred	4,282	3,571	4,391	3,906
Farm laborers, except unpaid and foremen	1,107	1,100	1,257	2,311
Laborers, except farm and mine	2,940	2,540	3,001	2,583

Source: *1960 U.S. Census of Population*, vol. 1: United States, part 1, table 98; North Dakota, part 36, table 68; Kansas, part 18, table 68; Washington, part 49, table 86.

a. Adams, Lincoln, Walla Walla, Whitman.

TABLE 1.4. Population change in cities and towns of south central Kansas, 1950–60

Size classes	Number	Change in population, 1950–60				
		Loss of 10% or more	Loss of 1 to 10%	No change	Gain of 1 to 10%	Gain of 10% or more
Under 250[a]	33	19	4	2	4	4
250–999	28	6	8	0	5	9
1,000–2,499	14	0	2	0	4	8
2,500–4,999[b]	7	0	1	0	4	2
5,000 and over	6	0	0	0	1	5
Total	88	25	15	2	18	28

Source: *Area Development: Inter-Disciplinary Approach to Research,* Kansas Agr. Exp. Sta. Bull. 440 (October 1961), p. 31.

a. Change not reported on two towns under 250.
b. Includes one town reporting in two counties.

technology has rapidly reduced labor needs, depleting the trade community. As a result of farm consolidation some farmers have had high incomes, but these higher-income farmers have tended to bypass the small-town businessmen.[18] In one study the conclusion was implicit that for the average small-town business, the customer base had declined past "the critical level." By living off his capital, the small-town businessman might linger on for a few years. Between 1957 and 1964, however, almost a third of the businesses had shut down in the "typical" small town.[19]

The smaller wheat towns have been in decline for two decades, during which time many have all but disappeared, some even in areas proximate to an industrial center (Table 1.4). Other towns have subsisted by gathering in the residents of surrounding farms and dying towns.

To illustrate the changing position of small towns within the wheat economy: In North Dakota in 1959 there were 358 villages, towns, and cities, of which 336 had populations of less than 2,000. Many of these smaller towns had lost population. The twelve North Dakota cities with more than 5,000 people had grown by an average of 35 percent during the decade. As of 1959 one-third of the population of North Dakota lived in these twelve cities; one-fourth lived in places of less than 2,500; about 40 percent of the population still lived on the farm.[20]

18. R. D. McKinney and Sandra Dawe, *Changes in a Southcentral Kansas Trade Area, 1937–1960,* Kansas Agr. Exp. Sta. Tech. Bull. 143 (November 1965), p. 15.
19. Ibid., pp. 13–15.
20. *1960 U.S. Census of Population,* vol. 1, part 36, table 3, p. 10.

Retrenchment in the small towns has been continuous though not rapid. The populations of some towns have grown by virtue of the fact that commercial farmers are moving in from the farms. The towns have gained support from an occasional military installation, state institution, or an extraction industry, and by the residence of seasonal or daily commuters to metropolitan areas. In small wheat towns, one or more businesses have often expanded beyond the traditional trade area by offering better prices or service than can be found in the surrounding towns. Attracted by these small-town specialities, customers may shop regularly in several towns, just as a suburbanite travels from one shopping center to another.

On the state level the continuing farm population decline has been offset somewhat by metropolitan and industrial growth. In Kansas, for example, the compensating growth of Wichita, Kansas City, and other cities is projected to result in a net population growth for the state of somewhat over .5 percent per year through 1985.[21]

The move toward an industrial base has been a tardy and relatively slight concession to urgings by outside experts over the past four decades. Occasional regional studies have all recommended a shift to a more diversified Plains economy. (See Chapter 9.)

The unstable one-crop economy probably helps explain the political strength of the Plains region. Help from government is often needed, and regional slumps have gained national sympathy even in the absence of national economic consequences—especially when the distress symptoms were awesome dust clouds.

In addition, the Plains Wheat Belt had fairly effective political representation. Legislators could be single-minded in their objectives, and they benefited somewhat from the method of distributing U.S. Senate seats. The nine states listed in Table 1.2 had only 7.4 percent of the population but 18 percent of the U.S. Senate seats. Furthermore, whenever wheat income was reduced or jeopardized, at least nine governors and state legislators were likely to become concerned, as were federated units from these states within the national farm organizations.

This concentration of political resources in support of wheat bore fruit in federal programs which stabilized and supported the price of wheat. These programs included substantial insurance features which made drought periods far more bearable for the region than previously. Stability through federal policy proved to be a feasible objective, whereas stability through diversification did not.

---

21. "Projections of Population by States," *U.S. Census Population Estimates,* no. 326 (Feb. 7, 1966), table 3, p. 25.

THE ORGANIZATION OF WHEAT FARMS, AND TRENDS

The Plains Wheat Belt was the last major farming area to be settled, the main period of settlement being between 1870 and 1910.[22] Despite the fact that wheat was, even then, a crop requiring extensive acreage, most of the land was acquired originally in lots of 160 acres per family, following the old rule of the Homestead Act of 1862. The exceptions occurred through special legislation applying to irrigable land and to rangeland in Montana, Nebraska, Wyoming, and Colorado.

Most settlers, who came from more humid farming areas of the United States or Europe, brought with them a pattern of farming suited to 160-acre farms but not well suited to the arid Plains. With the development of extensive farming techniques and specialized wheat farming in the 1890s, farms began to expand. At first, expansion occurred through purchase at low prices of land held by speculators or by those giving up farming, or through purchase of land within the public domain. After 1940, however, farmers were more likely to secure additional acreage by renting it from the owners.

During three-quarters of a century, the average size of farms in the wheat regions has expanded greatly, although no more dramatically in any one period than the growth in average national farm size (Table 1.5). These averages, however, obscure the fact that most wheat today is produced on farms several times the size of the original 160-acre homesteads (Table 1.6).

There have always been some large wheat farms. Even before mechanization there were rather cumbersome operations organized into subunits (which were later made into individual farms) in California, the Northwest, and the North Plains. With mechanization it became efficient for one family containing several adults to operate a farm of over 1,000 acres. Today large farms are generally more efficient than small farms, although presently efficiency per unit does not tend to increase beyond a certain point.

The minimum acreage of cropland for a wheat farm that can achieve economies of scale varies somewhat, depending on such factors as soil fertility, climate, region, and on the commodities with which the wheat operation is combined. In most of the commercial wheat area feed grains and beef provide a secondary source of employment and income, and Southern Plains farmers may raise both cotton and

22. A short history of the conditions of land settlement is found in Warren R. Bailey, "The Great Plains in Retrospect with a View to the Future," *J. Farm Econ.*, 45(December 1963):1092–1100.

TABLE 1.5. Growth in size of wheat farms

Location	1910	1920	Average size in acres 1930	1940	1950	1955	1959
All farms in United States[a]	...	148.5	157.3	174.3	215.8	...	302.8
Spring wheat region[b]	371	437	500	500	633	689	...
Pacific Northwest (western)[b]	453	509	...	329	629	677	...
(eastern)[b]	682	727	...	1,134	1,318	1,393	...
All cropland harvested[c]	379	399	...	482	593	666	...
North Dakota	...	...	276.0	215.8	322.9	...	367.6
Kansas	...	...	152.9	124.6	182.3	...	216.9

Sources:
a. *1959 U.S. Census of Agriculture*, vol. 2, General Report, p. 369.
b. Charles W. Hauheim, Warren R. Bailey, and Della E. Merrick, *Wheat Production: Problems, Programs, Opportunities for Adjustment*, ARS-USDA Info. Bull. 179, table 1.
c. *1959 U.S. Census of Agriculture*, vol. 1, parts 18, 21, state table 2.

TABLE 1.6. Increasing importance of large farms, as reflected in acres of cropland harvested, 1925–59

Year	Cropland harvested in North Dakota on farms of 1,000 acres or more	All cropland harvested
	(acres)	
1925	2,135,118	19,877,232
1930	2,432,677	21,254,660
1935	1,376,428	9,348,482
1940	3,186,168	15,536,632
1945	5,645,269	20,816,814
1950	5,645,269	20,342,560
1954	6,755,265	21,241,135
1959	7,382,947	19,485,204

Source: *1959 U.S. Census of Agriculture*, vol. 1, part 18, state table 2.

wheat. However wheat equipment and tillage practices are similar throughout the wheat areas.

Various studies indicate that per acre returns are maximized in the summer fallow areas[23] at the point where the cropland equals about 1,000 acres or more, and in areas of annual cropping where crop-

23. The more arid areas in which cropland lies idle every other year while gathering moisture for the next crop. Thus only about half the cropland acreage is available for planting each year.

TABLE 1.7. Acres of major enterprise needed for annual operator earnings of $3,500

Region	Acres required
North Central Montana	760 acres wheat
Washington Palouse area	261 acres wheat
Northwest Kansas	304 acres wheat
	308 acres grain sorghum
Oklahoma Rolling Plains	441 acres cotton
	591 acres wheat

Source: Adapted from *Resource Requirements on Farms for Specified Operator Incomes,* USDA Agr. Econ. Rept. 5 (1964), table 1.

land is somewhat over 300 acres.[24] All research thus suggests that farms with less than 300 acres of annual harvested crops do not achieve maximum efficiency per unit.

It is likely that most wheat farms still harvest fewer than 300 acres of crops annually. Using data from the *1954 U.S. Census of Agriculture,* one study indicated that while there are fewer small or inadequate farms in the wheat areas than elsewhere, nevertheless 60 percent of the Plains farms had less than 500 total acres—an average of less than 250 acres of cropland.[25] Therefore it may be concluded that at least half of the wheat farmers had farms of a size which would not maximize economies of scale.

The size of the large farms apparently has not grown as fast as average farm size. There have been and perhaps still are impediments to further growth beyond a certain point, some of which have been revealed in reduced per unit income levels.[26]

Another criterion for minimum size of farm additional to economies of scale is the level of income needed to support the farmer's family. One study suggested the required size in each region assuming that $3,500 in net income is a minimum level per family (Table 1.7).

Small or inadequate-sized farms have continued to exist for various reasons. A few small farms have been simply new enterprises. Young men have often begun farming on the inadequate holdings of

24. See the following: Henry H. Stippler and Emery N. Castle, *Wheat Farming in the Columbia Basin of Oregon,* Oregon Exp. Sta. Bull. 578 (March 1961), p. 10; Gordon E. Rodewald, Jr., Donald K. Larson, and D. C. Myrick, *Dryland Grain Farms in Montana,* Montana Agr. Exp. Sta. Tech. Bull. 579 (July 1963), p. 25; E. A. Tucker and O'dell L. Walker, *Adjustments in North Central Oklahoma Wheat Farms,* Oklahoma Agr. Exp. Sta. Bull. B-523 (March 1959), table 1; and James S. Plaxico and Daniel Capstick, *Optimum Wheat-Beef Farming Systems in North Central Oklahoma,* Oklahoma Agr. Exp. Sta. Bull. B-532 (August 1959), p. 14.
25. Howard L. Hill, "Farm Size and Land Use in the Great Plains," *Farming in the Great Plains,* ARS-USDA Prod. Res. Rept. 50 (1961), p. 12.
26. Stippler and Castle, p. 10.

a relative, estate, or other sponsor, in the expectation of renting or buying additional land. The number of these aspirants has been more than sufficient to meet needs, assuming the farm-size expectations given here.

A majority of smaller farmers, however, have been older men nearing retirement. Many are full owners of the land they farm. They receive the returns from the land as well as the returns from operating the farm and in that way may receive an adequate income. Small farmers may increase their current income by making no allowance for replacing existing equipment if they expect to retire before the equipment becomes obsolete or worn out. Also the planning horizon of an older farmer is understandably quite short. The reluctance of older men to expand their operations explains the fact that farm operators who are full owners tend to have smaller incomes on the average than those who are only renters or part owners.

In addition, most wheat farmers have some off-farm income. Up to 89 percent of the farm families in a western Oklahoma study had off-farm income.[27]

Perhaps an average of a third of farmers' incomes in the Great Plains comes from off-farm sources,[28] some of this from invested capital, pensions, or mineral rights. In the western Oklahoma study, 40 percent of those reporting off-farm income had been employed off the farm.[29]

The work cycle for wheat farms permits off-farm employment. The operator labor required to produce $5,000 in net earnings from wheat alone is apparently as little as 1,000 hours per year,[30] and this is highly seasonal labor. One finds among the operators of wheat farms teachers, students, lawyers, or businessmen. However most farmers with off-farm occupations in western Oklahoma were in construction work, service industries such as service stations, and agriculturally related industries such as cotton gins and grain elevators. Farmers who received more than 50 percent of their cash income from off-farm sources tended to have relatively low net farm incomes.[31]

Another method by which farmers can spread their work load is that of the "suitcase farmer," who owns land and often operates farms in more than one state. Suitcase farming is a phenomenon dating

27. Larry J. Connor, William F. Lagrone, and W. B. Back, *Farm and Nonfarm Income of Farm Families in Western Oklahoma–1956,* Oklahoma Agr. Exp. Sta. Bull. B-552 (March 1960), p. 8.
28. *Farming in the Great Plains,* ARS-USDA Prod. Res. Rept. 50 (1961), p. 29.
29. Connor et al., p. 8.
30. Harold E. Barnhill, *Resource Requirement on Farms for Specified Operator Incomes,* ERS-USDA Agr. Econ. Rept. 5 (1964), p. 19.
31. Connor et al., p. 10.

back to the World War II plowup of grass in the sparsely settled arid areas, and it has apparently become more common. Farmers from one area have had no difficulty in mastering the farming techniques of another. Widely scattered ownership has permitted the owner-operators to enjoy a longer work season and to provide a kind of insurance against crop failure.

Suitcase farming is illustrative of two ways in which the commercial wheat farmer does not fit the traditional farmer image. Unlike the bygone farmer, he travels constantly and travels far, by auto, truck, and even private airplane. If he is isolated in any sense, it is not basically because of distance. The other unique feature symbolized by the suitcase farmer is that the farm is no longer the preferred home. The major personal expense for many wheatgrowers during the past two decades has been the purchase of a home in town. Some farmers have preferred to reside in a nearby community; others have chosen to live in a far-away city and to commute irregularly to their farm businesses.

Wheat has been important to the Plains economy which produces it, but it has been much less important within the national economy within recent years. In 1959 Senator Frank Carlson (R., Kansas), whose state is the leading wheat producer, asked the U.S. Department of Agriculture to estimate the importance of wheat in the national economy. He must have been disappointed with the findings.[32] The value of domestic wheat production in 1959, including processing and sales, accounted for only 1 percent of the gross national product.[33] This amount was unimpressive even as a fraction of the annual growth rate of the national economy, which has been as much as 15 percent (1951) in recent years.

The wheat economy now supports relatively few people. It was estimated that in 1959 the total labor involved in producing wheat (not including processing or selling) was 109,000 man-years.[34] This would have been less than the labor spent making cabinets or for dressmaking.[35] Adding to this the 55,000 man-years required to produce the machinery and other inputs for wheat production, and the 360,000 man-years needed to process the product, the wheat economy required a total of only 524,000 man-years, compared with a total work force in 1960 of 68 million persons.[36]

---

32. "Wheat and the National Economy," USDA (September 1960); printed in *Congressional Record* (bound), Aug. 29, 1960, pp. 18118–20.
33. Ibid.
34. Ibid.
35. *1960 U.S. Census of Population*, vol. 1, table 206.
36. *Statistical Abstract of the U.S.* (1964), table 308.

As a national source of farm income, wheat has in most years ranked well behind beef cattle, dairy products, hogs, and cotton in cash receipts to the farmer.[37] It is obvious from the above comparisons that the national economy is not much affected directly by the shifts in the size and profits of the wheat economy.

The USDA's report evaluating wheat in the national economy did emphasize that wheat has been an important U.S. food. It has also been a substantial export and, as such, a critical increment permitting a "world food balance." If there should be such an entity as a world food policy, then U.S. wheat policy is clearly one of its most substantial and identifiable components. This perspective will be developed in Chapter 13.

Thus this domestic policy designed to attain prosperity and well-being in one region of the United States has greatly affected the designs of institutions whose more comprehensive objectives include world peace, world humanism, and world development. The dramatic interplay between the lofty national and international goals and the goals of U.S. wheat producers is a characteristic feature of wheat politics, as will be particularly apparent in the next two chapters.

---

37. *Cash Receipts from Major Products as a Percentage of State Totals, 1929–1934,* AMS-USDA Stat. Bull. 262 (April 1960), pp. 52–53.

USDA *Photo*

2 / DOMESTIC WHEAT POLICY IN REVIEW

THIS CHAPTER serves two purposes. At this point it presents a chronology of wheat commodity policies, each of which will be treated in a subsequent chapter. It also follows a thread of concern basic to all these programs: an assumed imbalance of supply and demand. Too much wheat has endangered producer income. Conversely, not enough wheat might mean privation or even starvation.

In practice, surplus rather than scarcity has been the catalyst of federal legislation, because the prime movers of farm programs until recently have been representatives of the commercial farmer. Market surpluses pressed prices downward—and brought forth cries for help —while scarcity was quite acceptable as an occasion for high prices. Federal commodity programs usually sought to prevent overproduction, but with less than complete success. When overproduction occurred the government sought to counteract its downward price pressures, usually by acquiring the surpluses.

Wheat surpluses have been linked with government programs. In the 1950s the word "surplus" usually referred specifically to large government stocks of wheat carried over from one year to the next, above and beyond the "working stocks" in bakers' inventories and elsewhere.

Critics asserted that surpluses would not have existed in the absence of government programs. With few exceptions the sizable carryovers throughout the world have in fact been owned or held by government agencies, usually in nations which frequently export a large part of their wheat crop. In this century the four big exporters—United States, Canada, Australia, and Argentina—all have had commodity programs under which the government has held stocks of wheat. The governments of France and Portugal and other marginal exporters have held wheat. In addition, governments of importing countries have maintained national granaries serving as a mechanism for stabilizing the price for their domestic wheat producers, for giving leverage in foreign purchases, and for assuring a food supply. Therefore in countries where wheat has had significance either as a product or as a food the national government has usually held stocks of wheat.[1]

Aside from government stocks, the word "surplus" has also referred to a capacity to produce more wheat than can be sold: that is, surplus productivity or surplus cropland. Still another meaning of "surplus" is the amount produced in excess of domestic needs— the amount ordinarily sold abroad. Prior to government commodity programs scholars and decision makers often referred to the "exportable surplus." These are related designations. Surplus productivity can easily become surplus stock if not adequately checked by the market, weather, or government production controls. The exportable surplus may also find its way into government granaries, in the absence of markets abroad.

The United States has had all three kinds of wheat surpluses. At times, particularly in the 1950s, large government stocks have accumulated. It was then possible, even necessary from the producers' point of view, to enact food programs designed to use these stocks. So these stocks became a food reserve available in emergencies and a means for guaranteeing steady supplies to regular customers abroad. Surpluses were used domestically to provide minimum levels of nutrition, and they were also distributed abroad presumably to advance foreign policy goals. These food-using policies in turn developed supporting interests, and an apparent supportive consensus, with which producers had to come to terms. In the 1960s

---

1. *National Grain Policies,* UN-FAO (1963).

production in excess of private market demand became an actual goal of federal policy, for the first time, rather than an aberrant result of it, and the policy under which government acquired that excess was determined for the first time by the users as well as the producers.

PRE-1914 SUPPLY AND DEMAND

Almost from the time of settlement the United States has been an exporter of wheat. In each decade wheat as a principal export has helped to buy goods for our people and to earn capital for developing industry. United States wheat exports grew rapidly from the middle until the end of the nineteenth century. This expansion of exports was due to the extension of railroads and population into the Midwest and the Plains, the development of harvesting machinery, and the growth of British and European markets. During most of these years the United States was the world's largest or principal wheat exporter. In the 1890s the United States exported about one-third of its production, and these exports averaged 44 percent of total world trade in wheat.[2]

United States production leveled off in the first decade of the twentieth century. Meanwhile exports from Russia, Argentina, Canada, and Australia increased. With U.S. population continuing to grow, it seemed for a time that U.S. production would not be able even to fill future domestic wheat needs.

This question was considered by the USDA's wheat expert, Mark Carleton, at the beginning of the twentieth century. Carleton undertook to predict whether the United States would still be self-sufficient in wheat production in 1950. Following trends of the past, Carleton accurately predicted a tremendous increase in yields, though without guessing that the improvement would be all in a spurt between 1940 and 1960. His projections of 1950 population and 1950 total acreage were also accurate.[3] (Notwithstanding Mr. Carleton's good fortune, yields and acreage have been difficult to predict since then, especially over the short run. Short-range predictions have been based mainly on projections of weather, the cycles of which are sharp and irregular in the Great Plains Wheat Belt. Predictions have often failed to take into account new methods of

2. Joseph S. Davis, *Wheat and the AAA* (Washington: Brookings Institution, 1935), p. 2.
3. Willard E. Swenson, "A Survey of Wheat-Crop Estimation Studies for Canada, Australia, and Argentina," *Statistics and Agriculture*, no. 3 (USDA, July 1941).

cultivation, new seeds, and technological improvements in general, so that the only thing fairly certain about predictions of future yields is that they were pretty consistently on the low side.)

WORLD WAR I

Wheat supplies were precarious during World War I, mostly because there had been no previous history of planning for food needs. In 1917 and 1918 Europe was very short of food; in the United States three consecutive harvests had been small. Scant supplies were hoarded in granaries in the expectation of higher prices, and European purchasers were ready to buy at almost any price. Facing inflation, the federal government set export quotas and fixed the wheat price—first through a gentlemen's agreement with the millers and subsequently through a federal corporation which controlled the price and distributed wheat. Breadlines were avoided in the United States by careful stewardship of available wheat and by persuading farmers to sell their farm-stored wheat. The government first appealed to farmers' patriotism and then offered them good prices and subsidies. Meanwhile the government augmented domestic wheat supplies by sizable imports from Canada.[4] In the subsequent postwar period enough wheat was produced to mount an impressive program of relief for Europe.

1920 LOW PRICES

In the 1920s the United States had an "exportable surplus" averaging about a third of the crop. This surplus was blamed for the farm distress of that decade, on the grounds that it linked U.S. prices to the depressed world price. This world-linked price for wheat was in contrast with that of nonexported American products whose prices could be raised above world levels by means of a tariff wall.

One explanation advanced was that the domestic wheat surplus was a result of wartime dislocation.[5] This was a convenient theory both for those wanting government price protection and for those who wanted to let the market find its own levels. Those favoring protection argued that the government was obliged to protect those farmers who generously responded to wartime appeals for expanded

4. William Clinton Mullendore, *History of the United States Food Administration, 1917–1919* (Palo Alto, Calif.: Stanford Univ. Press, 1941), p. 136.
5. Other explanations included the one advanced by McNary-Haugen proponents, and later by Secretary of Agriculture Henry A. Wallace, that foreign markets had been lost because the United States had changed from a debtor to a creditor nation.

acreage. Those opposed argued that wartime dislocations are temporary and prices would soon return to adequate levels without need for any federal intervention. The theory that wartime expansion causes postwar surpluses was advanced too after World War II.

This dislocation theory was too simple, because in both periods there were longer-term forces which had more effect on the wheat economy than did the war. World War I did add 20 million new acres of wheat, only half of which were retired at the end of the war. But wheat acreage had also expanded rapidly in the prosperous years before World War I, and acreage continued to climb in the 1920s despite depressed prices.

In the longer-run perspective, the war increase was only an upward wrinkle in the trend toward greater U.S. and world production. During the entire first half of the twentieth century, world wheat production trended upward at a higher level than world demand.[6]

There were also short-term explanations for low prices. Annual world production was fairly stable, due to counterbalancing regional variations;[7] world demand, however, was inflexible, causing prices to vary sharply in response to slight changes in supply. Thus the wheat price was erratic, but on the average wheat was a bargain-counter item. Wheat exporters including the United States were particularly affected, because tariff walls were erected against them by European governments. These major importers acted to stimulate local production partly out of a firm desire never again to be vulnerable to famine as in World War I.

AGRICULTURAL MARKETING ACT OF 1929

The Republican administrations of the 1920s resisted persistent pressure from commercial farming interests favoring federal measures to raise the U.S. wheat price. The Hoover administration finally made what was regarded as a token concession to the problem, with passage of the Agricultural Marketing Act of 1929. The main remedy in the law was to strengthen the price through nongovernmental market mechanisms. But after the price collapsed in 1929, with the onset of depression, the administering agency instituted a federal corporation in February 1930 with power to acquire and sell grain.

6. Wilfred Malenbaum, *The World Wheat Economy 1885–1939* (Cambridge, Mass.: Harvard Univ. Press, 1953), pp. 172–75.
7. V. P. Timoshenko, "Interregional Correlations in Wheat Yields and Outputs," *Wheat Studies of the Stanford Food Research Institute*, 20(July 1944):258–59.

In its unsuccessful effort to stabilize domestic prices in a chaotic world market, the corporation had acquired most of a 313-million-bushel domestic carryover at the end of the 1930–31 marketing year. This was the largest stock of domestic wheat in history. Lacking additional funds, the corporation was then obliged to sell most of its 250-million-bushel holdings either in the depressed domestic market or through subsidized exports, and to donate the remainder for relief. However private stocks grew due to the lack of acceptable markets, and the U.S. private and public carryover in mid-1932 was even larger than in 1931.

THE WALLACE PERIOD

THE IDEA OF WORLD ABUNDANCE

The Roosevelt administration of 1933 regarded this surplus productivity as both a short-run and a long-run problem. Secretary of Agriculture Henry A. Wallace supported a program of immediate income relief for farmers, and he also experimented with production controls. However Wallace believed the best route for America was to use the abundance which technology was about to bestow by developing a larger international trade. Although not confident of success, Wallace was a leader among those who would reverse the protectionist policies of his own and other governments.

Wallace envisioned a world economy, but not of the traditional laissez-faire order which he felt could lead only to further cycles of depression and war. His world economy would be a long-run product of education and laborious planning, whose function would be to use the world's vast resources to fulfill its tremendous food needs.:

> In an age when an advanced technology pours forth goods in a smothering abundance, fear of freezing to death and starving to death should be removed as a matter of common decency from the lives of civilized people as a whole. This is not a cloudy idealism which has no basis in facts. Only those really close to science can know the abundance that could be ours with even-handed justice and a generous distribution between groups. Our grinding efforts to subsist, in the mass, on the farm and in great cities alike, the world over, would drop into the far background in the light of the attainments we could command.[8]

Wallace feared that if the United States should fail to increase international consumption this country might be driven back to a policy of economic nationalism, of producing only for American

8. Henry A. Wallace, *America Must Choose*, World Affairs Pamphlets, no. 3 (1934), p. 11.

markets. This would require producers to retire 40 to 100 million acres of cropland and to shift many people off the farms. Wallace felt such a policy would require extreme regimentation of farmers. He did not think this was wise, precisely because he thought at first that farmers were indeed capable of enforcing this regimentation on each other, and would do so. He viewed this policy as a threat to political freedom.[9]

AGRICULTURAL ADJUSTMENT ACT OF 1933

Controls need not be so severe, Wallace hoped, if the agricultural economy could be organized on an international basis. Wallace took leadership in negotiating an International Wheat Agreement in 1933, under which the principal wheat exporting nations, including the United States, committed themselves to reduce their domestic production by 15 percent. This "domestic allotment program" for wheat, as implemented under his Agricultural Adjustment Act of 1933, gave income relief to farmers in return for which the USDA contracted with farmers to reduce wheat acreage.

Weather intervened to change the situation from surplus to scarcity. Severe, sustained drought (1933–36) left America short of wheat. The production control mechanisms functioned only as an experiment in administration. There was real doubt as to whether these voluntary control measures would prove adequate in normal weather, especially after the international wheat agreement broke down. Nevertheless this domestic allotment program was extended in 1935, only to be ruled unconstitutional by the U.S. Supreme Court in 1936.[10]

SOIL CONSERVATION AND DOMESTIC ALLOTMENT ACT OF 1936

Congress passed a substitute program, the Soil Conservation and Domestic Allotment Act (February 29, 1936). This act emphasized soil conservation rather than production controls, partly as a means of circumventing the Supreme Court's adverse decision on the 1933 act. Its theme was expressed in the statement "The nation that destroys the soil destroys itself."[11] However the act did provide payments to farmers for shifting land from production of surplus crops such as wheat, but it did not reduce supplies. The soil conservation provisions, which were in effect many years hence, no doubt raised productivity much over the long run.

9. Ibid., pp. 15–16.
10. U.S. v. Butler (297 U.S. Reports), Jan. 6, 1936.
11. *Saving the Soil,* USDA-AAA, G-53 (March 1936).

Like the earlier Wallace program, the substitute program did not provide for government purchase of surplus wheat. However it utilized the famous "section 32,"[12] which allocated 30 percent of all receipts from the tariffs to be used in disposing of "price-depressing surplus stocks through domestic relief agencies. Over one-fifth of the $15 million used from this fund in 1936 was for the purchase and processing of wheat (about 3 million bushels) for domestic distribution.[13]

EVER-NORMAL GRANARY

However Wallace did suggest a mechanism to moderate the chaotic and destructive cycles of the wheat market. During his first years in office he had weighed an idea that he called the "ever-normal" granary, and in later years he seemed always to regard it as his greatest idea. It became a subsidiary theme in the permanent farm program enacted in 1938.

The ever-normal granary, Wallace said, was derived from Chinese history and was related even to the rise and fall of civilizations. As a civilization becomes urban, Wallace suggested, it is ordered by a price economy, which may work well in the short run but which also moves in violent cycles, exaggerated in their response to scarcity or abundance of farm products. The farm economy takes the full brunt of the low cycle in sustained farm depressions, Wallace felt, and receives inadequate rewards at the peak of the cycle. Wallace believed that the farm depressions would lead to abuse of the land, would drive the younger generations away from the farms, and generally debilitate agriculture. So among many bad results of price instability, including political radicalism, Wallace feared a long-run food shortage, which would manifest itself in seasons of adverse weather. Wallace predicted a "serious food shortage over the entire world beginning sometime in the next ten or fifteen years, and that the shortage once definitely started will continue for a number of years."[14]

Wallace's ever-normal granary was not to be a stockpile assembled before a specter of famine, like Joseph's seven-year hoard against a

12. Passed in 1935 (Amendments to the Agricultural Adjustment Act, P.L. 320, 74th Cong.) and amended in 1936. The funds made available under section 32 were to be used: (1) to encourage exports, (2) to encourage domestic consumption by diverting commodities, by payments of benefits or indemnities or by other means, from the normal channels of trade, and (3) to reestablish farmers' purchasing power by making payments in connection with the normal production for domestic consumption.
13. *Agricultural Conservation, 1936, A Report of the Activities of the Agricultural Adjustment Administration,* USDA-AAA (1937), p. 80.
14. Henry A. Wallace, *New Frontiers* (New York: Reynal and Hitchcock, 1934), p. 232.

seven-year drought. Instead its function was to moderate the price cycle, to make agriculture abundant by keeping it stable.

The federal wheat granary which he proposed would be relatively small, perhaps confined to the hard wheats of the Plains, where yields are variable. An even smaller reserve would be required if foreign markets were regained because wheat usually exported could be used at home when needed.

While size was to be left indefinite, Wallace set several guidelines. If the reserve were too large, it would depress prices, and in addition would generate opposition leading to abandonment of the ever-normal granary program. "We have before us as a warning the experience of the Farm Board. We do not want to build up these adequate stocks in such a way as will continually depress prices and damage the farmer. We want the strong hand of the government in control of these stocks, but the plan must be such that no mere political attack can dislodge it."[15] Thus Wallace was impressed by the argument of his critics that such a granary might be "easy to fill but impossible to empty." He was also fearful, in view of the enormous increases in wheat acreages in 1936 and 1937, that government could not effectively control the wheat economy. He was certainly reluctant to put all wheat surpluses into government stocks.[16]

Wallace therefore began to question his earlier preference for a price support loan program as the mechanism for an ever-normal granary. Under such a program the cooperating farmers pledged their wheat to the government in return for a loan at a fixed price level per bushel. When market prices rose above the loan rate farmers redeemed their wheat and marketed it. When prices stayed below the loan rate farmers let the government take over the wheat. It was hoped the government would resell this forfeited wheat in years when crops were short and the price was high.

Wallace was worried that farm legislators might insist on using the loan mechanism not as a means for stabilizing supplies but as a means for boosting market prices. Higher prices would be an incentive for increased production and for increased stocks which government would then have no opportunity to get rid of. Wallace's fears were based on experience with other commodity programs:

> The outstanding danger I see in this program is a tendency continually to push the government loan higher, no matter what the situation may be. In the fall of 1933 we loaned 10 cents a pound on cotton. By July of 1934 requests were coming in that a new cotton loan pro-

15. Ibid., pp. 232–33.
16. *Why United States Wheat Farmers and Consumers Need a Stabilized Wheat Industry,* USDA-AAA (May 1937).

gram be established for the purpose of loaning 15 cents a pound on cotton. We settled at 12 cents. If we had loaned 15 cents a pound on cotton and escaped crucial trouble, the request would come for 20 cents a pound in 1935, and so on indefinitely until the crash."[17]

In addition to advocating reduced prices as a means of discouraging overproduction, Wallace still hoped for new markets abroad, but without his earlier enthusiasm. He welcomed increased consumer buying and research to find industrial uses for farm products. He commended governmental efforts to return marginal wheatlands to grass. In 1937 he came around to advocating production controls for wheat, as a further balancer:

> To keep government from committing a "farm board" it will be necessary after supplies under the loan program have reached a certain point to keep the granary from running over by some practical program of production adjustment. I call this part of the ever-normal granary program "storing the grain in the soil" instead of "storing it in the bin."[18]

Wallace was still opposed to pacing production for the domestic market only. With respect to wheat producers, however, he became less concerned about the effects of regimentation than about the possibility that they were too individualistic to accept stiff controls:

> The control that would be needed to cut acreage from 80 million down to 55 million acres or less would be far more rigid than anything wheat producers have ever thought about. Unless wheat growers should drastically change their whole point of view, it is doubtful that such control could be made to work.[19]

Thus increased international trade was still the slim hope for achieving balance.

Wallace sought to disentangle his ever-normal granary scheme for moderating production cycles from the other thorny problems of balancing supply and demand. He therefore suggested a different mechanism than price support loans for building his granary:

> Probably a sounder and better way to build the granary would be through the proposed plan for crop insurance, which may be taken as the fourth part of a wheat program. Under this plan, farmers taking

17. *New Frontiers*, p. 236.
18. Henry A. Wallace, "Definition of the Ever-Normal Granary," *Agricultural Situation*, 21(March 1937):9.
19. Speech at wheat meeting, Wichita, Kansas, Nov. 23, 1937.

out the insurance would pay their premiums and collect their indemnities in wheat or its cash equivalent. Whenever a farmer's yield fell below some specified percentage of his normal yield—say 75 percent—he would be paid an amount of wheat or its cash equivalent that would equal the difference between his actual yield and 75 percent.

Since the wheat representing the total of premiums paid in would be stored, it would be kept off the market in years of good crops and would be made available in the form of indemnities in years when crops were short."[20]

Wallace's view did not prevail. Instead a large farm organization, the American Farm Bureau Federation, was the dominant influence in the enactment of the Agricultural Adjustment Act of 1938. Farm Bureau was part of a coalition of farm congressmen and farm organizations which favored federal price guarantees for farmers, preferably at a level of fairness or "parity" reflecting expenses plus a fair profit. A statistical standard of parity had evolved, based upon the farmers' satisfactory income position during 1910–14.

PRODUCTION CONTROLS

Farm Bureau intended to achieve fair or parity prices by creating scarcity in the marketplace. Scarcity would be achieved through production controls, sternly enforced by government. With scarcity as their aim, Farm Bureau wanted a federal granary primarily as a means of removing any excess supplies from the market rather than for providing an ever-normal supply.

In the resulting legislation the federal government was charged with supporting farm prices at a percentage of the parity ratio. Both voluntary and compulsory production controls were authorized, the latter to be applied only when serious overproduction threatened. But these controls were not adequate; as Wallace had feared, the ever-normal granary became a depository for surpluses rather than a stabilizer of supplies. Minimum reserve levels were specified as a token to the ever-normal concept, but at the low level of 210–25 million bushels. The secretary could presumably affect supply levels by altering loan rates. Furthermore as supplies became large the control mechanisms would be triggered. Yet in practice the law provided no effective way to limit the growth of government stocks. Surpluses accumulated—first with voluntary controls in effect in 1939 and 1940—even with compulsory controls for the 1941 and 1942 crops. By 1942 all storage facilities were full.

20. Ibid.

WAR FOOD ADMINISTRATION

During the Second World War the USDA through its coordinator, the War Food Administration, was preoccupied with getting rid of these surpluses, although its wartime responsibility was to assure a food supply "adequate to meet all requirements."[21]

In 1942 the huge supplies of wheat which had accumulated under the wheat program overloaded storage capacity and impeded movement of wheat, resulting in some spoilage. One dividend of this developing surplus had been the construction of additional storage facilities, but these were not kept full in anticipation of postwar food needs. In surplus-ridden 1942 the Secretary of Agriculture had noted that "we have plenty of wheat for any emergency," but the USDA was then depleting these stocks by using them for animal feed. Largely due to USDA surplus disposal policies during the war, the stocks were no longer available when needed in 1946.

The USDA proved unable to shift its attention to its wartime responsibilities. Walter Wilcox[22] concluded that:

> Anyone reviewing the activities of the different peacetime agricultural agencies during the defense and early war period will become convinced that public agencies have difficulties similar to organized interest groups in relating their efforts to general welfare objectives in periods of change. Without exception each agency attempted to use the war emergency as an additional justification for continuing its particular line of work with little change. . . . The outstanding example without question was AAA activities in 1941, 1942, and 1943.

ESTIMATING POSTWAR NEEDS

Wheat reserves were not expected to be needed during the war, since domestic markets would not increase and major foreign markets would be temporarily cut off. Nevertheless a judgment had to be reached as to the amount of reserves needed to fill postwar relief needs.

There were differing opinions on this matter, stemming less from differing data than from the influence of divergent interests. The division of opinion tended to separate those interested in postwar farm policy from those whose interest was postwar food needs.

Those interested primarily in food needs included the Director

21. Exec. Order 9280, Dec. 5, 1942.
22. Walter Wilcox, *The Farmer and the Second World War* (Ames: Iowa State Univ. Press, 1947), p. 43.

of United Nations Relief and Rehabilitation Administration, Herbert Lehman, whose estimates of heavy postwar needs were labeled "alarmist" by agriculture groups.[23] Lehman, from the time he resigned as New York Governor to become UNRRA Administrator in 1943, stressed the gravity of the crisis. In September 1944 he concluded:

> Let the world not be deceived by reports from portions of the areas already liberated indicating that the suffering in a particular community or group of communities has not been so great as had been thought. These reports are far outweighed by others which indicate that the enemy has been even more ruthless in his treatment of the occupied countries and their peoples than had been known or anticipated. . . . The information that is now coming out of the liberated countries gives full confirmation to our fears of last November as to the size and difficulty of the task of relief and rehabilitation.[24]

Others who had urged that a margin of safety in the form of food reserves be ready at war's end included Herbert Hoover (who had administered U.S. relief after World War I) and the British minister of food, Ben Smith.[25] At least one USDA expert shared their view: Howard Tolley, head of the USDA Bureau of Agricultural Economics, charged in 1944 that USDA's lack of concern was leading to a world food crisis.[26]

The official USDA policy favored a "bare shelf" at the end of the war. The USDA took the view that postwar food relief needs would be small and probably could be met from army food stocks on hand at that time. Discounting predictions of massive hunger, the USDA and other farm program interests worried instead that unneeded stocks piled up at war's end might bring about a farm price recession. The following statement by a USDA official in May 1944 is a typical description of the "bare shelf" policy followed by the USDA in the latter years of the war:

> Food stocks now are large enough . . . to permit us to consider the postwar situation as well as what must be done more immediately. . . . From here on out we must exercise the greatest possible care with regard to food procurement in order that we may come out as even as possible at the end of the war.[27]

---

23. Ibid., p. 281.
24. *Journal of the Second Session of the Council of the United Nations Relief and Rehabilitation Administration* (Montreal, Sept. 19, 1944), p. 27.
25. Ibid., pp. 181–82.
26. Wilcox, p. 282.
27. Ibid., p. 279.

In his study of wartime food policy, Wilcox concluded that the Department of Agriculture had not met its responsibilities to provide adequate food for postwar relief, because it was more interested in postwar farm programs:

> War Food Administration officials not only underestimated the relief feeding requirements at the end of the war but accepted the prevailing analysis that the reconversion period would be marked by substantial unemployment. They were charged with the responsibility for supporting prices at 85 to 92% of parity for two years after the war, and without adequate appropriations. Quite naturally these officials were more concerned about having too much rather than too little food on hand when the war came to an end.[28]

Although the USDA had the duty to meet food needs, it was not alone in underestimating them. While administrators and supporters of farm programs were intent on giving acreage controls a fresh start, farm program opponents were just as anxious for "bareshelf" as a means of easing agriculture back into a free market. These critics included scholars at the Stanford University Food Research Institute, who had gained repute for their extended wheat studies. They were hopeful of a postwar economy uncluttered by surpluses, price supports, and controls. The leading scholar in the Stanford group, Joseph S. Davis, referred in 1942 to the "embarrassing accumulation" of wheat stocks which had "complicated defense-war efforts and raised difficult problems for later solution."[29] In September of 1943 Davis said:

> What we regard as seriously inflated notions as to the size and duration of the food shortage continue to be voiced in some official and trade quarters. These notions stem partly from exaggerated ideas of the current and prospective calorie-food deficit in Continental Europe. . . . One consequence is a disposition to hold reserves of wheat at very high levels, to expand production. . . . The danger of these notions lies in the prospect that they may promote overexpansion and maldistribution of wheat production, and both delay and make more difficult the process of postwar adjustment.[30]

WARTIME FOOD ADMINISTRATION

The huge U.S. wheat stockpile was emptied in midwar by subsi-

---

28. Ibid.
29. Joseph S. Davis, "World Wheat Survey and Outlook," *Wheat Studies of the Stanford Food Research Institute*, 18(May 1942):339–66.
30. Joseph S. Davis, "Wheat Outlook and Policies," *Wheat Studies of the Stanford Food Research Institute*, 20(September 1943):28. See also Helen C. Farnsworth, "World Wheat Outlook," *Wheat Studies of the Stanford Food Research Institute*, 20(July 1944):211–12, who at that late date suggested continued disposal of reserves.

dizing sales of wheat stocks for animal feed. One purpose of this "wheat-for-feed" program was to check inflation by encouraging livestock production. Meat served as one of the few alternative outlets for higher personal incomes. Yet the principal reason for pouring wheat into livestock, it appears, was simply the fear of postwar surpluses.[31]

The results of this wheat-for-feed program were mixed. It did dispose of reserves. Between July 1943 and July 1944 the Commodity Credit Corporation sold for livestock feed 514 million bushels, the bulk of its wheat stocks. The program also resulted in more meat. Earlier a black market item, meat became an oversupply. Not much meat could be stockpiled because of cost and shortage of cold storage and canning facilities, so citizens were asked on occasion to "eat their way out of" a temporary pork surplus.

Another unfortunate effect was an increase in the number of meat animals, which in turn produced a feed shortage crisis in 1946. As a result, this inflated animal population subsequently was fed abnormally large amounts of wheat which the federal government was desperately seeking to ship to humans abroad.

POSTWAR FOOD ADMINISTRATION

The world food deficit which developed in 1945 was partly the result of somewhat unfavorable weather in Europe. The main cause, however, was wartime resource and manpower shortages—and devastation. The European shortage had developed over a six-year period. It had been predicted by U.S. study teams in 1942 and 1943,[32] and in 1943 and 1944 by Hoover, Tolley, Ben Smith, and others. Yet in August of 1944 the WFA was still reminding farmers that they had recently faced surpluses. The agency recommended that for 1945 farmers plant 11 million acres less than the previous maximum acreage of 80 million acres in the 1936–37 year. In particular, the WFA asked that wheat not be planted where other crops could be grown, "nor on land better left in permanent grass."[33]

In mid-1945, the U.S. government was still dubious about reports from British sources of impending shortages of food in Europe. In July 1945 Secretary of Agriculture Clinton Anderson (in office July 1945–May 1948) stated that a continuation of the wheat-for-feed subsidy program was under consideration, although this would not be instituted at that time because of the large export requirements

31. Wilcox, pp. 171–72.
32. Ibid., pp. 281–82.
33. WFA news release, August 1944.

for wheat.[34] While not subsidizing wheat-for-feed in 1945, Anderson pointed out that there were no restrictions as yet on the use of wheat for that purpose. Three hundred million bushels were used for feed in the marketing year 1945–46.

Meanwhile a shortage of grains had developed in the Orient, normally a net exporter. By December of 1945 the desperate situation was clear to all. "World needs are very great and considerably exceed the available supply in the principal exporting counties," the USDA reported.[35]

During the winter of 1945–46 domestic transportation and distribution facilities were severely taxed in delivering the remaining U.S. wheat supplies to the war-torn countries. Needs, mostly in England and Europe, were for at least one-third more than could possibly be delivered. By March 1946 short supplies rather than transportation bottlenecks became the main problem. The WFA prohibited the use of wheat for alcohol and sought to reduce the amount being used for animal feed. Millers were required to extract a higher-than-normal percentage of the grain in making flour. Millers' inventories were subjected to size limits.

As a further way to increase the supply of wheat for export, President Roosevelt established a Famine Emergency Committee, which undertook to obtain voluntary reductions in the consumer use of wheat, by such means as movies, pamphlets, and press releases.

On April 1, 1946, domestic milling was restricted to 75 percent of the amounts milled in the same months of 1944. Numerous other restrictions included limits on the size of bread loaves and rolls. Still millers sometimes ran out of flour, and bread was sometimes in short supply.

As another way to obtain wheat for export, the CCC required that half of the wheat delivered to elevators by farmers must be sold rather than stored. Shipment of wheat overland out of the Southern Plains was prohibited so that the supply from America's principal bread basket could be funneled directly into export through Gulf ports. As of January 1946 half the U.S. wheat stocks had been located on the farms, and soon the only wheat remaining was that in farmers' bins. The USDA sent many emissaries to the countryside, urging farmers to clean out their grain bins in the interest of humanity. Remembering that farmers in World War I had tended to procrastinate in anticipation of higher prices, the USDA on April 2 offered to buy wheat for immediate delivery at the price farmers might

---

34. *Wheat Situation,* USDA-BAE, WS–89 (July 1945), p. 2.
35. *Wheat Situation,* USDA-BAE, WS–92 (November-December 1945), p. 3.

choose on any day during the coming year. Two weeks thereafter, as a further encouragement, the USDA announced a bonus of 30 cents per bushel (added to the option of future sales) to be paid for any wheat that farmers would deliver by May 25. A USDA bulletin informed farmers "there's just one reason for the 30 cents a bushel bonus offered under the emergency wheat purchase program. That's to get wheat off the farms immediately and moving into export channels to relieve the famine emergency overseas. The people abroad who need your wheat aren't just hungry—they're starving."

Wheat price ceilings were raised 15 cents, the purpose being mainly to encourage greater production during the following year, since the shortage was expected to continue indefinitely.

Wheat was sucked from every crevice during the late spring of 1946. Even the Soviet Union found some wheat to sell to France. Food-short Britain diverted 7.5 million bushels to Europe. As a last resort, "coarse grains" such as corn were shipped from the United States to be used as food abroad. With all this effort, European imports were still 40 percent below what was regarded as the minimum needed. This deficit was about equal to the amount of wheat fed to animals in the United States during the last six months of 1945. Stocks in all countries were practically exhausted when the new wheat harvest began in May. The United States had shipped 390 million bushels, and would have preferred to send twice as much had more been available. The amount sent was far from adequate. According to Wilcox, "1946 witnessed the greatest famine in the civilized world's history."[36]

As the 1946 harvest got under way, the CCC immediately entered the market to purchase more wheat for relief, boosting the ever-rising price of wheat above the $2-per-bushel mark for the first time in 30 years. Needs were again expected to exceed world supplies, and restrictions on U.S. domestic distribution and use of wheat were continued—in some cases tightened. Meanwhile the USDA urged that wheat acreage be increased to 71 million acres. Under the incentive of very high prices, U.S. farmers indeed found space for 78 million acres which, with high yields and somewhat reduced domestic food use, provided almost 500 million bushels for export during the marketing year July 1947 to July 1948. But as Secretary Anderson said, "Much more would be required to meet the urgent needs that exist."[37] Looking back on the year (1947–48) Anderson

---

36. Wilcox, p. 283.
37. U.S. House Appropriations Subcommittee on Agriculture, *Hearings on the Department of Agriculture Appropriations for 1949* (1948), p. 54.

remarked on the wisdom of Henry David Thoreau's remark, "How early in the year it begins to be late." He explained ". . . If there is anything that strikes me . . . it is the fact that conditions change quickly . . . in our food relationships, and sometimes almost before we know it it begins to be late."[38]

During the years 1944–48 one bright spot in the food situation was a succession of large U.S. wheat crops. No doubt these were in part the result of good weather and the high price incentives, but they were related as well to earlier federal policy which had sought to restrain production.

Among the paradoxes of wartime wheat policy was the fact that earlier efforts to control production and to raise farm income ultimately contributed much to U.S. capacity for food aid. Farm congressmen had insisted that farmers who had suffered through the Depression should not be deprived of the benefits of wartime inflation. Accused of unexampled greed, these farm legislators had brushed aside anti-inflationary price ceilings, raising wheat price supports first to 85 percent of parity in 1941, then to 90 percent in 1942,[39] and then to assurance of 100 percent of parity returns for farmers. The farm legislators included a legislative guarantee that supports would continue at 90 percent until two years after the war. Comparable supports were enacted for other crops.

With good crops during this period in contrast to the poor crops previous to it, net income per wheat farmer rose 1,000 percent in the Southern Plains and 500 percent in the Northern Plains during the six war years.[40] At the same time these powerful price incentives, reluctantly implemented by the administration, did much to boost wheat acreage to levels needed at the war's end.

Another inadvertent helpmate in increasing production was the system of acreage controls, which had been designed to reduce production. Although not adequate to prevent surpluses at that time, the controls idled and revitalized about 30 million acres of wheat between 1939 and 1943, effectively "storing food in the soil." When controls were lifted there burst forth a benediction of four fantastic crops, each in sequence an all-time record. With these crops the United States moderated famine throughout the world, and was

38. Ibid., p. 50.
39. The 90 percent price support did not apply to grain if the President should decide that a lower rate was required to prevent an increase in cost of food for livestock and poultry. As a result of this decision price support rates for wheat and corn remained at 85 percent until 1944.
40. Wilcox, p. 253.

credited with meeting the challenge of Communism which nearly triumphed in France and Italy.

During the three-year food crisis through July 1948 the United States was able to export just over 1 billion bushels of wheat. However between July 1942 and July 1948 the amount of wheat fed to animals was 1.25 billion bushels greater than during comparable time periods before and after, due mainly to the wheat-for-feed program. It is apparent that with advance planning emergency food exports could have been doubled—without any increase in the amount of storage space in use in July 1942.

By 1948 the USDA had begun to plan carefully to maximize food aid. Congress provided in 1947 that exports should not reduce the U.S. carryover below 150 million bushels; the amount remaining in the United States on July 1, 1948, was exactly that amount.

KOREAN WAR

SURPLUS THREAT

After 1948, billion-bushel crops were produced on extremely large acreages. Most of this wheat found outlets in the markets sustained by foreign aid funds, and also in cash sales under the International Wheat Agreement signed in 1949. President Truman's first Secretary of Agriculture, Clinton Anderson, expressed hope for continued exports but moved to decelerate production by advocating a reduction in price supports. This effort was frustrated by congressional opposition. Truman's subsequent Secretary of Agriculture, Charles Brannan, offered a farm program focused on income objectives, using regressively graduated direct payments to farmers. In 1949 Congress defeated Brannan's proposal as presented, which provided direct payments on perishable commodities and which would have continued loans and purchases as the method of supporting income from storable commodities. Brannan seemed less worried than were his predecessors about the prospect or the results of large stocks. With the defeat of the Brannan Plan, the administration was determined to maintain the support level for wheat and other basic commodities at 90 percent of parity, as during the war.

By July 1, 1950, the end-of-season carryover, largest in history, was of such size that Secretary Brannan was almost obliged to reinstitute the tight controls under the triggering formula of the 1938 act, as modified by changes in the formula under the 1949 act. The

Korean War began in mid-July of 1950. By July 1, 1952, supplies had worked down to the low levels assumed to be ideal under the provisions of the commodity programs.

STUDY OF RESERVE LEVELS

In 1952 a study by the USDA's Bureau of Agricultural Economics, done at the request of Senator Allen Ellender (D., Louisiana), Chairman of the Senate Committee on Agriculture and Forestry, suggested desirable U.S. reserve levels for wheat, corn, and cotton. The study noted the need for working stocks in millers' inventories of about 100 million bushels of wheat. Added to this was the amount that would be needed to offset shortages which might result from one very low annual yield followed by a moderately low annual yield. The annual carryover needed to offset such a production failure, they concluded, was about 450 to 500 million bushels.

Chances of another four-year drought as in 1933–36, resulting in a billion-bushel deficit, were regarded as too remote to prepare for. Nor was any consideration given to extreme fluctuations in demand or need such as that occurring during the war years. No comment was made about the prospect of World War III, nor was there any mention of using food aid as an instrument of U.S. foreign policy. No consideration was given to the size of domestic food stocks which might be needed in the event of nuclear war. The only justification therein for maintaining any reserves was to maintain cash markets abroad. "If it is desired to hold or increase export markets, the longer-run interest of wheat producers makes it advisable to meet normal export demand in full or certainly in substantial part, even in years of short domestic crops."[41]

Beginning in 1952, U.S. wheat producers were in the process of accumulating a surplus three times the size of the suggested reserves. At about the same time a Materials Policy Commission appointed by President Truman reported to him with respect to future food needs, not calculated in terms of stockpiles but in terms of capacity to produce. The commission found that food production would have to be raised to 40 percent by 1975 in order to meet rising domestic food needs. To meet this need, agriculture must be responsive to market demand rather than producing for government stockpiles, said the commission:

41. Quoted in *Wheat Situation*, USDA-BAE, WS-130 (August-September 1952), p. 14. Another study of appropriate levels, also in 1952, was made by Murray Benedict for the National Planning Association. Professor Benedict concluded 500 million bushels of wheat were needed, plus a billion bushels feed grain reserve.

A 40% increase in total agricultural production can meet the specific needs of 1975 only if it is made up of the right quantities of individual commodities. The gain in output must be not only large but well selected. The chief reliance to accomplish right selection should be on free play of market forces. It is important to have a price system in agriculture that will respond to the nation's changing needs and call forth approximately the required production of each commodity. But it is also important to protect farm income against sudden price fluctuations.[42]

The commission recommended reduced (flexible) price supports. However Truman's administration had already become committed to high supports for basic commodities, including wheat. The Republican candidate of 1952, Dwight Eisenhower, also promised a continuation of the high rigid price supports. The Truman administration therefore refused to impose quotas during the war despite predictions of record carryovers.

ADEQUATE STOCKS

An ample supply of wheat was on hand throughout the Korean War. Temporary shortages in the West were caused by logistical problems.

Under the circumstances of the war, Secretary Brannan made it clear that he preferred to be embarrassed by surpluses rather than to be faced with an unexpected food shortage beyond his means to satisfy, as had occurred after World War II.

In mid-1952 the official USDA forecast anticipated a very large harvest.[43] Exports were expected to decline. The 1953 carryover was predicted to be 450 million bushels, which also proved to be too conservative an estimate. Brannan explained why he did not impose quotas for the 1953 crop:

> The large 1952 crop makes it possible to establish a production level for 1953 which is below that of recent years. The goal for 1953, however, is kept on the side of abundance to play safe in the mobilization. . . . The goal also recognizes that wheat, being a universal grain, may be substituted for other grains in case an emergency should arise requiring such use of wheat.[44]

Indeed, Secretary Brannan seemed more concerned with the prospective need for farm abundance in peacetime than he was about

42. *Resources for Freedom, A Report to the President by the President's Materials Policy Commission*, 1(June 1952):49.
43. *Wheat Situation*, USDA-BAE, WS-128 (June 1952), p. 3.
44. *Wheat Situation*, USDA-BAE, WS-130 (August-September 1952), pp. 5-6.

the prospect of unmanageable surpluses. In 1952 the USDA issued a publication stressing continuous and expanding needs for food, due to military mobilization, increases in population, and per capita food consumption. Since additional cropland acres were not available, the USDA stressed that every five of the present cropland acres must be made to produce as much as six presently did. Among other food goals mentioned was an increase of 100 million bushels in the wheat carryover at the end of the marketing year.[45]

THE BENSON ADMINISTRATION

Brannan's intention to have a cushion of stocks against uncertainties was more than realized. As the Korean War came to an end, the carryover July 1, 1953, was well over twice as large as in the previous year. Despite reimposition of tight controls on the 1954 crop by Secretary of Agriculture Ezra Benson (1953–60), and despite the severe drought, wheat stocks climbed rapidly to a 996-million-bushel carryover on July 1, 1955.

Benson was highly critical of these large stocks of wheat accumulating during his administration. While favoring abundant productivity, he viewed the highly visible stocks as a scandalous waste of public resources. He hoped the mountainous surpluses would spark a public reaction against the high price support programs. In Benson's judgment price supports had perpetuated wartime production levels oblivious to the reduction in peacetime demand.

Secretary Benson was not the initiator of the various surplus-using programs begun in his administration, such as the P.L. 480 program for food aid abroad, the domestic food disposal, and school lunch and milk programs. He did subsequently embrace these programs, and he expanded them significantly. Expressing pride in the accomplishments of these programs, he nevertheless was continually concerned that they would become rationalizations for surpluses.

The principal surplus disposal mechanism was P.L. 480, passed in 1954, under which most wheat surpluses ultimately found noncommercial outlets abroad. The first P.L. 480 program followed the objectives of a proposal by the largest general farm organization, the American Farm Bureau Federation. To reduce government's role in the farm economy, Farm Bureau wished to use existing surpluses as a pump primer in expanding U.S. foreign markets.[46]

---

45. U.S. House Committee on Agriculture, *Hearings on USDA Reorganization* (1952), esp. p. 104.
46. U.S. House Committee on Agriculture, *Hearings on Famine Relief* (1953), pp. 111–23.

These trade expansion efforts under P.L. 480 did not fulfill expectations, and as surpluses grew other objectives came to be stressed. Another farm organization, the National Farmers Union, had urged the use of surplus food for political and humanitarian purposes. Farmers Union President James Patton had suggested in 1953 that U.S. food stocks could serve in the Cold War by reducing hunger. He suggested that the United States create special food reserves "that will be available to meet unforeseen contingencies that may arise in connection with the Cold War."[47] Spokesmen for the Farmers Union made it clear that they felt the U.S. government should be prepared to prevent famine anywhere in the world.

A wheat reserve or "set-aside" was established in 1954, but merely as a legislative device to prevent sharp acreage reductions under existing law. The set-aside provision did not recognize any food aid obligations.

The Eisenhower administration continued to stress that government surpluses were a temporary misfortune. This theme was somewhat in competition with the theme of some congressional Democrats, that agricultural abundance was a blessing. In any case, surpluses were distributed to the domestic needy in the increasing amounts asked by some legislators and labor and farm groups. In 1959 the Democratic Congress passed a food stamp program (which Secretary Benson did not implement) that shifted from disposing of surpluses to filling food needs. Also in 1959 the P.L. 480 program became the Food for Peace program. The new name stemmed from the idea of making U.S. food stocks a tool of U.S. foreign policy, as developed mainly by Senator Hubert Humphrey (D., Minnesota), an idea implemented more fully under Secretary of Agriculture Orville Freeman.

THE FREEMAN ADMINISTRATION

Secretary Freeman entered office determined to make constructive use of the abundant farm products. His administration moved vigorously to estimate domestic and foreign food needs and to implement programs for meeting these needs from U.S. stocks. At the same time he took pride that surplus stocks were being reduced. Initially more than a full year's supply was still in stock at the beginning of harvest, an amount far larger than regarded necessary. By 1965 this large carryover stock had been reduced almost by half. At that time the administration ordered a study to determine adequate reserve levels. The

---

47. U.S. House Committee on Agriculture, *Hearings on Wheat Marketing Quotas* (1953), p. 34.

resulting USDA study suggested a reserve level of 600 million bushels, an amount well below the existing expected carryover but probably well above the levels which would have been held in private stocks in the absence of any provision for a reserve. The criteria for arriving at this amount were never specified, although the functions of this proposed reserve were stated by President Johnson in his 1965 annual farm message to Congress. The reserve was to be used "for national security, for emergency relief purposes, and for domestic economic stabilization."[48]

In that message the President asked for authority to set aside an amount of grain for reserves. No stockpile was established, however, either by law or by administrative act. The 600-million-bushel level was subsequently referred to as a guideline, but the secretary was left free to vary the stock levels as he wished.

There appeared to be both advantages and disadvantages in refusing to fix specific levels. Some of the major purposes of a reserve might be best accomplished if the level were left indefinite. Grain would be used most constructively as foreign aid if recipients were not encouraged to relax their own development efforts by dependence on ever-ready U.S. abundance. Price stability could best be commanded by the Secretary of Agriculture if he had power to sell the entire U.S. stock, or to add to it without limit.

On the other hand, if reserve levels were not specified, reserves would likely fall too low to accomplish objectives, and this was the chief disadvantage. Farm policy was made largely by producer representatives in Congress whose interest was in promoting scarcity. Added to this dominant political pressure on the Secretary of Agriculture was the Budget Bureau's interest in reducing all costs, including storage fees. The secretary himself would be less embarrassed by shortages than by surpluses, as the historical record in this chapter bears out. The record suggests that the occasional large government stocks were the unintended consequences of a policy of scarcity, while all efforts to obtain a reserve for its own sake died aborning.

Yet the concept of a stockpile had some weight in the new circumstances. New and cogent reasons for food reserves had developed in the 1950s. Reserves would be valuable in the event of a nuclear war which might contaminate the land and animals. United States stocks were the only significant food reserves in a world population much of which had come to the threshold of Malthusian controls.

48. Lyndon B. Johnson, *Farm Message*, Jan. 4, 1965.

Furthermore the widespread drought occurring in India, Africa, and other areas during 1965 would clearly have resulted in serious famine and disorder on several continents except for the commitment of the balance of the U.S. surpluses accumulated during the 1950s.

As a further handicap in setting adequate reserve levels, USDA estimates of yearly demand tended to be biased on the low side. For example, estimates of exports were, on the average, 85 billion bushels below actual exports during the most recent ten-year period (1955–65). These institutional biases would be exaggerated by average yield predictions for poor crop years.

This tendency to overestimate carryover stocks was amply demonstrated with respect to the 1966 carryover. As a result of the widespread drought and large commercial sales from the Soviet Union and the People's Republic of China, opportunities for cash sales abroad as well as commitments under the food aid program increased very rapidly. Predictions with respect to the 1966 carryover began with 805 million bushels in May of 1965. This prediction was continually reduced due to domestic drought and to increased need abroad. The actual carryover was only 536 million bushels. Predictions for the 1967 carryover were 375–400 million bushels, an amount inadequate even for the limited purposes of the 1952 study. In the event of unexpected demands from food-deficit nations, the United States would be hard-pressed to meet them. In making new commitments for the use of U.S. wheat production, the Freeman administration had neglected to provide adequate supplies. Some commitments or intentions with respect to food aid were cut back sharply. The USDA found itself in the desperate position of the Anderson administration when the latter became aware of the European famine of 1946–47.

However the U.S. wheat producers were not dissatisfied. Due to lack of stocks, their government was powerless to prevent rapid increases in the domestic and world wheat prices and therefore increases also in the cost of the food aid programs.

In spite of considerable political opposition, the Freeman administration moved to replenish the reserve by increasing acreage for the 1967 crop. In 1967 acreage controls were relaxed, and harvested wheat acreage expanded from 49.8 to 60 million acres. Despite dry weather in the Southern Plains a record crop was produced, which together with larger crops elsewhere more than replenished world supplies. World and domestic prices declined to previous levels, with attending disappointment among domestic farmers.

During 1967 a new proposal for food reserves was considered in the Agriculture Committee of the House. This "Purcell bill" would have required the CCC to maintain stocks equal to 20 percent of annual domestic use and exports of wheat (about 300 million bushels). Some other commodities were to be included in the "national security" reserve. These stocks were to be used whenever needed to meet domestic and world food needs. By removing this amount from the market, an intended effect would be to raise prices. Opponents charged that as a price measure the reserve would be a "one-shot" device since, barring an emergency, these reserve stocks would be drawn from the market only once. However the history of surpluses suggests that the size of nonmarket outlets for wheat was related to, perhaps even dependent on, the size of the stocks available for use in those outlets.

The Purcell bill received formal support from the Freeman administration, although the administration seemed to prefer that no restrictions be placed on the use of reserve stocks (see Chapter 13). It was not reported from the Committee.

Meanwhile attention shifted away from the possibility of short-term emergencies and long-run shortages to the fact that U.S. agriculture possessed a short-run "overcapacity."[49] In 1968 attention was again to be placed on preventing surpluses rather than in using or preparing to use abundance.

SUMMARY

This chapter has brought together in preview the major commodity programs which will subsequently be discussed; it also has been convenient to give full coverage to the war policies. The focus here has been on the relationship of policy to supply and demand, and the conclusions reached about this relationship may perhaps be regarded as hypotheses for analysis of specific policies in the chapters which follow.

WHEAT STOCKS (RESERVES, SURPLUSES) SINCE 1920

During at least 28 of the 50 years since 1916, there has been too much or too little wheat. In 23 of these years the problem was too much wheat; in the rest, not enough.

49. Earl O. Heady, "Future Farm Production Potentials and Certain Policy Implications," speech at seminar on Grain Production and Stocks, Livestock Production, and Farm Policy, sponsored by the Center for Agricultural and Economic Development, Washington, D.C., Dec. 27–29, 1967.

PERIODS OF LARGE STOCKS

1. 1929–34—World depression and abundant harvests resulted in an unprecedented market glut. At first the federal government took up some of the huge surplus, which later was released to private traders until the oversupply was ended by drought. The trauma of overwhelming surpluses and futile public measures was an experience that had an impact on many future decisions.

2. 1940–42—Large stocks resulted from abundant production even under controls, when normal exports were eliminated by war. These war stocks were unwanted surpluses, fed to animals as quickly as possible.

3. 1953–60—Technological abundance, high prices, and policy deadlock combined to produce enormous surpluses as well as new storage facilities adequate to store the surpluses. Surpluses grew despite large-scale disposal programs. Experience with these disposal programs spurred interest in using farm abundance constructively, but huge stocks themselves were viewed negatively.

4. 1961–67—As stocks were reduced, due mainly to increased exports for food aid and for cash, there was discussion about appropriate reserve levels. No level was set, however.

PERIODS OF SCARCITY

1. 1916–18—Through vigorous and effective governmental intervention in the distribution of existing supplies, enough wheat was available to meet the critical domestic and war needs.

2. 1946–48—There was insufficient grain to fill policy requirements, particularly for postwar relief. With adequate storage facilities and continually high production, the sole reason for the food deficit was a negative view of stocks, as held by USDA administrators.

3. 1966—Most of the remaining food stocks were used to meet a world food deficit resulting from drought in India and other subsistence areas. Pressures on stocks came on two sides, from producers who were reluctant to increase supplies by increasing acreage and from the willingness of the government to meet contingencies—world food relief—that they had not planned for.

RELATIONSHIP OF FEDERAL POLICIES TO SUPPLY AND DEMAND

1. Production research—Farming was given a high value in the United States and was a principal beneficiary of the rapid progress of

technology in this century. Public research contributed enormously to productivity, but the supply of wheat on hand had little direct effect upon the amount of research done.

Therefore the continual increases in productivity were not intentional. They were largely the result of economic vigor, the availability of natural resources, and a cultural preference for farming.

2. Price guarantees—High price supports increased supplies over the long run by reducing the risk and raising the income from farming, and because of new technology higher incomes permitted farmers to risk new techniques and to purchase improved equipment.

3. Controls on acreage—These were designed to reduce production temporarily. Their ultimate effect, however, was to increase productivity by idling or rotating cropland and by paying part of the cost of making permanent improvements. The controls programs did not reduce production but instead created a kind of reserve and ultimately increased productivity.

RELATIONSHIP OF COMMODITY POLICY TO LEVELS
OF GRAIN STOCKS (RESERVES, SURPLUSES)

1. Government stocks have affected domestic productivity both positively and negatively. As a mechanism for supporting prices, they have resulted in increased production. At the same time the pressure of existing stocks available for sale prevented increases above support levels. In this way stocks stabilized prices; but since support levels were usually well above world price levels, their total effect was to increase productivity.

2. United States stocks also had mixed effects upon foreign productivity. United States stockpiling was a means both of stabilizing world wheat prices and holding them at higher levels than would otherwise have been obtained—in that sense leading to continued moderate increases in world wheat acreage.

In some ways foreign food development was spurred by the U.S. surplus disposal program which resulted from excessive stocks. This program in effect added to the U.S. resources committed to foreign economic development. With U.S. supplies available, however, some recipients tended to relax their own food-producing efforts. The all-important question was whether food aid was more a help than a hindrance to recipients. The answer was no doubt complex, varying by country, by year, and even by project.

3. Abundant stocks in the midst of world hunger drew attention to the mechanisms for distribution of agricultural commodities. Many

new and substantial political interests grew in connection with the processing, delivery, and use of food, as will be discussed elsewhere.

REASONS FOR RESERVES

The objectives or reasons stated for U.S. reserves of wheat discussed below have become more significant as the level of U.S. stocks has become the product of program plans rather than program deficiencies.

1. To assure adequate domestic food. Since the United States has annually produced far more food than was needed domestically, no one has worried about food shortage due to crop failure. Reserves would be needed only in the event of atomic attack, an eventuality for which the United States is unprepared in more ways than one.

2. To assure stable exports. Presumably the United States can gain additional foreign markets by guaranteeing supplies of the various kinds of wheat needed by buyers. Indeed, countries have often preferred to produce their own staples at great cost rather than to rely on irregular imports. For many years large U.S. supplies have provided security to all food-importing nations, even if they did not buy from the United States. When U.S. supplies were low, importers everywhere faced price inflation and even short rations.

3. Meeting world food deficits. With reserves lacking elsewhere, and with nutritive levels already dangerously low, any reduction in world food supplies recently has been likely to result in death and disorder. There is likelihood of a food deficit somewhere every year and ultimately of a world food gap even in years of normal crops.

The United States has taken some steps toward managing world supplies by meeting major food deficits from its own stocks during the past few years, by stabilizing world prices, by a political commitment to sustaining governments threatened by famine (such as India), by token aid for agricultural development and population control, and by seeking multilateral mechanisms for achieving world food sufficiency. These steps will be discussed in Chapters 3 and 13.

3 / EXPORT POLICY IN REVIEW

INTERNATIONAL MOVEMENT of wheat has long been substantial. Over one-fifth of total production went into international trade in 1900, as well as in the 1960s. The main flow of wheat trade in the late nineteenth century was from the United States and Eastern Europe —the big "breadbaskets"—into Western Europe, the major market. In 1898–99 the United States furnished 51 percent of the wheat shipped in foreign trade.

Trade patterns have since shifted, although the United States has remained a dominant influence in wheat exports (see Table 3.1). The Danube states of Eastern Europe have reversed their role—from major exporters to major importers of wheat.

Three new exporters entered the field as wheat moved into the world's arid and remote regions early in the twentieth century: as wheat spread from the Midwest to the Plains in the United States, it moved also into the sparsely populated plains of Canada, Argentina, and Australia. Total wheat trade expanded—indeed tripled—during this century, with these three countries claiming almost half of it. The

TABLE 3.1. Wheat and wheat flour: World exports, by principal countries (averages 1900–54, annual 1955–65)

Year beginning July	Total world production	Total world exports	Total U.S. exports	Percentage of total exports					
				U.S.[a]	Canada[b]	Australia	Argentina	France	Other countries[e]
	(million bushels)			*(percent)*					
1900–1909	...	596	155	26.0	6.4	4.4	14.1	...	49.1
1910–19	...	665	183	27.5	19.2	8.3	13.4	...	31.6
1920–29	...	840	222	26.4	31.8	10.5	18.4	...	12.9
1930–39	...	710	75	10.6	28.3	16.1	18.3	...	26.7
1945–49	...	878	415	47.3	28.7	9.4	8.7	...	5.9
1950–54	...	968	330	34.1	31.0	10.1	8.4	d	16.4
1955[e]	7,400	1,058	346	32.7	23.8	9.6	10.6	9.4	13.9
1956	7,800	1,323	549	41.5	21.3	9.5	7.5	1.1	19.1
1957	7,670	1,195	402	33.6	26.5	5.1	6.5	6.9	21.2
1958	8,710	1,320	442	33.5	22.7	5.7	7.8	3.0	27.3
1959	8,175	1,358	509	37.5	20.5	9.0	5.7	4.7	22.5
1960	8,185	1,575	661	42.0	21.7	11.6	4.5	3.6	16.6
1961	7,880	1,755	718	40.9	20.8	13.2	4.9	3.8	16.4
1962	8,760	1,605	638	39.8	20.6	11.3	4.1	6.8	17.4
1963[e]	8,346	2,074	847	40.8	26.6	13.7	4.9	4.7	9.2
1964	9,300	1,871	717	38.3	23.2	12.6	8.3	9.0	8.5
1965	9,108	2,311	858	37.1	23.6	9.0	12.5	7.6	10.2
1966[f]	...	2,070	733	35.4	26.3	12.3	5.5	5.4	15.1
1967[g]	...	1,975	750	38.0	19.0	12.2	3.3	8.7	18.8

Source: *Wheat Situation*, USDA-ERS (April 1963), table 23; (March 4, 1966), table 18; and (May 1968), table 22.

a. Excludes the wheat equivalent of exports of flour milled in bond. Includes principal products other than flour.
b. Includes imports of "wheat unfit for human consumption" into United States from Canada, in million bushels, as follows: 1950–54 average, 14; 1955–56, 7; 1957–58, 10; 1958–59, 7; 1959–60, 6; 1960–61, 7; 1961–62, 5; 1962–63, 4; 1963–64, 3; and 1964–65, 1. Includes wheat to the United States which was milled in bond and later exported by the United States.
c. Includes USSR. Beginning 1956, includes additional estimates of intra-Communist Bloc exports not fully accounted for in previous years.
d. Exports from France prior to 1955 are not entered in this table.
e. All years since 1955 exclude Communist China, North Korea, and North Vietnam; exclude USSR through 1961–62.
f. Preliminary.
g. Partly estimated.

United States at most times took much of the remainder, but its share of trade varied by periods. Normally heavy during and following wars, the market was relatively less and lightest during depressions. From 1960 to 1964 the United States controlled two-fifths of the total world wheat trade.

A fifth country, France, has made significant challenge in the export market since the mid-1950s. In fact the French share of world wheat trade occasionally has surpassed that of Australia or Argentina.

In short, though, the bulk of the wheat exports since 1900 have come from four countries, United States, Canada, Argentina, and Australia—sometimes misleadingly designated as "the club." Of these, Canada and the United States together supplied well over half the world exports.

Meanwhile the list of important importers has also changed. Since World War I, Western Europe has moved continually toward greater self-sufficiency.[1] Between the 1934–38 and the 1954–58 periods the proportion of world wheat imports to the four major European importers fell from 49 percent to 30 percent of the world's wheat trade.[2] Even as a long-run phenomenon, this loss of the main world wheat market was a most disturbing element affecting postwar wheat planning. Europe was expected even to have a food grain surplus by 1970.[3]

In the 1960s Asia replaced Europe as the principal wheat importer. China and the Soviet Union, who had usually consumed their own large wheat production, became importers, as did Japan, formerly a rice-eating nation.

However the largest single importer of wheat during the 1960s was India, who was unable to pay hard currencies for it. India and other populous countries had begun developing serious food deficits at about the same time that the commercial wheat market was developing a serious surplus. The result was the shipment of wheat exports into nonmarket channels, sometimes called concessional sales or food aid. In 1962–64 U.S. wheat exports for food aid totaled 1.6 billion bushels, or about 70 percent of total U.S. wheat exports.[4] Noncommercial or food aid shipments for 1964 amounted to about 30 percent of all world wheat trade and about 6 percent of total world production.

1. Table 3.1 indicates the trend in recent years, but it began before the turn of the century, according to Paul de Hevesy, *World Wheat Planning and Economic Planning in General* (London: Oxford Univ. Press, 1940), app. 18.
2. "Towards a Solution of Our Wheat Surplus Problems," Canadian-American Committee under the National Planning Association (U.S.) and Private Planning Association of Canada (1959), p. 20.
3. Bela Balassa, *Trade Prospects for Developing Countries* (Homewood, Ill.: Irwin, 1964), pp. 146–48.
4. Lyle P. Schertz and Richard J. Cannon, "U.S. Wheat Paramount in World Supply Situation," *Foreign Agriculture*, FAS-USDA, vol. 4, no. 10 (March 7, 1966), p. 16.

The existence of a food deficit in the developing nations and a market surplus in the wheat-exporting countries strongly suggested the continued or increased heavy distribution of wheat in nonmarket channels.

FUTURE WHEAT PRODUCTION

Future production and trade perhaps might be reduced by governmental actions. Production could decline with the appearance of a serious disease or other new hazard to wheat. However there are now tremendous resources for combating any such natural threat, as demonstrated in the successful campaign against rust which threatened durum wheat during the 1950s.

Improved seed varieties have increased yields recently. Within a four-year period, new Gaines varieties of wheat have doubled yields in the Pacific Northwest. These new varieties have been developed and widely adopted with even more impressive results in Mexico, Pakistan, India, and other developing countries. Hybrid wheat development is apparently feasible and may soon prove practical, but so far yield increases have been quite erratic and have been followed by periods of unfulfilled expectations.

Fertilizers can be extended with good results to additional acres of wheat cropland. Indeed wheat could be raised on most acreages now devoted to other crops. World production could be further increased simply by adding to the world's cropland those acres capable of growing wheat under existing technology. In addition, new techniques and seeds which prepare wheat for ever shorter seasons and ever drier climates may continue to be developed, thereby opening additional acreages not now usable.[5]

With so many possible increments, wheat production can presumably be greatly expanded. Indeed the trends in the direction of increasing yields, acreage, and total production of wheat have recently been underestimated. So have the trends toward increased use of wheat worldwide. Although the trend in per capita use is downward in industrial countries, the nutritional need for wheat is outracing world production.

FUTURE USES OF WHEAT

In poor countries cereals such as wheat, corn, rice, barley, and rye dominate the diet, but in countries with high per capita incomes cereals constitute but a small part of the average diet. As incomes go

---

5. For a history of specific progress on wheat breeding, see L. R. Reitz, "Wheat Breeding and Our Food Supply," *Econ. Botany*, 8(July–September 1954):251–68.

TABLE 3.2. Population growth by areas defined according to staple cereal foods

Consuming areas	1936	1956	1960	Increase per year	
				1936–56	1956–60
	(population in millions)				
Advanced wheat-eating	439.0	540.5	567.1	5.1	6.6
Mainly rice-eating	597.9	808.6	875.7	10.5	16.8
Other	327.7	478.0	525.5	7.5	11.9
Total	1,364.6	1,827.1	1,968.3	23.1	35.3

Source: International Wheat Council, *Review of the World Wheat Situation, 1961–62*, table 10.

up, people eat less grain. The U.S. cereal consumption per capita has dropped by one-third over the previous fifty years.[6] Flour consumption in the United States, per capita, stabilized in 1962–65 at the level equivalent to about 160 pounds of wheat per year.[7] Consumers in European countries who have been using as much as twice that amount (Greece, Italy, Turkey) may with increased income reduce the proportion of cereals in their diets.[8]

Wheat markets in most of the Western world are expected to shrink, as declining per capita consumption outweighs the impact of increasing numbers of consumers. The traditional wheat markets have all been shrinking.

In contrast, cereals are appropriate as the food staple for countries with very low income levels. In low-income countries agriculture production has not been keeping pace with population increases.[9] Most conspicuous among these countries is the Peoples Republic of China, whose people have the poorest diets in the world.

For a large share of the people in food-deficit areas, mainly in Asia, the staple food has been rice (see Table 3.2). However wheat is also raised in most Asian countries, where it is becoming a high-status food.[10] In other countries wheat is usually the preferred cereal, replacing staple corn, rye, and other cereals whenever wheat is available.

Wheat is the most likely of the cereals to bear the major burdens in filling the food gap, for several reasons. Wheat acreage is not limited by natural environment as is that of rice. Wheat yields have improved very fast, though perhaps rice yields worldwide will similarly improve shortly. More nutritious and generally less expensive, wheat

6. *National Food Situation,* USDA-ERS (May 1965), table 2, p. 2.
7. *Wheat Situation,* USDA-ERS, WS-95 (February 1966), p. 5.
8. *Wheat Problems and Programs in the United States,* North Central Reg. Publ. 118, Univ. of Missouri (1960), pp. 41, 55–56.
9. Lester Brown, *Increasing World Food Output,* USDA-ERS For. Agr. Econ. Rept. 25 (April 1965), p. 113.
10. Ibid., p. 79.

can now be processed to simulate rice. Wheat also requires less household fuel for cooking.

Countries experiencing food deficits are handicapped by low income and low education levels and by a very low ratio of arable land to people. The Far East has over half the world's population, but only a fourth of the world's agricultural land.[11] Even assuming maximum application of technology to all available land in the area, Asia would likely be obliged to increase grain imports substantially within a few years in order to upgrade diets to a level of minimum nutrition, and to feed the increased population. One USDA study of the trend in grain imports by geographic regions projected an increase from the level of 12 million metric tons in 1957–61 to annual imports of 54 million metric tons in the year 2000, even if Asia should develop the highest possible level of self-sufficiency. Other underdeveloped countries would be similarly in need, barring spectacular success in stabilizing population growth there. Exports from North America were projected to increase to almost 100 million metric tons, which is three times the size of the average U.S. wheat crop during the 1960s.[12]

India, Egypt, Indonesia, China, and other food-deficit countries have already had to import large quantities of grain as a means of preventing famine. It has been predicted that by 1970 the food deficit, as derived from an expected calorie gap, would be 54 million metric tons, which would be the equivalent of more than 2 billion bushels of grain.[13] All such predictions assume a continuation of trends such as population growth, which may or may not occur.

With respect to future supply and demand for wheat, present trends do indicate that there is an increasing capacity to produce in those nations in which per capita demand for wheat is declining. But in food-deficit countries containing most of the world's population, the need for food grows so much faster than the capacity to produce that ever-larger imports have been needed to ward off starvation. Yield improvement has led planners in some countries such as India to predict ultimate self-sufficiency. Economists, however, have differed on the question as to whether the effective world demand will exceed the supplies of food. Assuming that the United States were to act as the world's residual supplier, a 1965 analysis by the USDA suggested that U.S. production could fill the ever-widening food gap only until 1985.

11. *World Food Budget, 1970,* USDA-ERS For. Agr. Econ. Rept. 19 (October 1964), p. 15.
12. Lester Brown, *Man, Land and Food,* USDA-ERS For. Agr. Econ. Rept. 11 (November 1963), p. 122.
13. *World Food Budget, 1970,* p. 33.

However, economic analyses two years later suggested an increasing "overcapacity" to meet world food needs, permitting a reduction in U.S. grain acreage from 185 million acres in 1959 to 163 million acres in 1980.[14] The optimism pervading the latter projections, however, was apparently not shared by other social scientists and by natural scientists.[15] In the event that the amounts needed do surpass the full capacity of the existing structure of world agriculture, land and other resources could be diverted from production of foods with high resource input, such as animal products, to production of cereals. The transfer of food from the surplus nations to the deficit nations undoubtedly will be mainly in the form of wheat and to a lesser extent in the form of other grains.

Despite a market surplus of wheat during the past fifteen years, the market has been stabilized by restraints on production or by sales imposed by the governments of wheat-exporting nations. The United States in particular has reduced acreage while at the same time shipping as much as one-third of its wheat crop through special or nonmarket channels such as aid under the Food for Peace program. The level of such concessional exports projected for 1970 is $1.8 billion.[16]

In these concessional shipments, market mechanisms have been used to facilitate transfer, and may in the future play a role in decisions as to where food will be sent. The significant transfers of food during coming years may be in accord with political agreement, indirectly or even as a result of decisions on the battlefield.

HISTORY OF U.S. WHEAT TRADE POLICY

Constantly exercising great influence on international wheat trade during the past century, U.S. government wheat policies at the same time were a response to the circumstances of the international market. Several patterns of situation and policy can be noted, some of which were coterminous.

FREE MARKETS BEFORE 1920

Until 1920 America's domestic wheat surplus found markets abroad. World prices were often quite low, with farmer unrest oc-

14. Luther G. Tweeten, "Objectives and Goals for Farm Commodity Programs after 1969," presented at seminar of Center for Agricultural and Economic Development, Washington, D.C., Dec. 27–28, 1967.
15. K. S. Quisenberry (ed.), "Wheat and Wheat Improvement," *Agronomy,* vol. 13 (American Society of Agronomy, 1967), pp. 17–18. See also Center for Agricultural and Economic Development, *Alternatives for Balancing World Food Production and Needs* (Ames: Iowa State Univ. Press, 1967).
16. *World Food Budget, 1970,* p. 64.

curring during these periods. Rebelling farmers tended to blame internal conditions, such as the high cost of transportation and credit, rather than blaming the international price. In any case, there were taboos against price intervention by government, except through tariffs and other indirect devices. These taboos were suspended during the World War I crisis, the war being considered an adequate reason for controlling the price of U.S. wheat. Through joint action the allied governments successfully moderated an inflationary spiral in the world wheat price.

ECONOMIC NATIONALISM AND MARKET CHAOS, 1920–33

Between 1920 and 1933 the United States embarked on a foreign policy of "isolationism," seeking to avoid political commitments to other nations or to international agencies. At first wheat producers thought they might also retreat from international involvement, either through a farm program which would maintain a high domestic wheat price regardless of the state of international markets or by increasing U.S. consumption to the point where there would be no domestic surplus. Instead per capita flour consumption declined and no effective price programs were enacted—leaving U.S. producers at the mercy of the chaotic international market throughout the decade. From the experience of 1920–33 some economists and farm leaders began to lose confidence in the ability of the wheat market either to promote efficiency or to achieve balance between supply and demand. The market—according to theory and popular belief—was supposed to reward and encourage the efficient producer while eliminating the inefficient producer. However chronic short-run price instability had injured the efficient commercial producer relatively more than the inefficient subsistence farmer. With respect to the equilibrium goal, wheat prices exercised an inadequate control on production. In 1930 planted acreage increased despite the large stocks and despite wheat prices at levels far below the cost of production.

Wheat economist Paul de Hevesy reached the following discouraging conclusions about the wheat market in the Great Depression:

1. "The price of wheat . . . fell almost everywhere, but especially in predominantly agricultural countries, very much lower than the price-level of the industrial goods which are bought by the farmer and the agricultural laborer."[17]

2. For a period of several years, production costs were far higher than export prices for wheat.

---

17. de Hevesy, pp. 10–11.

3. "Wheat played an important part in bringing about, and later in relieving, the Great Depression, as well as in promoting the new economic crisis of 1938–39."[18]

Such events prompted de Hevesy to ask "whether it was, or ever can be, in the general interest to allow wheat to enter the world market at a price yielding no profit to producer, or at a price even lower than the cost of production."[19]

Inescapably, the free market for wheat did not work as it should in theory.[20] Research on wheat prices indicated several reasons for their chronic instability:

1. The inverse relationship between need and capacity to buy. The poorer a country was, the more likely was its population to subsist on cereal grains, and the more likely were its people to desire increased per capita consumption. By the same token, however, the less likely were that country and its government to be able to purchase food from abroad. Despite the fact that food was of basic importance to humans, governments have usually been willing to reduce nutritional levels as a means of achieving trade or domestic price objectives. Perhaps the most dramatic illustration was during the Great Depression, when wheat from hungry Russian peasants was confiscated to be sold abroad. Elsewhere tariff barriers against plentiful and low-priced wheat had encircled nations of hungry people. As a result, the lowest world wheat prices on record were accompanied by the smallest world market in a century.

On the other hand, countries with solvent economies were likely to be in the process of reducing per capita consumption of cereals. To overstate the tendencies described here, those for whom wheat was a staple food lacked purchasing power, and those who had purchasing power preferred to eat other, more expensive foods.

2. Production variations due to weather. Weather affected markets in two ways. In the first place, it caused sharp yield variations, locally, from year to year, and in turn caused sharp fluctuations in local market prices. Another effect of variable weather was to en-

18. Ibid., p. 8.
19. Ibid., p. 10.
20. Considerable evidence was presented supporting this conclusion, reluctantly, in several articles appearing in the *Wheat Studies of the Stanford Food Research Institute*. These articles include the following: Helen C. Farnsworth, "Decline and Recovery of Wheat Prices in the 'Nineties,'" 10(June and July 1934):289–344; Alonzo E. Taylor, "The Contractility of Wheat Acreage in the United States," 6(February 1930):151–88; Taylor, "Economic Nationalism in Europe as Applied to Wheat," 8(February 1932):261–76; and Holbrook Working, "Cycles in Wheat Prices," 8(November 1931):1–66.

courage farmers to plant even in the face of adverse prices; in other words, it deterred negative production responses to low prices and demand. Farmers would continue to plant wheat despite surpluses in the hope that a year of poor weather might eliminate a market surplus and restore good prices. They understood, for example, that poor weather was the temporary cure for the major price recessions of 1892–95[21] and 1929–37.

Good weather also encouraged overproduction. As we have seen in Chapter 1, a run of good weather in the arid areas—a few years of high precipitation—led almost inevitably to expansion of acreage onto marginal lands, which in turn increased production.

All these effects of weather have been most pronounced in those countries which export much of their production—Canada, Australia, Argentina, and the United States.[22] Thus the international market has been quite sensitive to weather whenever world stocks were not large, particularly when weather has caused similar yield changes simultaneously in two or more exporting nations.

While highly variable weather has encouraged irrational responses by individual producers, it has been a major incentive for national or international cooperation in the production and marketing of wheat. Because variations in the four exporting countries were the principal source of world supply instability, cooperation confined to these four governments could be quite fruitful.

3. Accumulation of surplus productivity over time. The wheat economy has often been faced with long-term overproductivity, induced by immigration, new technology, wartime prices, or some combination of these and other causes.[23] The 1920s were actually at the end of a long downward swing in world prices, and upward swing in productivity, both of these trends having been disguised by occasional unfavorable weather.

4. Governmental intervention in the marketplace. In the 1920s most of the countries which exported or imported wheat made private arrangements to escape the whipsaw effects of the international wheat market. These defensive measures were intensified when the market began its depression downswing. The resulting state of the international wheat market was described by Alonzo Taylor in 1932:

---

21. Farnsworth, "Decline and Recovery." The temporary effects of weather on prices in the past century are also discussed by Wilfred Malenbaum, *The World Wheat Economy, 1885–1939* (Cambridge: Harvard Univ. Press, 1953), pp. 177–81.
22. See the following articles in the *Wheat Studies of the Stanford Food Research Institute:* Holbrook Working, "The Changing World Wheat Situation," 6(September 1930):429–57; and V. P. Timoshenko, "Interregional Correlations in Wheat Yields and Outputs," 20(July 1944):258–59.
23. Malenbaum, pp. 177–78.

In Europe, in particular, the programs of self-containment are becoming state policies of ambitious extent. "Economic nationalism" is the political term applied in Europe. The movement is fostered by distress of producer classes. In particular, agriculturists in European countries seek preferential positions—Central Europe seeks preference in the wheat markets of Western Europe. The Dominions of the British Commonwealth seek preference in the wheat markets of Great Britain. Great Britain, Holland, Belgium, and France extend preferences to their colonies for feeding stuffs. In order to effectuate quotas and preferences, intricate internal regulations and extensive interstate barters become necessary. Russia, Argentina, and the United States stand outside the charmed circle. Of the exporting countries, the United States alone must sell export wheat at competitive prices in open markets.[24]

Like many economists, Professor Taylor was distressed by these policies. They were regarded as a useless product of retaliatory economic nationalism. Yet with respect to wheat, government intervention had sought quite specific objectives, and these were important enough that the price of wheat has been determined by governmental policies since that period.[25]

There were, and continued to be, various and sufficient reasons for widespread governmental control of wheat production and marketing. Among the reasons for this nearly universal control by nations over their wheat economy have been the following:

1. Conserving currency. Governments with an unfavorable balance of trade have frequently decided to reduce agricultural imports, either by increasing domestic production or by decreasing food consumption.

2. Desire for self-sufficiency. The people of Europe became desperately hungry when World War I limited access to their regular overseas food sources. This experience convinced them that it was quite necessary, for reasons of both self-preservation and national power, to seek self-sufficiency in food production. In practice, this has meant self-sufficiency in wheat production.

24. Alonzo Taylor, "Economic Nationalism in Europe as Applied to Wheat," *Wheat Studies of the Stanford Food Research Institute,* 8(February 1932):frontispiece.
25. In 1941–42 a world survey indicated that "practically everywhere in the world, wheat, flour, and bread . . . lay under governmental controls, which extended from farm marketings through prices and transport to flour milling and less generally to bread baking and rationing of consumption." In M. K. Bennett, Helen C. Farnsworth, and Rosamond H. Pierce, "Wheat in the Third Year: Major Developments, 1941–42," *Wheat Studies of the Stanford Food Research Institute,* 19(December 1942):87. A survey of grain policies in 1963 revealed about the same situation. See *National Grain Policies,* UN-FAO, 1963.

3. Aiding farmers. Wheat imports, unlike bananas or coconuts, have been almost invariably competitive with the product of local farmers. Most countries which have imported wheat have also produced it. Since local producers ordinarily could not profitably produce wheat at the world price, they sought and got price protection. One expert committee on international trade concluded that the principal reason for wheat programs in the various countries was to protect domestic producers.[26] The policy of protecting domestic farmers has been almost universal, including even countries highly committed to international trade, such as Switzerland. The reason no doubt includes both the political strength of producers and a general desire to maintain the peasantry as a "traditional mode of life."[27]

The total effect of these mutually defensive efforts to maintain farm income has been a matter for dispute. Paul de Hevesy said that the ultimate beneficiary of the various tariffs imposed on wheat was not the farmer, and certainly not the consumer, but rather the treasuries of the various taxing governments.[28]

In commenting on plans and programs from 1920–35, Joseph S. Davis argued that efforts to support domestic prices at a level higher than world prices tended instead to result in a reduction in world prices. Such efforts were defeated also by retaliatory measures undertaken by other governments.[29] Presumably this criticism no longer applied when the United States and Canada became able, as in recent years, to control the level of world as well as national supplies.

Benefits to farmers from protective policies have been particularly questionable when wheat protection was linked, as ordinarily it has been, with protection for the commodities and products which farmers must buy. As American farm spokesmen viewed protectionism during the 1920s, the key question was whether wheat was treated equally in relation to other products protected by the U.S. government. Some spokesmen were convinced that protectionist policies were effectively raising prices of farm equipment and other goods that farmers had to buy while making only symbolic contributions to wheat prices.

In any case, patterns of international trade in wheat have been

---

26. "GATT Programme for Expansion of International Trade," *Trade in Agricultural Products,* 2nd and 3rd Repts. of Comm. II (Geneva, 1962), p. 10.
27. Gerard Curzon, *Multilateral Commercial Diplomacy* (London: Michael Joseph, 1965), p. 206.
28. de Hevesy, p. 17.
29. Joseph S. Davis, *Wheat and the AAA* (Washington: Brookings Institution, 1935), pp. 417–19.

set by national policy as much as by relative efficiency. Wheat trade policies have been objected to on the classic ground that protective tariffs violate the "law of comparative advantage." According to this law, each nation should put its resources to their most efficient use. Regional differences in the comparative advantage of producing wheat, after transportation costs are deducted, have been neutralized by trade policies.

5. *Political aims and wheat policy*. It is sometimes argued that World War II might have been prevented if the more solvent nations had been less intent on extracting a pound of economic flesh from the less solvent nations during the 1920s. In that decade U.S. wheat policy was certainly free from any subsidiary aims of promoting international peace and cooperation. After 1933, however, international political aims became quite important—and generally over-riding—in the determination of wheat trade policies of the United States.

MULTILATERALISM, 1933–64

A multilateral policy is one which proceeds from consultation among several nations, and which takes the interests of these nations into account. Between 1933 and 1964 U.S. commodity policies took account of cooperative agreements with both importers and competing exporters. During much of this time the amount of wheat to be exported by the United States was determined by the government. Exports were regulated, directly or indirectly, by controls on production, levels of price supports, amounts of foreign aid grants and loans, and by willingness of the U.S. government to carry very large stocks. In addition, with domestic prices supported at levels above the world price, wheat could be exported only with the aid of a substantial per bushel federal export subsidy, which in effect determined the export price.

Wheat export policy was very much an adjunct of the pursuit of general U.S. policy goals during that time, including enhanced trade with other nations, political cooperation with other friendly powers, and opposition to unfriendly powers.

As an example, between 1954 and 1966 more U.S. wheat was shipped abroad primarily as food aid than as cash exports (Table 3.3). During periods of rapid surplus accumulation the United States usually sold less wheat abroad than at other times. Self-imposed restrictions on trade with Communist nations reduced the exports of wheat to these powers. The best illustration of the overriding

TABLE 3.3. Wheat exports for dollars and under government concessional programs, 1945–66

Year beginning July	Under concessional programs	For dollars	% for dollars
		(000 bushels)	
1945	169,754	218,620	56.2
1946	160,022	233,956	59.3
1947	325,838	152,954	31.9
1948	376,011	126,548	25.2
1949	256,790	41,680	14.0
1950	172,968	192,605	52.7
1951	159,341	315,374	66.4
1952	29,605	287,585	90.7
1953	100,544	115,968	53.6
1954	158,025	115,609	42.3
1955	240,693	104,871	30.3
1956	375,119	173,439	31.6
1957	246,826	154,936	38.6
1958	303,002	139,099	31.5
1959	374,552	134,472	26.4
1960	457,720	203,162	30.7
1961	491,072	227,945	31.7
1962	85,390	158,223	24.6
1963	503,414	352,530	41.2
1964	567,257	157,432	21.7
1965	568,973	297,835	34.4
1966	370,942	371,459	50.0

Sources: Data for 1945–47 from files of Food Grain Section ERS-USDA; 1948–54 from *Wheat Situation*, ERS-USDA (February 1961), table 3; 1956–65 from *Wheat Situation* (October 1966), table 10; 1966 from *Wheat Situation* (November 1967), table 8.

political aims of U.S. wheat policy, however, was the restraint used in marketing wheat. Throughout the entire period, the United States acted as a residual supplier. Some other exporters held moderate stocks during periods of peak surpluses, particularly Canada, but the United States was obliged to carry the bulk of the world's heavy wheat surpluses both in the period 1941–43 and in the surplus period from 1953 to 1964. The United States also took primary responsibility for disposing of these surpluses outside market channels—an expensive wheat policy that was one of the costs presumably offset by benefits derived from free-world leadership.

Exporters. As discussed above, most of the world's wheat exports during this period originated in North America, with the United States and Canada therefore being the main beneficiaries of stable world wheat prices. The economies of these two countries were very much interlinked. Canada's wheat exports, larger than those of the

United States and three-fifths of Canada's total wheat production,[30] were a mainstay of Canada's economy; Canada in turn was the biggest importer of U.S. goods. In addition, Canada's friendship and Cold War cooperation during this period were quite important to the United States, and it became quite clear that political harmony between the two nations rested on recognition of their economic interdependence.

Therefore U.S. wheat policy was responsive to pressures not only from the U.S. prairies but from the Canadian prairies as well. In a sense Canada was still a hostage, as in the nineteenth-century U.S.-British relations, but was now the hostage of other wheat-exporting nations. If the United States did not maintain a stable world wheat price, its neighbor with interlinked trade and political interests would likely be injured more seriously than other competitors.

For its part the Canadian government was ready to share responsibility for reducing production. The semigovernmental agencies in Canada which have purchased that country's wheat for export reduced the size of export quotas for individual farmers, and Canadian producer prices were held well below those offered U.S. farmers until the 1960s. But as a small country whose wheat exports were a major source of exchange earnings, Canada could not reduce cash exports or store surpluses to the degree that the United States did.

The other principal exporters, Australia and Argentina, were less able to play a responsible role in stabilizing markets. Argentina was ordinarily obliged to market its entire crop speedily because of inadequate storage space or because of pressure to overcome existing foreign-exchange deficits. Also the United States was the only major exporter offering all kinds and qualities of wheat, and thus relating all prices.

Exporter control over the world wheat prices was maintained by means of coordinating U.S. and Canadian prices. To maintain prices both countries shared in carrying over the hard wheat surpluses, although the U.S. carryover was usually far larger, and much of it was sent outside market channels as food aid. A total of 5,626 million bushels were shipped by the United States under some program of governmental assistance between 1947 and 1964, an amount equal to about one and a half years average world production of wheat between 1950 and 1964. (The average world production during this period was 7,961.9 million bushels.)

---

30. J. Anderson Walton, *Canadian Wheat in Relation to the World's Food Production and Distribution* (Saskatoon, Sask.: Modern Press, 1964), p. 73.

TABLE 3.4. Basic producer prices, 1965–66

Country	U.S. $ per bushel
Europe	
Austria	2.59
Belgium	2.65
Denmark	1.97
Finland	5.10
France	2.42
Germany	3.01
Greece	2.68
Ireland	2.34
Italy	2.67
Netherlands	2.67
Norway	4.04
Portugal	3.12
Spain	3.02
Sweden	2.94
Switzerland	4.29
United Kingdom	1.91
Yugoslavia	2.98
North and Central America	
Canada	1.38
Mexico	1.99
United States	1.25
South America	
Argentina	1.15
Brazil	3.09
Chile	. . .
Ecuador	1.51
Asia	
India	2.83
Japan	3.56
Pakistan	2.07
Syria	1.42
Turkey	2.42
Africa	
Algeria	2.76
Kenya	2.04
Libya	. . .
Morocco	2.37
South Africa	2.30
Tunisia	2.18
U.A.R. (Egypt)	2.11
Oceania	
Australia	1.70
New Zealand	2.03

Source: International Wheat Council, *World Wheat Statistics, 1966*, p. 52.

Importers. While the world wheat price was set by exporters, importers almost invariably determined at what price wheat would actually be sold within their countries (Table 3.4). In Table 3.4, the wide variation in market prices, even between proximate countries such as Denmark and Finland, indicates that governments have effectively determined the price of wheat. For much the same reasons as noted for the 1920s, virtually all importing countries sought to produce as much of their own cereal grains as possible. Importing countries invariably guaranteed a high price for locally produced wheat and then provided for a variable levy (the difference between the exporter's price and the domestic supported price) on incoming wheat to assure that wheat could not be sold at a level below the domestic supported price. The returns from these levies, as in the European Economic Community, were used to pay the cost of the domestic farm program or even to finance wheat exports, as in the case of France within the European Economic Community.[31]

By encouraging local producers to fill as much of the market as they could, the program for importers left exporters in the position of uncertain residual suppliers, thus adding to the instability of supplies and prices on the world market. An alternative to the variable levy was the deficiency payments device used by England, which subsidized producers rather than taxing the consumers. Under this mechanism wheat could be sold domestically at world prices, with government directly subsidizing local producers. Although this plan seemed to provide more market flexibility than the levies, and was recommended in one study,[32] another international representative group suggested that it was not preferable to the variable levy because "the essential feature of support measures is the level of support, and the degree to which production is thereby stimulated, with consequent effects on trade, rather than the particular techniques used in implementing the scheme."[33]

However production incentives did not result in wheat acreage increases in Europe, where the march toward self-sufficiency (Table 3.5) seemed powered more by sharp increases in yields than in acreage expansion. Yield increases were due immediately to technical change and in some measure to the subsidized farm incomes which made it possible to apply yield-raising practices. However some important contributors to yield increases, such as improved seeds, did not require much additional investment. In any case, it was a certainty, in terms of Europe's past food concerns, that she would pay the costs of the intensive practices needed to obtain higher yields.[34] These costs were paid through the guarantees of high domestic prices.

31. Curzon, p. 203.
32. *Haberler Report,* a report of a GATT study group. See *New York Times,* Oct. 3, 1958, p. 6.
33. "GATT Programme for Expansion of International Trade," p. 36.
34. Malenbaum, p. 103.

TABLE 3.5. Degree of self-sufficiency in wheat: Home production as a percentage of total supplies from internal and external sources

Country	Wheat (including flour)[a]					
	1909–13	1925–29	1934–38	1950–52	1952–53[b]	1965–66
			(percent)			
United Kingdom	21	20	24	35	34	. . .
Ireland	. . .	6	29	55[c]	47	. . .
Norway	8	9	20	12	10	. . .
Sweden	13	68	102	83	92	. . .
Finland	3	15	61	55[c]	43	. . .
Denmark	47	52	59	88	74	. . .
Netherlands	18	18	42	27	27	65
Belgium[f]	22	27	23	41	43	78
France	90	86	98	100	102	147
Germany	67	61	89	60[d]	58[d]	73
Austria	55	43	63	51	56	. . .
Switzerland	17	20	22	37	43	. . .
Italy	77	74	94	83	85	102
Spain	97	97	100	94[c]	97	. . .
Portugal	80	59	97	77[c]	81	. . .
Greece	66	38	63	83	80	. . .
Turkey	. . .	97	102	104	108	. . .
All the above	64[e]	63	·76	77	76	. . .
The above excluding the United Kingdom	74[e]	71	85	84	82	. . .

Source: International Wheat Council, "European Agriculture, a Statement of Problems, 1954," in FAO, *The World Wheat Situation and the International Wheat Agreement* (1954).

a. Converted to grain equivalent.
b. Computed from available data.
c. Average from 1950–51 to 1951–53.
d. Western Germany.
e. Excluding Turkey.
f. Plus Luxembourg.

Developing Countries. While concerned with the decline of traditional import markets, exporters became aware of the increasing demands for food in developing countries. It was clear that none of these developing countries (except Argentina) was likely to become an exporter of wheat in any future time. Most of them would strive for self-sufficiency in food because of a shortage of foreign exchange. Because of inadequate physical resources or agricultural organization, many would nevertheless need large cereal imports, which would have to be furnished as a gift or under unusual and very generous financing. In other words, a tremendous outlet for wheat existed in addition to commercial markets. Wheat shipped through that outlet was generally referred to as food aid.

MECHANISMS FOR MULTILATERAL ACTION

International trade agreements on wheat took two forms—cooperation within the wide front on the General Agreement on Tariffs and Trade and cooperation under the International Wheat Agreement.

General Agreement on Tariffs and Trade. United States farm spokesmen were among the champions of a movement following World War II favoring freer trade within the free world. In the postwar period several farm organizations emphasized that American aid for European recovery should be replaced as soon as possible by U.S. markets for European products. Their stress on "trade not aid" led them to support the multilateral General Agreement on Tariffs and Trade (GATT), a mechanism designed to negotiate reciprocal reductions in trade barriers.

However only a few farm spokesmen went so far as to support a proposed international agency (tentatively named the International Trade Organization) which would have been given power to reduce national trade barriers. Since many U.S. commodities benefited from U.S. trade barriers, farm groups wanted to retain constituency control over trade policies. Spokesmen for the protected commodities usually wanted tariff powers to remain in Congress or to be placed under the Department of Agriculture. Export-oriented farm groups, who recognized that U.S. agriculture exported more than it imported sought a decision-making framework under which tariffs could be negotiated downward, even while barriers were maintained against competitive agricultural imports. In practice this meant giving the U.S. President tariff powers, restrained on agricultural matters by congressional agriculture committees, the USDA, or other agencies responsive to farm interests.[35] This strategy seems to have worked well. In the postwar period from 1953 to 1965, U.S. farm exports doubled while agricultural imports remained stable.[36]

United States farm commodity programs met sharp criticism in the early GATT meetings. Most highly criticized were U.S. import quotas on a number of commodities, the purpose of which was to prevent any sizable imports. For example, almost no wheat to be used for human consumption was allowed to enter the United States.

35. Don F. Hadwiger, "Farm Organizations and U.S. Foreign Trade Policy, 1946–1955" (Ph.D. diss., University of Iowa, 1956), pp. 198–250.
36. Sherwood O. Berg, "Agriculture's Role in Expanding World Trade," *Proceedings of the Upper Midwest Conference on Agricultural Export Trade* (University of Minnesota, 1966).

Also criticized were U.S. export subsidies. Barriers on imports, linked with large export subsidies for wheat, enabled wheat farmers to enjoy domestic prices above world levels while exporting a large portion of the crop. These U.S. measures were viewed as particularly bad precedents by those desiring to liberalize world trade.

Later judgments of U.S. agricultural policies, however, were more favorable. With respect to wheat, for example, it had become clear that most nations were unwilling to permit their domestic prices to be determined by an unstable world market. It was also realized later that national wheat programs were needed to prevent overproduction, like the U.S. program which had reduced U.S. acreage by 25 percent.[37]

Surplus disposal programs in the United States also met hostility at first, because concessional sales of U.S. surpluses had undoubtedly displaced some commercial sales by competitors. GATT committees later concluded that surplus programs had increased total wheat outlets, on balance, in addition to having had other desirable results.[38]

GATT's objectives were threatened not only by U.S. unilateral action but also by the perspective developed by a regional organization, the European Economic Community. The EEC, organized by six countries which were traditionally a major market for world wheat exports, did not embrace the free-trade doctrine on which GATT had been built. That doctrine asserted that freer trade contributed to greater efficiency of production, wider choice of goods, greater equity for small nations, and greater international consultation and cooperation. With the spread of technological versatility, EEC did not assume that industrial complexes such as Europe, the United States, and Soviet Russia needed massive interchanges of goods in order to gain efficiency and wide choice. The EEC built upon successful experience with domestic and international price structuring rather than upon the unsuccessful experience with unregulated, chaotic markets. Economic goals were considered as an aspect of more general goals, and market forces as tools rather than sovereignties. Agricultural policy was conceived in the context of domestic and international policy rather than in the limited equation indicating the intereffects of tariff schedules. In this broader context the EEC regulated agricultural imports in the interest of obtaining agricultural self-sufficiency and to satisfy internal pressures for high

37. EEC meeting reported in *U.S. Agricultural Support: What It Is and What It Is Not, for Information of U.S. Personnel,* USDA-FAS (Aug. 4, 1960).
38. "GATT Programme for Expansion of International Trade," p. 36.

farm income. The EEC could also assure adequate domestic food supplies and could program foreign food aid to developing countries, as an alternative to seeking a precarious market balance of food supplies.

The earlier presumption that trade restrictions were probably contrary to both national and international interests had been the basis for continual criticism of U.S. agriculture programs.[39] Earlier reflecting this position, the U.S. Department of State, both in its international negotiations and in its recommendations for national policy, seemed embarrassed by U.S. agricultural policies. Many U.S. farm spokesmen were led to conclude that the State Department was hostile to U.S. agriculture. Certainly its more recent position suggests that it did lack adequate understanding of farm policies. The department came to agree that U.S. programs had beneficial results internationally, in that they underwrote world commodity price instability and generated resources to meet food deficits in developing countries. The department also came tardily to the position advocated by some U.S. farm leaders that agricultural development abroad was a first step in general economic development.

In summary, the free trade doctrine obscured significant national and international benefits deriving from farm programs of the United States and subsequently of the EEC. Yet the GATT mechanism did provide for communication between nations, and perhaps it did offset the constituency pull toward protectionist measures with no constructive purpose.

International Wheat Agreement. The purpose of GATT had been to reduce trade barriers. Another multilateral effort called the International Wheat Agreement (IWA) had the positive purpose of stabilizing both the quantity and the price of wheat moving in international trade.

After 1949 most of the wheat moving in international markets moved under the terms of the IWA, which was renewed in 1953, 1956, 1959, and 1962, and extended for a single year in 1965.

There were important precedents for this agreement as well as previous periods when such an agreement seemed needed. In World War I England and the principal allied countries had established an authority under a wheat executive agreement, which undertook to purchase and distribute all imports of wheat from October

---

39. See for example D. Gale Johnson, *Trade and Agriculture: A Study of Inconsistent Policies* (New York: Wiley, 1950).

1916 through the next three short-crop years.[40] Its purposes were to find as much wheat as possible, to ration it out equitably, and presumably to prevent competitive bidding by the participating nations, which would have further inflated the price. The U.S. government cooperated in all these objectives.

When wheat prices dipped down to or below prewar levels during the 1920s, proposals for international market regulation were discussed at several conferences in 1927, 1930, and 1931. However participating nations—most of all the United States[41]—were unwilling to agree to use export quotas, price fixing, or production quotas.

In 1933 the wheat economy was distressed by extremely low prices and large surpluses. Secretary of Agriculture Henry Wallace, who believed that international market control was the only realistic solution for those U.S. commodities with large export markets, led the way in negotiating an International Wheat Agreement, signed in 1933. Wallace tailored the subsequent domestic wheat program to the terms of this first IWA. The agreement established export quotas, including maximum shipments from the exporting countries. It also required a 15 percent reduction in acreage within the four major overseas exporting countries. Importers signing the agreement promised to reduce tariffs as soon as international prices returned to predepression levels.

Immediately it was clear that the exporter governments lacked the means to carry out the agreement. Argentina, which lacked the facilities to store its crop, was obliged to exceed its quota in the first year.

The world surpluses and low prices were soon dispelled by poor crops, but wheat experts during the mid-thirties nevertheless took a gloomy view of the long-run supply-demand ratio, forecasting chronic overproduction.[42] Surpluses did accumulate again, and with the onset of war a draft International Wheat Agreement was signed in 1942 between Argentina, Australia, Canada, and the United States, with the United Kingdom as principal importer also participating. The 1942 draft suggested thoroughgoing regulation of international

---

40. See two articles in *Wheat Studies of the Stanford Food Research Institute*: V. P. Timoshenko and Holbrook Working, "World Wheat Survey and Outlook, May 1940," 16(May 1940):378; and M. K. Bennett, "Wheat and the War, 1914–18 and Now," 16(November 1939):67 108.
41. See two articles by Alonzo E. Taylor, in *Wheat Studies of the Stanford Food Research Institute,* "International Wheat Conferences During 1930–31," 7(August 1931):439–66; and "International Wheat Policy and Planning," 11(June 1935):359–403.
42. See the remarks by Andrew Cairns and Merrill K. Bennett in de Hevesy, *World Wheat Planning,* pp. 863–70.

wheat export markets. It also provided for production controls (not just acreage controls); set the maximum and minimum levels for national stocks; and divided the world wheat market among four principal exporters, specifying an actual bushel quota for each as well as a percentage of the market. The United States at that time was to receive a small share—16 percent of the market or 80 million bushels.[43] This agreement never went into effect.

A draft was finally adopted in 1949 after a less ambitious agreement negotiated in 1947–48 failed to receive the requisite number of ratifications. Except for the Communist Bloc countries and Argentina, all major exporters and thirty-seven other major importers signed this four-year international wheat agreement (IWA).

No production controls were included. The new IWA of 1949 was basically a contract between specific importers and exporters fixing quantities and price ranges. Each exporter was to furnish a specific quantity and each importer was to purchase a specific quantity. The amount designated reflected existing trade patterns. The United States received 37 percent of the total guaranteed sales. A total of 456,283,000 bushels—just less than half of total world wheat exports in 1948–49—were included within the IWA.

The price range, with a maximum of $1.80, provided for a descending minimum beginning at $1.50, reflecting the expectation by importers that the world wheat price would return to prewar levels. Instead the price remained high. The issue in the 1953 renegotiation was the level of maximum prices, which was raised to $2.05. At that time the United Kingdom, to whom over a third of the total IWA shipments had gone under the 1949 agreement, concluded that the IWA tended to bolster the dominant position of the exporters in the marketplace and therefore refused to sign the 1953 agreement or to reenter at the time of the extension in 1956. In 1956 a maximum was set at $2.00. Some knowledgeable persons charged that Britain stayed out of the agreement in the hope of reinstituting ruinous competition between exporters.[44]

Britain reentered the IWA in 1959, but changes were made in this agreement which definitely favored importers. Maximum price was reduced to $1.90, and importers were given additional procedural protections. Most important perhaps, quotas to be accepted by each importing country were no longer expressed in terms of absolute

43. Andrew Cairns, speech to committee of the American Farm Bureau Federation, Chicago, Dec. 7, 1942 (dittoed).
44. Don A. Stevens, Vice-President of General Mills, Inc., and Gordon P. Boals, Director of Export Programs, Millers' National Federation, testimony before U.S. Senate Committee on Foreign Relations, *Hearings on the International Wheat Agreement* (1953), pp. 39–40.

quantities but rather as a percentage of that country's total wheat imports—that is, as a percentage of the residual market which domestic producers could not fill. This change permitted importers to use substitutes for imported wheat, if they wished, or become more self-sufficient in wheat production.

Exporters were guaranteed neither definite quantities of sales nor a percentage of the total sales under the IWA, even though a number of new objectives which were added to the IWA in 1959 tended to emphasize the problem of excessive supplies. The previous sales guarantees had not been fulfilled under earlier agreements. In 1954–55, for example, the United States sold only 139 million bushels from its quota of 196 million.

In short, the importance of the IWA had been reduced in practice to that of legitimizing the stated range of commercial wheat prices. This range was raised in the 1962 extension to $1.62½–$2.02½, despite the continued wheat market surpluses.

In asking U.S. ratification in 1962, Secretary of State Dean Rusk said, "The principal benefit of the agreement to the United States is the price range, internationally accepted as reasonable, notwithstanding the present imbalance of world supply and effective demand."[45] He also noted that the IWA was sympathetic to U.S. initiatives, both with respect to commercial sales and the large U.S. special disposal operations. "This is particularly so because the Wheat Council (the IWA executive) constitutes an international forum in which not only competing exporters may participate but also the importing countries which benefit directly from the U.S. special programs."[46]

In other words, the IWA was a useful vehicle through which existing U.S. national and bilateral policies could be implemented, with some accommodation to the interests of the other member nations. The IWA price range, for example, was less a determinant of prices than it was a reflection of the price policies of the two leading exporters, the United States and Canada. Indeed, the IWA had proven the point of those who had long argued that no international commodity agreement could determine prices. For a long time some pessimists had stressed the technical difficulty of establishing price relationships between differing qualities of wheat. Under the IWA an effort had been made to relate major wheat prices to the stated price for a particular kind and location of wheat, the one

---

45. Quoted in a Message to Congress from the President, transmitting the International Wheat Agreement, June 5, 1962.
46. Ibid.

chosen being Manitoba Northern wheat in bulk in port at Fort William/Port Arthur, Canada. Kinds and locations of wheat could be related on a scale, but quality differences had provided a major loophole for evading the IWA price range.

While the IWA could not adequately regulate prices, neither could it prevent exporters from managing prices in their own behalf. One of Britain's reasons for quitting IWA in the 1950s was that the agreement could not insure free movement of prices within the established range, nor could it prevent price collaboration between the United States and Canada or take steps to prevent a very effective duopoly of world prices.

BILATERALISM IN THE POSTWAR PERIOD

Actual control over the postwar international wheat market was maintained by the United States and Canada, with Canada assuming price leadership.[47] It was convenient for Canada to lead, because the Canadian Wheat Board was a direct seller of wheat, while the United States influenced the market indirectly through announcement of export subsidy levels following the closing of the market each day. Presumably, also, the United States as the chief economic power preferred to stay in the background.

Canada and the United States had parallel interests: both wanted to maximize income from North American wheat exports, yet both were wary of stimulating world overproduction through high prices at home and abroad. Tension between them arose from the different weighting of these interests. The Canadian Wheat Board felt constant pressure from producers to raise the world price, while the U.S. government, with greater responsibility for absorbing overproduction, favored greater world price restraint. United States producers could be subsidized instead through supported domestic price supports, export subsidies, and direct federal payments.

U.S. UNILATERALISM IN THE POSTWAR PERIOD

The United States' conduct in the postwar wheat market can be viewed in a series of concentric circles. In the outer comprehensive circle the United States maintained stable world prices by serving as the residual supplier of the world market. It transferred the world

47. Alex F. McCalla, "A Duopoly Model of World Wheat Pricing," *J. Farm Econ.*, 48 (August 1966):711–27.

surplus into nonmarket channels, a stabilizing action which served the larger objectives of the United States as responsible free-world political and economic leader.

In the next ring the United States was committed to cooperation with Canada in maintaining a desirable market for exporters.

In the inside ring, however, the United States engaged in unilateral market development activities. Restraints imposed by the outer rings were so severe as to make these activities in the inside ring sometimes almost symbolic in nature, even though much effort was expended on them. Unilateral market development was in deference to the American competitive spirit and the strong desire of U.S. farmers and wheat traders to maximize U.S. cash markets. It was also an attractive outlet for congressional desires to find new uses for farm surpluses, much like the fruitless search for major industrial uses for wheat and other farm surpluses. Finally, market development and sales promotion, as carried out under the USDA, was an expression of Secretary of Agriculture Ezra Benson's belief that agriculture could best solve its problems in a free market. The following short history of wheat market development activities reveals some frustrations resulting from the limited returns from the highly touted program, frustrations ordinarily released against the restraints imposed on the program. These limitations were the subject of continual conflict between the USDA and the State Department during the Benson administration.

Inner Circle of Wheat Market Activities. In 1953 the USDA began a vigorous pursuit of markets abroad, adopting the spirit of the "yankee trader." The USDA's small Office of Foreign Agricultural Relations was expanded, and a worldwide network of U.S. agricultural attachés was transferred to the enlarged agency (Foreign Agricultural Service) from the State Department.[48] Although the work of this expanded Foreign Agricultural Service (FAS) never attained great stature, the agency was quite successful in its relations with Congress.

The USDA also helped to finance the activities of private organizations working jointly with the FAS to promote U.S. sales abroad. All overseas market promotion work was on an extremely liberal budget, using foreign currencies generated under the surplus disposal program, P.L. 480, a major objective of which had been indicated in

48. Responsibility for agricultural attachés had been transferred from the USDA to the State Department under Reorganization Plan 2 of 1939. The responsibility was returned to the department in 1954. See *Century of Service*, USDA(1963), p. 562.

its title, The Agricultural Trade Development and Assistance Act of 1954.

Much of the overseas work initially was in the nature of sales promotion—that is, finding immediate buyers—rather than in market development. The FAS was particularly anxious to sell commodities such as wheat in surplus. As noted above, the surplus disposal program was designed to spur cash sales, by methods which drew strong protests from other wheat exporters. For example, "tied" sales were authorized: nations purchased some U.S. commodities for cash while receiving additional quantities as food aid. Considerable effort was also devoted to consummating three-way deals in which surpluses shipped to a country lacking dollars could be paid for with goods and services from a third country. Some surplus food stocks were bartered in exchange for raw materials to be added to the U.S. "strategic" stockpiles. Most of the surplus shipments were not direct grants but instead were concessional sales under which payment was in nonconvertible currencies. The United States was able to use a limited amount of these currencies within the recipient country for its own purposes, including loans to private enterprise, procurement for its own agencies, and for market development activities. Expectations with respect to the sales promotion campaign were not fulfilled, as cash wheat sales tended to decline during the time in which surplus disposal programs increased in size.

Among the efforts of FAS to develop permanent markets, perhaps the most effective was the outright grant of food for school lunch programs. Some governments of rice-eating poulations were quite pleased to see their children become accustomed to the less expensive, more nutritious bread.

Market development activities included efforts to establish meaningful standards for the kinds of wheat desired by overseas buyers and to persuade U.S. exporters to meet the standards on a consistent basis. Foreign users were introduced to techniques for processing U.S. wheat. Sales were facilitated by means of several types of credit assistance, from the forty-year, low-interest loans under which much food aid was moved into developing countries, to three-year loans for countries which were able to earn U.S. dollars.

The longer-range market development was one factor in opening new markets, and another indispensable factor, as experience with Japan suggests, was a reduction in U.S. prices. Japan became the prime illustration of achievement in wheat market development. Through cooperation of U.S. wheat producers, the FAS, and the Japanese government, Japanese consumers were introduced to bread;

and as processing facilities for baking bread were created, the food wheat market enlarged.

However the Japanese government then turned to Canada for over half its commercial wheat imports. In an effort to reverse this, the FAS and U.S. producer groups took steps to meet Japanese quality preferences. As an additional trade-priming device, the USDA subsidized internal transportation of wheat destined for Japan from central United States to the West Coast, and subsequently wheat producers and the USDA managed to obtain a reduction in rail rates on Plains wheat bound for the West Coast.

A key factor in returning the market to the United States was a decision in 1964 to sell to Japan at less than the Canadian price, whatever that price might be. As a result, in fiscal 1965 the Japanese market belonged to the United States and was absorbing 45 percent of all U.S. commercial wheat exports.

The Canadian government, no match for the competitive challenge of the USDA, accepted the locked price relationship under protest. The reasons for the new U.S. aggressiveness embraced more than the immediate sense of injustice over having lost a market that the United States had developed.

Price competition between the United States and Canada was a new development. Price cooperation had endured until late 1964 despite occasional strains. The main cause of the breakdown at that time was the decline of U.S. cash exports to a point well below any previous postwar year. The U.S. fair share of the cash export market had often been judged to be about 250 million bushels, but in 1964 it had dropped to 161 million. Meanwhile other exporters were increasing sales because of the huge new Communist markets. The USDA informally requested Canadian and other exporters to make way for somewhat larger U.S. sales in traditional markets, and when they refused to do so, the price competition ensued.

MULTILATERALISM AFTER 1965

In 1965 the United States abandoned the route of cooperation, instead threatening to use its economic power competitively in the wheat market. It ended its price partnership with Canada and emphasized its new independence by becoming reluctant to renew its membership in the International Wheat Agreement.

The United States continued to inform other exporters of its actions and also to respect their interests while conducting surplus disposal operations. However the United States reduced prices as much as 20–25 cents per bushel below those of other exporters—and announced its intention to outbid them in their own markets.

Viewing the new posture in terms of the three rings earlier discussed, this was not simply a return to the "yankee trader" philosophy of the inner ring but rather an effort to make wheat production and distribution a truly multilateral concern. The previous strategy as a benevolent pacesetter had failed, and the United States had shifted to the strategy of the taskmaster.

U.S. Objectives. United States objectives, as stated at the 1965 IWA negotiations, were in response to new circumstances in the world wheat market, in which the United States was incurring increasing costs while others were reaping increasing benefits.

One objective was to assure the United States access to world markets. The world wheat market had momentarily doubled in size, by virtue of Communist Bloc purchases, permitting an expansion of cash sales by most exporters. The United States had not got a share of these Communist markets, due mainly to domestic rather than international restraints. Added to domestic legal barriers against trade with the Communists were extraordinary demands by U.S. maritime interests, to the effect that any wheat sold to Communist countries must be shipped partly in American bottoms, which charged prohibitive rates. The U.S. government acceded to these demands to avoid a threatened maritime protest aimed at spurring public outcries against sending wheat to any enemy power.

While others were expanding exports by sales to Communist countries, the United States hoped to hold a fair proportion of the total market by assuming a larger share of the non-Communist commercial market.

Secondly the United States wanted a more equal sharing of world supply controls, assuming that the latter were needed. United States wheat acreage had been reduced in response to the actual world market surplus of wheat. This surplus had been hidden or isolated from the commercial market by U.S. storage and surplus disposal programs. Meanwhile world wheat acreage was increasing rapidly. The four major exporters had earlier (1955) agreed to institute policies which would reduce acreage, but with new Communist markets at hand in the 1960s the governments of Australia and Canada had instead effectively encouraged acreage expansion.

A third objective was to distribute the burdens of food aid among the developed nations. Although the United States was by no means bearing the whole load of food aid to food-deficit countries, its load was heavy by any standard. For example Canada's exports had almost doubled between 1960 and 1965, and 90 percent of these were for commercial sales. Only one-fifth of U.S. exports were commercial sales, the rest being food aid. Inadvertently the United States seemed to have accepted an open-ended commitment both to purchase world market surpluses and to prevent starvation in the developing countries. United States spokesmen pointed out that the burdens of market stabilization and food aid were falling increasingly on the U.S. government.

Low-Price Strategy. These U.S. objectives were to be achieved by the method of downward pressure on world prices. Recent changes in U.S. farm programs permitted the federal government to subsidize wheat farmers through direct payments while holding domestic wheat prices lower than those in any other country (see Table 3.4).

Reduced world prices would discourage wheat production elsewhere. Paradoxically, world prices promised to have a greater effect on world production in a system of highly regulated agriculture than in the unstructured market of the 1920s, since government policies responded more rationally to price than did individual producers. The government of France, for example, might well cease to export wheat and instead use its surplus for feed grain if the world wheat price dipped lower than the price of equivalent domestic feed grain. Under low wheat prices the Canadian government would persuade its farmers not to convert any more feed grain acreages to wheat.

The low-price strategy provided two alternatives with respect to food aid, either of which would reduce relative U.S. costs, with the choice of alternatives to be made by the actions of all developed countries. One alternative, if the United States were obliged to maintain low world price levels for an extended period, would be to reduce world production and thus to end market surpluses from which food aid had been granted. The other alternative would be agreement on a cost-sharing food aid program, in which case the United States could permit world prices and production to rise.

Progress in Multilateral Responsibility. The United States was successful in prodding other principal countries to share in the burdens of stabilizing wheat prices and providing food aid. The basis for cooperation was laid in agreements following the Kennedy Round negotiations of GATT, which took place between 1963 and 1967. In fulfillment of a Memorandum of Agreement by signatories from the Kennedy Round, a negotiating conference was held in Rome under auspices of the United Nations Committee on Trade and Development and the International Wheat Council. Attended by fifty-three countries and representatives of the EEC, this conference produced the International Grains Arrangement of 1967, which contained two separate conventions: a Wheat Trade Convention and a Food Aid Convention. Both went into effect as planned in mid-1968 after approval by the requisite group of signatories.

The Wheat Trade Convention substantially improved machinery for multilateral price control. Several basing points were established for determining price relationships for different kinds and locations of wheat, thus permitting more realistic pricing. To overcome the difficulty of fixing and enforcing price differentials a Prices Review Committee was established with authority to make and implement rapid decisions on prices. The wheat price range was increased by approximately 20 cents. New rules concerning food aid (or surplus disposal) were intended to further protect the commercial markets of competitors and of producers in recipient countries.

In the Food Aid Convention the signatories agreed to provide 4.5 million tons of grain annually for this purpose, of which less than half was to come from the United States. Other principal donors were to be the EEC (23 percent) and Canada (11 percent).

These conventions represented a major step toward multilateral management of the world wheat market, which had been seen as necessary and which had been much desired by earlier U.S. Secretaries of Agriculture. The conventions also seemed to make more realistic the oft-stated objective of eliminating hunger in the world.

SUMMARY

The United States has been the only consistent participant in the international wheat trade during the past century. Importers have come and gone, these being mainly consuming countries or customs unions intent on becoming nearly self-sufficient in food grains, and which have failed in this aim during certain periods or in years of poor crops.

The worldwide migration of wheat to the arid areas at the turn of the century resulted in a shift of U.S. wheat from the Midwest to the Central Plains and established a new set of competing exporters. The number of exporters has declined to a specialized handful of countries, whose export offerings have varied annually, due to weather vulnerability even more than to the needs of individual importers. The international wheat trade has been shifty and precarious, with the only safeguard of food adequacy being the tendency of regional variations in production to balance out on a world basis. When world wheat production was below average, distribution adhered to a priority system based on capacity to buy. When production was above average, a world wheat surplus could create panic in the marketplace (prior to World War II). Since for a number of reasons the market price of wheat had little short-range influence on acreage or production, surplus potential could grow over time, with exporter economies suffering heightening distress for a number of years. This was especially true after the advent of commercial farms in the twentieth century.

Before World War I U.S. wheat producers operated in a "free" market in the sense that no public or private controls over wheat prices existed in the United States or on an international level. The practicality of international market controls was proven in World War I, and the need for them was demonstrated in the decades following. The distress of the 1920s, and the market collapse of the early 1930s, produced a firm commitment not to return to unregulated wheat prices.

In addition to bad experience with unregulated markets, there were political pressures for market regulation. Farm groups lobbied effectively for domestic price supports; in the context of international policies, the political allies of the United States in war and in the Cold War were numbered among its major competitors and its best customers for food grains.

Beginning with efforts by Secretary of Agriculture Henry A. Wallace in 1933, the United States took the initiative in seeking a multilateral framework for controlling world wheat prices, meanwhile taking effective steps to stabilize domestic wheat prices. The international initiatives culminated in the International Wheat Agreement, entered into in 1949 by most wheat importers and exporters. The IWA never succeeded as a device for market regulation but was considered useful in legitimizing the price and supply arrangements implemented by some of the members.

Another international trade agreement receiving qualified U.S. support was the General Agreement on Tariffs and Trade, which many "free world" nations joined following World War II. In a timely and appropriate manner, GATT emphasized the futility of unilateral protectionism, but GATT also confused the issue by suggesting that the alternative was freer trade. Free trade in wheat, as an economic instrument, had been discredited by painful experience, and in any case, political considerations required that decisions on wheat production and prices be made by governments rather than according to a romantic theory of interacting supply and demand. Wheat was the basic food—a survival item—for many countries, and its political importance was reasserted in the policies of the European Economic Community and in the U.S. food aid program.

Wheat market control was also essential to preserve the close economic and political interdependence of the United States and Canada. Wheat was one of Canada's chief overseas exports, and a substantial export of the United States as well. In the two postwar decades world wheat prices were stabilized mainly by price cooperation between these two principal exporting countries. In this successful endeavor, however, the United States bore increasing financial burdens and received decreasing economic benefits. In addition, by virtue of its role as holder of the world's market surpluses, the United States was gaining the additional burden of meeting food deficits in noncommercial markets.

In 1965 the United States successfully put pressure on other industrial nations with the aim of getting better distribution of the burdens of price stability, food reserve maintenance, and food aid. The United States put downward pressure on the world wheat price and undertook other unilateral actions, to the consternation of other exporters. The apparent aim was not to discourage international cooperation in wheat policy but rather to replace the one-country umbrella with the firmer structure of collective responsibility. Another apparent aim was to move further toward integrating wheat policy with broader national political objectives. In the Kennedy Round agreements the United States obtained a multilateral commitment to supply 4.5 million tons of food aid annually over the ensuing three-year period, and there was reason to hope, due to the revised international grains agreement, that multilateral responsibility for stabilizing world wheat prices could be made a fact rather than a formality.

USDA *Photo*

4 / TWO-PRICE PLANS IN THE 1920s

THE FOLLOWING CHAPTERS each treat a major policy or policy proposal. The three questions to be answered are: Where did the policy come from? What was the policy? What were its results or effects? As these policies have been delineated, each tends to be associated with a particular time period. In fact, each policy is a product of its time, in the sense that a particular combination of measures was put together to serve the political interests on the scene, in response to the situation that these interests perceived. In addition, it has seemed appropriate to differentiate commodity policies based on the mechanism they used, since some programs and proposals have stressed a single remedy or panacea.

At the beginning of each chapter, the situation will be reviewed as it was perceived at the time and as it appears in retrospect. Those leadership groups initiating and gaining adoption of policies will be discussed, thus answering the question, "Where did the policy come from?" The policy will be described, and to the extent possible its effects will be assessed.

The present chapter is organized around the two-price idea which gained the support of most leading farm congressmen and organization leaders during the 1920s. Other program proposals were made during that decade, including some preferred by the presidential administration, but the two-price schemes tended to be the polarizing issue of that time.

Numerous proposals put forward by a coalition of rural legislators were referred to as "two-price" plans because they purported to be a way to hold the U.S. price at a level higher than the world price, thus enabling the farmer to get a fair return from the domestic market.

With respect to wheat, the circumstances in which such a plan would operate were as follows. The major market for wheat was domestic U.S. food. This was an inelastic market in that the price of the wheat had little effect on the size of the market (though the size of the market greatly affected the wheat price). The price of consumer products was not affected much by the price of the wheat components, and in any case consumers were not likely to switch to rye, cornmeal, or rice even if the wheat price rose very sharply. The domestic food wheat market seemed an ideal object for monopolistic control, and the two-price schemes were designed to rely on this market to provide wheat farmers' income.

Other markets would absorb the surplus, amounting to about one-third of U.S. wheat production. Exports were the major secondary market, other secondary markets being for seed and for animal feed. Two-price advocates at that time viewed these markets mainly as outlets for surpluses, not as important sources of income.

Most two-price supporters were willing to dump the surplus abroad, assuming, as the international environment seemed to require, that they could not be concerned about the consequences for foreign producers. However rural leaders seemed willing to link their income objectives with any humanitarian objectives that could command some domestic support. Senator William Kenyon (R., Iowa) said, in sponsoring an appropriation for purchase of U.S. commodities to relieve the Russian famine of 1921, "It blesseth him that gives and him that takes."[1]

The two-price plan was not unique to that decade; it was a feature in many subsequent programs. Like other instruments it proved to have some strengths and some shortcomings, to be appropriate in some

---

1. James H. Shideler, *Farm Crisis, 1919–1923* (Berkeley: Univ. of California Press, 1957), p. 181.

situations and not in others. Based on this experience, subsequent programs tended to make use of combinations of measures rather than to rely on a single mechanism as many seemed willing to do in the 1920s.

SITUATION IN THE 1920s

In view of a number of confusing trends during the 1920s, it is not surprising that most policy makers misperceived the situation with respect to the supply and demand for wheat. Most believed that the United States would soon consume most or all of its own wheat production and so would no longer be a major wheat exporter. This produced plans for a wheat economy based on the domestic market, when in fact the wheat economy was becoming more dependent than ever on foreign markets (Table 4.1) and more vulnerable than before to the influence of international wheat prices.

This misperception was due in part to the tendency of policy makers to imagine the situation as they wished it to be. America was seeking to retire from the world at the time, to find political and economic self-sufficiency. Farm interests hoped to achieve higher wheat prices behind a tariff wall. The business-oriented governments of the period viewed U.S. agriculture mainly as a source of cheap food for the industrial work force rather than as an export industry.

Yet the unawareness is explained partly by the inability of those on the scene to understand and predict the confusing trends of the times. For example, the United States had enjoyed a population boom which was suddenly slowed by a descending birth rate and by a virtual halt in immigration, beginning in 1923.

Per person wheat consumption had leveled out, after a long decline, and the leveling trend obscured the fact that it would decline much further in subsequent years (Table 4.2). Most misleading, however, were the interpretations of wheat acreage and production trends. The common judgment was that increased acreage and production during 1911–19 was a temporary product of wartime incentives. With respect to the question of government's proper role in the wheat economy, positions on both sides usually began with the notion that overproduction was due to wartime "dislocation." Some argued that farmers should not be made to suffer the effects of the overproduction boomerang, since they had responded to patriotic appeals for high war production. According to this argument the government should sustain farm income during the adjustment to a peacetime market economy.

TABLE 4.1. The wheat situation up to 1933

| Year beginning July | Supply | | | | Disappearance | | | | | | Total disappearance |
| | Carryover | Production | Imports | Total | Continental United States | | | | | Exports | |
					Processed for food	Seed	Industrial	Feed or loss	Total		
					(million bushels)						
1909	55	684	4	743	483	70	a	10	543	89	633
1910	110	625	4	739	485	73	a	8	543	71	614
1911	125	618	5	748	492	75	a	10	557	81	638
1912	110	730	4	844	492	73	a	9	574	145	719
1913	125	751	5	882	498	76	a	9	618	148	767
1914	115	897	2	1,015	501	81	a	45	612	336	948
1915	67	1,009	7	1,083	503	80	a	30	612	246	858
1916	225	635	25	884	510	79	a	29	598	206	804
1917	80	620	31	731	453	87	a	9	558	133	691
1918	40	904	11	955	455	97	a	18	583	288	870
1919	85	952	6	1,043	525	90	a	30	650	222	873
1920	170	843	58	1,071	407	89	a	35	578	370	947
1921	124	819	11	954	485	88	a	82	582	277	858
1922	96	847	11	953	482	86	a	9	605	216	821
1923	132	759	14	906	491	74	a	38	622	146	769
1924	137	842	1	979	491	80	a	58	615	256	871
1925	108	669	2	779	510	79	a	44	588	94	683
1926	97	832	a	929	513	83	a	10	613	207	820
1927	109	875	1	985	514	90	a	16	680	192	873
1928	113	914	a	1,027	517	84	a	77	656	144	801
1929	227	824	a	1,051	512	83	a	56	619	141	760
1930	291	887	a	1,178	501	81	a	24	754	112	866
1931	313	942	a	1,254	499	80	3	172	756	123	879
1932	375	756	a	1,132	510	84	a	173	722	32	754

Source: USDA.

a. Zero, or less than 500,000 bushels.

TABLE 4.2. Per capita consumption of wheat flour, and total per capita wheat disappearance for civilian food, 1910–68.

Year	Flour	Disappearance for food	Year	Flour	Disappearance for food
	(pounds per capita)			*(pounds per capita)*	
1910	214	310	1940	155	220
1911	213	310	1941	156	221
1912	211	306	1942	157	223
1913	209	302	1943	163	229
1914	207	301	1944	149	211
1915	205	299	1945	161	230
1916	204	298	1946	156	214
1917	191	272	1947	139	196
1918	179	247	1948	137	194
1919	192	277	1949	136	193
1920	179	263	1950	135	192
1921	167	245	1951	133	190
1922	180	259	1952	132	188
1923	180	260	1953	128	182
1924	180	256	1954	126	178
1925	181	260	1955	123	174
1926	182	259	1956	121	170
1927	181	260	1957	119	167
1928	179	255	1958	121	169
1929	177	254	1959	120	167
1930	171	247	1960	118	165
1931	168	240	1961	118	164
1932	170	242	1962	115	160
1933	162	232	1963	114	158
1934	157	222	1964	114	159
1935	158	225	1965	113	157
1936	163	235	1966	112	154
1937	159	228	1967	113	155
1938	160	229	1968[a]	112	154
1939	158	225			

Source: *Wheat Problems and Programs in the United States,* North Central Reg. Publ. 118, Univ. of Missouri (September 1960); and USDA.
a. Preliminary.

Those opposed to governmental intervention were optimistic that the transition from wartime to peacetime economy would be rapid and less painful if the government did not intervene.

In 1921 and 1922 prices did drop to prewar levels, sharply and painfully. The crop in 1923 was smaller than average. In 1924 U.S. farmers sold a large crop at improved prices because U.S. private investment flowing into Europe had restored purchasing power in that traditional market. The price stayed well above the prewar levels during the sale of a short U.S. crop in 1925, and in good crop years during 1926 and 1927. These prices, however, were regarded as inadequate when related to the increased costs of farming.

Contrary to the expectations of the "wartime dislocation" theory, acreage in the United States and in the world increased throughout the 1920s. World production did not exceed world demand during the early 1920s, but during the latter part of the decade production was increasing in all four major exporting nations—the United States, Canada, Australia, and Argentina—and all continued to accumulate large, unsold stocks. Meanwhile the major customers—the European nations—had been increasing their home production by means of a structure of import barriers.

Large world crops in 1928 and 1929 added further to the size of world stocks. The price collapsed in late 1929, coincident with the onset of general world depression.

LEADERSHIP

In the 1920s the important farm policy issue was the two-price program for wheat. The plan, promising increased income from wheat sold for domestic food, gained the support of most legislators representing the large commercial cropland areas. It was twice passed by Congress (1927 and 1928) and both times it was vetoed by President Coolidge.

Both the executive branch and Congress were vehicles for farm policy initiatives during the 1920s. Congressional initiatives were taken by a group of farm legislators in each house whose activities as a coalition were sometimes referred to as the Farm Bloc, although that name was originally applied to a specific group of senators only. The leaders of the congressional farm coalition in the Republican Congress of the time were rural Republicans from the central and western United States, who gained cooperation from southern and other rural Democrats. They came to be interested primarily in mechanisms through which government might assure adequate prices in farm markets. While their proposals did not become law during that decade, the ideas and commitments generated then were precedents for wheat policies enacted later.

The three Republican administrations also put forward policy proposals, largely to counteract or moderate the various congressional proposals. These counterproposals by the administrations of Warren Harding, Calvin Coolidge, and Herbert Hoover were aimed at avoiding action on farm policy issues to the extent possible.

RURAL COALITIONS IN CONGRESS

The rural coalitions in Congress, sometimes collectively referred to as the "Farm Bloc," were grievance committees rather than a radical force in the 1920s. Their clientele were specialized and well-capitalized farmers, who during a very brief war boom had modernized operations, acquired more land, and increased their level of living.

The tractor and other mechanically powered implements had become available, and farmers had quickly seen that they were far superior to horsepower in farming a large flat field. Automobiles became available too, to shorten the long distance to town. Commercial farmers assumed obligations during wartime inflation which became difficult to bear when wheat prices suddenly returned to prewar levels.[2]

Statistics of debt and bankruptcy, as well as the standing of farmers on an index of fair prices or "parity" which had been devised by the USDA, testified that, under the surface, the irreversible mechanization of farming had loaded the capital columns of the farm business, particularly for wheat farmers, without comparable increases in return.[3]

For most farmers the postwar effect was not unbearable in the way that the general depression proved to be at the end of the decade. Farmers were troubled—but not desperate enough to cross the high threshold of traditionalism and political indifference. So the Farm Bloc was supported mainly by a minority of activist commercial farmers who could make their personal weight felt in the congressional primaries but could not deliver the "farm vote" in presidential elections.

One vehicle for political action was the American Farm Bureau Federation (AFBF). The AFBF was a recent federation (1920) of community-level groups (farm bureaus) composed of innovative or progressive farmers. These groups had been formed around an agricultural specialist, originally to learn and in turn to disseminate to other farmers the scientific findings of the land-grant colleges. Membership in the farm bureaus was drawn from that stratum which had become saddled with the costs of wartime mechanization, and so the Farm Bureau became a political as well as a developmental organization.

The AFBF's Washington office was helpful in organizing the coalition of rural legislators in both houses of Congress. These legislators were given technical assistance and support by several farm economists, and by some sympathetic officials in the USDA, even including one Secretary of Agriculture, Henry C. Wallace (1921–24). The Farm Bureau leaders, cooperating legislators, some economists, and friendly

2. Shideler, ch. 2.
3. According to "parity" calculations of Cornell professor George F. Warren, the purchasing power of wheat in 1924 was only 72 percent of that in 1913. Noted in Gilbert C. Fite, *George N. Peek and the Fight for Farm Parity* (Norman: Univ. of Oklahoma Press, 1954), p. 11.

executive officials were able to muster a majority of votes in Congress on many of their key proposals, and in this way did battle against the presidential administrations of the 1920s.

Most members of the rural bloc gave obeisance to the same conservative economic and philosophic beliefs as the administrations of the time. Some participants, such as Senator George Norris (R., Nebraska) and Senator Robert LaFollette (Progressive, Wisconsin), were progressives or liberals, but leading members of the group, such as Senator Arthur Capper (R., Kansas), were intent on providing a respectable, moderate, and effective vehicle through which farm discontent could be voiced. Like the administration, they looked askance at views and activities of labor unions and other presumably radical groups; they were also quite suspicious of the federal government. The coalition's battles and victories reduced the appeal of more radical groups such as the Socialists, the Nonpartisan League of the Dakotas, the Farmer-Labor Party of Minnesota, and LaFollette's Progressive Party of Wisconsin.

In outlook, coalition leaders were in accord with the major views which dominated the government and the nation during that period. They were suspicious of activities by the federal government. They were political isolationists. They were opposed to labor unions and other presumably radical groups.

Indeed the main grievance of coalition leaders was that the institutions of the federal government and the Republican Party were being used against the economic interests of the farmer and of the great agriculture regions. It was their position that eastern industrialists, in control of Republican administrations, were using government, party, and the symbols of traditional conservatism as a means for exploiting American agriculture. Charges against big-business domination had long been taken seriously in the Plains, and the coalition was satisfied in this period that the policies of Presidents Harding, Coolidge, and Hoover were simultaneously pro-business and anti-farmer.

A number of laws were soon passed by the rural bloc which strengthened the farmer's economic power, including federal regulation of produce markets, better and more plentiful farm credit, and federal encouragement of farmers' cooperatives. These, however, contributed little to the primary objective of the group, which was to raise farm prices. The objective was made specific in the term "equality for the farmer," and in a mathematical formula which compared the costs of production with the returns and which yielded a price level indicating the "fair" price at any given time as measured by a standard of fair returns in a prewar period.

A more expedient expression of the objective was "make the tariff effective for the farmer." The advantage of this goal over that of "equality for the farmer" was its connotation that farmers were not asking for special protection from government but rather were asking for the very same protections that industrial America received through the tariff.

The objective "make the tariff effective for the farmer" seemed to assume that farmers should seek their income primarily in the home market rather than through exports. This assumption was in harmony with the protectionist and isolationist mood of the times. Indeed farm spokesmen were inclined to look upon exports, referred to as the "exportable surplus," as the cause of their problem. As Senator Arthur Capper (R., Kansas) asserted, "If America were a wheat importing nation . . . the farmer would have the better homes and schools to which he is entitled. . . ."[4] The exported surplus tied U.S. prices to world price levels rather than permitting domestic prices to be fixed by a protective tariff.

Although most persons in the rural coalition were protectionists by personal preference (such as Capper), quite a number in the group believed American agriculture would be more prosperous under free trade. But since there seemed no prospect for a general reduction in trade barriers, they felt that American farmers should get their fair share within a protectionist environment. Reliance on the home market was therefore justified as a corollary of the times.

The wheat surplus in particular was of concern to many farmers because wheat was widely raised as a cash crop and because the prices of wheat and a few other major commodities were assumed to have an effect upon other commodity prices. J. S. Lawrence stated in *The Annals* in 1929, "The unsatisfactory state of average farm income is due chiefly to the existence of uncontrolled surpluses in two dominant crops, wheat and cotton."[5]

Wheat policy, as we shall see, was of wide concern also because wheat was the commodity chosen by the rural bloc for policy experimentation.

Farm spokesmen became reconciled to living with the exportable surplus, at least temporarily. They made the best of it in public

4. Alonzo E. Taylor, "The Dispensability of a Wheat Surplus in the United States," *Wheat Studies of the Stanford Food Research Institute,* 1(March 1925):123.
5. J. S. Lawrence, "Stabilizing of Prices and the Farmers Income," *The Annals,* 142 (March 1929):168.

statements, often expressing the thought that a surplus capacity was a blessing to the American people. This thought appeared in the first version of the McNary-Haugen Bill on which farm policy debate focused in the 1920s. The bill spoke of "the necessity in part for the existence of such surpluses in order to safeguard the domestic market against the uncertainties of yield."[6]

The purpose of that bill, however, and of all the two-price plans proposed during that period, was to nullify the effect of this surplus upon the domestic price for wheat.

THE ADMINISTRATION

The presidential administration rejected two-price schemes throughout the 1920s. One supporter within the administration developed briefly—Secretary of Agriculture Henry C. Wallace (father of Henry A. Wallace), who served from 1921 until his death in 1924. Wallace, however, was not able to control administration policy while in office.

Secretary Henry C. Wallace began office with a "scientific outlook, a practical approach, a breadth of interest, and an independence of spirit which made him an able representative of agriculture in national councils."[7] Wallace's background and his experience as Secretary had also developed in him an "antibusiness" bias. He and many other farm leaders had concluded, though not so vocally as some midwestern Progressives, that their government was dominated by eastern business interests, who were willing to use for their own ends the prosperity and attitudes of the times.

In 1922 Wallace had condemned the price-fixing schemes presented up to that time: "Visionary schemes of all kinds are presented. Some would have the government take charge of the large business enterprises; others would have the government undertake to fix prices either arbitrarily or indirectly by buying up surplus crops. The experience of 3,000 years shows the impracticability of such efforts."[8]

Wallace changed his mind in 1923, when he became distressed over the effects of the farm depression and after his economists advised

---

6. S. 1682, 68th Cong., part 11, sec. 21, subsec. 4, quoted in Taylor, "The Dispensability of a Wheat Surplus," p. 123. Taylor noted in this article that reserve food stocks were not actually needed to assure food for American citizens. In the event wheat crops were short, he said, the United States could purchase wheat from nearby Canada or on the world market. He said there was little prospect of a world market shortage, but if so, rich America could outbid all others for this available food.
7. Shideler, p. 123.
8. Henry C. Wallace, "The Year in Agriculture," *USDA Yearbook, 1921,* p. 15.

him that overproduction and low prices in agriculture would be a chronic problem. Wallace concluded that America could not hope to increase its farm exports.[9] He came around to accepting the farm coalition's objective of "equality for the farmer," and he became convinced of the need for federal action to maintain farm prices. Under Wallace, USDA experts aided in constructing two-price legislation.

Wallace was an underdog in the Coolidge administration. The dominant farm policy voice within the administration throughout the decade, according to James Shideler, was Herbert Hoover. Hoover served first as Secretary of Commerce and finally as President. Wallace viewed Hoover, in Shideler's words, as a "representative of a commercial element of the nation whose aim it was to exploit agriculture."[10] However, Wallace's successors as Secretary of Agriculture, Howard M. Gore (1924–25), William M. Jardine (1925–29), and Arthur M. Hyde (1929–33), were generally disposed to agree with Hoover's point of view.

Hoover opposed two-price plans, even though they were mostly inspired by his own success in pegging wartime farm prices. Hoover had managed the World War I food program, one successful objective of which had been to restrain the inflationary spiral of farm prices. When prices dropped following the period of shortages, Hoover declared himself in sympathy with the farmer's plight, but he opposed peacetime intervention in the marketplace.

Hoover professed the view of dozens of prominent economists and conservative spokesmen of the time that farmers should not look to government for control of supply, demand, or prices. These conservatives felt that the distribution of rewards through the market was more equitable, on the whole, than a distribution based on political considerations.

Such conservatives as Hoover had supported—indeed initiated—many governmental actions which had influenced farm production, including research and extension activities, which had increased productivity. Hoover in particular stressed that government could and should do many things which, to use his categorization, had an indirect effect on the market, while government should avoid certain actions which, according to his categories, amounted to direct intervention. In the mind of many conservatives, the marketplace was an almost divine instrument, with which it was futile—and probably immoral—to tamper. This view was reflected in Coolidge's first veto

9. Henry C. Wallace, *Our Debt and Duty to the Farmer* (New York: Century, 1925), ch. 7.
10. Shideler, p. 142.

of the McNary-Haugen Bill, the most prominent of the two-price plans. Coolidge said the bill's provisions would "fly in the face of an economic law as well established as any law of nature."[11] Try as they did, the rural coalition was never able to frame a two-price mechanism which, like the tariff, would be categorized by the administration as an indirect action rather than rejected as direct intervention.

Some opponents of two-price legislation took a much less doctrinaire position. Joseph S. Davis, a prominent wheat economist of the conservative school, was dubious about the two-price plans of the 1920s on the ground that government had not yet developed the skill to manage them. "There is a tendency," he said, "in some business and academic circles to reason as if it were worse than sacrilegious for men to attempt to interfere with the natural operation of economic forces. This view is irrational. Most human advance has come through intelligent manipulation of natural forces so as to serve human ends. . . . Yet there is some warrant for the prevalent view. The social sciences are in their infancy. . . . For what might be termed social engineering the scientific foundations are inadequate."[12]

It should be emphasized that the positions taken by the Republican administration were reinforced by what could be called the "mood of the times." The appearance of general prosperity, relaxed government, and vigorous free enterprise were linked with the belief that America had developed a very satisfactory system. Minor problems, such as farm overproduction, would work themselves out through the price mechanism. The faith in free prices easily overcame the evidence that wheat production was unresponsive to moderate or short-term market price reductions. The chief threat to the system, in the eyes of its beneficiaries, was from those who, like the farm radicals, lacked confidence in the system.

Taboos flowed from this modified laissez-faire outlook, which two-price advocates found themselves bound to respect. It was held, for example, that one group of producers could not be helped at the expense of another. It was considered immoral for government to restrict farm production (though perfectly proper to stimulate it). "Efficiency" was regarded as an unmixed blessing, and governmental intervention inevitably a threat to it. Governmental restrictions or interference in the market were considered a threat to political freedom.

The first, most vehement, and apparently most potent criticism of new farm policy ideas was of an ideological nature. Some of the early

11. Fite, p. 179.
12. Joseph S. Davis, "The Voluntary Domestic Allotment Plan for Wheat," *Wheat Studies of the Stanford Food Research Institute,* 9(November 1932):61.

suggestions—price-fixing, government export corporations, and governmental responsibility for achieving equality in agriculture—were withered by ideological blasts; and although farm spokesmen tended to believe that ideology and attitudes were being used by industrialists as an instrument of class warfare against farmers, the fact remained that farmers themselves shared the basic assumptions of laissez-faire doctrine. So representatives of farmers busily tinkered with innocuous measures or worked on revisions which would make the McNary-Haugen Bill ideologically acceptable. The administration, by means of its two vetoes, made it clear that it was opposed to McNary-Haugenism in any form. Meanwhile it encouraged use of two other avenues—monopolistic cooperative bargaining and tariff increases—both of which were at least as objectionable under a classical laissez-faire doctrine, but both of which had also proved ineffective in accomplishing their farm price objectives.

Another fixed element in the mood of the times was protectionism—the belief that prosperity could be achieved and maintained by means of high tariffs. Whatever the theoretical conflicts between free enterprise and economic nationalism, these two systems were quite compatible in the mind of the times. This retreat toward economic and political self-sufficiency hurt American farmers, particularly wheat growers, who needed world markets. Except for a very few voices, however, farm spokesmen, agriculture analysts, and farmers themselves accepted and more often encouraged protectionism.

Still another element of the times was the subordination of agriculture policy to other considerations. The administration succeeded in making agriculture policy an adjunct of the national policy of the times. The Department of Agriculture had virtually no influence within the cabinet or White House after President Harding's death, and its ideas and actions had little or no impact on nonagricultural policies. Had there been effective communication from the USDA to the White House, the USDA might have made some contribution to overall national policy. The developing statistical and analytical resources of the department were superior to those elsewhere in government. The efforts to predict prices and production and to project the cost and effects of government programs, the development of a statistical standard of fair returns, and the concept that government could and should help producers to achieve a fair income were important precursors of later policy. But these achievements were not exploited at the time.

Another feature of the times was institutional opposition to change. We have noted the Department of Agriculture took no bold initiatives in the 1920s, though a few individuals within it brought forth crucial new facts and interesting ideas. American institutions were generally hostile to change, as is illustrated by those opposed to McNary-Haugenism at about midpoint in its career. The following is from Gilbert Fite:

> Thus by the spring of 1924, a majority of the business interests, the Coolidge Administration, many powerful Democrats, most professional economists, the metropolitan press, numerous farm journals and country papers, those who favored other agricultural relief plans, most cooperative marketing advocates, and a number of important farm leaders made up a formidable array of opposition to the McNary-Haugenites. . . . And as if this were not enough, the radical farm organizations also fought the measure.[13]

GENERAL HISTORY OF TWO-PRICE PLANS IN THE 1920s

For each of the various two-price plans introduced in the 1920s some unique advantages were claimed. Here we will briefly review the types of programs proposed during that decade, leaving for later consideration the domestic allotment plan which was formulated between 1929 and 1932. The latter became national policy in the early New Deal and is more appropriately discussed in that context.

RELIEF SHORT OF PRICE-FIXING

In the first wave of suggested remedies, after prices dipped low in 1921–23, were many proposals less bold than the price-fixing schemes that dominated later in the decade. Included were some old nostrums, such as induced inflation to aid the debtor, which no longer had adequate appeal. At the initiative of the newly formed farm coalition, several substantial measures were enacted during these years, including tariff increases for wheat and other agricultural products as well as long-considered measures to improve farm credit and legislation to regulate the middleman; this regulatory legislation was applied against packers and stockyards,[14] grain warehouses,[15] and grain exchanges.[16]

In seeking causes for low farm income, farm leaders often charged that the middlemen were making exorbitant profits at the expense of

---

13. Fite, p. 91.
14. Packers and Stockyards Act of Aug. 15, 1921.
15. Federal Warehouse Act, as amended Feb. 23, 1923.
16. Grain Futures Act of Aug. 24, 1921 (invalidated by the U.S. Supreme Court and repassed in revised form Sept. 21, 1922).

the farmers. Through the new, radical Nonpartisan League, the disturbed farmers of North Dakota had either replaced the middlemen by creating state-owned banks, grain warehouses, and insurance, or in other cases they regulated and taxed them severely. Subsequent experience under the national and state regulatory legislation proved, as economists had predicted, that regulation of the middleman was appropriate but would not result in major farm income improvement.

The same was true of credit measures. The farmers had inadequate sources of credit; but giving them a capacity to become more deeply indebted, even at lower interest, was at best a palliative, and if prices did not improve, easy credit could well add to farmer burdens.[17] Farmer-inspired measures to shift taxes to the "rich" also dealt with the results rather than the immediate problem. The problem for commercial farmers was low commodity prices.

Remedies short of direct government price intervention were much preferred. The question was whether they would be adequate. Secretary of Commerce Herbert Hoover recommended means for maintaining exports during the time while Europe was regaining the means to purchase more farm products. Hoover pushed for increased private loans to Europe, food relief shipments, and extension of the War Finance Corporation, which had extended credit for a few commodity exports. A few voices favored a policy of promoting freer trade, such as that of the industrialist Bernard Baruch, but these were powerless against the high wind of economic nationalism in this country and abroad.

Many turned to remedies which sought to recover the prewar "balance," such as "eat more bread" campaigns by small townsmen who did not comprehend that consumer shift toward animal products was an unavoidable result of higher per capita incomes. Similarly some urban spokesmen who had no idea how farm mechanization of agriculture had progressed during the war gruffly advised farmers to abandon wartime frills and return to the low-cost horse-and-buggy era. In the face of a well-advanced trend toward specialization in agricultural production, the Coolidge administration backed the Norbeck-Burtness Bill in 1923 which would loan Dakota wheat farmers

---

17. For a good description of the various farm relief measures of the early 1920s, see Shideler, *Farm Crisis*. Programs to raise prices during the 1920s are analyzed in the perspective of the times by John D. Black, *Agricultural Reform in the United States* (New York: McGraw Hill, 1929). The political history of two-price plans is covered in Fite, *George N. Peek and the Fight for Farm Parity*. The genesis and the New Deal operation of the domestic allotment plan for wheat are reviewed in Joseph S. Davis, *Wheat and the AAA* (Washington: Brookings Institution, 1935).

up to $1,000 to buy pigs, chickens, and dairy cows.[18] Coolidge and his Secretary of Agriculture, William M. Jardine, continually preached "diversification" as a means of raising income and reducing surpluses, as an alternative to price programs which would further encourage production of surplus commodities. Jardine's "diversification" scheme was finally challenged in a joint statement by the deans of the agricultural colleges and experiment stations. Their statement follows:

> Diversified farming has been offered as a sort of panacea for all agricultural ills. Diversity has been taken by many to mean a little of many crops and products and not much of any one. The trend in American agriculture is and should be towards a few well-chosen enterprises on each farm. Specialization in the production of two or three well-adapted products rather than wide general diversification is the rule on many successful farms. The application of science and technical skill to agricultural production favors specialization in a few rather than in many products. Increased use of machinery also favors specialization. Farmers cannot afford equipment for small areas of any one crop. To do the work by hand limits the amount that can be done and increases the cost. Farmers are therefore specializing in a few products for which their region is best adapted economically and naturally. Small areas and great diversity may be desirable in limited localities where production of home products are essential to a good food supply for the farm family, but commercial production demands specialization and concentration.[19]

EFFORTS TO CONTROL PRICES THROUGH PRIVATE ACTION

There were also efforts to control prices through private collective action, rejecting governmental assistance. Some of these seemed more radical than two-price proposals, in that some of their sponsors were angry men critical of both the economic and the political system, and their methods sometimes produced violence.

Farmers Union's President John Simpson urged farmers to hold their produce off the market as a means of forcing up the price, a scheme that had been tried on a number of occasions since 1870. It had

18. Alonzo E. Taylor of the Stanford Food Research Institute argued that diversification of production could and would occur as a result of low prices, except in a few arid states, and that this would solve the surplus problem. "If one were to go over the situation state by state and catalogue the wheat acreages in accordance with responsible definitions of diversified agriculture, as demonstrated in practice on the one hand, and of reversible one-crop cultivation on the other hand, one would secure a figure for acreage whose yield in average years would not furnish an exportable surplus of contract grade milling wheats." From "Dispensability of a Wheat Surplus," p. 136.
19. *Report on the Agricultural Situation by the Special Committee of the Association of Land Grant Colleges and Universities,* submitted to the 41st Annual Convention, Chicago, Nov. 15–17, 1927, p. 31.

failed again to obtain its objective in the 1920s when tried by a few nightriders in the cotton South. The latter threatened violence against farmers who sold cotton and burned gins which purchased the cotton.

A nonviolent form of collective action, also unsuccessful, was tried in Iowa. Henry A. Wallace, son of the Secretary of Agriculture, urged Iowa farmers through the columns of his magazine, *Wallaces Farmer,* to reduce their corn acreage in 1922 in order to create market scarcity. The poor results of this experiment in voluntarism were not lost on the Wallaces and on other farm leaders. Satisfied that they had demonstrated the ineffectiveness of this procedure, they later questioned the good faith of administration spokesmen and others who continued to advocate private collective actions as the best means to raise prices.

The main competitor to two-price plans was the cooperative movement, which swept the country from 1920 to 1923 via the powerful oratory of Aaron Sapiro and others. The cooperative idea was very attractive, in that it promised high prices without reliance on government. Sapiro preached that farmers could, by cooperatively "pooling" their products, control the supply and the price. This had been done by specialty crop producers in California, and Sapiro argued that growers of wheat and other major crops could also control their markets. However wheat growers' pools which organized in Kansas failed to work. A nationwide Grain Growers Cooperative was also organized under Farm Bureau suzerainty which proved to have a life span of only two years (1921–23). The efforts of several new regional or national cooperative marketing agencies also failed. It became clear that the only viable cooperatives were the small ones organized by local communities, and these were too few and too small to manage the price or supply of major commodities. Farm Bureau turned away from this route in late 1923, and so did the active farmers who had borne the heavy costs of pool administration and the heavy losses from holding wheat in a falling market.

As a means of market control for major commodities, cooperative marketing had been proved impotent under the conditions of the 1920s. Nevertheless the visibility of the scheme lingered on, and it became the administration program. The Coolidge and Hoover administrations promoted cooperative marketing as the major conservative alternative to two-price plans. The farm program of Secretary of Agriculture Jardine, submitted in the Tincher Bill of 1926, would have provided a revolving fund for loans to cooperatives, to enable them to channel off market surpluses and thus stabilize the price.[20]

---

20. Fite, pp. 158–60.

Congressional farm leaders had little patience for the Tincher Bill. By that time legislators in the Midwest and Plains had been pushing two-price plans for two previous years and by 1924 had converted many Southerners to their cause. Two-price advocates had even won over some champions of cooperative marketing by offering cooperatives a realistic role as administrators in their governmental program.

PRECURSORS OF TWO-PRICE PROPOSALS

The inspiration for all two-price plans was the World War I Food Administration Grain Corporation which, through purchases and sales on the market, had steadied the price of wheat for a period of over two years. The purpose of that corporation had been to parcel out scarce wheat to the allies and to domestic mills, thus preventing the inflation which would otherwise result from two short U.S. crops in the midst of great wartime demand. The corporation proved not only that it could hold prices down but that it could hold them up as well by means of massive purchases during the heavy marketing of the harvest season.

Many farmers had resented the government's wartime pegging of prices. As the price depression set in, farm spokesmen certainly did not all agree with the federal corporation's head, Herbert Hoover, that it was acceptable for government to hold prices down in war but not to hold them up in depression. Bills were introduced in 1920 by Congressmen C. A. Christopherson (R., South Dakota) and James H. Sinclair (R., North Dakota) to require government to fix minimum prices for wheat, corn, and cotton. More serious attention was given to a bill by Senator George W. Norris (R., Nebraska) which would create a federal export corporation, the purpose of which would be to buy raw farm products and sell them abroad on credit. Norris expected thereby to reduce "middlemen" costs and to keep prices at least up to cost-of-production levels.

Export Debenture Plan. One of several two-price schemes for farm price relief was the export debenture plan, championed by the Grange beginning in 1926. Under this plan the government would give to exporters of certain commodities (such as wheat) a certificate or export bounty, equal in value to the difference between an inadequate world price and the fair value of the commodity (stated as "cost of production"). Theoretically the prices both for wheat exported and for wheat used domestically would thereby be raised above world prices by the amount of the export subsidy.

Funds for this export subsidy program were to be derived as a certain percentage of the funds received from existing tariffs on imported goods, thus "making the tariff effective for the farmer" in a very direct way.

The export debenture plan was administrable, but the question was whether it would really raise prices. It could not accept the possibility that retaliation by other exporters, or the market dumping effects of the U.S. surplus, might cause sinkage in the world price to the point of canceling out the amount of the subsidy. It assumed, perhaps mistakenly, that the subsidies paid to U.S. exporters would be passed along through higher prices to farmers, rather than being in some way monopolized by the exporters themselves. Perhaps more than other two-price plans, the export debenture scheme rested on the hope that farmers would not increase their production much, if any, in response to expected higher prices. Rather, some advocates hoped that with higher incomes farmers would not feel it necessary to plant as much as before.[21]

McNary-Haugen Bill. The favorite farm relief plan of articulate rural America from 1924 increasingly to 1928 was the "equalization fee" or McNary-Haugen Bill. Coming on the heels of the collapse of the cooperative movement, its vigorous and persistent promoters gathered support for it, like a rolling snowball, until virtually all of America west of the Appalachians was counted in favor of it in the House of Representatives on a roll call vote in 1927 (Fig. 4.1). The snowball was fractured by the victory of Herbert Hoover in the 1928 presidential election.

The McNary-Haugen plan had several principal features, each of which had considerable appeal. One feature of course was its specific high price goal expressed as "equality for agriculture." This goal was stated in terms of a fair relationship between farmers' costs and the price of their products. The fair relationship, or "parity," was assumed to be the one which existed in 1910–14. This standard of "parity" was given statistical expression by the USDA's Bureau of Agricultural Economics.

The goal of parity proved a good rallying cry in the propaganda

---

21. Two economic analyses critical of the export debenture plan were Black, *Agricultural Reform in the United States*, and Joseph S. Davis, "The Export Debenture Plan for Wheat," *Wheat Studies of the Stanford Food Research Institute*, 5(July 1929):301–46.

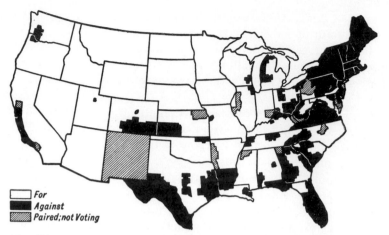

FIG. 4.1. House vote on the McNary-Haugen Bill, February 1927.
Source: John D. Black, *Agricultural Reform in the United States* (New York: McGraw-Hill, 1929), p. 253.

directed toward farmers, but the administration objected to it, being unwilling to take responsibility for guaranteeing a "fair" income for any group of producers. As an effort to please the administration, the price goal was restated as "equality under the tariff," or in other words, directed to obtaining benefits equal to those provided by the tariff to industrial producers. This skirted the objections to government "price-fixing" by stating domestic price goals as a relationship to world prices, rather than as a fixed amount.

The chief mechanism of the McNary-Haugen program was to be a federal grain corporation somewhat like that successfully operated during World War II. Such a corporation would, by acquiring market surpluses, support the domestic price of certain commodities at a fair exchange value. The corporation would dispose of these stocks by selling them abroad at world prices.

Although the McNary-Haugen plan was first included in an experimental program applying to wheat only, later bills included cotton, rice, and tobacco as a means of attracting southern support. As another attractive feature, the plan was expected to be self-financing. When they sold their grain, farmers would be paid partly in dollars and partly in scrip. The scrip represented the farmers' share in the returns from export of surplus wheat after program costs had been deducted.

The plan was attractive also because it appealed to protectionism and yet drew support from internationalists. Its author and chief salesman, George Peek, was and remained an outspoken economic nationalist.

Internationalists supporting the plan included southern cotton interests and also prominent farm economists who contributed to the rationale and the mechanisms of McNary-Haugenism and who subsequently moved agricultural leaders toward new plans when McNary-Haugenism began to flag in the late 1920s. One influential internationalist was Henry A. Wallace, who subsequently as Secretary of Agriculture moved the whole two-price bloc well into an internationalist position.

The internationalists advocated McNary-Haugenism only as a corollary of the existing protectionist structure, as something needed to provide economic justice or equality for agriculture. Like their protectionist allies, they had found abundant evidence that industrial America was quite deliberately using the tariff to exploit agriculture. "The strongest reason which the administration had for opposing the bill was scarcely mentioned in the first McNary-Haugen veto message," said the prominent agricultural economist, John D. Black. That reason, Black said, was that the McNary-Haugen Bill would raise the cost of industrial production, with the result that U.S. industry would be less competitive abroad. Black quoted Secretary of the Treasury Andrew Mellon's prediction as to the results of a McNary-Haugen Bill.

> "European labor could purchase American products at a lower price and could live more cheaply than American labor. Foreign industrial costs would be lowered and the foreign competitor assisted in underselling American products abroad and in our home market."[22]

Mellon felt the McNary-Haugen Bill would burden industry. Advocates thought it would unburden agriculture. It would end agriculture's subsidy to industry in the form of food for workers and fiber for mills furnished at a price below the cost of production. Clearly the fight over McNary-Haugenism was regarded by central figures in both industry and agriculture as a war between segments of the economy.

EFFECT OF THE MC NARY-HAUGEN BILL ON PRODUCTION AND INCOME

According to an analysis by John D. Black in 1928, the McNary-Haugen plan would have raised prices by 24 cents per bushel if production was not increased in response to the higher prices to a point

---

22. Black, *Agricultural Reform in the United States*, p. 248.

above the recent annual average production of about 800 million bushels. Overproduction, which had ruined prices, could also ruin the plan. In the event that farmers boosted wheat production to a billion bushels, the McNary-Haugen plan would provide them with a gross income no greater than they would otherwise have received, according to Black. If production went on up to 1.2 billion bushels, America's surplus would so overburden the world market that world prices would be reduced by more than the domestic premium per bushel, for a net loss to American producers of seven cents per bushel (not to mention the loss to foreign producers).[23] Of course any such increase in productivity would leave U.S. farmers under a cloud of future surpluses.

Alonzo E. Taylor and Joseph S. Davis suggested that the increased price (they assumed that the McNary-Haugenites wanted up to a 50-cent-per-bushel increase) would serve as a "profound stimulus" to production, adding at least 150 million additional bushels annually, much of it in low-quality wheat. Within a few years this would increase costs of the program to farmers to a point where the net price "would be little or no higher, and might even be lower" than if no such measure were adopted.[24]

Proponents argued that farmers might find it possible to reduce production under the McNary-Haugen program because they could maintain income on fewer acres. Yet this was not the lesson of war-time experience. A few McNary-Haugenites soft-pedaled the problem of production incentives under the plan by assuming that the U.S. food wheat market would also be growing. This assumption proved wrong.

In retrospect several other assumptions on which the McNary-Haugen and other plans were based proved false, not wholly true, or at best true only in relation to each other. The McNary-Haugenites were assuming without good reason that the dynamics of international action and reaction would somehow come to an end after passage of their bill. Instead other countries would have retaliated, although it is difficult to see how a McNary-Haugen program could have further accentuated the difficulties when the vicious circle of protectionism came full course with the passage of the Smoot-Hawley tariff of 1930.

IMPACT OF FARM ORGANIZATIONS

During the 1920s several farm organizations assumed policy roles and coincidentally experienced a tremendous growth in membership.

23. Ibid., p. 241.
24. Alonzo E. Taylor and Joseph S. Davis, "The McNary-Haugen Plan as Applied to Wheat," *Wheat Studies of the Stanford Food Research Institute*, 3(February 1927):234.

However farm organization leaders generally lacked both the imagination and the capacity for analysis that some leaders showed in later decades. The National Farmers Union, later instrumental in introducing both farm programs and general economic programs, was at that time strong on dissent and short on ideas. The Farm Bureau functioned well as legislative manipulator but not in generating ideas. Wheat commodity organizations were small and contributed little.

The farm organizations each seized upon a panacea and depended on it long after its inadequacies were known. Farmers Union advocated price-fixing, the Grange advocated export debentures, and the Farm Bureau advocated McNary-Haugenism during the latter part of the decade. It took considerable statesmanship—plus the Great Depression —to get them in harness behind the domestic allotment plan passed in 1933.

SUMMARY

Decision makers in the 1920s preferred to believe that they were dealing with temporary rather than chronic overproduction of wheat. They attributed overproduction to "dislocation" resulting from production incentives during World War I. The conservative presidential administrations of the decade expected that production would drop in response to moderately reduced prices and that demand for wheat would increase as U.S. population grew. A rural coalition operating through Congress sought to maintain wheat prices at "parity" levels, expecting to experience no difficulty in selling the surplus abroad.

The war was perhaps one factor generating productive capacity, but not just because it produced temporary price incentives. The war increased production, perhaps indirectly by spurring invention and innovation, and certainly directly by hastening mechanization of the wheat economy. Mechanization increased the overhead expenses of farming but also made it possible to expand total wheat acreage.

The trend toward overproduction was not checked by market mechanisms during the decade, and surpluses would likely have overrun a two-price program, had one been put into effect. The very serious consequence of overproduction at the end of the decade was the collapse of the wheat economy, which in turn helped to precipitate and aggravate the Great Depression. The wheat problem proved to be part of an overall problem with which decision makers lacked the wisdom, the freedom, and perhaps the technical competence to deal.

The Great Depression made clear the inadequacy of existing governmental and economic policies during the 1920s, including the

policy of approving protectionism in international trade while prohibiting governmental intervention in domestic markets.

While the wheat policy process thus did not deal with the important trend of the 1920s, it did have several functions. It provided a
channel for venting of grievances by commercial farmers hard pressed
to make a profit and by regions whose inhabitants felt themselves
discriminated against. It effectively raised the question as to whether
new kinds of governmental action were needed to assure some producers fair treatment by government and by the economy. It permitted
some measures to be tried and found wanting, such as private collective
action designed to control prices of a major product, and it permitted
other measures to be tried and found to be limited, such as measures
promoting cooperatives and preventing abuses in producer markets.
Finally, in this period there was much analysis of two-price schemes.
Experience in later decades was to prove that two-price mechanisms
had some value, combined with other measures, in policies designed
to control chronic overproduction.

USDA Photo

5 / THE AGRICULTURAL MARKETING ACT OF 1929

WORLD WHEAT ACREAGE increased sharply after 1925, while per capita wheat consumption was leveling off or declining in market countries. The developing wheat surplus (Fig. 5.1) was made fully visible as a result of an immense world crop in 1928 and another large crop in 1929 (Fig. 5.2). The surplus carryover from these and earlier crops accumulated in private and governmental stocks. In the severe depression beginning in 1929, the market demand for wheat declined along with the general decline in purchasing power, despite the fact that wheat was a food appropriate for persons and societies with low incomes. Meanwhile planted wheat acreage was increasing—in violation of the "laws" of supply and demand. It was in these circumstances of burdensome surpluses, decreasing demand, and increasing acreage that the Agricultural Marketing Act of 1929 was implemented.

107

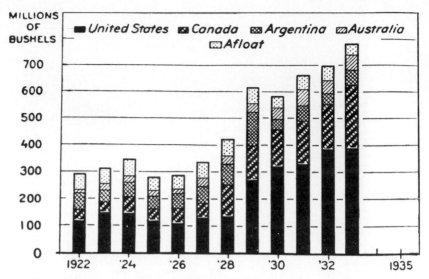

FIG. 5.1. Wheat: Carryover in principal exporting countries and afloat (as of July 1), 1922–33.
Source: *A Report of Administration of the Agricultural Adjustment Act, May 1933 to February 1934,* USDA-AAA, chart 7.

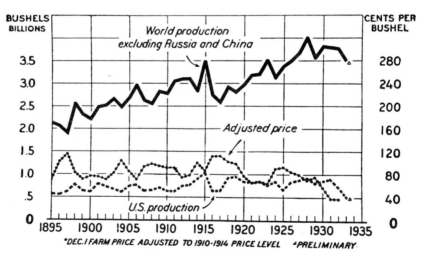

FIG. 5.2. Wheat: U.S. and world production, and U.S. adjusted farm price, 1895–1933.
Source: *A Report of Administration of the Agricultural Adjustment Act, May 1933 to February 1934,* USDA-AAA, chart 6.

LEGISLATIVE SOURCE

This law was the fulfillment of President Herbert Hoover's promise in the presidential campaign of 1928 to seek a remedy for the farm depression. In his campaign, however, Hoover defined tight perimeters for himself by reiterating his belief that government should not fix farm prices. He specifically condemned two-price proposals such as the McNary-Haugen plan, which his opponent Alfred Smith seemed to find acceptable.

The Agricultural Marketing Act was an executive bill, clearly labeled as Hoover's program. Passing through the hands of the disgruntled and hostile farm coalition, the bill emerged with provisions vesting considerable discretion in the appointed executive commission or Farm Board, which was to administer the law. However while the farm coalition used a broad brush wherever possible in defining the powers of the board, they were careful to meet Hoover's final requests with respect to the proper wording of the law.

The men nominated by Hoover to serve on the Farm Board included conservative industrialists and publishers who did not have the confidence of farm groups nor of leaders in many of the cooperative organizations they were supposed to serve. However most of the Senate rural leaders voted in approval of these candidates for the board, although some expressed pointed reservations about one or more of the prospective members.

Rural leaders accepted President Hoover's legislation and appointees, as they explained, because they wanted his program to be given a fair chance, in view of his election victory in the farm areas. They also wanted Hoover to bear full responsibility in the event that the program failed. Most of those in the rural coalition were convinced that the act would not accomplish even its own limited objectives.

OBJECTIVES

The Federal Farm Board was an agency designed to increase the farmer's "share" of the market rather than specifically to fix or raise commodity prices. There were two major lines of action specified in the act: improving merchandising and stabilizing the flow of commodities from the farm. Another major objective was to develop private instruments for these actions in the form of regional and national marketing cooperatives.

Related objectives included preventing loss or waste of wheat while in transit, standardizing the wheat output, discouraging the production of poor-quality wheat, and assuring premiums to the farmer in the sale of higher-quality milling wheat.

Another aim was to limit price fluctuations disadvantageous to the farmer. The board was empowered, in somewhat ambiguous phrases, to concern itself with "undue and excessive fluctuations" in the market and to take actions "preventing and controlling surpluses."[1] The context of the act suggested that the intent of these provisions was to minimize short-term fluctuations and surpluses, such as the decline in prices usually occurring during and immediately following the harvest season when most farmers were obliged to sell wheat in order to meet current obligations. The phraseology also suggests an intent to prevent extreme price responses to existing surplus or shortage.

These provisions were vulnerable to broad interpretation by the board. While the act was free of explicit two-price mechanisms, *Wallaces Farmer* noted, "The most hopeful farmers will take comfort from the fact that the powers of the Board and the President are great enough, under the bill, so that a great many desirable actions unspecified in the bill are possible."[2]

The board chartered a "stabilization corporation" and provided it with an operating fund of $500 million. Given these resources and the ambiguous legislative authority, and given the unexpected circumstances of the Great Depression, it subsequently became the board's objective to maintain the U.S. wheat prices at a level above tne world wheat prices, the same objective envisioned by the earlier two-price plans.

GENERAL HISTORY

After its creation the board began the process of creating a network of cooperatives to carry out the purposes of the act. But when the price depression occurred soon afterward, these cooperatives as well as their members were in distress. Beginning in 1929, the board began to offer loans to cooperatives, accepting as collateral the wheat held by cooperatives, in order to sustain the co-ops and also to maintain the price of wheat. The first loans led to additional loans and purchases to the same end, dictated by circumstances and by farmer pressures upon the board. Using its remaining funds in an effort to halt the drastic price descent, the board succeeded in steadying the

---

1. Discussed in *First Annual Report of the Federal Farm Board, 1930,* p. 24.
2. *Wallaces Farmer,* 54(June 1929):4.

domestic price between November 1930 and June 1931. At the end of that period corporation funds were exhausted. The corporation held 256 million bushels in wheat stocks, which crowded available storage and acted as a depressant on the market. In the face of a forthcoming harvest twice the size of normal domestic utilization, the corporation retired from the market, after which the domestic wheat price declined in conjunction with the world price to the lowest point in history.

Some of the wheat held by the board was exported under subsidy, some was donated to the Red Cross for domestic and foreign relief, and a small amount was sold on the domestic market.

RESULTS

The board, in its last *Report* (1932), noted that when it was active in the market it had kept domestic prices substantially above their ordinary relationship to world prices. Joseph S. Davis noted, however, that this action had not helped farmers much, since most farmers had already sold their wheat prior to the month of November when the board began pegging the price. Also farm prices for wheat were not as effectively supported by the board's action as were market prices. Davis noted a negative result, in that support of domestic prices had restricted exports and increased U.S. surpluses.[3]

The Farm Board's experience influenced subsequent policy, though this experience was the product of extraordinary circumstances. The unfortunate history of the stabilization corporation cast doubt upon the effectiveness of an export corporation in maintaining domestic prices, as had been envisioned under the McNary-Haugen Plan. The Farm Board fiasco made future planners cautious, and in addition the experience provided some explicit guidelines to be followed in future efforts to support prices. Indeed, reports of the board seemed to be highlighted by instructions as to what not to do in the future. From its experience the board suggested several cause-and-effect relationships in stabilization programs: it had learned that a very large quantity of wheat must be purchased if there is to be any effect on the market, and that in the process of making such purchases the structure of the market could be injured. It had learned that once stabilization purchases begin there is no convenient place to stop. Also there was inadequate storage for corporation grain, resulting in high costs and bottlenecks in the distribution of the grain.

3. Joseph S. Davis, *Wheat and the AAA* (Washington: Brookings Institution, 1935), pp. 22–23.

The corporation also found that "stabilization" was interpreted by farmers to mean "keep the price up." The corporation had undertaken to sell some of its stocks on occasions when prices rallied only to hear bitter protests from farmers. The corporation also noted that accurate information was needed about the size of the world carryover as well as information about other factors. The lack of this information explained in part the board's unsound decisions.

The most important recommendation of the board was that any effort to maintain prices must be accompanied by effective production controls:

> . . . no measure for improving the price of farm products other than increasing the demand of consumers can be effective over a period of years unless it provides a more definite control of production than has been achieved so far.[4]

The Board also gave the coup de grace to its strategy for maintaining farm income, which had been stressed in the Agricultural Marketing Act. The board suggested that the system of private or cooperative control envisioned by the act was not the solution for "the great staple products" such as wheat.

---

4. *Third Annual Report of the Federal Farm Board, 1932,* p. 62.

6 / THE DOMESTIC ALLOTMENT PROGRAM, 1933–35

THE AGRICULTURAL ADJUSTMENT ACT OF 1933 (the AAA),[1] containing a version of the domestic allotment program for wheat, was enacted May 12, 1933, in a period of extraordinary depression in the wheat industry. In December 1932 farm prices for wheat had fallen to "two-bits a bushel." The average wheat price for that marketing year was only 43 percent of the "parity price" as calculated by the Crop Reporting Board in the USDA's Bureau of Agricultural Economics.[2]

The economic circumstances of the time were indeed grave. Total cash income from wheat in the 1932–33 marketing year was $195 million,[3] compared with $1,751 million in 1919–20. Commercial

---

1. Abbreviation refers to the act, and also mainly to the administrative system, the Agricultural Adjustment Administration, which implemented the commodity programs. The abbreviation will be used both ways here, assuming it will be clear from the context whether the law or the bureaucracy is being indicated.
2. Joseph S. Davis, *Wheat and the AAA* (Washington: Brookings Institution, 1935), p. 451.
3. *Report of the Administration of the Agricultural Adjustment Act of 1933, February 15, 1934, to December 31, 1934*, p. 77.

farmers and rural areas were in distress as were their creditors and farm supply firms.

As the Roosevelt administration took office in 1933, U.S. and world wheat stocks were at all-time highs, although the Federal Farm Board had by that time disposed of most of its stocks. The wheat surpluses were temporarily removed, however, by the harsh remedy of crop failure. Dry weather and wind turned the Great Plains into the Dust Bowl, and in four consecutive U.S. harvests (1933–36) less wheat was produced each year than was consumed domestically. Prices rose somewhat in response to domestic wheat scarcity, but U.S. exports throughout the period 1932–37 were negligible. In 1937 the drought ended, and with the crop again larger than market demand, the United States was on the way to another surplus situation.

WALLACE ADMINISTRATION (1933–40)

Henry A. Wallace, editor of *Wallaces Farmer,* was also a plant breeder and statistician and son of a Republican Secretary of Agriculture. President Franklin Roosevelt chose him to be Secretary of Agriculture partly because he was highly acceptable to the major farm organization leaders and to rural congressmen, and because like his father he had a good reputation in rural areas. But Wallace also obtained crucial support from a group of his fellow progressives, some of whom had become Roosevelt's farm policy advisors.[4]

These progressives were for the most part agricultural economists, but unlike most economists this group wanted to participate in the decision-making process, by originating programs, by persuading decision makers to accept them, and then in helping to implement the programs. Prominent among these men were John D. Black, who was trained at the University of Wisconsin and later was professor of economics at Minnesota and Harvard universities, and who was one of the architects of the domestic allotment plan and a contributor to other ventures; M. L. Wilson, an economist and former extension agent from Montana, who devised the system of program administration through farmer committees, who synthesized ideas into comprehensive programs, and who also was a most successful policy salesman; Howard R. Tolley, who with Wilson looked toward comprehensive, multipurpose programs to develop rural America. Rexford Tugwell, another of the progressives, brought this group into contact with Franklin Roosevelt while Tugwell served the New York

4. Richard S. Kirkendall, *Social Scientists and Farm Politics in the Age of Roosevelt* (Columbia: Univ. of Missouri Press, 1966), p. 54.

governor as a campaign advisor. However Tugwell was different from the other progressive economists due to his nonrural background and biases. He and others lacking land-grant college degrees tended to become spokesmen for the interests of the noncommercial farming sector and thus to have only a peripheral interest in the commodity programs, or even to be in competition with them. Men like Tugwell became the politically vulnerable "left wing" of the Wallace administration.[5]

A hostile "right wing" existed in the persons of some Wallace appointees interested only in programs designed to support farm prices and actually opposed to programs designed for farmers who could not benefit from price programs. The most notable of this group was George Peek, salesman for the McNary-Haugen plan during the 1920s.[6]

Black,[7] Wilson, and the other farm economist progressives held the middle ground. They desired a many-faceted program which would emphasize conservation of resources, uplifting of communities, and rehabilitating marginal farmers, as well as increasing the efficiency and the income of the commercial farmers.[8] With Wallace, they understood that price and production programs for wheat and other commodities might help commercial farmers, but that complementary programs to attack basic social and economic problems of rural America also were needed. They were aware too that agricultural policy could serve national goals and inversely that an internationalist agriculture policy, which they preferred, was dependent upon the development of national and world policies in the direction of increased international trade.

Despite their broad view, these men, and in turn the Wallace administration, tended to be most concerned with the commodity programs which raised farm prices and reduced production, such as the domestic allotment program and other mechanisms in the Agricultural Adjustment Act of 1933. The professional and life experience of these men was on the whole in commercial agriculture, so the mental picture most pleasing to them was of the commercial family farm, while the other rural America appeared to them mainly as a set of tragic statistics. As economists they could conceptualize remedies for the problems of commercial agriculture, but there were no purely economic remedies

---

5. The activities of these men are described at length in Stanley Baldwin, *Poverty and Politics: The Rise and Decline of the Farm Security Administration* (Chapel Hill: Univ. of North Carolina Press, 1968).
6. The suggestion of the categories "right wing" and "left wing" is found in a quotation in Kirkendall, p. 102.
7. Black was a frequent consultant to the USDA, although he was not employed there.
8. The wide concerns of Black, Wilson, Tolley, Lewis Cecil Gray, and Secretary Wallace himself are noted in Kirkendall, ch. 1.

for the southern sharecropper, the subsistence farmer, the inefficient farmer, and the farmer on poor land.

Most important, the "voice of agriculture," as heard from Congress and from the constituencies, was the voice of commercial farmers. Wallace's middle-of-the-road group, as practical men, heeded that voice. Congressional leaders insisted, for example, that programs should serve the interests of private property in the capitalistic system.[9] Farmers themselves, including those who had no property, tended to be grass roots defenders of the rights of property. This was perhaps truer in the Plains area than elsewhere because of the importance of land, and because those who did not own property nevertheless managed property and had real hopes of acquiring some.

Therefore, despite the desperate times and the intent to write a comprehensive program for rural America, the Wallace administration gave the commodity programs most of the funds and energy, and these were hardly more revolutionary than the McNary-Haugen program of the 1920s. The Wallace commodity programs had no built-in social objectives as did the subsequent Brannan Plan, which sought to maintain family agriculture by scaling production payments so as to benefit small farmers.

OBJECTIVES OF AAA OF 1933

The objectives of the wheat commodity program, which was part of the Agricultural Adjustment Act of 1933, included the following:

1. Immediate relief. When the Roosevelt administration took office, farmers were suffering great hardship, and acts of violence in protest of these conditions were occurring in commercial farming areas. The highest priority for the program therefore was to provide a direct payment mechanism as a means of sending relief money to farmers immediately.

2. Increased farm income. This objective, dating from the 1920s, could hardly be expressed as full parity of prices, but there was the intent, consistent with the McNary-Haugen era, to achieve parity from returns on at least that portion of the production intended for the domestic market.

3. Production control. The world surfeit of wheat, and the failure of the Farm Board, had destroyed the hope that surpluses could be exported. It was thought that surpluses would have to be

9. U.S. Senate Committee on Agriculture, *Hearings on the Nomination of Rexford Tugwell for Assistant Secretary of Agriculture* (1935).

prevented mainly through production controls, beginning with home production, eventually to be made effective on a worldwide basis.

4. International regulation of wheat markets. Wallace believed that American agriculture should not, and would not be able to, shrink its production to the needs only of the American market.[10] But in order to make foreign markets profitable for American producers they would first have to be stabilized through international agreements and institutions.

5. Development of larger foreign markets. Internationalists and protectionists shared a desire to expand foreign markets for U.S. agricultural exports, wheat being among the prominent commodities in mind.

STRATEGIES OF LEADERSHIP

The Roosevelt administration provided leadership in achieving passage of the Agricultural Adjustment Act of 1933. Roosevelt's previous election mandate, and the needs of the moment, permitted him a freer hand in passage of the legislation than any other administration has had. The major challenge to this administration (aside from developing remedies for the serious economic crisis) was in securing cooperation among farming regions, farmers, and farm leaders. The crucial judgment on the Roosevelt programs was to be made in future Congresses and in future elections, presumably after the country had emerged from crisis. Therefore a successful program would anticipate the restraints and supporting influences of post-depression times.

PRELIMINARY AGREEMENT AMONG FARM LEADERS

President Roosevelt insisted that the farm programs of his administration must gain wide preliminary support among farm leaders.[11] "Farm leaders," apparently, included roughly the rural coalition which had supported the McNary-Haugen Bill during the 1920s.

While he was candidate in 1932 Roosevelt promised to accept any farm program on which farm leaders could agree.[12] As President in 1933 he rejected the advice of his aide, Rex Tugwell, that he formulate a workable program and then "coerce the farm leaders into its acceptance by going over their heads to the farmers themselves.[13]

---

10. Henry A. Wallace, *America Must Choose*, World Affairs Pamphlet 3(1934), p. 27.
11. Kirkendall, p. 45.
12. Ibid., p. 42.
13. Ibid., pp. 45–46.

President Roosevelt wanted farm leaders not only to approve but to take credit or responsibility for the New Deal farm programs.

The burden of securing preliminary agreement, and even farm group sponsorship, fell upon program architects. The social scientists who wrote the 1933 wheat program had the task of persuading rural leaders to accept their proposals, or if not succeeding, to modify the proposals until they became acceptable. This strategy had its price, in that it proved necessary to incorporate the panaceas of some farm leaders as well as to conclude with a program which favored the commercial farmers with little recognition of other potential groups such as consumers, small farmers, or taxpayers.

But legislative passage was not so extraordinary, considering that a farm coalition had twice passed the McNary-Haugen Bill, an antecedent of the domestic allotment program. However farmers' destitute conditions certainly influenced most to participate in the program. During the 1920s relatively few farmers had been active and interested in the political fight for farm income programs, and the others were difficult to communicate with—little involved in politics and indeed suspicious of government.

GRASS ROOTS ADMINISTRATION

As a way to gain farmer acceptance and continuing support for the program, and to achieve satisfactory administration, it was decided to vest local administration in the hands of farmer committees. In practice this device helped bigger farmers gain control of the program. Through this committee system, the extension education system, and subsequently through the locally oriented USDA bureaucracies, the bigger farmers gained a position of dominance over agriculture decision making within the executive branch comparable to their control within Congress.

NATIONAL AND INTERNATIONAL POLICY

The Wallace administration viewed agriculture as part of a larger policy network, in which agriculture should receive its fair share while making its fair contribution to the whole. Obligations to the system were recognized, for example, in proposals by the USDA to provide a place in the countryside for the industrial unemployed. Most impressive was the Wallace administration's leadership in reviving international trade. The USDA took a leading role in enactment of the Reciprocal Trade Agreements Act. The USDA also negotiated the first International Wheat Agreement and tried to fulfill its terms.

In important ways, painfully recognized within the USDA, agriculture policy even when paralleling a general recovery program was not wholly compatible with the commonweal. Production control measures in agriculture meant, over the short run, that a poor, hungry nation would have less food at higher prices. Reduction of crop acres meant, in practice, that some farmers were forced off the land and into a migrant existence.

TEST OF PROGRAMS AND ADMINISTRATION

Although those in the Wallace administration had developed some favorite remedies, none was considered sacred or comprehensive. For example, the domestic allotment plan on which leaders in the USDA had labored was revised in crucial respects to fit the circumstances. The domestic certificate, as we shall see, was replaced by a direct federal payment. Program performance was surveyed extensively, with administrators intent on profiting from mistakes.

As one result the Wallace group managed pretty much to avoid defensiveness or group paranoia which might have limited their ability to profit from the unique depression experiences. Their willingness to make objective appraisals is apparent among many USDA publications during this period, in which praises for the programs are invariably intermingled with confessions of doubt and shortcomings. Wallace himself seemed to set the tone for a balanced view, always looking ahead to possibilities and problems, always uncertain about present as well as past efforts.

LONG-RUN PERSPECTIVE

The Wallace administration had to be concerned with present problems as had perhaps no other administration, and yet more distant problems were kept in full view. The distant view was a basis for judging current programs; for example, the need for stable overseas markets prompted the choice of production controls rather than export subsidies as a way to avoid surpluses. There was an effort to work around some prospective problems, illustrated in the unsuccessful effort at each policy step to provide adequate economic and legal rationalizations for the 1933 act, hoping thereby to persuade the courts that the act was in accord with the Constitution.[14] The research-communications function was given high priority, as the USDA sought to analyze its future tasks and sought to prepare an institutional and attitudinal basis for more sophisticated programs.

Recognition of long-range problems conditioned the participants to expect shortcomings in their own measures. For example, the drought was given its due as the "awful balancer," so that the USDA was under no illusions about the weaknesses of the production controls administered under the 1933 act, and was able to face squarely the prospect of post-drought surpluses even in the absence of acceptable remedies for them.

GENERAL HISTORY OF DOMESTIC ALLOTMENT PROGRAM

The Roosevelt administration's wheat program, in the Agricultural Adjustment Act of 1933, was first regarded as experimental and temporary, although it was renewed for a four-year period several months before the U.S. Supreme Court ruled it unconstitutional in January 1936, principally on the ground that processing taxes could not be used as a mechanism for enforcing production controls.[15] Despite the adverse decision, some aspects of the program continually bobbed up as legislative proposals thereafter. The domestic wheat certificate programs of 1963, 1964, and 1965 are its recognizable kin.

The wheat program in the Agricultural Adjustment Act of 1933 was named the domestic allotment plan. It was a wedding of two features, each with different histories. One feature was production controls. The other was the reward or income mechanism, in the form of government payments distributed in proportion to the amount of normal production on allotted acres. The payments were funded by a use tax paid by the processors of wheat used for food in the United States. As with other major farm income-raising plans of the 1920s, the domestic allotment plan was a general farm program which had been conceived with the problems of wheat primarily in mind.

PROCESSING TAXES

The processing tax device was developed over a four-year period by a small number of economists. The idea apparently originated

---

14. One early and impressive rationale for the Agricultural Adjustment Act of 1933, intended for those who would question whether it was needed or whether it was constitutional under the circumstances, was *Economic Bases for the Agricultural Adjustment Act*, by Mordecai Ezekiel and Louis H. Bean (USDA, 1933).
15. U.S. v. Butler (297 U.S. Reports 1), Jan. 6, 1936.

with the USDA's William J. Spillman, who suggested it in 1926 through an article, "Getting the Tariff to the Farmer."[16] This device was to enable government to support the domestic wheat price without having to enter the market, as was the case with the McNary-Haugen export corporation device.

The processing tax, a major feature of the domestic allotment plan, was suggested by Henry I. Harriman, president of the U.S. Chamber of Commerce, and by Harvard economist John D. Black. In 1929 Black presented an anlysis of the domestic allotment plan in testimony before the Senate Agriculture Committee and in a book *Agricultural Reform in the United States*.[17] Another contributor to the domestic allotment plan was Mordecai Ezekiel, a USDA economist who served as an advisor to the Federal Farm Board. In a pioneering econometric projection, Ezekiel presented new evidence that the McNary-Haugen scheme was not practical.[18] Thus there was need for a new, different device by which to exploit the domestic market.

It is interesting that the Federal Farm Board, representing the presumably obsolete export corporation principle, nevertheless served as the setting in which the new plan evolved. Economist Black served as consultant to the board, as did economist M. L. Wilson and Henry A. Wallace, then a farm editor in Des Moines. Wilson developed the administrative features of the new plan and promoted it successfully with farm organizations, congressmen, and ultimately with President Roosevelt.

In April of 1932 a group of interested and influential persons including businessmen whose firms dealt with farmers (lenders and mail-order companies) discussed the domestic allotment program at a conference in Chicago. They unanimously approved the version of it presented by Wilson and Ezekiel. A bill had already been roughed out by Ezekiel and Stanley Reed, counsel for the Farm Board. This was reworked by a subcommittee of the U.S. House Committee on Agriculture, and received attention in both houses during that session, though early adjournment killed hope of passage. At that time the Grange, the Farm Bureau, and the Farmers Union were sponsoring a competitive measure which included each of their separate remedies, and which was therefore called the "three-headed monster." However the farm organizations became interested in the domestic allot-

16. As attributed in the testimony of John D. Black, before U.S. Senate Committee on Agriculture and Forestry, *Hearings on Farm Relief Legislation* (March 1929), pp. 68–69.
17. (New York: McGraw-Hill), ch. 10.
18. "A Statistical Examination of the Problem of Handling Annual Surpluses of Nonperishable Farm Products," *J. Farm Econ.*, 11(April 1929):193.

ment plan and began to lean toward it after two October meetings attended by farm organization leaders and the authors of the plan, and especially after Roosevelt's victory in the election. These farm organization leaders then helped to work it into a form to which they gave unanimous support.[19] Neither of the political party platforms of 1932 contained a direct reference to the domestic allotment plan, but the presidential candidates discussed it. Incumbent President Hoover, in his speech accepting renomination, condemned all such plans. Roosevelt, at the urging of Tugwell, who had become converted at the 1932 Chicago conference, decided to use the main features of the domestic allotment plan as his farm program, though without using its name. Wilson and Ezekiel then wrote his "Topeka" campaign speech on the farm issue in which Roosevelt spelled out its features.

FEATURES

The domestic allotment plan was different in several ways, and presumably superior to, the McNary-Haugen export corporation. Under the domestic allotment plan, the market prices would not be supported, nor manipulated, by the government. Instead growers would be issued certificates for that portion (or allotment) of their wheat that was used for domestic food (the allotment was to be derived by multiplying each farmer's production expressed in terms of acres times the fraction of national wheat production used for domestic food). These certificates would be sold by farmers for a value equal to the difference between the inadequate market price and the higher, statistically "fair" price that farmers were presumed to deserve (whether using the "fairness" standard of equality under the tariff, parity, or some other measure). These certificates would be purchased by millers in conjunction with the purchase of food wheat. The advantages were these:

1. There was to be no worrisome government storage and, strictly speaking, no price-fixing. The price of wheat would be determined in the market.
2. The plan would not stimulate production as much as had the other two-price plans, since price subsidies were for only part of existing production (not for the additional or marginal bushels) and since the domestic allotment would be divided on the basis of past

---

19. Davis, *Wheat and the AAA*, p. 34.

production rather than on the basis of present or future decisions as to how much to produce. Some said the plan would not increase production at all, although Black was inclined to think that since the certificates would cover fixed costs, farmers would be free to expand production as long as returns on additional acres were above the bare operating costs.[20]

3.   Other countries would be less likely to object to and to retaliate against the wheat certificate plan than in the case of the mechanisms which actually altered the domestic price. In May of 1932 Great Britain had enacted a measure similar to the domestic allotment plan for wheat, and this precedent apparently had been accepted by other countries.

4.   The plan involved no interference with the existing marketing system. Black's original proposal even permitted imports of certain desired grades of wheat not abundant in the United States. Of course not everyone viewed nonintervention with the market as an advantage; some congressmen still felt that the existing marketing system operated to the advantage of "robber" middlemen.

5.   Because the domestic allotment certificate would be issued to farmers whether or not they planted or harvested wheat, it served as a kind of income insurance. As Black pointed out, the mechanism went directly to the primary purpose of all the farm plans: to support farm income. Producers received a direct income supplement rather than waiting for support to trickle through the market mechanism.

6.   The plan was self-financing. The consumer ultimately paid the bill.

Also acknowledged were several minor disadvantages. Farmers who had not grown wheat in the past could not get certificates. The plan would therefore tend to rigidify production patterns. Secondly, the bill would apply initially only to wheat and cotton. Other measures were to be used for other products, including the export debenture plan for some commodities which were not exported in large quantities. Finally, since the processing tax might be regarded as a tax on bread, the staple of low-income diets, proponents explained that it should not be considered a tax but rather an "equalization fee" exacted as a matter of economic justice.[21]

---

20. For analyses of the plan at that time, see the following: Joseph S. Davis, "The Voluntary Domestic Allotment Plan for Wheat," *Wheat Studies of the Stanford Food Research Institute*, 9(November 1932): 23–62; Black, *Agricultural Reform in the United States;* U.S. Senate Committee on Agriculture and Forestry, *Hearings on Farm Relief Legislation* (1929), pp. 53–91; Davis, *Wheat and the AAA.*
21. Davis, *Wheat and the AAA*, p. 188.

PRODUCTION CONTROL

The other feature of the wheat program in the AAA of 1933 was production control. The farm plans of the 1920s, including the domestic allotment plan just discussed, had not assumed the need for production controls because the earlier surplus had seemed relatively small. With tremendous surpluses overhanging a reduced world market in 1932, and with the Federal Farm Board's failure serving as a warning, it seemed to many that production controls were a necessity. Accordingly a provision for reduction of wheat acreage on each cooperating farm was included in the domestic allotment bill introduced in the summer of 1932. However farm organization leaders did not agree to production controls until after the presidential election.[22] Even then, Farmers Union refused to endorse controls, but Farm Bureau's convention of December 1932 was recorded as strongly in favor of production controls as an integral part of farm relief.[23] Some farm policy leaders such as George Peek, who became the first administrator of the program, remained strongly opposed to controls even after they had become part of the law.

It was not assumed that the U.S. production controls would by themselves prevent world surpluses. The U.S. product was largest next to that of the USSR, but it was still only 19 percent of total world wheat production (1924–29). Advocates of production controls were presuming that other wheat-exporting nations could be persuaded to cooperate in reducing production. The principal exporting nations did subsequently agree on acreage reductions of 15 percent in the International Wheat Agreement of 1933.

Controls provided in the AAA of 1933 were voluntary rather than mandatory in the sense that individual farmers reduced acreage whenever requested by the government, if they wished to share the payments generated by the processing tax. But the main purpose of the depression wheat program was not to control production (which it failed to do as well as had been agreed to under the IWA) but rather to raise farmers' income. It did this successfully.

PROVISIONS OF AAA OF 1933[24]

The bill Congress passed in 1933 permitted the executive branch to choose from among several oft-advocated mechanisms for raising

---

22. Ibid., p. 46.
23. *Bureau Farmer,* 8(March 1933):7.
24. The administration of wheat programs under the AAA of 1933 is the subject of a thorough study by Davis in *Wheat and the AAA.* Much of the information here was gleaned from that study.

farmer income. The administration chose to use the federal corporation for market control on some commodities, while choosing for wheat the domestic allotment plan which had evolved during the discussions of 1929 to 1932.

Black's original domestic allotment plan of 1929 had been considerably revised. No certificates were issued to wheat farmers in the way Black had first envisioned. Instead the plan had been revised in the spring of 1932 to provide for direct federal payments to farmers. The payments offered a way to persuade farmers to reduce their acreage and to compensate them for doing so.[25] Therefore by December of 1932 the proposed subsidies had come to be viewed by some as land rental payments rather than as price supplements.

Under the act, farmers contracted with the USDA to reduce their average wheat acreage (average of 1928 through 1932) by as much as 20 percent, depending on how the USDA viewed the supply situation. In return they were guaranteed benefit or adjustment payments on that percentage of their wheat to be used for domestic food. In 1933–34 the domestic allotment for each cooperating farm was calculated as 54 percent of the average production in the four-year base period.

To finance the payments a use tax was levied directly upon the millers, which they were obliged to pay upon wheat processed into human food. The proceeds were quite adequate to finance the program.

The administrative mechanism of the act was novel in that it provided for grass roots decision making. The AAA's Washington office determined the basic formulas for allotments and for apportioning benefits, but the actual distribution of acreage and enforcement of contracts was made by farmer committees formed at the state, county, and community levels.

As a means of apportioning allotments, farmers' committees in each township had first to determine the average wheat acreage raised on each farm during 1930 to 1932, the period on which allotments were to be based. With no previous records available to be used for this first program, the acreage history had to be based on the farmers' own report. To encourage honesty the reported acreages were to be published and neighbors were invited to call attention to errors. Since farmers had to share a given county quota, they would presumably be alert—in their own interest—against dishonest reporting by a neighbor.

This strategy of pitting the interests of all farmers against the greed of each was successful on the whole, yet some farmers apparently

25. Davis, *Wheat and the AAA*, p. 141.

overstated their acreage. The reported county acreage—the sum of individual farmers' estimates—was often much larger than the "official" estimate which had been made annually by the USDA's Division of Crop and Livestock Estimates. Since accuracy of the official estimates themselves was subject to some question at that time, they were often revised upwards in order to be more nearly reconciled with farmers' estimates. For the United States as a whole the official wheat acreage estimate was increased by a total of 1,800 thousand acres, over half of which (975 thousand acres) was in Kansas alone.

After the estimates had been adjusted upwards, the reported acres were usually still 10–20 percent larger than the estimates. At this point the AAA farmer committees were given the task of reducing the reported county acreage to the amount of the estimate, either through discovering and correcting individual overstatements or by reducing all acreage bases across the board. This done, each farmer was allotted an acreage on which he could raise wheat.

Compliance with the allotment for each farm was at first checked out by locally trained farmer supervisors, using a simple device for measuring acreage, such as a chain or metered wheel. Subsequently air photos were perfected as a means for accurate measurement.

The farmer committeemen were on the whole respected farmers who worked conscientiously and suffered much in the abrasive process of apportioning and checking acreage. They were rewarded with the considerable prestige of the job and substantial per diem payments. They were assisted during the first three years of the program by the agricultural extension agent in each county, whose main function previously had been to teach new agricultural techniques. These county agents, as the chief federal employees on the local agriculture scene, were often obliged to administer the adjustment program single-handedly during its first year, during which committees were being formed or were not yet ready to take responsibility.

RESULTS OF PRODUCTION ADJUSTMENT

Since crops were poor and income was depressed during the life of the 1933 act, production control became secondary to the main objective of raising farm income. Nevertheless the control measures were regarded as a serious experiment in administration. Administration of the program was remarkably excellent, according to conclusions in the careful study by Davis.[26]

Did the acreage control program reduce production? It was

26. Ibid., p. 412.

difficult to separate its effects from those of the drought and depression. Many acres idled under the program would have been barren anyway. On the other hand, the farmers' financial plight, the wheat scarcity resulting from drought, and the return of the unemployed to the farms all encouraged larger plantings by farmers who decided not to participate in the program, including a considerable area of newly broken land in the Southern Plains.[27]

Since the 1933 program got underway late in the crop year, co-operating farmers were not required to reduce acreage below their 1930–32 average (the allotment base). For the 1934 crop an effort was made to remove 15 percent of the wheat base, but the actual planted acreage was only 5.2 percent below their 1930–32 average. In 1935, due to the drought, cooperating farmers were asked to reduce acreage only 10 percent. This reduction was further softened by allowing farmers to harvest acres borrowed against the following year's allotment. Planted winter wheat acreage for 1935 was the largest in three years, due in part to a provision permitting farmers to plant their entire allotment under the agreement that they would use the excess acres only for winter pasture.[28]

According to the estimates by Davis,[29] an amount of land producing about 75 percent of the 1930–32 production was enrolled in the 1933–35 program contracts. This land was held by only about half the wheat farmers eligible to participate. The great majority of farmers in the commercial wheat areas signed, but those elsewhere tended to be indifferent toward the program. The year 1934 provided the main test of the effectiveness of controls. The USDA claimed that about 8.5 percent of the 1930–32 average acreage—about 12 million acres—was not harvested as a result of production controls in 1934. However they estimated only a 50-million-bushel reduction in 1934 due to controls[30] (with a 314-million-bushel estimated reduction due to drought).

Davis, even more skeptically, said controls had little effect on production. He suggested that about 90–93 percent of the 1934 reduction in bushels produced was due to the drought and that the 1935 crop also "bids fair to differ little from what it would have been in the absence of the AAA."[31]

In the absence of drought, the effects of acreage controls would have been more evident, since more of the idled acres would have

27. Ibid., p. 108.
28. Ibid., p. 139.
29. Ibid., pp. 347–54.
30. *Agricultural Adjustment, 1933–1935, A Report of Administration of the Agricultural Adjustment Act, May 12, 1933, to December 31, 1935,* USDA-AAA, p. 152.
31. Davis, *Wheat and the AAA,* p. 98.

otherwise produced a crop. Still, said Davis in his study of the program's administration, "had nature chosen to smile instead of to frown in 1933 and 1934, I do not believe that the wheat adjustment efforts would have led to important reductions in the 1935 carryover from what it was on July 1, 1933. More probably, shrinkage of exports would have largely or wholly offset crop curtailment by the AAA, and the carryover might even have increased."[32]

Because controls seemed to him ineffective, Davis questioned whether the voluntary controls program should be continued after 1935.[33] He suggested that it should be replaced by compulsory controls binding on all farmers if the AAA really expected to control production.

The Wallace administration, although not so openly unenthusiastic about the results of voluntary controls, took note of the fact that although complying farmers reduced their acreage by 19 percent in 1935, this reduction was more than offset by an increase of 70 percent in noncomplying acreage.[34] This negative balance of acreage reductions was to be compared with the 30 percent reduction presumed to be needed during years of normal yields.

Nevertheless the voluntary program was extended, though almost immediately to be voided by the Supreme Court.[35] In the 1936 extension farmers were offered a new four-year contract, with these minor changes:

1.   Compliers could be asked to take out as much as 25 percent (formerly 20 percent) of their acreage base.

2.   They could drop out of the program after two years if they wished.

3.   Adjustment payments were to be based on the actual average farm price during the crop year rather than being based on the price during the previous year.

4.   The county committee was directed to protect tenants and sharecroppers against dishonesty by landlords; in general, administrative responsibility was shifted somewhat toward the local level.

The new program was approved overwhelmingly in a producer referendum, but it attracted somewhat less acreage than had been contracted under the first program.

---

32. Ibid., p. 413.
33. Ibid., p. 433.
34. *Agricultural Adjustment, 1933–1935,* p. 154.
35. U.S. v. Butler.

Apparently the program was extended partly out of lethargy, in the absence of immediate surplus pressures or falling prices. It also seemed at least as good as the alternatives. To move away in one direction was to rely more, as Davis urged, on "economic forces" as regulators of production. But the 1920s had revealed the inadequacy of the wheat market as a regulator, and in any case the Roosevelt administration was politically committed to rapid farm income improvement.

The Wallace administration was even more reluctant to move in the other direction, toward compulsory controls for wheat production. Wallace considered compulsory controls to be a threat to freedom, particularly dangerous for Americans, who in his judgment were preinclined toward mass regimentation and comformity. Wallace wrote in 1934:

> Regimentation without stint might indeed, I sometimes think, go farther and faster here than anywhere else, if we once took the bit in our teeth and set up for a 100 percent American conformity in every-thing. We are people given to excesses. I recall particularly the pressure toward conformity brought to bear during our wartime Liberty Loan drives; and we all have seen the same thing more or less repeated on a smaller scale whenever a town had a Y.M.C.A. or something of the sort to build. These outbursts of local high-pressure are not necessarily plotted and pushed from above. During the first year's cotton plow-up campaign in the South, for example, time did not permit sending out anything from national headquarters at Washington very much more than the contract itself. We had no slogans or banners, and very few set speeches. We had no insignia for the farmer who signed up to put on his mail-box. We knew what pressure would fall on the man who had no mark on his mail-box; and we purposely wished to avoid things like that. We wanted the thing put as a plain take-it-or-leave-it inducement to voluntary cooperation; and all our national plans and directions were drawn with that in mind.
>
> Immediately, however, many local communities formed drives in the old 100 percent "come along or be accounted a traitor" spirit; and before the thing was over there was even, I am told, a little night-riding, with the neighbors coming in to take out the cotton of the man who refused to sign. The American spirit as yet knows little of moderation, whichever way it turns.[36]

Another reason for continuing the voluntary program was the everlasting hope that wheat exports might increase, taking much of the load off controls. Exports had not developed in the first three years, nor were the omens good. The International Wheat Agreement had proved unsuccessful and economic nationalism had continued to

36. Wallace, *America Must Choose*, pp. 15–16.

flourish abroad. In short, experience permitted no optimism that the controls program was adequate for the surplus situation.

INCOME PROVISIONS

Adjustment payments were made to farmers which were designed to equal the difference between the market price and the parity price, but just for that portion of the wheat to be used for domestic human consumption. These payments, on about 54 percent of compliers' production, were prorated without regard for the amount of wheat actually produced on allotted acreage and without regard for the fact that a relatively small part of the production of some wheat growers, particularly those in the Northwest, was used for domestic human consumption. Federal payments per bushel were 28 cents in 1933, 29 cents in 1934, and 33 cents in 1935. These payments amounted to about one-third of the total income from the wheat crop in each of the three years. The cost of the payments and of the wheat program was recovered, up until the last few months of the program's existence, by the 30-cents-per-bushel processing tax paid by the millers.

The Supreme Court's 1936 decision overruling the processing tax brought pandemonium to the existing program. In expectation of the decision, many processors had obtained court injunctions impounding processing taxes obligated to the government. When these funds were returned to the processors and tax collections were terminated, the federal government met its remaining obligations to farmers by means of a special congressional appropriation.

The price of wheat had increased rapidly after enactment of the program, from an average of 37.9 cents per bushel in the 1932–33 marketing season to 74.1 cents in 1933–34, 84.7 cents in 1934–35. It had risen to 90.1 cents by December of 1935. However Davis attributed "nearly all" the striking price rise to the drought, which reduced supplies below domestic requirements. Another reason for increased prices was the devaluation of the dollar in 1933. Even so, prices never rose above 80 percent of parity. Davis concluded that the goal of parity prices under the domestic allotment program was entirely impractical,[37] although he conceded that cooperating farmers in effect received the equivalent of parity prices on their domestic allotment. Income advances were made, due both to the program and to the drought. Total cash income from wheat had stair-stepped from $196 million in the 1932–33 marketing year to $481 million in 1935–36 despite the smaller crops. The benefit payments had been widely

---

37. Davis, *Wheat and the AAA,* p. 413.

though not equally disseminated. The majority of recipients, who had been in great need, had spent the funds in ways that had rejuvenated the economy of rural communities[38] and which had revived their own spirits as well.

GROUP INTERESTS

The principal opponents of the program were the millers against whom the tax had been levied and the grain exchanges through which wheat was bought and sold.

In late 1932, when the bill embodying the domestic allotment plan had been under consideration, spokesmen of the milling industry and grain trade had taken very strong positions against it. They diagnosed the situation as one requiring acreage controls but not market intervention. The Millers National Federation, representing the vast majority of the millers, resolved that the surplus problem was due to carryovers from previous crops and from excessive acreage; they concluded that "the immediate problem, therefore, reduces itself to the disposing of existing surpluses, and of providing means by which burdensome surpluses may be prevented in the future."[39]

This group had sought to pass an "acreage rental" plan during the closing days of Hoover's administration. Meanwhile the group condemned the domestic allotment proposal on a number of grounds. They said it was unconstitutional as well as impracticable, and would result in a large increase in bureaucracy and in later legislation detrimental to farmers. It would increase production and would cause up to a 10 percent decrease in flour use as consumers switched to oatmeal, corn, rye flour, and potatoes. "Bootlegging" flour (avoiding the processing tax) would develop on a large scale, the group predicted.

After the act was passed, one group, the Southwestern Millers' Association, asked for quick implementation in behalf of their dust bowl region, but the Northwestern Millers continued to campaign for repeal of "the wheat tax" on the ground that it was a burden on the "millions who are struggling for means of existence."[40]

After a year the latter group's organ, *Northwestern Miller*, acknowledged that they had failed to ally bakers, the grain trade, the consumers, or the farmers in a campaign to repeal the act. At about the same time, the Millers' National Federation, which had at first pledged full cooperation in administering the act, declared that the program was ineffective and ought to be abandoned.

38. Ibid., pp. 162–67.
39. Ibid., p. 373.
40. Ibid., p. 377.

The baking industry had pledged a willingness to accept whatever program farmer representatives should agree upon, and the grain merchants or grain trade seemed inclined to let the new administration give the bill a fair trial. Both the grain trade and the millers protested strongly against Wallace's additional ambition to develop a government-financed "ever-normal granary" of wheat reserves designed to stabilize prices and supplies.[41]

An interesting array of ideological opposition greeted the domestic allotment bill. Ideological opposition came from economists in considerable measure. Most general economists at that time were, as Joseph Davis said, "prone to condemn destruction of crops or livestock and restraints on acreage or production as shortsighted and uneconomic . . . ," and many "have no faith in the ability of the government to improve upon the adjustments which economic forces tend to bring."[42] These economists were undoubtedly the most self-assured defenders of the pre-New Deal legislative status quo.

There were other ideological critics. Former President Herbert Hoover called the AAA programs "a threat to liberty." Socialist leader Norman Thomas, noting the malfunction of a system which must restrict food production in the midst of a hungry world, was most distressed over the fact that well-intentioned men felt obliged to take this course of action.

Farm organizations and farmers united in support of the program. Except for the National Farmers Union, the major farm groups interested in wheat supported the domestic allotment program and were highly pleased with its results during the first two years. Farmers Union felt that farmers deserved far better than this program. This organization continued to believe that farm production for the domestic food market should be rewarded through fixed prices at "cost of production plus a profit," and that government should eliminate the private "middlemen." Since Farmers Union also felt that production controls were unworkable and unnecessary, the union was far closer in its position to the old McNary-Haugen Bill than to the new agricultural adjustment program.[43] Despite constant criticisms of the program by the National Farmers Union, whose main strength was in the Plains Wheat Belt, its membership and local leaders in the Wheat Belt apparently cooperated in the administration of the program.

41. All the information about opponents of the 1933 wheat program is from Davis, *Wheat and the AAA*, pp. 369–81.
42. Ibid., p. 370.
43. John A. Simpson, *The Militant Voice of Agriculture* (privately published, 1934), esp. pp. 54–55.

The other major farm groups had not kept to rigid preferences with respect to the measures to be used to bring about farm relief. At that desperate moment none of the organizations had many members because farmers could not pay their dues, so there was more interest in getting relief to farmers than in getting credit for it. Roosevelt's administration was ready to give these groups some of both. Like the farm groups, the New Deal wished to move on many fronts, promoting better credit, preventing foreclosures, reducing currency values, regulating middlemen, strengthening farmer cooperatives, and increasing farm prices. For the most part the farm groups were contented at first to let the administration determine the emphasis, the timing, and the specific mix of mechanisms to be employed within the range of those acceptable. Most important to them, Roosevelt did accept "their" plan as the basis of his program, recalling that the farm organizations had been won over to the domestic allotment plan before the new administration took office, and they were consulted frequently in the final formulation of the bill. Thus they were able to share in the credit for its enactment and for the benefits which followed.

The Farm Bureau was outspoken in favor of the AAA, and claimed the new program as its own. Its claim was partly based on the initial support by the Montana Farm Bureau for M. L. Wilson's efforts, partly also based on the participation by Farm Bureau's President Ed O'Neil and Vice-President Earl C. Smith in writing the program, and partly in helping to coordinate farm organizations and legislators in support of the bill. Like the other general farm organizations, Farm Bureau activists at the grass roots joined the ranks of the farmer committees that would have to persuade farmers to cooperate with the program. Farm Bureau had still another reason at that time to support program administration, in that the Extension Service with which Farm Bureau was linked was the bureaucracy through which the initial program was carried to the farmers.

Farm Bureau called a conference of organizations friendly to the program in January 1934, the members of which included the American Farm Bureau Federation, the National Cooperative Council, the Farmers National Grain Corporation organized under the Federal Farm Marketing Act of 1929, and the National Agricultural Editors Association.

The conference urged further increases in farm income, using increased market prices as the means to do so. To this end they approved controls, as a temporary measure, but preferred development of foreign trade and industrial outlets, plus reduction in distribution costs, as good long-run measures. The conference also supported several recommendations for amendment to the act designed to strengthen its administration which had already been made by the Agricultural Adjustment Administration.[44]

One continuing worry of all the cooperating farm organizations was that the AAA farmer committees might become merged into a new, bureaucratic farm organization. Farm Bureau had developed its own organization from the farmer groups set up around the federal-state-county extension education program and did not want to see the experience repeated in behalf of a competitor organization. But it was not until the 1940s that the AAA came to be seen by Farm Bureau as a real threat—one to be opposed by Farm Bureau.

In short, the economic circumstances certainly encouraged co-operation with the administration, because the stricken farm organizations needed help more than the administration needed their assistance. They were generally pleased with the legislation and indeed claimed it as one of their own programs. They continued to seek the "image" and the substance of farm policy leadership and to be careful that the program would complement rather than compete with their individual operations.

FARMER REACTION

Farmers were passive elements in the evolution of the AAA. Subsequently they were expected to participate in making administrative decisions, but it proved difficult to involve them. This was to be expected since relatively few farmers took part in local affairs or in farm organization activities. However the circumstances prompted a quick response by most farmers, as participants in program benefits. Most were apparently eager to join the program as a means of receiving the much-needed subsidy, and criticisms from farmers arose mostly over slight delays in implementing the program. As the price of wheat rose during 1934–35, the domestic allotment program received general support in the commercial wheat area. In contrast, farmers in the areas where wheat was a minor crop were less enthusiastic about the program—sometimes indifferent or hostile to it.[45]

SUMMARY

Weather rather than government policy was the main influence on production and prices in the three harvest years during which the

44. Davis, *Wheat and the AAA,* pp. 385–86.
45. Information about farmer reaction was drawn largely from Davis, *Wheat and the AAA,* pp. 381–84.

Agricultural Adjustment Act of 1933 was in effect. Yet these were years of policy innovation. Social scientists for the first time were permitted to construct policy, subject to approval by congressional and farm organization leaders.

The depression provided the occasion for the acceptance of new measures. Direct payments to wheat farmers were introduced and re-luctantly accepted. A farmer cooperative system for administering commodity programs was organized and perfected. Procedures were worked out for reducing acreage on each participating farm, although the drought was not a good time to test the effectiveness of production controls. Experience with voluntary controls did suggest that produc-ion could not be controlled by persuasion alone, at least given in-centives no more persuasive than those offered under the 1933 act. At the end of the three years, when the wheat program was extended in 1935, it was apparent that controls would be inadequate even to keep U.S. production within the bounds set by an International Wheat Agreement of 1933, much less to bring it down to the level of domestic demand. In fact, the International Wheat Agreement had not been implemented by foreign producers either, so another world surplus era seemed in prospect.

The social and political impact of the act was apparently great but perhaps different than intended. Notwithstanding the fonder hopes of some framers, the program had not been revolutionary (in that it had been subject to approval by the rural coalition) and had been quite responsive as it went along to political pressures and to the lessons of its own experience. Its intent was to increase the power of farmers in government and in the marketplace, and it certainly took steps in that direction—in the face of opposition from most but not all wheat processors. However the program also affected the distribu-tion of power within the farm economy, enhancing the power of those farmers at the upper end of the income spectrum. The AAA was a means of access to USDA policy decisions tailormade for the large specialized commercial farmers; and by passing a federal program sup-porting their incomes the USDA assured that farmers would be inter-ested in policy. The act reinvigorated the general farm organizations, which were another means of access for commercial farmers. Spokes-men for these farmers, although willing to logroll in behalf of other recipients of federal services and protection, were not in basic sympathy with many New Deal aims. They were particularly unsympathetic toward programs for small farmers, tenants, and farm laborers, and subsequently they reduced these to a token status.

In short, the conservative commercial farm coalition (with wheat well represented), which had differentiated itself in the farm economy of the 1920s, was given control of agricultural policy by the Roosevelt administration. A coalition representing commercial farmers wrote the next major commodity law, the Agricultural Adjustment Act of 1938, and this proved to be the most enduring of all the landmark commodity laws.

7 / AGRICULTURAL ADJUSTMENT ACT OF 1938

SEVERAL FACTORS which made it likely that major commodity legislation would be passed converged in 1938. The first Agricultural Adjustment Act, passed in 1933, had been invalidated by the Supreme Court in early 1936, and had been replaced on a stop-gap basis by the Soil Conservation and Domestic Allotment Act of 1936. The latter act, which made an enduring contribution to farm legislation, emphasized soil conservation and provided a means for continuing to channel federal payments to farmers. But the 1936 act did not embody adequate mechanisms for restraining production and for maintaining price levels. Increased prices and reduced surpluses, which were the main goals of farm decision makers, had been achieved in 1936 due to reduced world production and prolonged drought in the United States. Wheat plantings sharply increased despite the voluntary control provisions in the 1936 act; and with the return of "normal growing conditions"[1] during the 1937 crop year, the USDA

---

1. *Agricultural Adjustment 1937–1938*, USDA-AAA, p. 98.

137

became concerned about the need for framing permanent, or long-range, commodity programs. Congress came to share this concern when the 1937 wheat crop indeed proved large and when planted acreage the following fall was much increased despite falling prices. Reduced farm prices were one aspect of a severe economic recession which began in 1937.

A special session of Congress was called, during which the Agricultural Adjustment Act was passed on February 16, 1938. Under the mandatory controls of the new act wheat acreage was sharply reduced. During 1939–43 harvested acreage was reduced to between 50 and 56 million acres, the minimum national acreage allotment having been legislated at 55 million acres. Yet U.S. stocks grew, due to increased per acre yields and because the war in Europe prevented substantial exports. The wheat carryover increased yearly until it reached 631 million bushels on July 1, 1942, which, adding the 1942 crop of 969 million bushels, was equivalent to a two years' supply of wheat on hand.[2] (See Table 7.1.) Wheat surpluses were burdensome, so they were channeled into secondary uses, such as production of alcohol and animal feeds. While they lasted, stocks were a reassuring reserve of food to be used by America and her allies during World War II.

By devoting wheat stocks to secondary uses, surpluses were reduced rapidly, even after production controls were removed. Stocks remaining at the end of the war proved smaller than were needed for human food in the postwar years. Thus the Agricultural Adjustment Act of 1938 was a timely effort to accommodate the strong and often unpredictable influences upon supply and demand during the decade following the passage of the act.

CHARACTER, OBJECTIVES, AND STRATEGY OF LEADERSHIP

Leadership for developing and enacting the Agricultural Adjustment Act of 1938 was provided by the American Farm Bureau Federation and the Department of Agriculture. Other farm organizations were cool toward many features of the basic framework developed by the AFBF and the USDA. So were leaders on the congressional agriculture committees, who were more interested in income measures for specific commodities—especially cotton—than in obtaining comprehensive, permanent legislation.

---

2. *Report of the Secretary of Agriculture, 1942,* p. 72.

TABLE 7.1. Wheat: supply and disappearance, United States, 1935-52

Year beginning July	Supply[a]				Disappearance							
					Used in United States							
	Carry-over	Production	Imports[b]	Total	Food[c]	Seed	Industrial	Feed[d]	Total	Exports[e]	Shipments	Total
					(million bushels)							
1935	146	628	35	809	490	87	f	85	662	4	3	669
1936	140	630	35	805	492	96	f	101	689	10	3	702
1937	83	874	1	958	494	93	f	115	702	100	3	805
1938	153	920	f	1,073	497	74	f	142	713	107	3	823
1939	250	741	1	992	488	73	f	102	663	45	4	712
1940	280	815	3	1,098	489	74	f	112	675	34	4	713
1941	385	942	4	1,331	487	62	2	117	668	28	4	700
1942	631	969	1	1,601	523	65	54	306	948	28	6	982
1943	619	844	136	1,599	533	77	108	518	1,236	43	3	1,282
1944	317	1,060	42	1,419	533	80	83	256	992	144	4	1,140
1945	279	1,108	2	1,389	494	82	21	297	834	391	4	1,289
1946	100	1,152	f	1,252	504	87	f	176	767	397	4	1,168
1947	84	1,359	f	1,443	484	91	1	181	757	486	4	1,247
1948	196	1,295	1	1,492	477	95	f	105	677	504	4	1,185
1949	307	1,099	2	1,408	488	81	f	111	680	299	4	983
1950	425	1,019	12	1,456	489	88	f	109	686	366	4	1,056
1951	400	988	32	1,420	493	88	1	103	685	475	4	1,164
1952	256	1,306	22	1,584	484	89	f	83	656	318	4	978

Source: USDA.

a. Includes flour and other products in terms of wheat.
b. Excludes imports of wheat for milling-in-bond and export as flour.
c. Includes military food use at home and abroad.
d. This is the residual figure after all other disappearance is accounted for. It has been assumed roughly to represent feed.
e. Actual exports, including exports for civilian feeding under the military supply program.
f. Less than 500,000 bushels.

FARM BUREAU

Farm Bureau, a federation of groups originally formed by county agents to disseminate good farming practices, had been influential in forming and guiding the congressional farm coalitions of the 1920s, as noted in Chapter 4. In behalf of commercial farmers these coalitions had obtained legislation regulating middlemen, encouraging producer cooperatives, and subsidizing farm credit. A champion of the unenacted McNary-Haugen Bill, Farm Bureau had subsequently acquiesced in the creation of President Hoover's Federal Farm Board,[3] and the group participated along with others in the enactment of the New Deal's Agricultural Adjustment Act of 1933.[4]

Depression severely reduced the membership of all the farm groups, but by 1938 Farm Bureau had reestablished roots in the midwestern and southern commercial farming areas. Under President Edward A. O'Neal, who was very effective both as an organizational leader and lobbyist, Farm Bureau was the most influential participant in forming the 1938 act.

Objectives. The overriding legislative objective of Farm Bureau was "parity" for farmers.[5] Parity could be expressed as parity prices or as parity of income. Farm Bureau spokesmen approved both concepts. Parity of income was the income that would provide the farm family a corresponding return for their work and investment as that afforded in other professions. Parity prices based on the relationship of costs and prices in 1910–14 were the preferred measure because the legislative objective could be made statistically specific. Furthermore, comparing parity price levels with the lower actual market prices during the 1930s, the parity price objective was adequately ambitious and yet not out of reach (Table 7.2).

President O'Neal, in lobbying for a farm program during 1937, did not insist that the program achieve parity prices immediately. Rather he insisted that the program should, at a minimum, bring prices "within shooting distance of parity."[6]

Farm Bureau had organizational as well as legislative objectives. The organization understood that as farm income improved more

3. Christiana McFadyen Campbell, *The Farm Bureau and the New Deal* (Urbana: Univ. of Illinois Press, 1962), p. 41.
4. Theodore Saloutos, "The American Farm Bureau Federation and Farm Policy: 1933–1945," *Southwestern Soc. Sci. Quart.*, 28(March 1948):314; Orville M. Kile, *The Farm Bureau Through Three Decades* (Baltimore: Waverly, 1948), ch. 10–16.
5. Saloutos, p. 314; Campbell, pp. 53, 55.
6. *New York Times*, Nov. 14, 1937, p. 4.

TABLE 7.2. Wheat prices as a percentage of parity

Year	Percent	Year	Percent	Year	Percent
1932–33	34	1937–38	79	1942–43	81
1933–34	81	1938–39	49	1943–44	93
1934–35	78	1939–40	61	1944–45	94
1935–36	74	1940–41	60	1945–46	97
1936–37	93	1941–42	82	1946–47	115

Source: Grain Division, CSS, USDA, March 1960.

farmers would be willing to pay dues. In addition, as Saloutos noted, "Experience had taught it that to have something over which to agitate kept up the interest of members, gained new converts, and impressed legislators."[7]

Strategy. As used here, strategy refers to the legislative mechanisms chosen as means of achieving increased farm income; and it also refers to the procedures chosen to achieve passage of the legislation. While the two aspects are related, separate consideration is helpful.

1. Legislative mechanisms. Farm Bureau's chief imprint on the 1938 act, and consequently upon farm commodity policy for subsequent years, was that it successfully emphasized supply controls as the main mechanism for increasing farm income.

Supply control was to be obtained mainly through stern controls on production. Farm Bureau leaders had become disillusioned with voluntary mechanisms of earlier New Deal programs, in which farmers reduced production in return for federal payments. New Deal experience had also convinced them that farm income could not be raised much in the absence of effective controls. Farm Bureau advocated mandatory or compulsory controls, later to be called "marketing quotas." These were, in President O'Neal's words, "drastic control measures."[8]

Marketing quotas for wheat were authorized in the 1938 act, despite the opposition of leading congressmen and the reluctance of the Secretary of Agriculture.

Linked with an emphasis on stern production controls was an emphasis on price supports as a means to higher income.[9] Farm Bureau thought it more feasible to obtain federal price guarantees, and

7. Saloutos, p. 314.
8. Campbell, p. 112.
9. *New York Times*, May 15, 1937, p. 32; Nov. 14, 1937, p. 4. See also Kile p. 237, and Campbell, pp. 114, 120.

in this way to achieve parity in the marketplace, than to seek parity of income each year by means of federal payments to farmers supplementing inadequate prices. Since under the first procedure mentioned prices were to be guaranteed through federal nonrecourse loans to farmers, using farmers' wheat as collateral, any market surplus would be lifted off into government stocks. Therefore the burden of balancing production while achieving fair farm income fell upon the USDA. Understandably Secretary Wallace preferred not to accept this burden.

While Farm Bureau did not expect surpluses to accumulate under strict production controls, its program did specify that federal stocks could not be resold in the domestic market except at prices well above the supported price. The organization took pains to assure that the USDA had adequate funds available for commodity storage, just in case surpluses did accumulate.

2. Lobbying strategies. Farm Bureau pursued several lobbying strategies in seeking passage of a general farm program. One of these strategies was alliance with the administration. The administration was of course the major political force in 1937, and it shared Farm Bureau's desire for prompt enactment of a permanent program which would apply to all major commodities and which would balance production. This position was in contrast with that of senior figures in Congress, particularly the House and Senate Agricultural Committee chairmen who were preoccupied with individual commodities and with short-term income increases rather than with long-term balance of supply and demand. In 1937 President O'Neal noted the kinship between the administration and Farm Bureau, in opposition to Congress: "As I have been telling farmers, I am on the side of President Roosevelt who has shown by every word and act that he is for the farmers and with Secretary Wallace and against the Democratic leadership in Congress."[10]

To facilitate cooperation with the Secretary of Agriculture, Farm Bureau passed a resolution favoring Wallace's ever-normal granary concept,[11] although Farm Bureau in fact preferred a policy of high prices through enforced scarcity. Farm Bureau chose not to emphasize its differences with the administration until after the bill was well along towards passage. Then it urged congressional committees to set low grain reserve levels while permitting high price supports.

It was unusual for Farm Bureau to be in opposition to the agricultural wing in Congress. Cooperation with the executive branch in 1937 and 1938 was not without strains. The conservative Farm

10. Campbell, p. 112.
11. *New York Times*, Jan. 13, 1937, p. 14.

Bureau leaders had become increasingly uncomfortable in working with other groups in the New Deal coalition such as labor unions.[12] Farm Bureau lacked sympathy for many Roosevelt measures of the time, including the Farm Security Administration program for low-income rural citizens.[13] In addition, Farm Bureau was obliged to submerge its own fears that the farmer committees set up under the farm program agency, the Agricultural Adjustment Administration, were looming as its chief competitor in organizing the grass roots of rural America. In pressing for enactment of the 1938 act, however, Farm Bureau acted as a staunch supporter of the AAA.[14]

Farm Bureau leaders exerted heavy pressure on farm congress-men. O'Neal, outspoken in criticizing congressional delays, informed legislators they were out of touch with rural constituents. He described the bill developed in the House Committee as being "wholly inadequate, ineffective, and entirely unsatisfactory,"[15] and he organized mass meetings in the constituency of the House Committee Chairman, Representative Marvin Jones (D., Texas), who subsequently complained that Farm Bureau was "using the whip and spur" on him.[16]

As in its earlier lobbying efforts, Farm Bureau tried again, this time less successfully, to play the role of farm group coordinator. Farm Bureau leaders were prominent in a conference of general farm organizations called by Secretary Henry Wallace early in 1937, and subsequently they were well represented on the Committee of Eighteen which worked with the USDA in drafting the bill. The bill that emerged was identified with Farm Bureau and consequently did not gain active support from most leaders of other farm organizations.[17] This bill, later called the Pope-McGill Bill, emerged from the Senate as the basis for the legislation finally enacted.

THE WALLACE ADMINISTRATION

In character, the Wallace administration of 1938 was much the same as in 1935. During several years in office, however, the Wallace administration had developed programs supplementary to commodity programs, such as those for low-income farmers. It had also

---

12. Saloutos, p. 319.
13. Ibid., p. 327. See also Grant McConnell, *The Decline of Agrarian Democracy* (Berkeley: Univ. of California Press, 1953), ch. 9, 10.
14. Saloutos, p. 314.
15. *New York Times*, Nov. 14, 1937, p. 4.
16. Kile, p. 240.
17. Kile, p. 239.

learned the strengths and weaknesses of various production and income measures, and the Secretary of Agriculture had become wary of implementing mechanisms which were likely to burden or to embarrass his administration.

Objectives. Among the ten or so major farm program objectives of the Wallace administration,[18] a few were associated directly with the commodity program. Secretary Wallace said in 1937 that the proposed wheat program had three goals—to conserve soil, to maintain farm income, and to assure adequate supplies for consumers.[19]

1. Conserving soil. The objective of soil conservation was much desired on its merits, although the fact that it was given first ranking was due not to grass roots support for it but due to the hope that the Supreme Court would find it more worthy than the income objective of the 1933 Agricultural Adjustment Act, which was the objective important to the agricultural constituency.

2. Maintaining income. Up to a certain point, the Wallace administration was in harmony with its constituents' desire to raise farm income. As income increased, the USDA's job became more difficult, requiring it to obtain increased federal budget outlays; or if higher prices were to be the route to higher farm income, it was incumbent on the administration to find ways to offset the production incentives resulting from higher prices. Higher domestic prices also endangered export markets and presumably affected consumers adversely.

Therefore Secretary Wallace and the Roosevelt administration posited more moderate income objectives, specifically abandoning the goal of "parity prices."[20] Less specific income objectives were stated. It was once proposed to give the "average farmer the same purchasing power that he had in the fifty years before the World War."[21] President Roosevelt spoke of setting farm prices "at reasonable levels."[22] Wallace spoke of "sustained income." Wallace favored the norm of "parity of income," which he once defined as giving farmers that which they must have in order to make their effective contribution to the welfare of the nation.

The administration assumed that parity prices were unattainable. Wallace said "I don't think there is any way of getting enough money

18. H. R. Tolley, "Objectives in National Agricultural Policy," *J. Farm Econ.*, 20 (March 1938):24–36.
19. Speech to wheat producers, Wichita, Kansas, Nov. 23, 1937.
20. *New York Times*, Sept. 23, 1937, p. 12.
21. Ibid.
22. *New York Times*, May 15, 1937, p. 32.

out of the Treasury to give farmers parity prices during the next ten years for cotton, wheat, corn, hogs, or any other product that is exported. . . . You might be able to get enough for a year or two to do this. But the consumers would soon rise up in protest."[23]

Wallace implied also that parity prices might indeed reduce farm income by reducing outlets,[24] or by flooding the market.[25] As World War II approached, Wallace maintained that the best net income for agriculture in the long run, and also the best results from the standpoint of general welfare, depended upon the maintenance of a correct balance between supply and price."[26]

In 1940 several economists further developed the theme that inflated farm prices hurt farmers in the long run. John D. Black and Nora Roddy said ". . . Most of the difficulties following the last war grew out of the inflation part of it. The overexpansion of agricultural production induced by inflation caused the agricultural surpluses of the twenties."[27]

Farm income objectives in any case gave way to goals for the whole economy, as inflation threatened during the early war period. One means chosen for preventing inflation was to restrain farm prices as much as possible, and the effort to do this led to sharp conflicts with farm groups over the proper level of price ceilings.

3. Assuring adequate supplies. Wallace's third goal was to assure adequate supplies to consumers. This was a basic objective in the long-run sense, since Wallace was convinced that a neglected agriculture would finally fail to feed the nation. It was a derived objective in the short-range sense, however, since the commodity programs, by restricting purchases from abroad, created the possibility of food shortages.

Other goals, not always specifically stated as such, included the desire to limit governmental involvement in agriculture pricing. Experience during his first term had made Wallace wary of mechanisms such as price support loans which could generate ever-increasing federal costs and responsibilities, and mechanisms such as production controls which could bring ever-increasing intervention by government in the affairs of farmers. Wallace clearly approached such mechanisms with great caution, because in 1937 he wanted to minimize government involvement in agriculture.

Still another objective was preservation of the family farm, al-

23. *New York Times*, Sept. 23, 1937, p. 12.
24. Speech to Kentucky Farm Conference Committee, Louisville, Ky., Oct. 2, 1937.
25. *Report of the Secretary of Agriculture, 1938*, pp. 19–20.
26. Ibid., p. 15.
27. John D. Black and Nora Roddy, "The Agricultural Situation, March, 1940," *Rev. Econ. Stat.*, 22(May 1940):73.

though by this time Wallace had become aware that rural America's social needs were better served through programs to aid low-income farmers than by measures to increase returns from specific commodities.

Strategy. To implement his programs, and to try to insure their success, Wallace emphasized the following legislative mechanisms:

1. Adjustment to supply and demand. The uniting theme of Wallace's policy suggestions was "adjustment," a word which gained significance as a result of experience under the 1933 act. Government's role in agriculture, in Wallace's matured judgment, was to help achieve a healthy adjustment between supply and demand. Wallace did not believe agriculture would benefit from efforts to hold prices higher than were needed to achieve given production levels or by tariffs or production controls designed to achieve artificial scarcity. In 1937 Wallace spoke of a "middle course" in which government would minimize the pain of shifting to reduced world markets and to advanced technology. The ever-normal granary would level out the hills and valleys caused by differences of annual yields, and the federal government would regrass those marginal acres which should never have been farmed. However government would not seek to be the major influence upon supply and demand but rather to help commercial farmers achieve the most favorable short-term adjustments to the long-run supply-demand relationship. In this basic strategy Wallace differed from the American Farm Bureau Federation, which wanted government to assert definite sovereignty over both prices and production. Therefore the Farm Bureau and the USDA programs were often quite different even when they advocated many similar mechanisms.

2. Moderate production controls. Wallace continued to reject the alternative of gearing wheat production to a protected U.S. market, even though export markets were not significant during the midthirties. Such an objective was expected to require severe production controls, which he felt would be disapproved by farmers and which he believed should not be an ordinary mechanism in a democratic society. In Wallace's original proposal in 1937, controls would be established only in the event of an emergency and only in the event that other measures had failed to prevent accumulation of surpluses.[28]

On the other hand, Wallace felt farmers were discriminated against as the result of a Supreme Court decision voiding agricultural

---

28. *New York Times,* Feb. 9, 1937, p. 22.

production controls. He maintained that most regimentation in the economy was accomplished by large corporations with full permission of government. " 'Corporate regimentation' is so omnipresent, so much a part of the air we continually breathe, that we have ceased to recognize it. The great corporations were first in the field of regimentation, and apparently some of them are jealous of agriculture and labor. . . ."[29] In 1937 Wallace advocated voluntary production controls, under which farmers would be paid "according to the sacrifice involved."[30] Wallace subsequently expressed approval for the use of compulsory controls for wheat during periods of extraordinary surpluses, provided that a large majority of farmers approved. He felt that experience under the first New Deal had proven the usefulness of such controls. "An utterly unguided, ruthlessly competitive agriculture would not fit into present conditions," according to Wallace, "with practically all urban industry under centralized control of one kind or another."[31]

3. The ever-normal granary. Wallace gave major emphasis to the concept of an "ever-normal granary" whose stocks would assure adequate food during poor crop years and which would be replenished with surpluses when these would otherwise burden the market. The granary concept would be first tested with wheat, and to implement it Wallace preferred the mechanism of crop insurance. The insurance would have the added virtue of compensating farmers for losses due to crop failure. Premiums would be paid in kind, so that in good years the federal government would remain in possession of as much as one-fourth of the total wheat crop. Loss payments would also be in kind, providing the means for marketing government stocks whenever crops happened to be short.

Congressional and farm organization spokesmen, who were far more interested in maintaining prices than in stabilizing supplies, preferred the price support loan as a means for acquiring and disposing of federal stocks. Under the loan mechanism the federal government would acquire stocks whenever the market price fell below the loan price, regardless of the supply situation. Wallace feared farm groups would push the support price ever higher, leaving the USDA with a large stock of surpluses.

While Wallace worried that huge surpluses would build inadvertently, farm interests worried that ever-normal granary stocks, accumulated by intent, would depress the market. "Secretary Wallace

29. *New York Times Magazine,* Jan. 3, 1937, p. 19.
30. Wichita speech.
31. *New York Times,* Sept. 23, 1937, p. 12.

favors big granary supplies, and we just can't go along with him on that idea," said President O'Neal of the Farm Bureau.[32]

5. Price-adjustment payments and adjusted prices. Wallace expected his ever-normal granary to stabilize but not to fix prices. Anticipating that wheat would soon be in oversupply, Wallace expected that adjustment to the demand siuation would require price reductions. Meanwhile farmers' income would be maintained through price adjustment payments, the prospect of which would also serve as a principal incentive for production controls.[33]

Wallace wished to reinstitute a processing tax as a means of financing these payments to farmers.

6. Measures for industrial growth. Secretary Wallace felt that American farms should continue to become more efficient rather than turning back toward a stage of more numerous, self-sufficient farmers.[34] Therefore new jobs and purchasing power would be found not on the farm, but through industrial recovery and development. "In a progressive economy industry and not agriculture would bear the brunt of providing new jobs. . . . Unless more can be employed in industry there is trouble."[35]

Lobbying Strategies. In 1937 the administration faced pressure from Congress and from the farm organizations for farm subsidies which would have no purposes other than relief, and which in the administration's view would not be in the direction of adjustment to demand. Administration efforts to counter this pressure took several forms.

1. President Roosevelt emphasized that any new expenditure for agriculture should be covered "100 percent by additional receipts from new taxes."[36] Roosevelt's rule seemed to require the passage of a processing tax, or alternatively a program of price-supporting loans, losses on which could be reimbursed from future budgets. Even under the latter program, it would be necessary to pay a subsidy on any exports equal to the difference between the world price and the domestic supported price. Congress had already provided revenues to cover export subsidies by setting aside 30 percent of tariff receipts for this and other purposes in a 1935 law,[37] but Secretary Wallace indicated considerable reluctance to use this fund for export subsidies incident

32. *New York Times,* Dec. 14, 1937, p. 4.
33. Wichita speech.
34. *Report of the Secretary of Agriculture, 1938,* pp. 4–5.
35. *New York Times,* Jan. 1, 1937, p. 25.
36. *New York Times,* Oct. 24, 1937, p. 1; "The Extraordinary Session of Congress Recommending Certain Legislation," in *The Public Papers and Addresses of Franklin D. Roosevelt* (New York: Macmillan, 1941), 1937 volume, p. 495.
37. Public Law 320, sec. 32, 74th Cong., 1st sess. (49 Stat. 641), ch. 641, p. 744.

to supporting domestic wheat prices above world levels. In this case Wallace's desire to put pressure on Congress coincided with his belief that export subsidies were self-defeating.

2. In 1937 the administration would not support additional farm relief—though farm legislators pleaded for it—except as a consequence of a comprehensive adjustment program or in clear anticipation of such a program.

3. Wallace sought a flexible bill, one that would allow the Secretary of Agriculture considerable discretion in responding to circumstances. Rather than engender conflict over the choice of specific provisions, Wallace apparently preferred to seek a variety of mechanisms which the secretary could then decide how and when to employ.

4. The Wallace administration hoped to gain the support of all major farm groups. Conferences of farm groups called by the administration were expected to achieve consensus on the program, although the unconciliatory Farm Bureau tended to dominate, ultimately with loss of support from some other groups.

Also in the direction of group unity, Wallace emphasized the point that "wheat is wheat," even though he administered some special measures for specific regions, such as special export subsidies for western wheat. All wheat regions did join together, although with varying enthusiasm, in supporting the enactment of the Agricultural Adjustment Act of 1938.

GENERAL HISTORY OF THE AAA

At the December 1936 convention of the American Farm Bureau Federation, President O'Neal expressed disappointment that the 1936 Soil Conservation and Domestic Allotment Act had not balanced production or raised farm income. He said, "The farmer wants definite measures for production control through legislation and will be satisfied with nothing else."[38] The convention resolved in favor of constitutional amendments or legislation such as might be necessary "to maintain price levels of farm products in line with the American standard of wages and American standard of living, and to assure to farmers of America their rightful share of the national income."[39]

In January 1937 the AFBF executive committee met with Secretary Wallace and his staff, at which time both groups agreed that the farm problem was a responsibility of the national government which could not be dealt with by the states or by interstate compact. It was

---

38. Kile, p. 234. See also Campbell, p. 111.
39. Kile, p. 234.

agreed that a new program should incorporate Wallace's "ever-normal granary" as a main feature.[40]

Following this, Wallace called a conference of farm organizations in February. This conference, in its final report, failed to adopt Wallace's crop insurance scheme as the basic mechanism for the ever-normal granary but instead recommended the use of commodity credit loans, emphasizing that the loans should be made at the "uppermost" level to keep prices from declining below parity. For purposes of further implementing its suggestions, the conference selected a Committee of Eighteen, with ten Farm Bureau members and with O'Neal as chairman. The Farm Bureau staff, working with experts from the USDA, drafted a bill by mid-April, which was further revised before being approved in early May by Farm Bureau's executive committee and by the Committee of Eighteen. Enthusiastic support came from M. W. Thatcher of the National Farmers Union, but representatives of other organizations tended to be undecided, opposed, or absent from committee sessions.[41] Thus the measure came to be known as the Farm Bureau Bill. It was also called the Pope-McGill Bill, named after the senators who cosponsored it.

When introduced in late May the bill met a cool response in both the White House and in the congressional agriculture committees. Secretary Wallace, O'Neal, and other farm leaders called upon President Roosevelt, who said that he favored the legislation in principle. Roosevelt, however, would not express a commitment to press for passage of the bill during the current session.[42] Neither the ever-normal granary nor the concept of compulsory controls was favorably received by leading farm spokesmen. The House Committee on Agriculture preferred to give consideration to a bill supported by the Grange which provided for voluntary rather than compulsory controls.[43] The Senate Agriculture Committee decided to conduct cross-country hearings prior to the passage of a permanent program,[44] and later in July the two committees agreed to postpone action during the 1937 regular session.

Meanwhile, however, farm prices of some commodities were dropping in response to large supplies and general depression in the economy. Several senior committee members implored the President to implement a price support loan program for cotton, but Roosevelt responded that he had not yet received sufficient assurance that a

---

40. Ibid., p. 236.
41. Ibid., p. 238.
42. *New York Times,* May 22, 1937, p. 6.
43. Kile, p. 239.
44. *New York Times,* July 24, 1937, p. 1.

permanent program of crop control legislation would be enacted. When cotton congressmen concluded that these were the only terms on which the administration would be moved, they reached a White House agreement,[45] the consequence of which was the announcement of cotton loans by the administration and a congressional resolution which provided that at the next regular or special session Congress would enact a measure providing for an ever-normal granary, production controls, crop insurance, price-pegging loans, and other features of a permanent program.[46]

In the fall, as the farm depression became more serious, President Roosevelt called a special session of Congress and charged them to enact an "all-weather" farm plan, in which any new expenditures would be offset by additional revenues.[47] The Senate Agriculture Committee adopted the Pope-McGill Bill, despite the reluctance of its chairman, Senator "Cotton Ed" Smith (D., South Carolina). The House committee refused to accept compulsory controls, instead agreeing tentatively on a voluntary controls bill.[48] But the committee then added a provision for compulsory controls to be implemented only following crop years in which production had been very large.[49] House committee Republicans generally criticized the House bill, for example expressing doubts about the constitutionality of the use of farmer referendums to approve compulsory controls.[50]

Secretary Wallace served notice that he supported the Pope-McGill Bill in principle, although he asked that the loan and payments rates be reduced.[51] Leading legislators accused Wallace of applying pressure on them.[52] Chairman Smith charged, as the bill went to conference committee, that the administration was creating discord among committee members,[53] but by that time disagreement between Farm Bureau and the administration had also come into the open. President O'Neal complimented the "fighting Secretary of Agriculture" while noting that "Secretary Wallace favors big granary supplies, and we just can't go along with him on that idea. . . . The Secretary wants a flexible bill, while we want a measure with definite control written into the law. We hate to disagree with our good friend, the Secretary, but we cannot and will not compromise on this fundamental issue."[54]

45. *New York Times,* Aug. 14, 1937, p. 1.
46. *New York Times,* Aug. 21, 1937, p. 4.
47. *New York Times,* Nov. 6, 1937, p. 14.
48. *New York Times,* Nov. 25, 1937, p. 10; Nov. 17, 1937, p. 17.
49. *New York Times,* Nov. 25, 1937, p. 1.
50. *New York Times,* Nov. 17, 1937, p. 17.
51. *New York Times,* Nov. 18, 1937, p. 17.
52. Ibid.; *New York Times,* Dec. 14, 1937, p. 4.
53. *New York Times,* Nov. 17, 1937, p. 17.
54. *New York Times,* Dec. 14, 1937, pp. 4, 24.

The final compromise, which received large majorities in both houses, was supported by Farm Bureau leaders. Although the Farm Bureau no longer claimed paternity for the legislation,[55] the new Agricultural Adjustment Act of 1938 did provide for compulsory controls when needed, did seek the objective of parity prices, and did provide for "parity payments" to farmers although without providing a mechanism such as a processing tax by which money for such payments would automatically be available. Later in the session Farm Bureau obtained appropriations for parity payments in 1938 of $212 million with the help of urban labor support. Farm congressmen returned the favor by voting for the Works Relief Act.[56]

The USDA applauded the elements of flexibility in the act and supported the act on final passage, despite its use of commodity loans to achieve ambitious price and production goals.[57] Secretary Wallace called the act "the Nation's well-matured answer to the challenge of an undisputed need for profound agricultural readjustments."[58]

PROVISIONS OF THE AAA OF 1938

The major provisions of the 1938 act were not novel; they had previously been implemented on a temporary or on a nonstatutory basis. For example, commodity loans, used earlier as emergency devices to raise farm income, had never been specifically provided for in law. Under the new act nonrecourse loans were available, using wheat as collateral, whenever the price at the close of the crop year was below 52 percent of parity. The secretary could set the loan rate for wheat between 52 and 75 percent of parity. The loan rate in effect served as a support price or price floor, and the loan served as a method by which farmers could hold their crops off the market during seasons of market surplus.

In addition the act directed the secretary to make parity payments to producers of wheat and other "basic" commodities (corn, cotton, rice, and tobacco), if and when funds were provided through appropriations. This would provide a return for them as nearly equal to parity prices as the available public funds would permit. Parity prices for wheat used the base period August 1909–July 1914. The parity payments were made on "normal" production, an amount determined on the basis of a reported history of production per acre in prior years. These parity payments were in addition to conservation payments, also

---

55. Campbell, p. 113.
56. Ibid., p. 115.
57. Wallace believed the loans involved "hazards" which could be avoided. See *Report of the Secretary of Agriculture, 1938,* pp. 13–15.
58. Ibid., p. 9.

made on normal production, which had been authorized in the 1936 act.

As a condition for receiving loans, parity payments, and conservation payments, cooperating farmers had to observe acreage allotments. These allotments were designed to produce an annual supply equal to a year's domestic consumption and export, with 30 percent left over for reserve. The annual carryover under this arrangement was expected to be about 100 million bushels more per year than the average carryover during the 1920s.[59]

Compulsory controls were also provided. These were implemented in terms of acreage controls under the allotments; however, in deference to the 1936 Hoosac Mills Case, in which the Supreme Court voided production controls, the new controls were called marketing quotas, thus in form regulating the marketing of wheat (under the "commerce clause" of the U.S. Constitution) rather than regulating production.[60] Marketing quotas were to be proclaimed whenever supplies—crop plus carryover—exceeded 135 percent of a normal year's domestic consumption and exports. Before being implemented, quotas had to be approved by two-thirds of the wheat farmers voting on the question in a referendum. If farmers disapproved, there would be no farm program for that farm commodity for the ensuing year. The act also contained a crop insurance program for wheat only, with both premiums and indemnities to be paid in kind or in cash equivalent.

INCOME SUPPORTS

Federal outlays for farm measures to support wheat farmers' income consisted of price supporting loans, conservation payments under the 1936 act, parity payments, export subsidies, and crop insurance.

1938. The act required that price-supporting loans must be made if the farm price of wheat on June 15 were less than 52 percent of parity. This percentage compared with the average price at 93 percent and 79 percent of parity respectively in 1936 and 1937. But prices were high in these previous years due to scarcity, and the USDA correctly anticipated that supplies would become more than adequate in 1938. Therefore loans were offered to cooperating farmers during the 1938 crop year, but the amount of wheat placed under loan in 1938 (9 percent of the crop) was inadequate to support the price at the loan rate, due mainly to uncertainties and problems in administering the new

59. *Agricultural Adjustment, 1938–1939*, USDA-AAA, pp. 32–33.
60. *New York Times*, Feb. 15, 1938, p. 6.

law. Secretary Wallace was quoted as saying that the wheat loan program had been "a headache to us all."[61]

With only 86 million bushels placed under loan, the market price for the 1938–39 marketing year averaged 10 cents below the support rate, although most of the wheat under loan was ultimately redeemed for sale. Farmers taking out loans received 7 cents per bushel payment toward storage costs.

Export subsidies, which earlier had been used for only a few shipments mainly from western states, had not been expected to be used much under the Agriculture Act of 1938. The farm program maintained the U.S. price well above the world price during 1938—as much as 35 cents above its normal relationship—but Secretary Wallace hoped to reach an international agreement resulting in higher world price levels. This agreement failed to materialize, and in August 1938 Wallace reluctantly announced a program of export subsidies as a means of maintaining a share of the world market. Under the subsidy program a federal corporation, the Federal Surplus Commodity Corporation, purchased U.S. surplus wheat at the market price and sold it to exporters at a price enabling them to sell abroad. Of the 107 million bushels of U.S. wheat and flour exported in the 1938–39 marketing year, about 94 million bushels were assisted by the Federal Export Program.[62] The effective subsidy was about 29 cents per bushel of wheat, and 22 cents per bushel equivalent for flour.

Complementing export subsidies was the high 42-cent tariff on wheat imports. Import quotas were subsequently proclaimed for wheat, beginning in May of 1941, which limited annual imports to 800 thousand bushels of wheat and a small amount of flour.[63]

Per bushel federal payments to farmers included 12 cents per bushel for following conservation practices under the 1936 act.

1939. The support rate for the 1938 crop had been 59 cents per bushel, and as set at the upper level for 1939 (55 percent of parity) it was 63 cents per bushel. The average market price during the 1939–40 marketing year held almost at the support level. In addition growers received conservation and parity payments equaling 28 cents per bushel (17 cents and 11 cents respectively), thus receiving over a fourth of their total income from the federal treasury.[64]

---

61. Joseph S. Davis, "The World Wheat Situation, 1938–39," *Wheat Studies of the Stanford Wheat Research Institute,* 16(December 1939):133.
62. *Agricultural Adjustment, 1938–39,* USDA-AAA, p. 34.
63. *Report of the Administrator for the Agricultural Conservation and Adjustment Administration, 1942,* USDA-AAA, pp. 11–12.
64. Joseph S. Davis, "The World Wheat Situation, 1939–40," *Wheat Studies of the Stanford Food Research Institute,* 17(December 1940):191.

In 1939 crop insurance for wheat went into effect. It was intended to establish a "wheat reserve" with the premiums paid in, in furtherance of Wallace's ever-normal granary concept. However, under the actuarial scheme as administered by the AAA county committees, the Federal Crop Insurance Corporation incurred a deficit in each of its first three years despite generally good crop weather. The ratio of losses paid by FCIC to premiums collected was 152 in the 1939 harvest year, 165 in 1940, and 142 in 1941.[65]

A larger share of the 1939 crop—about 22.6 percent—was placed under loan, and almost all the wheat placed under loan was redeemed.

1940. In 1940 the price support level was held at 57 percent of parity, although the conservation and parity payments were reduced to a total of 18 cents per bushel. More than a third of the large crop was placed under loan, and two-thirds of this was never redeemed. The CCC took ownership of 174 million bushels.

1941. In May of 1941 Congress raised the maximum price support level to 85 percent of parity, and this maximum became the effective price support despite the existence of large CCC stocks. Exports during 1940 and 1941 marketing years were small, taking place mainly with assistance of export subsidies averaging 29 cents and 21 cents per bushel respectively for the two years.[66] Well over a third of the 1941 crop was placed into CCC stocks.

In response to a storage crisis, the USDA sought in various ways to dispose of its surplus wheat. A major means was domestic sales of wheat for feed grain, sold domestically under subsidy despite strong protests from Farm Bureau and other farm spokesmen.[67]

Conservation and parity payments for 1941 again totaled 18 cents per bushel. With inflation threatening the economy, the administration preferred to use federal payments rather than price increases as a means of achieving the income goals insisted upon by farm interests. Federal parity payments were considered as a means of closing the gap between market prices and income goals. In 1939 and 1940 the goal had been to achieve 75 percent of parity prices. In both these years Congress specified that the payments should not exceed the amount by which the average price was less than 75 percent of parity. No such limitation was stated for 1941; for 1942, over the objections of

65. J. C. Clendenin, "Federal Crop Insurance in Operation," *Wheat Studies of the Stanford Food Research Institute,* 18(March 1942):250.
66. Helen C. Farnsworth, "The World Wheat Situation, 1940–41," *Wheat Studies of the Stanford Food Research Institute,* 18(December 1941):151.
67. Helen C. Farnsworth, "World Wheat Survey and Outlook, May 1942," *Wheat Studies of the Stanford Food Research Institute,* 18(December 1941):342.

the administration, Congress revised the statement to direct that if the price or loan plus the payments should be higher than needed to achieve *parity* prices, "the parity payments shall be adjusted so as to provide a return to producers which is equal to but not greater than parity price."[68]

Secretary of Agriculture Claude Wickard, speaking for the administration in April 1942, protested, "We just can't keep on getting parity for all the wheat from 55 million acres." The administration was aware of the increasing costs of the wheat program, and also that good returns from wheat would increase production, without any prospect for increasing foreign markets.

1942. As the administration sought to control prices throughout the economy, Congress specified, in the Second Price Control Act[69] of October 2, 1942, that no maximum price should be established on wheat or its products which would fail to reflect to producers either parity price or the highest prices received by producers between January 1 and September 15, 1942. Also specified was that adequate weighting should be given to the high cost of farm labor, which was not fully reflected in the old parity formula.

There ensued a period of disagreement between price control authorities and farm legislators over the correct way to calculate parity price. One question in dispute was which federal payments to farmers should be added in as subsidized income to be subtracted from the parity price as a means of determining a proper loan and market price. Meanwhile both the market price and the calculated parity price of wheat rose sharply after the harvest of 1942. As the market price of wheat moved well above a dollar, it was supplemented by per bushel payments of 23.4 cents for cooperators. Economist Helen C. Farnsworth protested that such prices would have serious consequences for rationing and price control programs, as well as diversion of scarce industrial resources and for determining postwar price and farming readjustments.[70]

1943. In 1943 the wheat price moved well above the loan level, which was at 85 percent of parity, while federal payments tended to boost the total income of wheat farmers to 100 percent of parity prices. In the 1944 marketing year, and as it turned out in all the years until 1955, the price support rate was at 90 percent of parity. The actual market price was 93 percent and 94 percent of parity during 1943 and

68. Joseph S. Davis, "World Wheat Survey and Outlook, May 1942," *Wheat Studies of the Stanford Food Research Institute,* 18(May 1942):343.
69. Public Law 729, sec. 3, 77th Cong., 2d sess. (56 Stat. 766), ch. 578.
70. Helen C. Farnsworth, "Wheat in the Fourth War Year: Major Developments, 1942–43," *Wheat Studies of the Stanford Food Research Institute,* 20(November 1943):56.

1944, respectively. The price received in 1945 was 97 percent of parity, and the average annual price for 1946 was 115 percent of parity.

Throughout the war years the federal government undertook to maintain support levels at somewhat below the price ceilings implemented for wheat and other commodities. So long as the wheat price could be stabilized through sale or acquisition of federal stocks, this endeavor was successful. When stocks were exhausted through use for animal feeding and industrial alcohol, and subsequently for foreign aid and relief, this endeavor proved unsuccessful.

PRODUCTION CONTROLS

In the 1936 Soil Conservation and Domestic Allotment Act, wheat was one of several commodities lumped together in a general "soil-depleting acreage base," and the efforts to control wheat production under the act were spectacularly unsuccessful.

For the 1937 crop planted acreage was the largest in history despite a plea by AAA to wheat farmers that they plant only 80 percent of their "soil-depleting base acreage" designated under the 1936 act.

The 1938 act provided for a national wheat allotment, defined as the acreage which at average yields would produce, with carryover from the previous years, not less than 130 percent of a year's normal domestic consumption and export requirements. As compared with the approximately 80 million acres planted to wheat for the 1937 and 1938 crops, the formula in the act would have specified an allotment of only 62.5 million acres for the 1938 crop. However, since the 1938 program was not implemented until after most of the wheat had been planted, the allotment was used only for calculating benefit payments rather than for acreage control.

Under the act, allotments were distributed to the states and thence to counties and individual farms, based upon average seedings of wheat for the preceding ten years.

1939. According to the formula, it appeared that the acreage needed for 1939 would be 46 million acres, an amount only 40 percent of the 1937 acreage. Rather than require a reduction of this magnitude, Congress in June 1938 passed a resolution providing that the national allotment for 1939 should not fall below 55 million acres.[71] In a resolution passed in April 1939 Congress extended this 55-million-acre minimum allotment for subsequent years.

Compulsory marketing quotas were not established for 1939, since the expected supply was slightly less than a billion bushels while the

---

71. *Agricultural Adjustment, 1937–1938,* USDA-AAA, p. 115.

amount needed for domestic use and reserves under the formula was slightly more than a billion bushels. However, in order to receive program benefits in 1939 farmers were obliged to reduce their wheat acreage to comply with the 55-million-acre allotment. Seedings for the 1939 crop were thus reduced 19 percent below the 1938 planted acreage, to about 65 million acres. Harvested acreage was less than the 55-million-acre figure.[72]

1940. Under the reduced acreage 1939 wheat production was small enough that the 1940 allotment could be increased to 62 million acres, still without need for marketing quotas. An estimated 75 percent of wheat growers participated in allotments during 1940, with seeded acreage nationally only slightly exceeding the allotment.[73]

1941. The 1940 crop was relatively large, on top of a carryover of 280 million bushels, and with the prospect of a positive response to higher price supports in the coming year, 1941, the secretary was obliged according to the formula to proclaim marketing quotas for the 1941 crop, under an allotment of 62 million acres. Although there was some speculation as to whether wheat farmers would provide the necessary two-thirds approval for the quotas, a majority of 81 percent of those voting did approve them.

With marketing quotas in effect, any noncooperating producer with more than 15 acres of wheat could not secure a marketing card for sale of wheat until he had presented evidence that any wheat produced on nonallotment or "excess" acres had been stored under seal, or that he had paid the penalty (half the loan rate) on the "excess" wheat which was to be marketed or fed, or as a third alternative that he had delivered his "excess" wheat to an agent of the Secretary of Agriculture. As a noncooperating producer he could not use the wheat-loan program, except to secure restricted loans on his "excess" wheat at 60 percent of the regular rate. In addition the noncooperator was given reduced parity and conservation payments according to the formula which decreed a 10 percent reduction in payments for every percentage point by which a farmer's acreage had been overplanted. Given this combination of penalties along with rewards to encourage compliance, the AAA was able to announce after the 1941 harvest that only about 1 percent of the crop was to be marketed under penalty.[74]

1942. Despite effective marketing quotas, the 1941 crop was very large, on top of a 385-bushel carryover; excessive supplies prompted a new concern about the viability of the permanent wheat program, al-

72. *Agricultural Adjustment, 1938–1939,* USDA-AAA, p. 35.
73. *Agricultural Adjustment, 1941,* USDA-AAA, p. 21.
74. Farnsworth, "Wheat in the Fourth War Year," p. 40.

though Secretary of Agriculture Claude Wickard noted that an ample wheat carryover would be desirable during and after a war.[75] Wickard was advised by some to seek a repeal of the 55-million-acre minimum in order to maintain a viable program, since the actual wheat acreage needed for 1942 was probably not much more than 40 million acres. However, while predicting that production would be in excess of demand, Wickard said it was not practicable to ask wheat growers to make further reductions.[76]

Although planted acreage for the 1942 crop was smaller than in any of the past 20 years,[77] good yields produced the largest U.S. crop in history. This billion-bushel crop, added to a 1942 carryover of 631 million bushels, taxed all resources for storage space in spite of the fact that storage had been expanded in anticipation of the crop.

1943. Quotas were again announced for the 1943 crop, and farmers approved them by an 82 percent majority in 1942. In addition farmers were urged voluntarily to hold plantings at 52.5 million acres, and the estimated 1943 planted acreage turned out to be just over 54 million acres. During 1943, however, wheat stocks began to decline as the amount of wheat used for animal feed tripled under a USDA subsidy program and as substantial quantities of wheat were used for production of industrial alcohol. As a result of this increased use, and also perhaps from a fear that farmers would disapprove 1944 quotas in a referendum originally scheduled for the spring of 1943, Secretary Wickard on February 23, 1943, suspended quotas for the 1943 crop, thus permitting farmers to exceed allotments and still be eligible for AAA payments and wheat loans. The suspension was retroactive in allowing 1942 crop wheat produced on excess acres to be marketed without any penalty.

In 1944 and during the immediate future years, the emphasis in farm programs shifted completely from production controls to farm production practices, with the chief objective being to improve the fertility of the soil as the war demanded more production.

RESULTS OF THE 1938 ACT

EFFECT ON PRODUCTION

Under the program, beginning in 1939 through 1941, the acreage at 80 million acres in 1937 was reduced by an average each year of

75. *Report of the Secretary of Agriculture, 1941,* p. 102.
76. Ibid., p. 103.
77. Farnsworth, "Wheat in the Fourth War Year," p. 41.

18 million acres, and in 1942 by more than that amount. Using as a measurement the average yield per seeded acre during those years, the annual reduction in wheat production due to acreage controls would have been about 200 million bushels.[78]

Some acreage idled under the wheat program was converted to production of other commodities, and vice versa. Yet the AAA estimated that as a result of the wheat commodity and other programs the total acreage devoted to "soil depleting crops" (cotton, wheat, feed grains, tobacco, and rice) was 30 million acres less than the average of 299 million acres planted in 1928–32.

Offsetting acreage reductions, however, were the effects of new conservation practices inaugurated by the program. Many millions of acres benefited from conservation practices under the program including summer fallowing, crop rotation, fertilization, and control of wind and water erosion. In 1941 the USDA asserted, "Conservation farming is the surest means of getting greater production on a continuing basis from year to year for as long as the war lasts. Sometimes conservation is thought of in terms of saving up soil fertility for future generations. Actually, it is the most effective way to boost output *now* as well as for the future."[79]

In 1942 Joseph S. Davis expressed agreement with the USDA about program results, but with a different judgment as to the value of increased production: "In this country so-called 'production control' measures have been enforced for years, but they have facilitated instead of prevented embarrassing accumulations of wheat stocks."[80]

EFFECT ON FARM INCOME

Observers also would have agreed, in general, that "wheat prices and incomes of wheat producers were higher from 1939 to 1943 than they would have been without any wheat program."[81] However experts disputed whether the long-run effects or impact on farm income would be beneficial or not. In 1942 Davis concluded that "the price of wheat has risen noticeably in the past two seasons with increasing surplus. This has been due primarily to the operation of price-boosting legislation, adopted and maintained under the influence of the farm bloc."[82]

In the regional study referred to above, economist John A.

78. *Wheat Problems and Programs in the U.S.*, North Central Reg. Publ. 118, Missouri Agr. Exp. Sta. Res. Bull. 753(September 1960):15.
79. *Annual Report of the Administrator of the Agricultural Conservation and Adjustment Administration, 1942*, USDA-AAA, p. 5.
80. Davis, "World Wheat Survey and Outlook, May 1942," p. 341.
81. *Wheat Problems and Programs in the U.S.*, p. 15.
82. Davis, "World Wheat Survey and Outlook, May 1942," p. 341.

Schnittker concluded that from 1938 to 1942 wheat prices would have been much lower, perhaps 50 percent lower than the actual price, in the absence of the price support program. On the other hand, he noted, the sale of CCC stocks between 1942 and 1946 helped to restrain wartime wheat price increases.[83]

There was dispute as to whether domestic price increases represented real income gains. The AAA stressed that the spread was reduced between U.S. and Liverpool (world) prices, estimating as much as 34 cents per bushel in favor of the American wheat grower. V. P. Timoshenko, however, argued that the export subsidy substantially depressed world wheat prices, so that the actual benefit to the U.S. grower was only about 7 to 8 cents per bushel.[84] The USDA's *Wheat Situation*, taking into effect the impact upon world prices, maintained instead that the prices of wheat to growers during the prewar period September-June of 1938–39 was increased by a net of 17½ cents.[85]

Federal payments to wheat growers were also a substantial contribution to farm income, for example in 1938 providing as much as a 25 percent increment over cash income from sales of wheat.[86]

COST TO THE FEDERAL GOVERNMENT

Major costs associated with the wheat program included subsidies on wheat exports, losses under the price support loan program, and payments to farmers. Export subsidies required substantial expenditures as compared with other program costs, although the subsidized exports were significant only in the 1938–39 marketing year. In that year 93 million bushels of wheat were exported at an average subsidy of 27 cents per bushel, for a total cost of $25.7 million.[87]

Losses from the wheat price support program were not large under the CCC system of accounting, particularly as compared with the program for cotton (Table 7.3). The largest federal costs were for payments to farmers, which totaled somewhat over $100 million annually during program years after passage of the 1938 act (Table 7.4).

ADEQUATE FOOD TO THE CONSUMER

Due to the conservation practices incorporated in the program, and due also to improved technology, per acre yields were so large as

83. *Wheat Problems and Programs in the U.S.,* p. 15.
84. V. P. Timoshenko, "Wheat Subsidization and Exports," *Wheat Studies of the Stanford Food Research Institute,* 17(October 1940):85.
85. *Wheat Situation,* USDA (Sept. 25, 1939), p. 18.
86. Timoshenko, p. 66.
87. *Agricultural Adjustment, 1939–1940,* USDA-AAA, p. 27. Subsidized costs for other years: 1939–40, 35 million; 1940–41, 21 million; 1941–42, 19 million; 1942–43, 20 million. From Farnsworth, "Wheat in the Fourth War Year," p. 50.

TABLE 7.3. Realized loss by CCC on wheat, corn, and cotton

Fiscal year	Wheat	Corn	Cotton
1939	$ 3,456,400	1,070,726	52,446
1940	1,953,001	3,399,837	786,360
1941	790,059	15,607,901	12,190,194
1942	5,089,029	9,478,707	74,425,846
1943	28,505,494	4,461,707	25,525,792
1944	28,412,822	273,751	28,799,078
1945	17,940,086	8,071,978	24,835,610

Source: Agricultural Stabilization and Conservation Service, Financial Analysis Branch, February, 1964.

TABLE 7.4. Payments under agricultural adjustment, agricultural conservation, and parity payment programs, by program years, 1933–43

Program year	Adjustment or conservation	Parity	Total
	($000)		
1933	93,806	. . .	93,806
1934	105,554	. . .	105,554
1935	114,988	. . .	114,988
1936	43,389	. . .	43,389
1937	. . .	. . .	. . .
1938	50,126	. . .	50,126
1939	83,941	53,614	137,555
1940	47,754	55,884	103,638
1941	49,127	58,226	107,353
1942	57,442	79,741	137,183
1943	59,675	80,774	140,449

Source: Agricultural Statistics, 1945, USDA, table 652.

to provide an abundance of staple foods during wartime, presumably with the expenditure of fewer resources than would have been required to produce the same amount on a much larger acreage. In addition idle acreages were being restored to fertility, while held in reserve to meet the extraordinary postwar demands. The large surplus stocks were also useful because they were available on demand and because when converted into meat products they reduced inflationary pressures on U.S. food prices during the war. In the following statement of Secretary Claude Wickard, the contribution of the commodity program to the war is summed up:

> Outstanding among the assets which agriculture brought to its task was the reserve power it inherited from the 1930s, the years that saw the birth and early growth of our national farm program. Features of this program which had been adopted to reduce farm surpluses and

raise farm prices were also, as it turned out, preparation for the war emergency. The acreage adjustments it promoted favored precisely the crops we now require. Commodity loans accumulated reserves in the Ever-Normal Granary. Soil conservation stored production capacity in the land. Contrary to a popular impression, the adjustment system was never a scarcity device; it merely reduced the output of things not needed for the sake of getting more production of things required. Our total farm production rose; it increased 10 percent between 1938 and 1940, and the increase was mainly in the commodities that help us now to win the war. The program enabled us to begin with large stocks of breadstuffs, meats, and fruits, with a record supply of food-stuffs, and with a record number of meat animals on farms and ranches.

In a word we did not have to begin from scratch. When Great Britain asked for more foodstuffs, when Russia needed some of our farm products, and when our own needs mounted we had the means to respond. Our stocks in the Ever-Normal Granary and our renovated soil gave us a head start which allowed us to increase our own food consumption and at the same time to be a food arsenal of democracy. Corn on hand became meats and dairy products quickly; wheat stocks became available as feed for livestock and also for the production of ethyl alcohol.

Also the program prepared farmers as well as farms for the ordeal of war. Farm prices sagged after Germany's early successes. Cash wheat at Kansas City, for example, dropped from 107 cents a bushel on May 13, 1940, to 79 cents on June 5, 1940. Hogs and other livestock dropped. Export outlets for wheat, cotton, and tobacco shrank to nothing. But commodity loans supported farm prices, tided farmers over, and brought them through with their finances as well as their land and crops in fair adjustment. The agricultural front was firm and ready to advance.[88]

REACTION TO THE AAA OF 1938

Some voices of dissenting groups, including the Grange, were heard during and after the passage of the 1938 act. In a 1938 speech to the AAA state committeemen, Wallace noted efforts to aggravate regional conflicts, including efforts to differentiate between producers of spring and winter wheat. Many court suits were brought against the new legislation. Some business leaders condemned major aspects of the program.[89] Five Brookings Institution studies published in the mid-thirties generally approved the New Deal farm program but were in some respects critical of production controls and of the ever-normal granary scheme, the main features of the 1938 act.[90]

Appeals for support of the 1938 program, however, were appar-

---

88. *Report of the Secretary of Agriculture, 1942,* USDA, p. 2.
89. "Fortune Round Table on Agricultural Policy and National Welfare," *Fortune,* 22(July 1940):68–69 ff.
90. *New York Times,* Mar. 1, 1937, p. 3.

ently heard by more farmers and were more credible to them than
were the voices of opposition. One reporter looking for evidences of
"farm revolt" in 1938 found that, despite the very large acreage reductions and election year criticisms, the great majority of farmers
accepted the need for programs and appreciated the benefits flowing
from them. Farmers in opposition were the same minority of "ideal-
ists" who had always opposed New Deal farm programs.[91] As noted
earlier, the two referendum votes were in overwhelming approval of
the program.

SUMMARY

The Agricultural Adjustment Act of 1938 was a reflection of past
experience—and a product of existing depression conditions and of
prospects for a difficult future. The AAA of 1938 proceeded from
experience under two New Deal farm statutes. Experimentation under the AAA of 1933 had revealed that numerous mechanisms, earlier
conceived as partial or complete solutions to the problems of overproduction and low prices, all had numerous shortcomings. The fact
that no foolproof program had been discovered for raising farm prices
and stabilizing production was reflected in the 1936 Soil Conservation
and Domestic Allotment Act, which was modest in its goals and which
emphasized moderate subsidies rather than market control as a first
step toward a permanent program.

Indeed, the 1936 act had registered little impact on farm income.
Income had improved temporarily due to drought but was in jeopardy
by 1937. Nor did the act affect production, which had been inadequate
to the point of scarcity during the extended drought of the mid-thirties
but which in 1937 amounted to more than the market could use. In
1937, the year in which the Agricultural Adjustment Act of 1938 was
first considered, it seemed clear to all that in "normal" times income
incentives would have to be moderated, or else strong production controls would have to be applied, in order to prevent overproduction of
wheat.

The coinitiators of the 1938 act were the leadership of the American Farm Bureau Federation and the Wallace administration. Both
desired to enact a permanent program in conjunction with the granting of depression relief in 1937. Both were dedicated to a farm income
objective, although the USDA was inclined to stabilize prices at non-
incentive levels while Farm Bureau wished to raise farm prices to
parity. The USDA had the additional objectives of conserving soil
and providing adequate food for consumers.

91. A. R. Buckingham, *New York Times,* May 15, 1938, sec. 4, p. 3.

As an organizational objective the USDA desired to maintain and improve its capacity to gain new policy and to keep viable its existing functions. Farm Bureau's organizational aim was to increase its own membership and its prestige in the policy-making process.

Farm Bureau, for its lobbying strategies, chose to work in alliance with the administration and therefore sought areas of agreement, such as mutual support of the ever-normal granary scheme and willingness to accept voluntary production controls during some years. Farm Bureau also sought to lead a coalition of general farm organizations on the 1938 bill, without much success. Farm Bureau did arrange for a trading of votes with labor groups, and in addition the organization generated very heavy grass roots pressure upon rural legislators.

The legislative mechanisms chosen by Farm Bureau were compulsory production controls to be applied as a means of inducing scarcity, and price support loans which would be used to maintain and to raise the market price of wheat.

While Farm Bureau's proposals would put the burden of adjustment upon the federal government, Wallace's legislative strategy would have cast government only as a moderator of economic trends. Wallace's "middle course" would have required U.S. agriculture to adjust to domestic and foreign demands over the long run. He asked Congress to make provision for mandatory production controls (marketing quotas), but he sought a market environment in which such compulsory controls would seldom be used.[92] He would have maintained an ever-normal granary the size of which would reflect anticipated food needs rather than solely the amount of grain in surplus at a given time. Wallace would have allowed prices to fluctuate, within limits, in response to supplies, and he would have relied on an expanding industrial economy as the major solution for depression in agriculture as well as in the total economy.

As strategies for gaining passage of the desired policies, President Roosevelt emphasized that any new expenditure should be paid for with additional taxes, that no new farm relief should be granted except as a part of a permanent program, that a permanent program should permit adequate discretion by the Secretary of Agriculture, and that the law should if possible have the support of all farm groups.

Thus Farm Bureau's proposals would have made the USDA the focus, and the mediator, of enormous economic and political forces; in the light of past experience, it was doubtful that even severe production controls could restrain the dynamic production incentives loosed by high prices and advancing technology. Wallace resisted such re-

92. Testimony before the House Committee on Agriculture, *Hearings on General Farm Legislation* (May 27–28, 1937).

sponsibility, feeling in any case that compulsory controls were inappropriate to a democratic society except in emergencies. Wallace felt that farmers would themselves reject such controls.

The 1938 act was a compromise between the USDA and Farm Bureau positions. It posited a goal of parity prices, but its minimum requirement was for loans at 52 percent of parity. It provided for compulsory controls but only during those years when annual supply was expected to be 30 percent larger than would be expended or would be needed for reserves.

As implemented, the act came closer to what Farm Bureau had recommended. Congressional leaders, many of whom had been reluctant to enact a long-range program vesting discretion in the Secretary of Agriculture, found that power indeed lay in congressional hands—in the capacity to specify the lower limits of price supports and the lower limits of acreage allotments. Congress could also determine the size of appropriations from which farm subsidies would be paid and could place limitations on the disposal of CCC surpluses.

Compulsory controls, which were inaugurated in addition to the voluntary acreage allotments, functioned well but without achieving the objective of reducing production to effective demand. Farm income rose, even in the absence of large foreign markets, and until 1942 increased income could be attributed largely to the price program. After 1942 the program achieved the objective of meeting large demands for food, thus preventing inflation in domestic food prices while enabling huge food shipments to allies and for postwar relief.

Program costs included export subsidies and losses on commodity loans but consisted mainly of payments to farmers. Costs were large in comparison with some past programs but apparently quite small in terms of the benefits provided to farmers, to the general economy, and in terms of service to the war effort. The virtues of the program were no less real because some were unanticipated.

8 / MOVING AWAY FROM RIGID PRICE SUPPORTS, 1953–60

THE WHEAT COMMODITY PROGRAMS were designed to raise commercial farmer income, but the method usually chosen for doing so—and the immediate aim—was to raise commodity prices. The statistically determined goal of the "parity price" was postulated as the ideal price, but government was usually not expected to achieve full "parity." Instead programs were judged by their ability to stabilize prices at levels somewhat above what they might otherwise have averaged. These levels were considerably below the ideal goal of parity. In the 1938 act, for example, price support loans were initially available only when the market price fell below 52 percent of parity or when the July estimate for wheat was in excess of a normal year's domestic consumption and exports.[1]

During World War II, however, a rural coalition achieved temporary income guarantees equivalent to 100 percent of parity price

---

1. The world price did fall during the first year of that program to 50 percent of parity so that from the beginning of the program the loan rate was in effect acting as a price support.

supports; they also gained guarantees of 90 percent of parity supports for wheat and the other basic crops during two years following the war. In postwar farm politics a rural coalition developed similar to those Congress-oriented coalitions in the 1920s and 1930s; the coalition rallied around the goal of maintaining 90 percent of parity prices as the minimum support level in future programs. This group branded all efforts to return to the "flexible support levels" (permitting levels to be reduced within a certain range when production exceeded demand) as an abandonment of the parity objective.

Meanwhile an opposing coalition including the American Farm Bureau Federation had begun to question whether the federal government should even be involved in managing commodity prices. In the conflict between these groups, positions tended to become polarized. Program mechanics, as subjects for serious discussion, gave way to ideological disputes about the proper role of government.

Secretary of Agriculture Ezra Taft Benson (1953–60) viewed the 90 percent of parity coalition as advocates of "big" government. In return, Benson's opposition claimed that his intent, as suggested in his more extravagant statements, was to put an end to commodity programs. With neither group willing to compromise, and with both generally able to veto the other's initiatives, a policy stalemate existed throughout the 1950s. Technology was quite dynamic during this period, and very large surpluses of wheat accumulated in government stocks.

THE SITUATION

Secretary Benson entered office at a time when the wheat situation was shifting rapidly out of balance. Government stocks were still inadequate, according to a 1952 yardstick of needed reserves,[2] but a year and a half later (July 1954), stocks were twice the size needed, as measured by that yardstick. This increase in carryover was due in part to a sharp reduction in exports, as the European Recovery Program and the Korean War both came to an end. It was due also to the fact that the world wheat crop in 1953 was the largest in history.

Little relief from surpluses was provided by an extended drought in the Great Plains beginning in 1953, even though the drought was as severe, according to one authority,[3] as during the dust bowl years

2. "Reserve Levels for Storable Farm Products," USDA-BAE, prepared at the request of Senator Allen Ellender, U.S. Senate Committee on Agriculture and Forestry, Sen. Doc. 130 (1953). The study concluded that about 450–500 million bushels carryover would be adequate.
3. E. G. Heine, personal communication quoted by Louis M. Thompson, in *Evaluation of Weather Factors in the Production of Wheat* (Iowa State University Center for Agricultural and Economic Adjustment, 1962), p. 14.

of the 1930s. The fact that the effects of drought were not much reflected in U.S. per acre yields and did not empty the bins as in the Great Depression was impressive evidence, not much heeded at that time, that the technology of wheat production had quietly taken another huge step during the decade of war and recovery.

Mandatory controls were imposed beginning with the 1953 crop. Acreage was further reduced with the implementation of the Benson administration's soil bank program for the 1957 crop, but acreage reduction and poor weather combined could not contain production much below previous levels. Large amounts of U.S. surpluses were sent abroad as food aid, and in this way U.S. wheat stocks were held steady for the 1955 crop and reduced slightly for the 1956 and 1957 crops.

Increased yields per acre in 1957 signaled the end of the drought. In 1958 the yield on the 55-million-acre allotment was a fantastic 27.5 bushels per acre. As a result the surplus grew to 1.3 billion bushels. High yields continued on the minimum allotments in 1959 and 1960. Despite very large food aid shipments, the carryover on July 1, 1961, had grown to 1.4 billion bushels, enough to satisfy bread and other flour needs for the U.S. population for three full years.

Secretary Benson had hoped that production would decline as a result of reduced wheat price supports, but it did not. He had also hoped for an increase in U.S. exports for cash, but exports during the Benson years, despite vigorous promotional efforts, were well below the twentieth-century average. Benson left to his successor a legacy of huge surpluses and policies inadequate to prevent future surpluses.

LEADERSHIP CHARACTER AND ASPIRATIONS

Tenets of religion and ideology have long been interwoven with federal farm policy, but never so explicitly as in the Benson administration—and never with such discordant effects.

In his basic beliefs, Secretary Benson was in harmony with much of the Christian fundamentalism and political conservatism found in rural America, and he valued the efficiency ethic which has motivated farmers and farm policy makers. According to Benson himself,[4] these beliefs guided his personal interrelationships as well as the positions he took on farm policy, but neither of these endeared him to those whose cooperation he needed for passage of farm policy.

The unfavorable impact of his creed (and the psychological

---

4. Ezra Taft Benson, *Cross Fire* (Garden City, N.Y.: Doubleday, 1962). An unfriendly biographer, Wesley McCune, agreed to the importance of Secretary Benson's religion and philosophical beliefs in his book, *Ezra Taft Benson: Man with a Mission* (Washington, Public Affairs Press, 1958).

stance springing from it) on his ultimate relations with his constituency is suggested here. First, while sharing rural values and a rural background as well, Benson's first identification was with a religious minority, the Church of the Latter Day Saints, with a nonconformist psychology and a history of being frequently persecuted in America. He approached American culture with a missionary spirit rather than in an attitude of reconciliation and compromise. As a member of the highest body in this church, Secretary Benson stressed that he was first a religious leader and secondarily a statesman. Rather than drawing a line between his private norms and his public responsibilities, as President Kennedy later attempted to do, Secretary Benson constantly judged his official conduct by the norm of his private judgment rather than by the norms of success in solving public problems or in winning political support. He also stressed the great public significance of an exemplary private life.

Regarding the process of bargaining in politics as a necessary evil, Benson had no respect for the political pragmatists whose decisions reflected mainly a reconciliation of interests. On his desk was a sign, "Oh, God, give us men with a mandate higher than the ballot box," and often after talking with congressional leaders he reaffirmed to himself the shortage of such men.[5]

Benson tended to judge men by the policies they advocated. He found it incongruous that a good man should be able to support policies viewed by Benson as immoral. He remarked to one of his associates about USSR Ambassador Menshikov, "It seems out of character, doesn't it, that such a congenial person should be representing such a godless, murderous, cold, and forbidding government?"[6]

Secretary Benson apparently discovered relatively few good men in public life. He did mention in his autobiography several political personages whom he admired highly, all of them conservatives: Herbert Hoover, Douglas MacArthur, Robert Taft, Styles Bridges, Everett Dirksen, John Bricker, William Knowland, Barry Goldwater, Harry Byrd, and Frank Lausche.[7] Inadvertently Secretary Benson communicated to his opponents the fact that he lacked respect for most of them as persons.

The science of economics was brought to bear in the decisions of the Benson administration, but economics was not the main basis of these decisions. Benson himself was an agricultural economist, as were several of his staff members. Some of his major policy proposals

5. Ibid., p. 299.
6. Ibid., p. 392.
7. Ibid., pp. 23–25, 106.

were attributed to a "Cornell group" of agricultural economists which included his principal advisor, Don Paarlberg, whose academic training was at Cornell University.

Other prominent Cornellians consulted by Secretary Benson were Dean W. I. Myers, Chairman of the Cornell College of Agriculture, and Dr. Carl Butler, who was instrumental in Benson's selection as secretary, according to Benson's autobiography[8] and according to *Wayne Darrow's Farmletter.*[9] President Eisenhower's brother, Milton, another Cornellian, was a Benson supporter in the White House.

Despite the presence of economists in the Benson group, economic analyses and projections were not sovereign guides to policy outcomes. Farm economist G. E. Brandow, in reviewing Benson's book *Freedom to Farm,*[10] concluded that for Benson economic policy merged with and was an extension of theology.[11]

Secretary Benson believed that there were absolute truths which could serve as immediate guides to public policy.[12] These included certain economic beliefs, particularly the right to own property and freedom of the marketplace.

Benson viewed himself as less willing than many other men to compromise principles—in this case, conservative political principles. He said that he preferred to apply the principles consistently rather than bend with the circumstances. He quoted George Washington with approval, "We should raise a standard to which the wise and honorable can repair. The event is in the hands of God."[13] In another speech dealing primarily with farm policy, delivered early in his administration, Benson said, "*We need a nationwide repentance* to rid this land of corruption. We must return to the fundamental virtues that have made this nation great."[14]

Secretary Benson believed that his unwillingness to compromise explained the fact that President Eisenhower supported him on crucial issues. Benson related that he persuaded Eisenhower to veto the farm bill of 1956, against the unanimous advice of the White House staff and Republican party leaders, and that he succeeded by virtue of the following statement to the President:

---

8. Ibid., p. 14.
9. *Wayne Darrow's Washington Farmletter,* Dec. 19, 1959.
10. (Garden City, N.Y.: Doubleday, 1960).
11. *J. Farm Econ.,* 43(February 1961):52–53.
12. At Eldora, Iowa, June 26, 1956, Secretary Benson said, "There are enduring values and eternal principals that never change. Truth has never changed and never will: Right hasn't changed and that will never change either."
13. As in his speech to the Pennsylvania State Grange, Oct. 22, 1956.
14. The italic appeared in the original text of the speech, delivered at St. Paul, Minn., Feb. 11, 1953.

> Mr. President, do you remember not too long after you came into office, we had a discussion in your office in which we agreed that if a thing is right it ought to be done and that if it is right it will also prove to be the best politics? This bill is not right. It is not right for farmers. It's not right for the country. The only right thing to do is to veto it.[15]

In general Benson's unwillingness to mesh his principles with the differing views of others was not a successful strategy. Yet in fighting for a good cause, he could find some satisfaction in defeat. One congressional farm leader is reported to have said: "Ezra dearly loves to play the role of martyr." Congressional critics commonly accused Benson of dogmatism. Benson saw his critics in the same light. In testifying before agricultural committees in Congress, he thought he was often treated as the potential heretic in an ecclesiastical court.[16]

OBJECTIVES

Among the objectives of the Benson administration, one had overriding salience: the objective of reducing government involvement in the farm economy. This was highly desired as a means of increasing individual freedom, and the relationship between reduced government and individual freedom was stressed by stating the objective as "reversing the trend toward government invasion of farmer freedoms." Freedom was, to Secretary Benson and some of his advisors, most valuable for its own sake and as a means to other goals.[17]

In viewing commodity programs, for example, members of the Benson administration were less concerned about inequalities in the distribution of benefits than about the stifling of opportunities to enter farming. Paarlberg stated, "The real long-run interest of the disadvantaged groups is in keeping the society open, not in having it closed.[18]

As the elusive word "freedom"[19] tended to be applied, a core issue was dependence on government for farm income. As farmers came to be more and more under the patronage of politicians, farmers would find it more and more difficult to make independent political judg-

---

15. Benson, *Cross Fire,* p. 318.
16. Ibid., p. 99.
17. See the discussion by Secretary Benson's former advisor, Don Paarlberg, in his book *American Farm Policy: A Case Study of Centralized Decision Making* (New York: Wiley, 1964), pp. 94–95.
18. Ibid., p. 131.
19. For an eloquent discussion of the use and meaning of "freedom" in agriculture policy, see Harold F. Breimyer, *Individual Freedom and the Economic Organization of Agriculture* (Urbana: Univ. of Illinois Press, 1965), ch. 2.

ments. They would become wards of government.[20] Almost by definition, then, government subsidies were not expected to enhance freedom. There could be no question that under a socialist dictatorship
the Russian peasant had lost his freedom. Frequent references to the
Russian system indicated that Benson's mission was to save American
farmers from that fate, by reducing the level of government involvement in the farm economy. With respect to wheat policy in particular,
his aim was to return to a fully free market.

Less governmental involvement was also expected to achieve some
of the objectives of the commodity programs, such as improved farm
income and adequate food supplies, which suggested that commodity
programs, in the view of the Benson administration, had hindered
more than they helped in the achievement of these objectives.

In their view, the incapacity of farm commodity programs to
achieve their objectives had been demonstrated in each year and each
period. Among the several reasons given for their failure was the
tendency of governmental bureaucracy to be inefficient and also to
proliferate. Professor Paarlberg compared public service unfavorably
with private enterprise in the following statement:

> In competitive enterprise, stern checks are placed on unwanted
> growth. These checks are lacking in a bureaucratic maze. The growth
> of a business firm is determined by its ability to use scarce resources in
> a manner approved by its customers, an ability readily measured by
> its earnings. The growth of a government bureau is determined by
> its service in support of a broad public purpose; its performance is not
> subject to accurate measurement or the discipline of the marketplace.[21]

A second reason for governmental incapacity was the expediency
of elected decision makers, a characteristic which constantly amazed
Secretary Benson. Public policy, to many congressmen, seemed simply
a method of obtaining votes. Paarlberg commented:

> There are some politicians who are not interested in "solving the
> farm problem." Politically, the issue is more valuable to them than
> a solution. . . . Nobody feels that he has enough votes. So they pres-
> sure for more spending, more programs, more promises.[22]

Commodity programs also reduced agricultural efficiency, in Benson's judgment. His ordinary example of the reduction in efficiency
caused by these programs was the fact that wheat acreages had been

---

20. Statement by Benson to the Pennsylvania Grange, Oct. 22, 1956.
21. Paarlberg, p. 121.
22. Ibid., pp. 114–15.

moved onto marginal lands while good lands were held idle.[23] This efficiency argument was dubious or even untruthful, and most economists preferred to stress merely that some of the private and public resources drawn into or held in agriculture by high farm prices could have been better used elsewhere.[24] Unlike some of his advisors, however, Benson would have been equally reluctant to see some of these public resources employed in some other federal program for rural areas, such as aid to rural public education.

On occasion it was also held that the price programs perpetuated small uneconomic units, although it became apparent during the late 1950s that programs tended to speed farm consolidations to the extent that they had any impact on farm size at all.

For these and other reasons, Benson, Paarlberg, and others in the Eisenhower administration did not believe that governmental regulation of production and markets could ever succeed. Aside from having failed to balance supply and demand, the price supports, in their judgment, had not achieved their primary objectives of raising income for farmers.[25] Their belief that farm price programs were an exercise in futility tended to make them unenthusiastic in administering them. Under haphazard leadership bureaucracy indeed could prove inefficient.

STRATEGIES

REDUCING GOVERNMENT INVOLVEMENT

Idealogy which suggested policy also suggested a strategy, in holding that government involvement was self-generating. The growth of government must be reversed before it reached a point, as in totalitarian Russia, where it could not be reversed. It became the strategy of the Benson administration, based on this one-dimensional view of change, generally to initiate or support laws or administrative actions which reduced governmental intervention, and generally to disapprove those which increased it. While the strategy was regarded as a clear guide to action, it was visible also to opponents who constantly looked for policy issues on which the administration would, if it acted consistently with its strategy, take an unpopular position. This strategy emphasizing consistency rather than flexibility resulted in stalemate.

23. As in his speech to Annual Farm and Home Week, Cornell University, Mar. 24, 1959.
24. See for example the analysis by D. Gale Johnson, "Efficiency and Welfare Implications of U.S. Agriculture Policy," *J. Farm Econ.*, 45(May 1963):331–42.
25. Paarlberg, p. 71.

The strategy of reducing governmental involvement was in a sense a master strategy linking all other strategies. It was implemented directly with respect to policy stands. The policy strategy for the wheat commodity programs was to bring to an end the two major functions of the wheat commodity program—supporting prices and controlling production.

High price supports were regarded as the main source of farm trouble. It was assumed that wheat production had been increased by high wartime prices. Continuation of these price levels into peacetime by virtue of price supports had caused surpluses, both by discouraging adjustments to smaller markets and by pricing some products too high to be competitive in all potential markets. For wheat, price was not regarded as a barrier to food markets so long as the federal government subsidized exports, but it was assumed by the Benson administration that less wheat would have been produced if prices had been lower.

This explanation for surpluses denied weight to other factors, especially the many inexpensive technological improvements such as improved seed which would have been applied regardless of the wheat price. Benson stoutly maintained that slightly lower price supports, such as he obtained in the Agriculture Act of 1954, would reduce future production, especially if farmers were convinced that lower prices would persist.[26] His confidence was not borne out by events, or by economic studies.[27]

Benson's proposal for reduced price supports was politically vulnerable because lower supports did mean lower farm prices over the short run. The Benson administration was reluctant to acknowledge this, emphasizing instead that over the long run there was little evidence that price supports increased average income for any commodity.[28]

Reducing supports meant also reducing the controls for which they had served as incentives. Secretary Benson was willing to forego existing controls which he regarded only as token measures to salve

26. Testimony of Benson before the U.S. House Committee on Agriculture, *Hearings on Price Supports for Basic Commodities* (Feb. 17, 1955), pp. 14–15.
27. The following studies suggested that wheat production would be adequately reduced only at very low prices: Geoffrey Shepherd et al., *Projections for the Feed-Livestock Economy,* Iowa Agr. Exp. Sta. Special Rept. 27 (August 1960); USDA, *Projections of Production and Prices of Farm Products for 1960–1965, According to Specified Assumptions,* in U.S. Senate Doc. 77, 86th Cong., 2d Sess.; "Possible Effects of Eliminating Direct Price Support and Acreage Control Programs," *Farm Econ.,* 218(October 1960):5813–20; *Economic Policies for Agriculture in the 1960's,* prepared for the Joint Economic Committee, 86th Cong., 2d sess.
28. Paarlberg, *American Farm Policy,* p. 71.

the consciences of price support recipients. In 1956, under pressure of surpluses, Benson did accept some production control in the form of voluntary acreage rental measures by the federal government. But these restraints were designed as a complement to lower prices rather than as a complement to high price support. With lower farm prices sufficient land could be rented and retired at the lower rates.

OPENING LOOPHOLES

Without controls, presumably, no system of high price supports could be justified for long. Without high supports, in Benson's judgment, controls would be unnecessary. Believing the existing acreage controls ineffective, Benson took steps to wash them out.

His view that existing controls were futile put him at loggerheads with congressional farm leaders whose presumed objective was to make the controls system more effective. They deplored Benson's cavalier administration of the controls and his willingness to allow legislative as well as administrative loopholes in the existing system. Early in his administration, for example, Secretary Benson wished to increase the size of the small farmer acreage exempted from controls and also to permit production of wheat for feed use. In 1958 he gained authority to extend price supports to corn producers who did not abide by their allotments, and he desired to provide price supports for noncompliance wheat as well.

"RIDING IT OUT"

In general the Benson administration did not seek to control events through governmental action. Their aim was, after all, to reduce governmental intervention, and they were pessimistic about the capacity of government for effective action regardless of the quality of its leadership.

They also felt that time was on their side, so their response to the farm problem was to "ride it out," cooperating meanwhile with the economic forces at work. Two of the trends which they assumed to be favorable to their objectives are discussed below.

Farmer Movement to the Cities. One explanation of the "farm problem," acceptable to many farm economists at the beginning of the 1950s was that an excess of labor existed in agriculture. This situation, however, was presumably coming to an end as the less efficient farmers retired, permitting the remainder to achieve a higher per capita income with a smaller total product.

Some members of Secretary Benson's administration and some White House advisors wanted to speed this trend by programs to facilitate farmer migration, including federal aid for rural education and better counseling for farmers and farm youth. They were also supporters of the long-term acreage rental programs which offered small landowners a source of income during the transitional period from farm to city employment.

In fact, however, little was done by the USDA to facilitate off-farm migration. Farm interests generally were opposed to such policies, and Benson himself was a strong opponent of federal aid to education and similar measures which might have made rural Americans more mobile.

The proposal for lower price supports was at first expected to catalyze off-farm migration. The remedy of making farming unprofitable for the least efficient producers was based upon the same simple reasoning advanced by Joseph S. Davis in the depression of 1932, and which proved to be erroneous then. Davis had said:

> Wheat can be produced very cheaply now. Prices that have been regarded by wheat farmers as merely remunerative are far above levels now required to induce production sufficient for what the world will use for seed and food. To produce more necessitates lowering the price to feed grain levels, and prices are not low today. The world can spare for other work wheat growers whose costs are relatively high. Attempts to make all wheat farmers prosperous tend to bring them all to distress.[29]

In the Great Depression, however, more people returned to the farms than left them, and studies of off-farm migration during the 1950s generally agreed that farmers move to town more in response to the pull of employment opportunities than in response to the push of low farm prices. Off-farm migration was in fact relatively low during the Eisenhower administration, as compared with the previous Truman administration, especially during the years of relatively high urban unemployment.[30]

29. Joseph S. Davis, "The World Wheat Problem," *Wheat Studies of the Stanford Food Research Center*, 8(July 1932):437.
30. See studies by C. E. Bishop and Larry Sjaastad in Iowa State University Center for Agricultural Adjustment, *Labor Mobility and Population in Agriculture* (Ames: Iowa State University Press, 1961).

Self-defeating Surpluses. It was also believed that the price support programs would in time be the cause of their own ruin, because both political and economic pressures went in the direction of surplus accumulation. The pressure of surpluses on the market would offset the efforts to raise market prices and would ultimately discredit federal efforts, as the Federal Farm Board had been discredited in 1932.

GENERATING A PUBLIC REACTION

Secretary Benson has related that in the late 1950s he had concluded as follows:

> The one massive soft spot that I could see was the fact that the old program was a failure. If we could lay out the fallacies in the existing program for wheat especially, but for tobacco and peanuts, too, so plainly, so starkly, as to show the nation the Congress might have to move. This became the strategy.[31]

Benson pointed in particular to the extraordinary surpluses as highly visible evidence of program failure. In numerous speeches in 1958 he reminded his listeners that the cost of handling the billion-bushel wheat surplus was one-half million dollars per day.[32]

In 1959 Secretary Benson "went to the country," as he said, "over the head of Congress," seeking an end to surplus-causing programs. He told the California Wheat Growers as he told other audiences, "My fellow citizens, the situation is critical. The present price supported acreage program as it applies to wheat is bankrupt."[33]

His audiences in 1959 included such groups as industrialists, farmer cooperative leaders, various producer groups, processors, Chambers of Commerce, university groups, bakers, soil conservationists, and luncheon clubs. His speeches were reported in the mass media, sometimes with sympathetic editorials. However sympathy for his efforts was not translated into congressional votes, nor was the farm issue an advantage to the Republicans in the 1960 election. Quite the contrary, the farmer polls as well as the results of the congressional and presidential elections clearly indicated that dissatisfaction with farm policy was directed largely toward Secretary Benson and the Republican Party rather than toward program supporters in Congress and the Democratic Party.[34]

---

31. *Cross Fire,* p. 429.
32. As in a speech to the Vegetable Growers of America, Dec. 9, 1958.
33. Speech, San Francisco, Jan. 30, 1959.
34. Don F. Hadwiger, "Political Aspects of Changes in Farm Labor Force," in *Labor Mobility,* p. 70–71.

In short, Benson's effort to rally other groups against producers elicited some interest but no effective response. There was in fact no vehicle available through which these groups could respond except by registering some generalized protest.

DEVELOPING FRIENDLY BUREAUCRACIES

It was evident to the Benson administration that the leading individuals in a number of USDA agencies, and many in middle positions, were in personal disagreement with the policies and objectives that the Benson administration would pursue. In addition those in some agencies seemed to feel that their institutional interests would be adversely affected by the Benson policies. Many officials in the powerful farm program agency, then called the Production and Marketing Administration, had come through the ranks of farmer committees which had administered the commodity programs at local levels. These persons were highly committed to the programs which Secretary Benson hoped to phase out. He also wished to change the shape of some other well-rooted agencies, such as the Rural Electrification Administration and the Soil Conservation Service.

As a means to accomplish these reorganization plans, he achieved the implementation of Reorganization Plan No. 2, which vested in the secretary all statutory functions and powers of the various subordinate USDA agencies, thus permitting him to dissolve agencies and to transfer their functions at his pleasure. Resulting changes brought into effect two reconstituted agencies, the Agricultural Marketing Service and the Foreign Agricultural Service, both designed to increase agriculture's income in the free market.

Secretary Benson abolished a major farm program agency, PMA, and reorganized the agency for economic research within the USDA. In the process there was a considerable shuffling of career officials. Powers were redistributed among the geographic levels to favor maximum control by the Benson administration. Nevertheless Benson was never able to place full confidence in either the Economic Research Agency or the program agency. This is one reason among others why it was difficult for that administration to assert legislative leadership.

DIVERSIONARY PROPOSALS

Secretary Benson pointed up other remedies as alternatives to the income measures, placing a confidence in these alternatives which later proved unrealistic. For example, he continually noted that one way out of the cost-price squeeze was to reduce farm costs, and since there was not much else to be done about this matter, he continually lectured against labor unions and other instigators of increased farm costs.[35]

Other minor remedies, such as market development and industrial uses for farm commodities, proved to have far less potential than Secretary Benson suggested or implied for them.

RESPONDING NOT LEADING

It is useful to compare Secretary Benson's situation, objectives, and legislative response with those of the Republican administrations of the 1920s. As in the twenties, Secretary Benson faced pressures from within both parties in Congress favoring programs of assistance to commercial farmers. In Benson's case, however, the programs were already written in law for the most part, whereas in the twenties the objective was to prevent them from becoming law. Also Secretary Benson could play a defensive role. He possessed the leverage of the veto because existing laws had to be serviced through annual appropriations, extension of terminal dates, and amendments to accommodate change. In addition to the executive veto, he had considerable administrative discretion. Deciding to take a defensive stance, he chose not to take legislative initiatives for the most part but rather to respond to those from Congress. His legislative strategies were usually counterstrategies. He indicated his policy preferences in general terms and then reacted vigorously to specific proposals coming through the congressional committees. In cases where he did make a specific recommendation, as in the case of the 1956 Soil Bank Act, his decision to take the offensive was less a result of his own inclinations than of the pressure brought upon him from within the administration and from Republican Party leaders.

No doubt there were several reasons for Secretary Benson's tendency to pursue legislative objectives through counterstrategy. He believed the function of lawmaking belonged to Congress. He said early in his administration:

> While I do have a definite agricultural policy in which I believe, I have no program of my own to offer. It is my conviction that farm programs are made, and should be made, in the Congress. Our job is

35. As in the case of labor unions whose actions would raise rail rates (*Cross Fire*, p. 188).

to execute the laws and to administer the programs that the Congress establishes as efficiently and effectively as we can. We shall always be ready to help the Congress by means of testimony, by presentation of factual material, and by such recommendations as are proper to the executive branch. But the making of farm programs is a legislative function, not an executive one.[36]

In expecting Congress to frame complex farm legislation, however, Secretary Benson was laying upon them a greater burden than they had been willing to assume in recent decades.

Another reason for Benson's reluctance to take the initiative was his firm belief that certain kinds of governmental measures were displeasing to God. He wished to avoid incurring personal guilt for them, and therefore he preferred to let Congress serve as the vehicle for necessary compromises. In cases where USDA initiative was unavoidable, Secretary Benson usually delegated the responsibility for initiating action. When the White House insisted in 1955 that the USDA suggest a farm program to alleviate distress during the 1956 presidential election year, Benson agreed that an acreage rental program was probably the least offensive way to do this. But he said, "I could not for a long time bring myself to accept the idea, much less recommend it."[37] He directed his economic assistant, Don Paarlberg, to work something out "as unobjectionable as possible," while he and Mrs. Benson made a tour of Europe.

In smaller measure, some other leaders in his administration shared Benson's distaste for submitting to demands for new federal activities. Undersecretary of Agriculture True D. Morse quite unhappily oversaw the enactment and administration of the 1956 Soil Bank subsidies.

As a bargaining stance this reluctance to take initiatives attracted some support from commodity interests who desired no subsidies, as well as from some whose programs had already gained Benson's approval (wool, tobacco, sugar). It also fostered some discord within the rural coalition which supported wheat and other controversial programs, whose members were under pressure from Benson to join in weakening other commodity programs as a condition for the servicing of their own. However the "do-nothing" aspect of this negative strategy proved damaging to Benson's and the Republican Party's image, both in Congress and in rural America. At the same time, permitting programs to go out of focus resulted in surpluses whose tremendous

36. "Legislative-Executive Relationships in the Administration of Programs as Viewed by the Executive," speech at the USDA Graduate School, April 30, 1953. Quoted in *Organization of Professional Employees of the USDA* (June 1953), p. 2.
37. *Cross Fire*, p. 295.

costs served as precedents for higher program expenditure in the future.

Another disadvantage for Benson, resulting from his conflict with the rural coalition in Congress, was congressional harrassment of the administration. Congress was reluctant to delegate to Benson the discretion which was needed for proper administration of the program.

GENERAL HISTORY OF PRICE SUPPORT PROGRAMS

Although Secretary Benson's principles and objectives identified him with those opposed to government farm programs, his policy suggestions were almost identical to those offered by the Roosevelt and Truman administrations under which these programs were developed. Benson wanted in effect to return to the flexible price supports mechanism of the basic law, the Agricultural Adjustment Act of 1938. "Flexible"[38] supports, designed only to stabilize prices throughout the marketing year and to set a price floor, had been replaced during the war by high rigid supports designed to peg commodity prices at a level near parity. A brief review of the debate over high versus flexible price supports (which began almost as soon as the high supports went into effect, early in World War II) will help to clarify how this dispute became the chief issue in the farm policy deadlock of the 1950s.

The 90 percent of parity loan rates legislated during wartime had been scheduled to end on December 31, 1948, two years following official termination of hostilities. The wartime law directed, and policy makers fully intended, that after the termination date government should help farmers to adjust to a peacetime economy. There was question, however, as to the price level at which farmers should adjust. The dispute over flexible versus high price supports, which came to symbolize the impasse between Benson and Congress, may be traced from that time. As early as 1944 the USDA had become concerned that high price supports would cause postwar overproduction, and this in turn would bring a burden of stored surpluses. Secretary Wickard recalled in 1944:

> A glance back to the years before the war indicates some of the things we must watch out for in the future. . . . Everybody realized that we were coming face to face with the time when the granary would be full . . . , that the rising level of supply eventually would bring a day when the dam would burst.[39]

---

38. The level of the loan rate or support level would vary, at a range less than market price normally would vary in response to supply and demand.
39. Address to the Farmers' Union Grain Terminal Association Convention, Dec. 13, 1944.

So Wickard apparently believed the farm economy should adjust to the new levels of higher price and income set during the war, with help from the government in controlling production and reducing surpluses.

Proposals for a return to flexible supports surfaced during the administration of Secretary Clinton Anderson. In this confused transitional period, there was considerable miscalculation, on several sides, with respect to three factors: the size of future farm markets, the likely effect of prices upon future production, and the political context of the price support programs.

OVERESTIMATING POSTWAR WHEAT MARKETS

The demand for U.S. wheat in war-torn countries had led Secretary Anderson to hope that the traditional level of U.S. cash exports could be much increased. He told the Senate Agriculture Committee in 1947:

> Some people seem to feel that American farmers cannot expect a sizable continuing market for such products as cotton and wheat. We have to say, I think, that there are some real problems ahead, especially as European and Asiatic agriculture recovers to normal. But I don't want to be classed in the defeatist school, and I don't see why American farmers should reduce production schedules in advance on the assumption that we can't hold reasonable export markets. Aside from our desire to relieve suffering abroad, it's good business for American farmers to export 400,000,000 bushels of grain as they did last year and as they might again this year. . . . In fact, a rather happy solution to many of our price and production problems could be worked out if we were sure that maximum employment could be restrained and that we could find ways of maintaining or increasing our foreign trade in such commodities as cotton and wheat.[40]

Increased markets were to be obtained through lower, competitive prices. Farm income would be maintained through greater volume of production per farmer. Farmers with too little production could shift into nonfarm work.[41]

OVERESTIMATING THE EFFECTS OF PRICES

It was also assumed that flexible price supports would permit producers to shift away from commodities in oversupply and to produce others for which additional markets could be found. This result would be in contrast with the results of rigid supports. High

40. U.S. Senate Committee on Agriculture and Forestry, *Hearings to Establish a Farm Price Support Program* (Jan. 23, 1947), pp. 3–4.
41. Ibid., p. 4.

rigid supports would serve as incentives for production and in the long run would lead to self-defeating surpluses. This belief, generally held since the beginning of price programs, was not borne out by experience with the basic commodities. It was reinforced when Secretary Anderson had to destroy or otherwise dispose of stocks of perishable commodities accumulated under price support guarantees during World War II, at heavy financial loss to the government.

The flexible supports proposals were justified ordinarily on the basis of experience with commodities other than wheat, because wheat surpluses had accumulated during periods of relatively low prices (1929–33 and 1939–42) rather than in periods of high price supports.

Fear of surpluses and moderate optimism that supply and demand would balance in the marketplace were the bases for the flexible supports policy under President Truman as well as previously under Wallace and subsequently under Benson. Rather than supporting income, the purpose of the flexible supports was simply to prevent extreme or destructive fluctuations in prices. President Truman said, in the 1948 Economic Report prepared by his Council of Economic Advisors:

> Commodity price supports are desirable as assurances against special dislocations which might arise in case of recession. I emphasize, however, the need for keeping support levels flexible.[42]

Truman emphasized that price supports should not be used to raise or peg prices. In his budget message of 1949, he stated:

> As I said a year ago,[43] price supports should be regarded chiefly as devices to safeguard farmers against forced selling under unfavorable conditions and economic depression. Their purpose is to bring an element of stability into agriculture. At the same time, they should not place excessive burdens on the Treasury and taxpayers or inhibit shifts in production needed to meet peacetime demand and to promote adequate conservation of soil resources.[44]

HOSTILITY TO FLEXIBLE SUPPORTS

However it soon became apparent that flexible supports were politically vulnerable. The congressional agriculture committees were reluctant to relinquish control over farm prices in favor of market

---

42. *The Economic Report of the President, 1948,* p. 93.
43. *Farm Message of 1948.*
44. *Budget Message of 1949.*

determination, and producers of supported commodities were reluctant to move to a lower price.[45]

During the 1948 consensus of administration and farm organizations a flexible supports program was authorized for 1949, but it was never permitted to go into effect for wheat. Under this scheme and as revised somewhat in a 1949 law, the legislative minimum of price support loan rates for wheat would vary between the minimum support of 75 percent of parity (in situations when the total wheat supply was greater than 130 percent of normal) and a high floor of 90 percent of parity (when the total supply was less than 102 percent of normal).

Wheat prices would have moved even lower due to another provision in the 1948 program, also not implemented. This was a modernization of the parity scale, taking account of changed demands for agricultural commodities. "Modern" parity, as it affected wheat, was about 10 cents per bushel below the old parity. The move to new parity was to take place in annual steps of not more than 5 percent of the old standard, or in other words to be accomplished for wheat within two years. From the combined effect of the new parity and the sliding scale, wheat price supports would ultimately fall by as much as one third from the wartime 90 percent level. In the Republican 80th Congress both Republicans and Democratic leaders had supported these measures. Opposition had come from southern and western Democrats and from some midwestern and Plains Republicans.

The Senate approved the program in 1948, while the House Agriculture Committee instead reported a bill freezing price supports at 90 percent of parity for another year and a half. As a compromise, supports were frozen for one more year, and both the sliding scale and transitional parity were scheduled to take effect January 1, 1950.

45. This political context hostile to flexible supports had been predicted by John D. Black in 1944. Black had said, "Government is committed to full 'parity' prices for cotton and wheat and most other products for another year, and if the Congress of 1944 could put this over, why not the Congress of 1945? . . . Considering the strategic political position which the corn belt and cotton belt congressmen and senators now hold and will continue to hold so long as the party balance is about even in Congress, what reason have we for thinking that the 90 percent guarantee will not be extended? Indeed, it may very well be raised to a 100 percent guarantee, its present level, when the time comes to apply it." Because he had felt that the federal government would be compelled to maintain high supports, Black, like Wickard, had suggested the two-price scheme for wheat as a way to satisfy the price goals while enjoying the advantages of a flexible market price. (The quote is from J. D. Black and C. D. Hyson, "Postwar Agriculture in the United States: Problems and Policies," *Seminar in Agriculture, Forestry and Land Use Policy,* USDA Publ. 10 (1944),p. 43.

Before that date arrived, however, the Democratic administration became committed against reduction in farm prices or income, apparently as a result of the influence of this issue in the 1948 presidential election. Although flexible support proposals were not an issue in that election, incumbent President Truman charged that the Republican Congress had sought to return the farmer to depression prices; and presumably on the strength of this charge, he carried three crucial "farm" states (Iowa, Wisconsin, Ohio) which Roosevelt had lost in 1944.

To fulfill President Truman's commitment to maintain farm income, Truman's Secretary of Agriculture, Charles Brannan, proposed to continue price supports for wheat and other basic commodities at a level comparable to 90–100 percent of parity, but with an upper limit on the amount of production per farm eligible for price supports and loans. Meanwhile Brannan proposed to shift resources away from production of surplus wheat and other basics by offering attractive federal payments on high-nutrition perishable commodities. These federal payments would be equal to the difference between the market price and a price support level and would be scaled to provide proportionately more to farmers with small sales.

This effort to support family farm income without inducing surpluses was opposed both by conservatives who had favored flexible supports and by some of the high-supports coalition, whose effective constituents were larger commercial farmers. The principal argument against the Brannan Plan, however, was that government subsidies were subject to the whims of Congress, and in any case farmers were reluctant to accept them. The Brannan Plan was defeated, so the administration supported a one-year extension of the 90 percent supports for wheat and other basics, which was approved.

The flexible supports mechanism for wheat never went into effect during President Truman's administration. Although the sliding scale became available for use in 1951 and 1952, Secretary Brannan decided to keep supports for "basics" at 90 percent of parity for both years, due to the needs of the Korean War.

In 1952 President Truman asked that the sliding scale be repealed outright. Congress fulfilled the intent of his proposal by continuing the 90 percent of parity supports on wheat and other basics for 1953 and 1954, and in the 1952 elections both presidential candidates committed themselves to a continuation of the high price supports.

In keeping with this campaign pledge, the Benson administration did not suggest any revision of the price support laws during

its first year in office. Following an extensive review of policy alternatives during 1953, Benson sent his first farm program to Congress
in 1954. It suggested, simply, that Congress put in effect for 1955
the sliding provisions enacted in 1948–49 and that the transition to
modernized parity also enacted in 1948 should begin effective in
1956. To prevent a precipitate drop in supports under the formula
due to the large existing surplus, Congress was asked to authorize
a "set-aside" of 400 to 500 million bushels of existing CCC stocks,
which would then be ignored in computing the formula. The emphasis was thus on gradualism in the move toward improving the
"functioning of market prices." Secretary Benson noted, "Farmers
do not wish to be left to the unimpeded forces of the market."[46]

This approach was much less attractive than it had been in
1948. By 1954 there was far less confidence that lower prices could
induce market balance, because outlets happened to be decreasing
irrespective of price. As the chairman of the House Agriculture
Committee, Clifford Hope (R., Kansas), reported in 1953, it was
clear that wheat exports would be small in the future unless they
were subsidized under foreign aid programs. Domestic wheat consumption was also declining. And it was apparent to Representative
Hope that price reductions on the flexible scale would not, by
themselves, adequately reduce production. It would probably still
be necessary to have controls.

The most important element in the changed outlook was the
evidence, convincing to many farm congressmen, that high price
supports had definitely benefited postwar wheat farmer income. Hope
said, "Since 1948 support prices on wheat at 90 percent of parity have
kept prices considerably above what they would have been otherwise."[47]

Aided by price supports and export subsidies, the price of U.S.
wheat had averaged 63 cents per bushel higher than the world price
during the years July 1, 1949, to July 1, 1953. Hope noted, however,
that there was a "question of whether we can maintain a policy in
this country of supporting prices on all wheat at 90 percent of parity
and export part of it at the world price. . . ."[48] As a way to capitalize
on foreign markets without paying export subsidies, Hope favored
a two-price plan.

---

46. Testimony of Benson before the Joint Committee for the Economic Report,
Hearings on the January 1954 Economic Report of the President (Feb. 4, 1954),
p. 155.
47. Speech to the National Association of Wheat Growers, Jan. 30, 1953; printed
in *Congressional Record* (daily), Feb. 24, 1953, A900.
48. Ibid.

Despite opposition from Hope and other rural congressmen of both parties, Secretary Benson won approval of flexible supports in the Agricultural Act of 1954. Benson was obliged to accept as the minimum support level 82½ percent parity rather than 75 percent, for the 1955 crop only. Following that, the 75 percent of parity minimum would be in effect. Transition to the new (lower) parity was to begin with the 1956 crop.

The year 1955 was the trial year for Benson's theory that reduced price supports would reduce production by encouraging production shifts, by reducing capital investment and by discouraging marginal acreages. The effect was not immediately apparent. On the 55-million-acre minimum, wheat farmers still produced nearly a 1-billion-bushel crop despite severe drought in the Southern Plains. Meanwhile exports had fallen off notwithstanding Benson's vigorous marketing efforts (see Chapter 3).

Benson had been reluctant to attribute surpluses to technology (and particularly to suggest that price supports had spurred technological improvement), but in 1955 even he expressed amazement at the impact of technology as it overbalanced the effects of the serious drought. In February of 1955 Secretary Benson concluded " . . . wheat supplies next year will probably be greater than they are now despite everything we are doing."[49]

It was clear by midyear 1955, as Secretary Benson later said in his autobiography, that "it was a losing game." He said, "I knew how a ship captain must feel as he watches his badly leaking vessel take water—watches the sea creep higher and higher in the hold. . . . Would this sea of surplus crops overwhelm us and sink us before we could plug the leak?"[50]

As another sign that surpluses were expected to grow, the USDA strongly encouraged the development of commercial storage facilities during the years 1954 and 1955 by guaranteeing the use of these new facilities for periods sufficient to pay off the investment and by offering very attractive storage rates. A temporary but embarrassing shortage did occur in late 1954, but between April 30, 1955, and December 31, 1956, commercial storage capacity grew by one-fourth.

Some supporters of flexible prices, particularly the leadership of the American Farm Bureau Federation, were emphasizing that since the effects of price upon production were not immediately

49. U.S. House Committee on Agriculture, *Hearings on Price Supports for Basic Commodities* (Feb. 17, 1955), p. 10.
50. *Cross Fire,* p. 257.

apparent, an interim program was needed. Farm Bureau suggested a $1 billion federal land rental program—the soil bank—which was introduced in 1954 and 1955 by leading farm congressmen of both parties. The Benson administration recommended against enactment of these bills.

As surpluses piled up in mid-1955, however, Secretary Benson later recalled, "It became evident that some kind of crash program of this nature would have to be forthcoming."[51]

As a bandwagon began to roll favoring the soil bank, Secretary Benson set his staff to work on it. In fall hearings by the Senate Agriculture and Forestry Committee in locations throughout the country, witnesses in each region called for a soil bank; the pressure on the Benson administration both from farm legislators and from national Republican leaders appeared irresistible. Some congressional Democrats wanted to use the soil bank as a device for strengthening the existing price support program by requiring participation as a condition for receiving price supports. However Congress respected Secretary Benson's wish that the programs be kept separate, although it did include with the first Soil Bank Bill (H.R. 12, 1956) an unrelated provision fixing price supports at 90 percent and still another provision embodying a two-price measure for wheat. These measures were unacceptable to Benson, and on his advice President Eisenhower vetoed the bill.[52] However Eisenhower stated, contrary to Benson's advice, that he would freeze supports at present levels during 1957.

Congress was unable to override the veto, though it then passed another Soil Bank Bill, which also suspended for one year the implementation of the new parity formula. Thus began a legislative battle lasting several years in which high-price-supports advocates, sparked by some House rural Democrats, sought to pass high-price-supports bills, while Secretary Benson sought to frustrate passage. All searches for a compromise during this period seemed futile.

The primary issue between Benson and his critics was over the level of actual farm prices. Benson told the House Agriculture Committee in 1955:

> The inappropriateness of parity prices as a sole objective of farm programs is evidenced by this fact: since 1910–14 farm prices have fallen 11 percent relative to nonfarmer prices but per capita farm income has increased 29 percent relative to per capita incomes of nonfarmers. Thus, since 1910–14 farmers have improved their net income position relative to nonfarmers. They did this by turning out greater

51. Ibid., p. 259.
52. Ibid., pp. 314–20.

volume, and by increasing their efficiency, and in spite of a relative decline in prices.[53]

The House Committee, in reporting the 1959 High Supports Bill (H.R. 7246) took a contrasting position with respect to the proper level of wheat prices.

> The committee refuses to follow the President in his recommendation that we abandon the parity principle for agriculture, in favor of price supports based upon a percentage of market prices in past years. The parity principle is the only means in the law by which farm prices may be measured in fair relationship with prices in the rest of the economy. The Nation accepts this principle as sound and just, and this committee is unwilling to return agriculture to a standard of income based solely on market quotations where the farmer, unlike any other producer in America, has no voice whatever in the price of what he sells.[54]

After 1956 the major price support measures dealt with commodities other than wheat. In 1957 and 1958 cotton and rice interests sought legislative revisions, particularly to avoid sharp acreage reductions under the controls program. As a means of getting presidential approval of these changes, cotton and rice representatives of these commodities supported a Benson corn program under which controls were abolished and prices were supported at 65 percent of parity. Since relatively few producers had been in compliance with the controls program, the effect of the new corn program was to raise the effective market price of corn. Benson took pride in this measure and would have liked to enact a companion law for wheat. In 1957 he had suggested both to the cabinet and to the chairmen of the agriculture committees that the flexible supports formula should be eliminated for wheat; instead the Secretary should be given discretion to set supports at any level, "consistent with certain safeguards written in the law, to prevent his action from being arbitrary."[55] The Benson administration did not campaign for such legislation, apparently because they were convinced that Congress could not be persuaded to pass it.

Meanwhile the congressional committees made proposals for tighter controls for wheat linked with higher supports. In early 1958 Congress passed another price freeze measure preventing any price supports reductions below 1957 levels for wheat and other basic

---

53. House, *Hearings on Price Supports for Basic Commodities*, p. 4.
54. House Rept. 384 on H.R. 7246 (1959), U.S. House Committee on Agriculture, p. 5.
55. *Cross Fire*, p. 352.

commodities except tobacco. The President vetoed the bill, again on Secretary Benson's recommendation, and over the protests of the Republican party leaders and many midwestern Republican legislators including House Leader Charles Halleck. Another serious congressional effort at legislation was a bill containing a two-price plan for wheat, reported out of the House Agriculture Committee and defeated on the House floor in 1958.

The administration's legislative influence was weakened by the defeat of many farm state Republicans in the 1958 elections. Surpluses also grew in 1958 as an extremely large wheat crop increased by half the 800-million-bushel carryover remaining from 1957. In 1959 the administration again suggested the reduction of wheat price supports as a measure to reduce production, while proposing to dispose of the huge wheat stocks through the food aid program. The President suggested that Congress permit supports to be reduced to 90 percent of the average market price over the preceding three years (a three-year moving average), or alternatively that all supports be made discretionary, to be fixed by the secretary between 0 to 90 percent of parity. A proposal for a moving average, as applied to wheat, was rejected when offered as an amendment to a farm bill on the Senate floor in 1959.

Congressional Democrats instead sought tighter controls linked with higher supports maintaining income. In 1959 a conference committee ironed out a measure offering an increase in wheat supports from 77 to 89 percent of parity, in return for an additional 20 percent cut in acreage. This conference bill was defeated on the floor of the House, with pressure from the administration. But the Senate then accepted the provisions of the original House bill providing for 90 percent of parity and a 25 percent cut in acreage. President Eisenhower vetoed this bill, again over the objections of Republican leader Halleck and other congressional leaders. The one measure passed in 1959 was a limit of $50,000 on nonrecourse price support loans which could be received by any single producer. This limit had been requested by the President and was applied, without much effect, for the 1960 crop.

In 1960 President Eisenhower suggested removal of all production controls on wheat with price supports at 90 percent of the three-year moving average. Given the surplus situation, the administration stated that the only alternative was much tighter production controls, which congressional Democrats still preferred. A House agriculture subcommittee under the leadership of Carl Albert (D., Oklahoma) made a determined effort to write a controls bill acceptable to the administration, finally proposing supports at 85 percent of parity with a 25 percent cut in quotas (which would reduce national wheat acreage to about 42 million acres). Farmers were also to receive federal payments-in-kind from existing wheat stocks as compensation for the acreage reductions. This bill was rejected on the House floor, mostly for reasons not having to do with the wheat provisions.

The Senate passed a measure holding supports at only 75 percent while reducing acreage by 20 percent, indicating pressure to reduce the costs of the wheat program.

EFFECTS OF THE BENSON ADMINISTRATION

INCOME FROM WHEAT

With exporting countries holding huge stocks of wheat during the Benson administration, the market was anything but buoyant. Meanwhile the parity price (100 percent of parity) increased due to the fact that the index of prices paid for commodities used in wheat production climbed, indeed faster than that for most other crops.[56] Since this parity increase was more than offset by the reduction in the percentage of parity at which price supports were set, the season average wheat market price which reflected the price support loan price declined from $2.32 in 1952 to $1.94 in 1960 (Table 8.1). Notwithstanding increased production costs and higher volume of production, the farm value of wheat was lower during Secretary Benson's tenure than during the postwar period preceding his administration.

PRODUCTION CONTROLS

It may be remembered that two kinds of production controls had been authorized under the Agricultural Adjustment Act of 1938. Under the voluntary type, called acreage controls, farmers who complied were eligible for price support loans and other benefits. The other type of controls, called marketing quotas, employed the same acreage base, expressed in terms of normal yields per acre. Quotas were subject to approval by a two-thirds vote in a producer referendum for each year in which they were proclaimed. The voluntary acreage controls had to be announced each year except during a national emergency. (Thus none was announced for the 1944 through 1949

56. *Possible Methods of Improving Parity Formula, Report of the Secretary of Agriculture Pursuant to Sec. 602 of the Agricultural Act of 1956,* U.S. Senate Doc. 18 (1957), table 3.

TABLE 8.1. Postwar income from wheat

Year	Farm value of production[a]	Average price per bushel[b]	Average price support level per bushel[c]	Price support as % of parity per bushel[c]	Effective parity prices[d]
	($000)	*($)*	*($)*	*(%)*	*($)*
1946	2,201,036	2.09	1.49	90	...
1947	3,109,445	2.52	1.88	90	...
1948	2,577,191	2.19	2.00	90	...
1949	2,061,897	2.16	1.95	90	...
1950	2,042,296	2.28	1.99	90	2.21 (Old)
1951	2,088,739	2.43	2.18	90	2.42 (Old)
1952	2,720,402	2.32	2.20	90	2.45 (Old)
1953	2,390,936	2.27	2.21	91	2.46 (Old)
1954	2,082,485	2.37	2.24	90	2.49 (Old)
1955	1,858,518	2.18	2.08	82.5	2.52 (Old)
1956	1,976,239	2.21	2.00	82.6	2.42 (Trans. 95)
1957	1,848,437	2.15	2.00	82.6	2.51 (Trans. 95)
1958	2,543,688	1.94	1.82	75	2.43 (Trans. 90)
1959	1,974,891	2.00	1.81	76.7	2.41 (Modern)
1960	2,365,154	1.94	...	...	2.36 (Modern)

a. *Agricultural Statistics, 1962* (USDA).
b. At Kansas City, No. 2 Hard and Dark Winter, computed by weighting selling prices by number of carlots sold as reported in the Kansas City Grain Market Review. From *Agricultural Statistics, 1962* (USDA).
c. As of July 1, *CCC Price Support Statistical Handbook* (February 1960).
d. USDA (Mar. 7, 1960). Reference is to old parity formula, transitional parity formula, and new parity formula.

crops and for the 1952 and 1953 crops. Those for 1943 and 1951 were suspended after they had been announced.) Marketing quotas were compulsory, in that producers who did not comply were obliged to pay a penalty on each bushel of wheat produced on nonallotment acres. Compulsory quotas had to be announced and enforced whenever the carryover at the end of the marketing year was expected to be more than 30 percent of the crop, except during national emergencies.

As stocks grew after World War II, Secretary Brannan narrowly avoided having to proclaim marketing quotas for the 1950 and 1951 crops, and certainly would have had to proclaim them for the 1953 crop under the legislative formula except for the state of national emergency.

Benson had no such alternative, with war at an end in 1953, and he quite reluctantly proclaimed quotas for the 1954 crop. Quotas had to be announced for each year thereafter during his administration. The carryover was so large that under the formula the total allotment had to be held at the 55-million-acre minimum, except for the transitional 62-million-acre allotment permitted in 1954, the first year of postwar quotas.

TABLE 8.2.   The postwar wheat situation

Marketing year (July 1– June 30)	Yield per harvested acre	Acres harvested	Production	Exports For dollars	Exports Total	Carryover[a]
	(000)		*(mil. bu.)*	*(%)*	*(mil. bu.)*	
1946–47	17.2	67.1	1.152	59.3	397.4	83.8
1947–48	18.2	74.5	1.359	31.9	485.9	195.9
1948–49	17.9	72.4	1.292	25.2	504.0	307.3
1949–50	14.5	75.9	1.098	14.0	299.1	424.7
1950–51	16.5	61.6	1.019	52.7	366.1	399.9
1951–52	16.0	61.8	.988	66.4	475.3	256.0
1952–53	18.4	71.2	1.306	90.7	317.8	605.5
1953–54	17.3	67.8	1.173	53.6	217.0	933.5
1954–55	18.1	54.4	.984	42.3	272.4	1.036
1955–56	19.8	47.3	.937	30.3	346.3	1.033
1956–57	20.2	49.8	1.005	31.6	549.5	908.8
1957–58	21.8	43.8	.956	38.6	402.9	881.4
1958–59	27.5	53.0	1.457	31.5	443.3	1.295
1959–60	21.7	51.8	1.121	26.4	510.2	1.313
1960–61	26.2	51.9	1.357	30.7	661.9	1.412

Source: Data on percentage of exports for dollars derived from *Wheat Situation,* ERS-USDA (February 1961), table 3; (October 1966), table 10. Other data obtained from Grain Division, Program Analysis Branch, ASCS, USDA, June 1962.

a. June 30, end of the year.

The harvested acreage, however, remained well below the 55-million-acre minimum. Thanks largely to drought, only about 44 million acres were harvested in 1957 (Table 8.2). During the Benson administration most wheat acreage was in compliance with quotas, particularly in the commercial wheat area. In the last Benson year (1960), for example, 43.1 million acres of wheat were in compliance on a total allotment of 50.6 million acres. Only 8.8 million acres were not in compliance, including a noncompliance allotment of about 4.2 million acres.[57]

Legislative controversies over controls centered not on the basic issue (though this was debated elsewhere) but rather over proposals to permit concessions or "loopholes" or to eliminate them, and over proposals to encourage compliance.

Loopholes in the Controls. Secretary Benson was often accused of seeking to destroy the program by watering down the controls rather than performing the ordinary USDA role of disciplinarian. But there were pressures from Congress, cumulatively very strong, favor-

57. ASCS Grain Division (April 1962).

ing special concessions. While both Congress and the executive permitted loopholes, both took some steps to tighten provisions. Decisions as to which provisions to tighten and which to loosen were judged by their presumed effects on regional competition. Legislators from the Plains wheat states felt that Secretary Benson usually sought provisions favoring the midwestern feed grains areas. The following are some of the "loopholes" at issue during the Benson administration.

1. Fifteen-acre exemption. Any farmer with less than 15 acres was not subject to mandatory quotas. In the absence of an acreage allotment, any farmer could grow up to a total of 15 acres and sell the product on the market. However, based on his history of 15-acre plantings, he could then claim an allotment base of 15 acres, after which he would be eligible for price support loans if he abided by the acreage cuts established under the price support program.

In 1958 the USDA estimated that cumulative production under this loophole for producers of small wheat acreages totaled 385 million bushels.[58] Most "15-acre" growers were in the Midwest and South. Since the 15-acre amendment had the double effect of weakening the administration of the program at the same time that it generated geographic support for the program, the positions of Secretary Benson and of the wheat state legislators tended to shift, depending upon which effect seemed most important at the time. Initially Secretary Benson did not object to this provision and in 1953 even proposed to increase the exempted acreage to 25 acres.[59] But in 1959 and 1960 he argued instead that the exemption should be totally repealed. Wheat state legislators continually opposed the 15-acre exemption, but most were convinced that repeal would jeopardize congressional support for the program.

2. Wheat for feed. Another exemption supported by Secretary Benson and resisted by wheat state legislators, finally passed in 1957, permitted noncommercial wheat farmers to harvest up to 30 acres so long as the total production was fed on the farm. This and a Benson-supported provision for exempting whole states with fewer than 25,000 acres of wheat seemed to have little effect on total wheat production.

---

58. Brief prepared by the National Agriculture Advisory Committee, USDA, (September 1958). See Chapter 3 for details.
59. U S. House Committee on Agriculture, *Hearings on Wheat Marketing Quotas* (1953). p. 8.

3. Hot wheat. No penalty had to be paid on wheat harvested on nonallotment acres so long as it was stored under seal. This "hot wheat" could be sold without penalty during years when wheat production on the allotment acres was below "normal." Thus in the high-risk areas the stored hot wheat served as insurance, to be sold in years of crop failure. As a further encouragement to produce "hot wheat," the sealed wheat could be marketed just before harvest-time (normally at the peak of the market) on the condition that it be replaced with new wheat within 30 days after sale.

4. Allotment to new farms. Following World War II the total wheat acreage in the United States increased by 10 million acres; much of it was newly broken ground in the arid portions of the Great Plains and the Northwestern Palouse areas. Wheat state legislators insisted that these new areas should be given allotments. In the first year that this was done these allotments were granted as additions to the 55-million-acre minimum, but henceforth a portion of the pre-established allotments had to be released for grants to new acreages. The direct effect of this provision was, if anything, to reduce production, because acreage was moved from traditional to marginal areas. But the larger per farm acreage cut needed to accommodate the new area within the 55-million-acre national allotment no doubt increased resistance against further reductions in the national minimum acreage.

5. Changing to a harvested-acre basis. After 1954 compliance with quotas was on a harvested-acreage rather than a planted-acreage basis. Thus farmers could plant their entire cropland and subsequently pick the most promising acreages for harvest. The USDA desired this provision as a means for facilitating the administration of quotas. Farm congressmen were quite happy to give their farmers this flexibility.

6. Lack of cross-compliance. The most generous loophole in the controls program was the absence of any requirement for cross-compliance between programs. That is, acres taken from wheat production could be planted to noncompliance cotton or feed grains. Secretary Benson was particularly aware of the fact that wheatland idled under the allotment program was often simply shifted to production of some other price-supported crop. As a result, despite the sharp reduction in wheat acreage under quotas from 80 to 50 million acres, the total of U.S. farmland used for crop production while various control programs were in effect in 1954 was only 5 million acres less than the average during the period of uncontrolled production from 1944–53. To prevent the flight of acreage from wheat to other surplus crops

when wheat quotas were applied in 1954, Benson directed that if farmers were to participate in the wheat program, they would have to participate in programs for any other price-supported commodity grown on their farms, and vice-versa.[60] But he rescinded his cross-compliance directive after being subjected to election pressures from rural legislators. Secretary Benson proved unwilling to fight for controls since, as he said, he had little faith in their effectiveness anyway.[61] Benson's willingness to relax on controls was in contrast with that of another critic of existing programs, the Farm Bureau, which continued to advocate cross-compliance.[62]

7. Poor administration. Prominent farm state legislators and farm organization spokesmen constantly charged that Secretary Benson was seeking to discredit the program by providing inadequate administration. Charges were rarely specific. The Senate Agriculture Committee did explore the impact of changes in personnel and shifts in authority within the farmer committee system which administered the program;[63] they concluded that the appointment of persons either inexperienced or unfriendly to the program had damaged both the agency and the program itself.[64]

Incentives for Compliance. During the Benson administration, program rules came to be structured somewhat more in favor of the non-compliers or violators, to the point where the advantage for many producers seemed definitely to be in noncompliance with the program. This tended to embitter those farmers who had continually supported the program out of loyalty.

The fine for exceeding allotments was inadequate. The penalty was payment of a percentage of parity on each bushel of "normal" production on excess acres. The penalty was only 15 percent of the parity price until 1941, then 50 percent of the support price, and under the act of 1954, 45 percent of the parity price (in 1965, raised to 65 percent of parity). With yields increasing, many farmers ordinarily produced far beyond "normal" production so that the extra amount produced for which no fine had to be paid was large enough to justify payment of penalty on "normal" production.

There was even a reward for exceeding allotments, in that farmers could increase their allotment base by virtue of a history of over-

60. *Wheat Situation,* USDA-BAE, no. 139 (1954), p.14.
61. *Cross Fire,* p. 145.
62. *Wayne Darrow's Washington Farmletter,* Feb. 19, 1955.
63. U.S. Senate Committee on Agriculture and Forestry, *Hearings on Administration of Farm Programs by Farmer Committees* (1956).
64. U.S. Senate Committee on Agriculture and Forestry, *Abuses and Disruptions of the Elected Farmer Committee System* (Sept. 10, 1956), committee print.

planted acres. Thus those violating the program received successively larger acreage allotments—at the expense of compliers elsewhere. In 1957 the Congress decided to prohibit counting of excess acres as history (unless the excess production was not marketed), and in fact to reduce the acreage base of noncompliers, but this change did not go into effect for individual farms until 1959.

Effects of Controls. Secretary Benson, as noted, had little confidence in the acreage controls connected with the price supports programs. He maintained that much of the reduced wheat acreage under programs was simply planted to other crops, usually feed grains, thus adding to other surpluses.

Opponents of the price supports programs also suggested that yields improved when controls were in effect. It seemed logical that farmers would use their best acres in the allotment and farm these acres more intensively than before. In the summer fallow areas where much wheat is produced, the program might even have helped farmers to resist the temptation toward self-defeating annual plantings. Also the system of cultivation followed under a controls program was more resistant to dust bowl conditions.

However there seems little doubt that the major factor in increased yields has been new technology, particularly new seeds and new dryland farming techniques, not control programs. In the 1950s yield increases were most striking in the hard winter wheat areas where new varieties incorporated many improvements. In the early 1960s there were breakthroughs in durum wheat, in soft red winter, hard red spring, and most dramatically in the white wheat of the Northwest. The tempo of yield increases thus varied with weather and technological change far more than with changes in the price supports program. New wheat technology has been adapted very quickly in other countries, and this fact no doubt explains why yields increased in Canada, Mexico, and European countries at about the same pace as in the United States irrespective of the type of farm program which happened to be in effect.

Thus it can be concluded that the acreage taken out of wheat by virtue of the controls program would have added to the national production. An additional 20 million acres of wheat even at yields only half the national average, for example, would have produced considerably more wheat than was exported for cash during the Benson administration.

FARM ORGANIZATIONS

In the postwar era the general farm organizations were influential, though in somewhat different ways than previously. These groups were responsive to the political changes of the times and were also affected by changes within the organizations themselves.

The American Farm Bureau Federation, formerly coordinator of congressional commodity interests, lost its inside role in the congressional committees, taking policy initiatives instead through the executive branch under Secretary Benson.

Farm Bureau was an originator of the existing price supports–mandatory controls program (see Chapter 10). Under new leadership in the postwar era, however, Farm Bureau's confidence in governmental measures was exchanged for a confidence in the capacity of the marketplace to return adequate farm income. Farm Bureau was influential in the defeat of the Brannan Plan, became a consistent strong supporter of the flexible price supports, and enthusiastically espoused a brand of strong economic conservatism similar to that preached by Benson.

However Farm Bureau stressed the need for supplementary measures to remedy overproduction. Farm Bureau sought to tighten existing wheat controls by instituting cross-compliance, eliminating 15-acre exemptions, and reducing the minimum national allotment. In addition to being the chief early sponsor of the soil bank (see Chapter 9), Farm Bureau also sponsored the P.L. 480 surplus disposal programs (see Chapter 13) and was instrumental in persuading the Benson administration to approve the surplus disposal effort.

After its bitter battles against the Brannan Plan and against high price supports, Farm Bureau found itself sharply at odds with most national Democratic leaders, including Southerners, and with rural Republican legislators. Conversely, it was in close alliance with other conservative organizations and with the conservative wing of the Republican Party.

Farmers Union moved into the organizational vacuum left by Farm Bureau's move to the right. Although Farmers Union had been closely associated with the defeated Brannan Plan, the organization's subsequent arguments favoring high price supports were welcomed by the friendly congressional committee leadership and within most Democratic groups. Farmers Union's overriding objective was high aggregate farm income. The group was oriented toward abundant production, with large stocks and large disposal programs. Farmers Union also contributed to the development of the soil bank.

Whereas Farm Bureau's policy proposals were most acceptable in the traditional farming areas (particularly in the Midwest) and in the eastern states, Farmers Union's programs were most compatible with the interest of commercial farming areas in the north central and southern areas, which were the areas most influential in congressional decisions on agriculture policy.

The fixed policy of the Grange throughout this period was its advocacy of a two-price program for wheat. In 1954 the Grange minimized the need for high price supports, but by the end of the decade the organization had become alienated from the Benson administration. It supported the Democratic price freeze measures.

The commodity organizations apparently played a relatively small role in wheat legislation during this period, as contrasted with their more important role in the subsequent Freeman administration. Wheat interests were most directly represented by the congressional agriculture committee members from the wheat areas, such as Senator Milton Young (R., North Dakota) and Representative Clifford Hope (R., Kansas). The small number of legislators from commercial wheat areas was offset somewhat by the high seniority of individuals such as the two just mentioned.

SERVICE INDUSTRIES

Grain storage interests were quite prominent during the 1950s due to their interest in federal expenditures for handling, storage, and disposal of large stocks. (Their interest in the administration of stocks is described in Chapter 12.) Both the cooperative and private agencies were interested in the wheat program itself, because they wished to continue an abundant production. The effect of their desires upon decisions is difficult to assess.

Labor unions, particularly the CIO United Auto Workers, were also interested in farm legislation. They had been ardent supporters of the Brannan Plan (which would have presumably slowed the migration of farm workers to the city) until its defeat when they came to the support of high supports programs as allies of rural liberal groups.[65] Labor groups also spurred expansion of domestic food disposal programs.

---

65. See testimony of Walter Reuther (President of the United Auto Workers) before House, *Hearings on Price Supports for Basic Commodities* (1955), pp. 267 ff.

CONGRESSIONAL INFLUENCE

Congress was successful in its battle with Secretary Benson, as they had been with former Secretaries of Agriculture. Congress had often lost the principle while winning the decision point. Experience in Benson's administration demonstrated again a tendency of the administration to embrace a comprehensive program with ideological embroidery, to which rural legislators would be willing to give obeisance only if income guarantees could be preserved in the bargain.

While congressional farm leaders were revealing some signs of weakness during the last two years of Benson's administration, they came off well in the last analysis—with an enlarged agriculture budget and an enlarged contingent of program-oriented legislators with which to begin the decade of the 1960s.

SUMMARY

The supply situation during Benson's eight-year administration was one of overproduction and large surplus stocks. The dominating element in the supply situation was the production technology generated and applied during and after World War II. Technology increased per acre productivity and also helped to stabilize the arid Wheat Belt. Serious drought throughout the dust bowl during the Benson years failed to serve as the awful balancer, and moderate reductions in wheat prices had relatively little effect on production. Production controls were applied, and they reduced acreage sharply. Declining cash wheat exports were more than compensated for by large food aid exports during Benson's second term, and still enormous surpluses accumulated.

Price support levels were the main technical issue in the bitter farm policy conflict during the 1950s. Prewar programs, as well as President Truman's first postwar proposals, had assumed that support levels must be flexible so that they could be reduced as a remedy for overproduction. Flexible supports became the central feature in Secretary Benson's various farm program proposals, but their significance had by then changed. High fixed supports had developed political strength and status, both in Congress and as a popular measure in national elections. The price-oriented rural coalition had resolved by that time not to abandon the precedent of full parity prices set during wartime. This coalition, which included commercial wheat farmers, desired to use price supports to obtain the full benefits of postwar prosperity and to use 90 percent of parity as the minimum at which prices could be supported. They had decided to rely on other devices for the task of controlling production.

The tendency to rely mainly on federal price supports for maintenance of farm prices and income prompted an ideological reaction. The flexible supports approach as advocated by Benson was intended not mainly as a farm income measure but rather as an instrument to reverse a perceived trend toward big government or tyranny. This objective was, for Secretary Benson, a feature of his religious mission, but it also cohered with the program of this administration and served the political ideology and the group interests descendent from Republican administrations of the 1920s. The general farm organizations, except Farm Bureau, tended to become hostile to this conservative coalition.

Benson supported steps to reduce governmental involvement in the farm market and to oppose steps which would increase it. Rather than taking policy leadership, however, he preferred to respond to initiatives from Congress, even if this stance resulted in policy stalemate, believing that the trend of his time was leading toward a reduced role for government.

Yet the interplay between Benson and Congress, and the changing supply situation, prompted numerous policy proposals and some changes in policy, including variations in production control regulations, new acreage rental programs (see Chapter 9), and changes in price supports. In addition, much administrative experience was gained. Indeed, most of the years in which mandatory wheat quotas were in effect occurred during the Benson administration. Benson also met major challenges in administering surplus stocks (see Chapter 11).

Secretary Benson succeeded in reducing price support levels, but this action did not, on balance, reverse the trend toward "big government." Due to surplus accumulation, Benson set a precedent in enlarged farm program budgets which was valuable to the next administration. He also alienated farmers, farm leaders, and political liberals as well, inversely contributing to the prestige of the farm coalition which had opposed him, both within Congress and within the rural constituencies. This enhanced prestige was subsequently used in behalf of "big government" for agriculture.

Comparing the Benson administration's experience with that of other administrations seems to provide a lesson that efforts by the executive branch to reduce federal subsidies for commercial agriculture should be spearheaded by someone other than the Secretary of

Agriculture, who is expected to be the farmers' advocate rather than their critic. Opposition to farm subsidies that came from Republican presidents and from Secretary of Commerce Herbert Hoover in the 1920s, and from the Budget Bureau and Council of Economic Advisors in the 1960s, proved to be more tolerable than Secretary Benson's campaign against high price supports during the 1950s.

USDA *Photo*

9 / SOIL CONSERVATION MEASURES

MOST COMMODITY LAWS have specified several objectives. In addition to the goals of increased income and production control, a third objective of high priority has been conservation of agricultural resources, particularly soil. Soil conservation has been felt to be a national interest, and since most farmland is privately owned, the federal government has undertaken to compensate farmers for soil-conserving practices. Soil conservation, as an attractive goal in the eyes of citizens, farmers, political organizations, and official policy makers, has been stated as a major objective in several agricultural laws.

In two commodity acts—Soil Conservation and Domestic Allotment Act of 1936 and the Soil Bank Act of 1956—soil conservation was a foremost goal. Both acts were passed during periods when soil erosion had become visible in the form of dust storms on the drought-stricken Plains.

Both laws had income and production objectives, and both assumed a compatibility between the objectives of soil conservation, production control, and income improvement. The logic of this assumption is that farm income is improved both by payments to the farmer for his contribution to conservation and by the increased returns from improved land; idling land provides a means of production control as well as an opportunity to rest it and to perform conservation practices upon it.

In practice, however, these objectives have not always been in harmony. Soil conservation measures have increased the acreage and yields of surplus crops. Income incentives have prompted owners to abuse the land in search of profit. Furthermore legislative priorities have not always been followed. Laws passed under the banner of "public interest in conservation" have been used as a channel for farm subsidies.

This chapter will be devoted primarily to discussing the 1936 and 1956 laws cited above. However it will also touch upon other commodity programs which included conservation measures, beginning with the Agricultural Adjustment Act of 1933.

LAND RENTAL IN THE AGRICULTURAL ADJUSTMENT ACT OF 1933

As noted in Chapter 8, payments to farmers in the Agricultural Adjustment Act of 1933 were sometimes regarded as "rental," since farmers agreed to idle a certain percentage of the land previously devoted to wheat and other designated commodities. The main function of this land rental program was to "serve as a mainspring of the adjustment of production."[1]

Drought intervened as the adjuster of production so that acreage taken from wheat was used wherever possible to produce the feed grains needed to sustain animals in the drought areas. The rental payments functioned mainly as a means of channeling income to hard-pressed farm families. For many farmers in drought areas, "benefit payments served as crop insurance and constituted a large part of the year's farm cash income."[2]

THE SOIL CONSERVATION AND DOMESTIC ALLOTMENT ACT OF 1936

The dust bowl conditions prompted attention to the need for soil conservation at the same time that the Supreme Court, in overruling

1. *Agricultural Adjustment, 1933–1935, A Report of the Administration of the Agricultural Adjustment Act,* USDA-AAA (1936), p. 6.
2. Ibid., p. 28.

the Agricultural Adjustment Act of 1933, raised the need for acceptable legislative objectives for future farm subsidies. The legislative
purpose of the next commodity law, the Soil Conservation and Domestic Allotment Act of 1936, was "to provide for the protection of
land resources against soil erosion, and for other purposes." The first
four stated objectives in the act all related to soil conservation, leaving
farm income improvement as the last stated goal.[3]

The administration insisted that the new emphasis was not simply
to please the courts but instead was the product of long-term agricultural planning, in contrast with the emergency planning of the
early depression.[4] It was noted that President Roosevelt had said two
months before the adverse court decision that "the long term and
more permanent adjustment program will provide positive incentives
for soil conservation."[5]

Nevertheless the new law did seek to reduce acreage of certain
crops, including wheat, although with a different mechanism and
presumably for different reasons. Rather than contracting for acreage
reduction, as in the 1933 act, the 1936 act provided payments for
converting land from certain cash crops to "conserving uses." Payments were both for the purpose of reimbursing farmers for income
lost by not planting crops (diversion payments) and to share the cost
of conservation practices performed on the diverted acres and elsewhere on the farm. Some of these conservation practices, such as
fertilization of the land, would actually increase productivity per acre.

The diversion of crop acres to a nonproductive status was justified as a soil conservation measure on the assumption that those crops
which offer "larger immediate cash returns" tended to "exhaust soil
fertility rapidly and expose soil to destruction through erosion by
wind or water."[6]

Yet administrative decisions seemed responsive to the supply situation rather than wholly responsive to the purpose of the act, which
was to "maintain soil fertility and control erosion."[7] An official review of the program administration, in which it was reported that
farmer committees recommended a 4-million-acre reduction in wheat,

3. *Summary of Provisions of Soil Conservation and Domestic Allotment Act,*
USDA-AAA, G-52 (1936), p. 1.
4. *Soil Conservation—Its Place in National Agricultural Policy,* USDA-AAA (May
1936), pp. 25–26; *Agricultural Conservation in 1936, A Report of the Activities of
the Agricultural Adjustment Administration,* USDA-AAA (1937), p. 1; *Agricultural
Adjustment, 1937–1938, A Report of the Activities Carried on by the AAA, January
1, 1937, through June 30, 1938,* USDA-AAA, G-86 (1939), pp. 131–37.
5. *Soil Conservation—Its Place in National Agricultural Policy,* p. 26.
6. *Agricultural Adjustment, 1937–1938,* p. 36.
7. *Agricultural Conservation, 1936,* p. 26.

noted that "the price, supply, and prospective demand situation, no doubt, influenced to a certain extent the recommendations made in the various subregions.[8]

ACREAGE DIVERSION

Whatever the administrative objectives, the Soil Conservation and Domestic Allotment Act did not reduce wheat production during the two years the act stood alone prior to the enactment of an explicit controls program in 1938. Under the 1936 law wheat was not one of those commodities on which specific reductions were made and whose production was apparently reduced. Instead wheat acreage was included in a general crops base from which diversion could be made. Payments were made for diversion of 21.8 million acres from that general base in 1936[9] and for 18.1 million acres in 1937.[10] Yet the planted acreage of wheat increased rapidly during these two years, from 69 million acres in 1935 to an all-time high of 81 million acres in 1937. As reasons for this increase despite the program the AAA report cited the absence of any specific restrictions on total production in either year and the higher market price resulting from the prolonged drought which served as an incentive to expand acreage.[11] Other sources make it clear that the financial plight of many farmers had led them to maximize their wheat crop acreage, even when prospects for growing a crop were not good.[12]

SHARING COST OF PRACTICES

The farm crisis caused by extreme drought and prolonged low prices called attention to the inability of the Great Plains economy to withstand the unstable market and climate. Like the grasshopper in Aesop's fable, the farming practices and the economy as a whole were geared to exploit the "good times" and were unprepared for the "bad times" which seemed inevitably to follow. To live satisfactorily in the area, man had to find ways to accommodate himself to the long dry spells.

A notable research report by the USDA in 1936[13] suggested that

---

8. Ibid., p. 33.
9. *Agricultural Adjustment, 1937–1938*, p. 258.
10. Ibid., p. 264.
11. Ibid., p. 164.
12. U.S. Great Plains Committee, *The Future of the Great Plains* (Washington, D.C., 1936).
13. Ibid.

many changes in the human element were needed, including new farmer attitudes, new owner-tenant relationships, larger farms, less burdensome governmental legal structure, better credit, and other improvements.

Through its farmers' committees and other agencies the USDA tried to stimulate research, planning, and action toward overall structural change in the Great Plains. Yet most of the federal funds spent for special measures for that area were devoted only to soil conservation, beginning with an appropriation of $2 million for emergency tillage of windblown land in 1935. As a principal long-range remedy both for wind erosion and economic instability, the USDA wished to convert to grass those croplands which were judged to be unfit for farming. In some areas parts of farms would be regrassed, but in the regions with little rainfall or unsatisfactory soil entire farms would be returned to pasture. According to one estimate, about 15 million acres in the Great Plains as a whole "should no longer be plowed."[14] Another estimate suggested that 6 million acres in the Southern Great Plains[15] should be permanently retired.

One method for accomplishing this was for local agencies such as Rural Conservation Districts to purchase the marginal acreages or for the federal government to do so in cooperation with these local groups. As an incentive for local groups to gain title to the land and remove it from production of cash crops, these agencies were able to collect some of the federal payments made for diverting acreage and for conservation practices.

No estimate could be found as to how many acres were returned to grass as a result of land purchase by public agencies. Nor is it known on how many acres the private owners decided to convert cropland "permanently" to grassland. Since payments and practices after 1935 were only on a year-to-year basis, land put into conserving uses one year could be and often was returned to production. Marginal croplands removed from production during the dust bowl years were plowed again during the war and postwar years (Table 9.1). The principal method by which wind erosion was brought under control was not by regrassing marginal acres but rather through improved cultivation on the land which continued to be used for wheat production. The important conservation practices were summer fallowing,

---

14. Ibid., p. 5.
15. Address by Roy I. Kimmel, "Activities of Federal and State Agencies in Solving Agricultural Problems of the Southwest," at Kansas State University Farm and Home Week, Manhattan, Feb. 1, 1939, p. 6. A recent estimate of land which should have been returned to grass in 1931 in the Southern Plains also suggested 5 to 6 million acres. See *Facts about Wind Erosion and Dust Storms on the Great Plains*, USDA-SCS, leaflet no. 394 (June 1955), p. 3.

TABLE 9.1. Wheat-seeded acreage of land in farms in the Great Plains, specified
years, 1929–49, with net changes for each period

Region[a]	Land use				Net change		
	1929	1939	1944	1949	1929–39	1939–44	1944–49
				(million acres)			
Northern Plains	19.3	14.4	17.9	21.5	−4.9	+3.5	+3.6
Central Plains	19.5	19.6	18.8	25.2	+.1	−.8	+6.4
Southern Plains	6.9	6.8	9.2	8.7	−.1	+2.4	−.5
Great Plains	45.7	40.8	45.9	55.4	−4.9	+5.1	+9.5

Source: *Wheat Production—Trends, Problems, Programs, Opportunities for Adjustment,* USDA-ARS (March 1958), table 6.

a. Northern Plains: North Dakota, South Dakota, and Montana. Central Plains:
Wyoming, Colorado, Nebraska, and Kansas. Southern Plains: Includes 93 counties
in the Plains area of Oklahoma, Texas, and New Mexico. Great Plains: All three of
the above areas.

strip farming, ridging of surfaces, and other temporary protective
measures financed in part by federal funds. These temporary practices
were the ones for which most federal funds were spent.

A variety of conservation measures was undertaken under a special
program for the Great Plains beginning in 1937.[16] Restoration land
program payments were made in ten states to retire land unsuited to
production. In addition, federal cost-sharing payments were also made
under a permanent program established in the Soil Conservation and
Domestic Allotment Act of 1936. This Agricultural Conservation Payments Program, still in effect, has been administered by the commodity
program agency. It has not had production control as an objective,[17]
and no effort has been made to estimate the effect of the annual ACP
programs upon total production of wheat and other commodities.
Efforts of ACP to conserve and improve the nation's farmland, if
successful, have more likely increased the nation's land base rather
than decreased it. On occasion ACP cost-sharing funds have been
linked with production control programs. They were used to improve and conserve acreages diverted from wheat and other commodities under the act of 1936, and in 1940–42 a special program was
undertaken by ACP to convert acreages from unsound land use (usually from production of wheat) in a number of counties in the Southern Plains.

Since 1961 ACP cost-sharing practices have again become linked
with production control measures by virtue of a requirement in the

16. One list of measures is in the mimeographed "Report of the First Five Years
of the Regional Agricultural Council for the Southern Great Plains States," Office
of Land Coordination, Amarillo, Tex. (1942).
17. *Conservation Through Cost-Sharing—One of the Tools Available for Achieving
Coordinated Resource Development,* USDA-ASCS-PPA (July 13, 1964).

production controls program that a percentage of the allotment base be placed in conserving uses. Cost-sharing funds of ACP were available to share the costs of converting these acreages from production of surplus commodities. All of these ACP programs, however, are on a one-year basis, differing in this respect from the long-term contracts authorized under the Soil Bank Act of 1956.

THE SOIL BANK ACT OF 1956

Passage of the Soil Bank Act was at a climactic point in the conflict between individuals, parties, and agencies of government—a conflict which had gone on throughout the first three years of the Benson administration. Disaccord sharpened in 1956 due to drought, surpluses, and election-year political considerations.

The soil bank scheme was not itself a very divisive issue, having been sponsored from all sides once the general idea became visible. Basically it was a suggestion that U.S. farm productivity be stored in the soil, by enabling the federal government to rent unneeded acreages and thus to retire and restore them. Soil bank programs had been proposed in 1954 and 1955 by Representative H. Carl Andresen (R., Minnesota) and Senator Hubert H. Humphrey (D., Minnesota), among others. The most notable sponsor of the soil bank from 1953 to 1955, however, was the American Farm Bureau Federation. Soil bank was a principal feature of Farm Bureau's legislative program, and it gained a modest place in the programs of other farm organizations, including Farmers Union.

Soil bank proposals generated considerable congressional support in 1955, while the Benson administration reacted adversely to some of the proposals and was noncommittal with respect to the others. In the fall of 1955 the U.S. Senate Agriculture and Forestry Committee held hearings at locations throughout the United States, at each of which witnesses urged passage of a soil bank. In October Farm Bureau leaders as well as prominent Republicans urged Secretary Benson to introduce such a program in 1956. Meanwhile White House advisors were urging Benson to introduce a major program of some kind. By that time considerable study had been given to the soil bank within the USDA. However decisions needed to give substance to the program (what its objectives and mechanisms were to be and which agency would administer it) were not made until early January 1956. Then Benson outlined the administration measure before the Senate Committee on Agriculture and Forestry on January 12, and the administration bill was forthcoming on January 17 (S. 2949).

The timing of the legislation became a major issue. At the beginning of the year all parties wanted the legislation to become effective for the 1956 crops and therefore wished to expedite passage. But congressional committee Democrats believed Benson should have introduced the legislation in late 1955 to give adequate time to Congress for enactment, and for administrative planning.

Congress passed a soil bank bill on April 11 (H.R. 12). This bill, though, also contained a provision freezing price supports at 90 percent and a two-price wheat measure, both opposed by the administration. The bill was vetoed. Following mutual recriminations over the failure to implement a program prior to the planting season, suggestions for further action were made.

In his veto message President Eisenhower urged that an unencumbered soil bank measure be enacted immediately. Congressional opponents countered that a program could be implemented quickly under existing law (the Soil Conservation and Domestic Allotment Act of 1936), and they offered to appropriate the necessary funds immediately. The administration refused this option, noting that the existing legislation limited contracts to one-year periods, and that it had other unacceptable restrictions.[18]

Congress then enacted a second soil bank bill (H.R. 10875) on May 28, too late—in Benson's judgment—to be implemented for 1956. As a means of providing drought relief in 1956, Benson preferred that Congress permit him to make advance payments on 1957 land rentals. Instead Congress directed him to put the program in effect immediately and specifically denied him the power to make advance payments.

OBJECTIVES

The various interested groups differed as to what objectives the soil bank program should be given. Within the administration there were advocates of controlling production enough to reduce government surpluses quickly, and also advocates of a longer-term program to retire marginal croplands permanently while reducing the number of farmers. As a way to accommodate both views, the long-term and short-term objectives, the administration bill included one program representing the long-term conservation objective and another to deal with the short-term surplus problem.

Farm Bureau's proposal had also laid heavy emphasis on production reduction, but the main objective of many other organizations, political party leaders, and many supporters of the soil bank in Congress was apparently to use the soil bank, particularly in 1956, as a

18. U.S. Senate Appropriations Subcommittee on Agriculture, *Hearings on Department of Agriculture Appropriations for 1957* (1956), p. 474.

means of compensating farmers for losses suffered in the prolonged, widespread drought.[19] The Benson administration and Farm Bureau were interested in increasing farm income, but they expected income improvement to occur as a result of better prices in a balanced market rather than through land rental payments.

The Benson administration was also interested in reducing federal program costs, hoping that the major costs could be met by sale of existing surpluses. With surpluses out of the way, the cost of the price support programs would be greatly reduced.

ACREAGE RESERVE PROGRAM

Of the two measures included in the Soil Bank Act, one emphasized soil conservation and long-term reductions in land and in the number of farmers. Called the conservation reserve, it provided for retirement of marginal crop acreage for periods of several years in anticipation of permanent retirement of this land. The other measure, called acreage reserve, was conceived as a temporary provision with the purpose of reducing production and carryover of wheat and other specific "basic crops."[20]

At Secretary Benson's insistence the acreage reserve (as well as the conservation reserve) was not closely linked with the price support programs. For corn producers in particular the relationship between programs was voluntary in both directions. Corn producers were not obliged to abide by the ordinary acreage allotments as a condition for soil bank participation, although producers of other supported commodities were obliged to so so. Since few producers were in compliance with corn allotments, it is likely that few corn acres would have entered the acreage reserve if compliance with the existing supports program were a condition for participation. Benson rejected an alternative proposal that the price support program for corn be revised so as to attract more participants. Instead a special soil bank corn base was established based on the existing acreage planted to corn. Acres rented to the federal government under the acreage reserve were subtracted from that soil bank corn base. This base was 18 percent larger than the national corn allotment, which led spokesmen for other commodities to charge favoritism for feed grains producers.

Benson had also rejected the proposal by Farm Bureau and many congressional farm leaders that participation in the soil bank be made a necessary condition for receiving price supports. Benson did

19. See discussions among legislators and lobbyists in U.S. House Committee on Agriculture, *Hearings on General Farm Legislation* (1956).
20. Testimony of Benson before the U.S. Senate Committee on Agriculture and Forestry, Jan. 12, 1956.

so because of his belief in free economic choice—and no doubt because he did not want the soil bank program to serve as a tool for increasing the effectiveness of price supports programs.

The idea of using land rental payments as a way to update the price supports programs, as the Freeman administration subsequently did, had impressive support in 1955. Benson's unwillingness to consider any soil bank proposal during 1955 and subsequently his insistence on voluntarism made the acreage reserve much different in its effects than as proposed in 1955.

The linked objectives of income support and surplus reduction were no longer very compatible. By the time the acreage reserve program became law in late May of 1956, wheat harvest was already at hand, and the spring-planted crops would be well along by the time a program could be implemented. In this drought year the acreage to be offered most eagerly for federal rental would be that on which crops had already failed or on which crop failure could be foreseen. If this acreage were accepted, production would be reduced very little. On the other hand, federal rental payments on these barren acres would provide the direct relief which congressional leaders insisted on, an effect similar to the benefit payments made under the Agricultural Adjustment Act of 1933. In any case, it was all but impossible to institute tight and equitable administration so late and so speedily.

A USDA memo noted as early as April, for example, that it would be physically impossible to establish fair and equitable farm feed bases for the 1956 crops. Past experience indicated that the farmer-reported acreages were inflated by 15 percent, and since there would be inadequate time to "solidify" these farmers' estimates, the soil bank would likely bring "little or no adjustment in acreage."

Nevertheless the Benson administration apparently tried to include production control among the objectives of the 1956 program.[21] Secretary Benson was quoted in early June: "I intend to see that the Nation gets a dollar's worth of surplus reduction or a dollar's worth of conservation for every dollar paid out."[22]

Congressional leaders countered that the law in effect directed payments for drought acres, and their view was reinforced by election-year pressures. Drought relief became the only major objective of the acreage reserve program in 1956. As Assistant Secretary of Agriculture Marvin McLain explained:

> We early had indicated that because of the delay, we thought it better that we not put it in operation for 1956, but by law we were required to do it.

21. *Wayne Darrow's Washington Farmletter*, June 9, 1956.
22. *Congressional Record* (bound), June 5, 1956, p. 9558.

> We even went to the point, after we got the law, of reviewing just how far we should go with the members of the Joint Committees of Agriculture and we got our direction very firmly as to what we should do and, of course, the law itself, if you look at it closely, spells out very firmly, and I think in the testimony that the Secretary made earlier, and certainly it has been generally known, that we did not accomplish much in 1956 simply because the crops were all planted, and the only crops we got were those that did not amount to anything. So this did not surprise us and I am sure it doesn't surprise you.[23]

Those chosen to administer the acreage reserve program were primarily concerned with finding a framework in which authorized funds could be spent in the available time. The law was signed May 28, and general regulations were sent out June 8. Under criticism from Congress that the administration was moving too slowly, "final" instructions for acreage reserve were sent out June 17. Training meetings were held at each geographic level of the farmer committee administrative system during the week of June 15–22. At that time most counties began signing acreage reserve agreements.[24]

A number of rule changes were made thereafter, usually in the nature of relaxing requirements or delaying deadlines in order to enable greater participation. In the interest of speedy communication, rules were often announced by means of a press release. Some farmers were inclined to interpret press releases more liberally than was intended, prompting further revisions of the rules in order to prevent injustice so as not to penalize those who had misunderstood the rules. By this process terms of the acreage reserve became ever more generous as the season progressed.

Under the wheat acreage reserve, farmers in compliance with wheat acreage allotments and marketing quotas could place in the reserve up to half of their wheat acreage allotment (or 50 acres, whichever was larger). Acreage of less than 10 percent of the allotment (or 5 acres, whichever was larger) would not be accepted. The acreage reserve could not be grazed or harvested or cut for hay during the entire calendar year, and the only requirement with respect to cultivation was that noxious weeds must be controlled.

Since the wheat crop had long been planted, payments in 1956 had to be made on acres already committed either to crops or to nonproductive uses. Four categories of eligible acres were announced:

1. For spring wheat, allotment acreage which had not been planted because of anticipation that the soil bank would be enacted

---

23. U.S. House Appropriations Subcommittee on Agriculture, *Hearings on Department of Agriculture Appropriations for 1958* (1957), p. 1617.
24. USDA press release, June 27, 1956.

or because of adverse weather conditions. Payments were to be at the "standard" rate, which was calculated to equal the income farmers would have earned from the production on the reserve acres. The formula for the standard rate was the number of acres times the "normal" production[25] times the established rate per bushel (the national rate of 60 percent of parity or $1.20 per bushel).

2. For winter wheat, unplanted allotment acres were eligible for the reserve in the event that the failure to plant was due to adverse weather. Payment for such acreage was to be only $4 per acre. This much lower rate for winter wheat was due to the fact that winter wheat farmers had made their planting decisions before there was any reason to anticipate soil bank passage.[26]

3. The USDA could contract for allotment acreages where crops had failed due to natural causes. For these acres the payment rate was the appraised yield for that year (if the acres had been harvested) or the normal yield for that acreage, whichever was smaller, but not less than $6 per acre. Most land in this category rented at the minimum rate.

4. Planted allotment acreages could be included by plowing down the crops. The compensation for these acreages was the same as the third category. About four-fifths of the 1956 wheat acreage reserve was from this "plowed-down" cropland. Actually much of the land was permitted to be grazed off rather than plowed, due to the animal feed shortage during the 1956 drought.

Results in 1956. The Soil Bank Act authorized a total payment of $750 million annually for all crops, of which $375 million could be paid for the wheat acreage reserve. Since the average per acre payment in 1956 was only $7.89[27] (most acres were rented at the minimum $4 or $6 per acre), the cost of the 1956 program was much less than the authorized expenditure. In an effort to reach a goal of 5 million acres for the wheat acreage reserve, the deadline for complying with 1956 soil bank provisions was extended several times. The June 30 deadline was extended to July 15, by which time only 2.2 million acres had been signed up. By moving the compliance deadline to July 31, and finally to August 3, the acreage goal was finally achieved.

As a remedy for injustice due to lack of time or information, the program agency was permitted to revise the agreements of farmers

25. "Normal" yield was the average yield per acre on the acreage during the past several years, as calculated in the county farm program office.
26. U.S. House Committee on Agriculture, *Hearings on H.R. 11958* (July 11, 1956), pp. 4–5.
27. U.S. House Appropriation Subcommittee on Agriculture, *Hearings on the Department of Agriculture Appropriations for 1959* (1958), part 1, p. 259.

who did not fulfill the terms because of an incorrect understanding of the program.[28] In practice, this permitted farmers additional time to decide whether or not they wanted to comply with the program once they had signed. Apparently few if any farmers were penalized for violation of contracts.[29]

As noted earlier, the 1956 acreage reserve program was not intended to reduce production much. The Benson administration viewed the 1956 effort as a drought relief operation for which Congress was obliged to take major responsibility. The administration looked to 1957 experience for evidence that the acreage reserve program would reduce surpluses.[30]

Although 10 percent of the wheat allotment was put under acreage reserve in 1956, wheat production was 7 percent above the previous year. Production was 13 percent below the 1945–54 average, but this was most appropriately explained by effects of the drought[31] and also by the reduced acreage due to the quotas under the price support acreage program which had been in effect since 1953. The USDA estimated that the reduction in production due to the 1956 acreage reserve, after all the variables had been weighed, was about 25–30 million bushels.[32]

The 1956 program succeeded in its income objectives, although some winter wheat spokesmen would have preferred that payments on planted acreage be on the basis of normal yields rather than on the basis of expected yields—which were often near zero—or at the low minimum-per-acre figure. The total wheat acreage reserve payments of $44 million were, for all practical purposes, a net addition to wheat income and were distributed to those farmers hardest hit by the drought. South Dakota program officials and farmers were reported to have agreed that the program was a "lifesaver" for the farmer.[33] It had been possible to make rather large payments to the states in the Southern Plains, despite the lateness of the program, with Texas receiving more than Kansas the first year (Table 9.2).

Yet for the entire United States the USDA was able to use only 17 percent of the total funds authorized for wheat, which was small compared with the $180 million paid in 1956 for the corn acreage reserve (Table 9.3).

28. USDA press release, Sept. 21, 1956.
29. U.S. House Committee on Agriculture, *Hearings on Soil Bank Program* (1957), pp. 7–9.
30. Testimony of Benson before House, *Hearings on Soil Bank Program,* esp. pp. 2–4.
31. House, *Hearings on Agriculture Appropriations for 1958,* part 6, pp. 180, 186.
32. Ibid., part 4, p. 1661.
33. Ibid., part 6, p. 190.

TABLE 9.2. Acreage reserve payments for wheat per state

State	Acreage reserve payments 1956[a] ($)	1957[b] ($)	Production 10-year average 1946–55[c] (000 bu.)
Arkansas	1,068	39,580	770
California	80,042	2,912,644	11,137
Colorado	4,587,448	22,220,374	41,278
Delaware	. .	51,940	1,060
Georgia	15,131	804,666	2,091
Idaho	766,568	4,921,047	39,528
Illinois	1,985	859,008	39,280
Indiana	55,577	1,741,041	35,497
Iowa	112,507	169,259	4,131
Kansas	5,008,386	78,864,012	194,917
Kentucky	29,607	692,744	4,751
Maryland	3,676	266,279	5,620
Michigan	55,697	4,262,467	32,201
Minnesota	1,001,111	2,809,192	17,673
Missouri	58,728	2,717,534	30,959
Montana	1,714,910	8,816,397	86,019
Nebraska	515,846	11,544,433	79,801
New Jersey	3,838	172,519	1,823
New Mexico	1,074,915	982,110	2,795
New York	68,758	3,417,454	10,726
North Carolina	26,252	1,709,021	7,144
North Dakota	13,689,191	21,040,485	118,467
Ohio	77,612	4,895,551	50,834
Oklahoma	3,064,391	16,219,205	72,900
Oregon	177,684	3,203,975	26,813
Pennsylvania	26,282	1,068,182	19,425
South Carolina	5,482	958,057	2,847
South Dakota	5,511,315	10,044,542	40,069
Tennessee	36,465	601,083	4,063
Texas	6,229,561	12,724,261	47,339
Utah	267,322	1,873,803	7,984
Virginia	5,429	840,130	7,588
Washington	199,734	6,454,548	72,058
West Virginia	662	109,359	1,264
Wisconsin	78,758	154,767	2,148
Wyoming	187,951	689,857	6,166

a. Maximum compensation approved under the 1956 acreage reserve program; revised report from the U.S. House Appropriations Subcommittee on Agriculture, *Hearings on the Department of Agriculture Appropriations for 1958* (1957), part 7, pp. 159, 161–62. Due to late implementation of the 1956 program, the allocation was approved after payments had been made, so that this column in effect contains the amounts received.
b. Amount received by each state for participation in wheat ARP 1957, from the U.S. House Appropriations Subcommittee on Agriculture, *Hearings on the Department of Agriculture Appropriation for 1959* (1958), part 1, p. 267.
c. Ibid.

TABLE 9.3. Wheat in the acreage reserve program

	1956[a]		1957[b]	
	Obligation of ARP funds by commodity	% of total obligation of ARP funds	Obligation of ARP funds by commodity	% of total obligation of ARP funds
Corn	$179,664,064	69.00	$196,417,873	32.00
Wheat	44,739,889	17.18	230,851,526	37.61
Peanuts	595,626	.23	. . .	. . .
Rice	1,394,294	.54	15,466,625	2.52
Cotton	27,336,091	10.50	153,296,122	24.97
Tobacco	6,633,081	2.55	17,806,424	2.90
Total	$260,362,982	100.00	$613,838,570	100.00

Sources:
a. U.S. House Appropriations Committee on Agriculture, *Hearings on Department of Agriculture Appropriations for 1958* (1957), part 6, p. 160.
b. U.S. House Appropriations Committee on Agriculture, *Hearings on Department of Agriculture Appropriations for 1959* (1958), part 1, p. 260.

1957 Acreage Reserve. The conflict over objectives persisted in the 1957 program. Congress stressed drought relief. Farm Bureau stressed production control, and so did the administration, but the latter failed to exert strong leadership toward this objective.

Farm Bureau wished to make the 1957 program an effective control measure. To assure wide participation and to reduce costs, Farm Bureau urged again that acreage reserve participation should be required as a condition for receiving price supports. To assure a reduction of government stocks, Farm Bureau urged again that acreage reserve payments be made "in kind"—from surplus stocks—rather than in cash.[34]

In-kind payments had not been required in the 1956 act (though they could be used to a limited degree) due to fear by producer representatives that surpluses would thereby be dumped into the marketplace, causing reduced farm prices.

Farm Bureau also advocated measures to assure against productive use of reserve acreage, including a proposal that contracts be for longer than one year and a proposal that a soil bank base be established to prevent additional cropland acres from slipping into production. Farm Bureau urged "that success of the soil bank program in 1957 and subsequent years will depend upon the extent to which the Department of Agriculture and Congress resist pressures to convert the program into free crop insurance and disaster relief.[35]

The Benson administration, while lacking Farm Bureau's enthu-

34. House, *Hearings on Soil Bank Program,* p. 112.
35. Ibid.

siasm for implementing production control, officially shared the view that the 1957 program should be used primarily to reduce production.[36] The USDA could have further tightened the program without any further congressional action, had it felt capable of "taking the heat" from Congress and criticism from many farmer spokesmen.[37] Despite abundant evidence of wide loopholes in the acreage reserve program, however, the USDA did not take major steps to reduce slippage, except to establish in the final year of the program a soil bank base for each farm as a means to assure against switching of acreage from one commodity to another.[38]

In Congress there was considerable support for continuing the income relief emphasis—and little for restoring the original objective of the program—despite the immediate need for production control. By 1957 there was already a definite feeling that the acreage reserve program was adrift, with all interests determined to realize the most from it in its remaining short life.

The administration concentrated on reducing wheat acreage in the 1957 reserve program. Wheat contracts jumped to 38 percent of the total 1957 acreage reserve program. Almost 13 million acres (23 percent of the national wheat allotment) were placed in the reserve.[39] Harvested wheat acreage was reduced sharply—to 44 million acres as compared with 49 million in 1956 and 65 million acres for 1946–55 average. Wheat production was down only about 50 million bushels from the previous year, but this reduction was in the face of increasing yields. The administration estimated that the total wheat reduction due to acreage reserve in 1957 was 175 million bushels[40] (at a cost of 230 million dollars in payments).

Continued productivity despite acreage cutbacks suggested that the drought had ended, but the acreage reserve was reduced rather than increased in size for the coming year. By mid-1957 both the policy and the administration of the acreage reserve were so highly criticized that the entire program was in jeopardy.

Criticisms of the Acreage Reserve. From the beginning there were numerous criticisms of the acreage reserve program. Some of its major flaws were reported by periodic investigations of the Agriculture Subcommittee of the House Appropriations Committee.

---

36. House, *Hearings on Agriculture Appropriations for 1958,* part 4, pp. 1626–35.
37. House, *Hearings on Agriculture Appropriations for 1959,* part 1, p. 265.
38. Ibid., p. 1976.
39. Ibid., p. 265.
40. Ibid., part 4, p. 2008.

1. In a report of its first investigations of the 1956 program, the committee staff noted that in all the wheat belt areas studied, most acres placed in the acreage reserve would have yielded little or nothing.[41]

2. In the spring wheat area, due to the overlapping with the new law encouraging the planting of durum wheat, producers who had underplanted their 1956 spring wheat allotments were able to receive payments based on normal production on these acres, and at the same time in some cases to raise a durum crop on this soil bank acreage.[42]

3. Some producers collected both soil bank payments and federal-subsidized crop insurance indemnities for acreage on which crops had failed.[43]

4. In one South Dakota county land values had climbed as speculators purchased farms, exercised their right as new owners to evict tenants, and placed the land in acreage reserve.[44] Senator Henry Dworshak (R., Idaho) charged that low-value land in Idaho was also being placed in acreage reserve at very high returns for values.[45] The House Appropriations Committee investigators also produced evidence that the "normal" yields on which acreage reserve payments were calculated were far higher than the actual average yields[46] in some marginal areas. This and other evidence made it clear that the acreage reserve program tended to be attractive not only in drought areas but on marginal acreages in general.

5. In 1957 producers had to make decisions early, but they succeeded in getting released from their agreements on acreages for which good crops were in prospect.[47]

6. In the summer fallow areas producers were able to contract the fallow acres for acreage reserve permitting them to raise a feed grain crop on the idled allotment acreage. Sorghum production doubled. The national increase in sorghum production was several times the national decrease in wheat production in 1957.[48]

7. The acreage reserve program was giving a bad public image to all farm programs. Much criticism of acreage reserve was being received from town merchants and agricultural service industries who claimed that by idling cropland the program reduced the volume of business with farmers. This criticism began to be taken seriously by

41. House, *Hearings on Agriculture Appropriations for 1958*, part 6, pp. 179–91.
42. Ibid., pp. 181–82.
43. Ibid.
44. Ibid., p. 190.
45. Ibid., p. 27.
46. House, *Hearings on Agriculture Appropriations for 1959*, part 1, p. 271.
47. Ibid., pp. 275–77.
48. Ibid., p. 263.

the rural legislators.[49] In addition, the explicit practice of "paying farmers for not producing" became a symbol of the wastefulness of farm programs.[50]

8. A conflict between the expressed income aims of farm programs and the actual results was most obvious in the acreage reserve program. Farm income payments were defended as a way to sustain small family farmers, but huge acreage reserve payments were being made to big farmers, and in some cases without reducing production of these large farm firms much if any.[51] To meet this criticism, Congress stated in the Soil Bank Appropriations Act for 1958 that no payment could be in excess of $5,000. However producers were able to circumvent this rule.[52]

It also appeared that tenants had not been adequately protected despite provisions for them in the law. The division of payments was often more favorable to the landlords than was the customary division of returns in the community.[53]

9. An inherent flaw in this voluntary one-year program, particularly in the Wheat Belt, was the fact that farmers had a basis for predicting crops before planting time. In dry cycles farmers would choose to enter the acreage reserve, while in wet cycles few farmers would be attracted to it. As a result it would attract acreage when production was needed and it would not attract acreage when surpluses threatened. This tendency was clear in the decision on acreage reserve sign-ups for 1958.

The 1958 Program. For the 1958 acreage reserve program the USDA apparently requested the full amount authorized for payments[54] ($750 million) but did not insist upon it.[55] In contrast, the House Appropriations Committee proposed to hold payments at $500 million, and the House of Representatives voted to delete the entire appropriation for the 1958 acreage reserve program. The Senate voted to set the limit at $500 million, and the appropriations bill which passed Congress used the Senate figure.[56] (Congress later raised this amount to the authorized limit, as a result of an unexpected heavy participation in the cotton areas due to poor crop prospects.)

Apparently this reduction in appropriations did not affect the

49. House, *Hearings on Agriculture Appropriations for 1958,* part 4, p. 1572.
50. Ibid., p. 1623.
51. House, *Hearings on Agriculture Appropriations for 1959,* part 1, pp. 272–75.
52. Ibid., part 4, pp. 2038–50.
53. House, *Hearings on Agriculture Appropriations for 1958,* part 6, p. 187.
54. Ibid., part 4, p. 1596.
55. House, *Hearings on Agriculture Appropriations for 1959,* part 4, p. 1992.
56. Ibid., pp. 1993–94.

size of the 1958 wheat acreage reserve program as much as did the good weather. An expenditure of $178 million was planned for wheat, but in January 1958 this amount was revised downward to $100 million,[57] apparently because due to good crop prospects[58] winter wheat producers did not participate in the expected degree. The amount of 1958 wheat acreage payments turned out to be $105 million, less than half of that for the previous year.

Meanwhile, with good weather in the offing, wheat farmers chose to increase their planted wheat acreage. With an increase of 10 million harvested acres (to 53 million acres) simultaneous with an increased yield per acre—27.5 bushels per acre, the highest in U.S. history—the total production in 1958 was 400 million bushels more than could be used in the forthcoming marketing year. The excessive production of 1958 became the largest single addition to the U.S. carryover.

In 1958 the Benson administration proposed to Congress that the acreage reserve program cease at the end of the 1958 crop year. As its replacement, funds were asked for an increase in the longer-term conservation reserve (the other soil bank program). No doubt there was real question as to whether Congress could have been persuaded to appropriate any acreage reserve funds for another year. The administration noted this fact among the other reasons it gave for bringing the acreage reserve to an end. Assistant Secretary Marvin McLain explained to the U.S. House Appropriations Subcommittee on Agriculture:

> The decision to change the emphasis of soil bank programs to the conservation reserve approach was made after careful review of accomplishments under both soil bank programs in relation to the objectives as indicated in the Soil Bank Act and related legislative history. Also, the views of members of Congress, including the members of this committee, who studied the operations of the programs have been given weight.
>
> The record of accomplishment clearly indicates that both the acreage reserve and the conservation reserve programs have been and are effective means to divert cropland from the production of excessive supplies of agricultural commodities. . . . It is our considered judgment, however, that the conservation reserve approach will result in more concrete and more permanent benefits per dollar spent in both the areas of crop reduction and enduring conservation. The acreage reserve deals with basic commodities only and takes the land out of production for a one-year period. The producer in the following year may use this land and choose the commodity he produces. In many

57. Ibid., p. 1998.
58. Ibid., pp. 1992–94.

cases, this has acted as a means of crop rotation. On the other hand, the conservation reserve program retires the land for periods of 3–10 years in protective cover and in many instances results in a permanent change in land use.[59]

Review of the Acreage Reserve. In 1957 McLain was still not ready to concede that "the baby has gone inwards."[60] However his allegory is a good one to illustrate the fate of the soil bank acreage reserve program. A continuing problem for the acreage reserve program was the fact that the administration sponsored it only as a result of outside pressure. These pressures on the administration were the ones present in behalf of any commodity program. In the case of more successful programs, however, the administration had been able to orient the various interests so as to satisfy a number of objectives, including some defensible as in the public interest. In the absence of a vigorous brokership by the administration—and dedicated, self-interested administration of the program—the acreage reserve failed to contribute significantly to production control, despite heavy expenditures.

The acreage reserve was an effective drought relief measure for producers of the basic commodities, and no doubt it was of assistance to incumbents seeking another term in office. It achieved some reduction in production (Table 9.4) but at a high cost per bushel.

Another result of the act, however, was to emphasize some of the "unattractive" features of the commodity programs which were perhaps equally significant but somewhat obscured in the price support programs, particularly the tendency of controls to be juggled until they removed only the less productive acres, and the tendency for farm program rewards to go to a relatively few large farmers. Experience with the acreage reserve program contributed much to the unfavorable image of farm programs which came into being in the late 1950s. Secretary Benson and other opponents of the commodity programs made the most of this unfavorable image, while others tried to minimize its impact.

CONSERVATION RESERVE PROGRAM

The acreage reserve was one of two measures in the Soil Bank Act. The other was the conservation reserve program. Rather than bidding directly for acreages producing surpluses, the conservation reserve at first aimed at shifting the least suitable and usually least

---

59. Ibid., p. 2003.
60. House, *Hearings on Agriculture Appropriations for 1958*, part 4, p. 1691.

TABLE 9.4. Production control under the acreage reserve

Commodity	Approximate reduction of acreage	National allotment	% of allotment reduced	Payments
Wheat				
1956	5,670,441	55,000.000	10.0	43,450,000
1957	12,783,192	55,000,000	23.2	229,853,000
1958	5,289,477	55,000,000	9.6	105,111,500
Corn				
1956	5,315,578	43,280,543	12.3	179,649,500
1957	5,233,478	37,288,889	14.0	194,416,000
1958	6,658,093	38,818,381	17.2	282,255,190
Cotton				
1956	1,121,151	17,391,304	6.4	26,465,000
1957	3,015,630	17,585,463	17.1	152,567,000
1958	4,925,957	17,554,528	28.1	270,207,699
Total (including rice, tobacco, peanuts)				
1956	12,211,834	120,339,170	10.2	249,000,000
1957	21,354,018	114,309,871	18.7	610,000,000
1958	17,158,343	115,799,253	14.8	696,032,300
Grand total	50,724,195	350,448,294	14.5	1,555,032,300

Source: USDA, in U.S. House Appropriations Subcommittee on Agriculture, *Hearings on the Department of Agriculture Appropriations for 1960* (1959), part 3, p. 2235.

productive cropland to forage, trees, or water storage.[61] In order to accomplish this, such acreages would be rented by the federal government for periods of three to fifteen years (as implemented, the maximum was ten years). It was hoped that much of the acreage placed in conservation reserve would never be returned to crops unless needed for food production at some future time.[62]

As an incentive for participation, the USDA offered small annual per acre rental payments. The national average rate was $10 per acre for 1957, with state averages varying from $8 to $13. This rate, lower than the 1957 average wheat acreage reserve payments of $18, was raised to a national average of $13.50 when the conservation reserve program took over the functions of both the acreage programs after the demise of acreage reserve at the end of 1958.

The conservation reserve program was unique in seeking to subtract acreage from the total cropland rather than from the acreage devoted to particular commodities. A "soil bank base" was established for each participating farm. Consisting of the average cropland acres farmed during the past two years, this acreage was eligible for participation in the conservation reserve. However it was provided that

61. Testimony of Benson before U.S. Senate Committee on Agriculture and Forestry, Jan. 12, 1956.
62. House, *Hearings on Agriculture Appropriations for 1959,* part 4, p. 2004.

any additional cropland—idle or in tame hay—was also eligible at a reduced annual payment rate (30 percent and later 50 percent of the regular rate). As an additional incentive for participation, the federal government offered to pay up to 80 percent of the cost for converting cropland into conservation uses (although the federal share of the cost averaged less than 80 percent).

The administration depended heavily on negative incentives for participation. It assumed that returns from the nation's marginal cropland would soon become so unattractive that producers would enter the conservation reserve as a means of retiring these acres. Changing technology was reducing the value of some farmlands (although it was improving productivity of some land in the arid Wheat Belt). It was expected that new opportunities for urban employment would bid many farmers away from their traditional employment. In addition, it was assumed that as a result of reduced farm price supports much existing cropland would probably become unprofitable and would therefore be offered for the conservation reserve. For this reason, some officials felt that the conservation reserve program was seriously weakened at its inception by the decision of President Eisenhower not to reduce price supports for 1957, as planned.

1956–58 Program. Dividing the soil bank into two programs had not eliminated controversy over the proper objectives of the conservation reserve. Those responsible for instituting it as a separate measure did not expect the conservation reserve to contribute much immediately to production control. They were not distressed by the fact that the program did not get underway until late in 1956 and that only 6.5 million acres had been enrolled by the end of 1957. They hoped to develop the program slowly, outside the spotlight of political controversy which is likely to surround large expenditures. The skimming-off of unsuitable croplands, such as those subject to wind erosion in the Plains, was to take place over a period of several years.

Others in the administration and in Congress expected the conservation reserve to make an immediate contribution to production control, particularly in the Wheat Belt (Table 9.5). Excess wheat production had often been attributed to the breaking-out of "new lands" in World War II. With the Wheat Belt stricken by drought, two-thirds of the acreage entered in conservation reserve during 1957 came from seven Wheat Belt states (Texas, North Dakota, South Dakota, Oklahoma, New Mexico, Minnesota, and Colorado).[63] As indi-

---

63. Ibid., p. 2024.

TABLE 9.5. Conservation Reserve Program in the Wheat Belt

State	1957 conservation reserve goal	State	1957 conservation reserve goal
	(000 acres)		*(000 acres)*
Wheat Belt		Maryland	100
Texas	1,680	Massachusetts	35
Kansas	1,385	Michigan	485
North Dakota	1,200	Minnesota	735
Nebraska	790	Mississippi	355
Montana	760	Missouri	830
Oklahoma	710	Nevada	17
Colorado	640	New Hampshire	24
South Dakota	620	New Jersey	50
Washington	430	New Mexico	135
Other		New York	450
Alabama	360	North Carolina	275
Arizona	50	Ohio	480
Arkansas	435	Oregon	260
California	495	Pennsylvania	365
Connecticut	27	Rhode Island	4
Delaware	18	South Carolina	195
Florida	125	Tennessee	520
Georgia	390	Utah	85
Idaho	265	Vermont	70
Illinois	680	Virginia	260
Indiana	505	West Virginia	110
Iowa	900	Wisconsin	640
Kentucky	585	Wyoming	120
Louisiana	280		
Maine	70	National goal	20,000

Source: USDA, in U.S. House Appropriations Subcommittee on Agriculture, *Hearings on Department of Agriculture Appropriations for 1958* (1957), part 4, p. 1613.

cated in Figure 9.1, this emphasis on wheat acreage became even more pronounced as the program reached full development.

With demise of the acreage reserve by mutual agreement in 1958, the Benson administration suggested a much enlarged conservation reserve program to bear the load of surplus reduction. They asked that the conservation reserve appropriation be more than doubled,[64] despite the fact that previous appropriations had been far larger than were needed to fulfill controls offered at existing rates. Annual rate increases and liberalization of some rules for eligibility, plus the transfer of some acres from the acreage reserve, were expected to permit an enrollment of twice the amount signed up in the previous three years.

While the administration had become more enthusiastic about the program, congressional support had waned. The chairman of the House Appropriations Subcommittee which handled appropriations

64. Ibid., p. 2002–3.

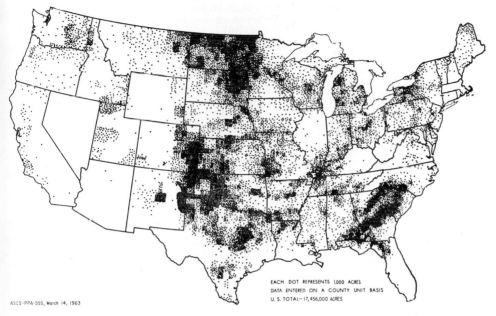

EACH DOT REPRESENTS 1,000 ACRES
DATA ENTERED ON A COUNTY UNIT BASIS
U. S. TOTAL—17,456,000 ACRES

ASCS-PPA-SSS, March 14, 1963

FIG. 9.1. Conservation reserve program acreage under contract as of January 1, 1964. As intended, much of the retired cropland was in the Wheat Belt. Retired acreage was highly concentrated geographically.

Source: Conservation Reserve Program and Land Use Adjustment Program. *Statistical Summary 1963,* USDA-ASCS (April 1964).

for the program suggested instead that a one-year moratorium be declared on new contracts, pending further study of program experience.[65]

Congress had already reduced the calendar year authorization for 1958 from the $450 million authorized in the statute to $325 million.[66] Yet in response to the administration's plea for more funds for 1959, Congress raised the authorization for calendar 1959 to $375 million,[67] and the administration did succeed in doubling conservation reserve acreage during 1959, although not spending the full appropriation. The $375-million authorization was continued for 1960, permitting a further moderate increase in contracted acreage (Table 9.6). After 1960 no new contracts were made, since the amount appropriated just equalled the funds necessary to service existing contracts. At the peak

---

65. Ibid., p. 2026.
66. Ibid., p. 1963.
67. U.S. House Subcommittee on Agriculture, *Hearings on Department of Agriculture Appropriations for 1960* (1959), part 3, p. 2122.

TABLE 9.6. Total acreage under contract of Conservation Reserve Program, 1956–61

Year	Acres
1956	1,428,722
1957	6,427,169
1958	9,886,594
1959	22,463,574
1960	28,660,679
1961	28,511,526

Source: "Conservation Reserve Program and Land Use Adjustment Program," *Statistical Summary, 1963,* USDA-ASCS (April 1964), p. 6.

of the conservation reserve acreage in 1960 it was estimated that the program had retired about 3 million acres of wheat, accounting for a production of about 62 million bushels (Table 9.7).

Problems. From the beginning of the soil conservation program there were considerable criticisms of the program administration. Objections as to the goals or likely results of the program also were raised. These became most significant when Secretary Benson decided to make it a principal mechanism for production control.

Among the objections relating to program administration was evidence presented by the staff of the U.S. House Appropriations Subcommittee on Agriculture that the USDA was not receiving full value under its contracts, even recognizing that rental payments were low. Additional evidence was subsequently provided by the U.S. General Accounting Office which reported that 23 percent of the "cropland" on which payments were being made was not in production and had

TABLE 9.7. Wheat adjustment attributable to conservation reserve

Year	Acreage adjustment	Production adjustment
	(mil. A.)	*(mil. bu.)*
1957	0.5	9.4
1958	.8	17.8
1959	2.3	46.1
1960	3.1	61.6

Source: USDA, from U.S. House Committee on Agriculture, *Hearings on Wheat* (1960), p. 191.

no record of previous production.[68] It appeared that some farmers, landowners, and firms were getting windfall profits from participation in the program. In addition, the provision in the law limiting payments to $5,000 per producer was being evaded in many cases.[69]

However the most significant congressional criticisms were directed to the priority of goals or objectives. Paramount was the low priority given to farm income in a program on which a considerable portion of Department of Agriculture funds were proposed to be spent. As noted, the program was to be made workable by virtue of reductions in farm prices and income. There were other unsatisfactory provisions for distribution of income, as judged by informal congressional norms. Payments under the program would go to a minority of farmers (only 89,000 were participating in 1957). A substantial portion of these payments would be invested in soil conservation and improvement rather than in income for farmers.

By concentrating its benefits and effects on marginal acreages, the program had another undesirable result. The marginal lands were geographically concentrated (Fig. 9.1) so that the acreage retiral would tend to reduce the activity and population of communities in these areas, a consideration more important to the spokesmen for these communities than the fact that individual program recipients may have benefited much from retirement or migration to new employment.[70]

In short, the conservation reserve mechanism had been well designed to achieve the objectives of soil conservation and efficient land use, which were usually subordinate to the objectives of income improvement and production control in major farm commodity pro-

68. U.S. House Appropriations Subcommittee on Agriculture, *Hearings on Department of Agriculture Appropriations for 1961* (1960), part 1, p. 19. Benson suggested that the GAO findings reflected the fact that some acreages had previously been in tame hay, summer fallow, or temporary pasture, or had suffered crop failure due to drought or similar extended disaster. Benson noted that the law permitted rental of such acreages (USDA press release, Jan. 7, 1960). Subsequent research suggested that "slippage" of acreage was small, and that the two soil bank measures had removed a larger proportion of cropland for each acre in the program than did the Freeman programs. (See Luther G. Tweeten, "Objectives and Goals for Farm Commodity Programs after 1969," *Abundance and Uncertainty—Farm Policy Problems,* Iowa State University Center for Agricultural and Economic Development, Rept. 31 (1968), pp. 149–74.
69. House, *Hearings on Agriculture Appropriations for 1959,* part 1, pp. 345–78.
70. Among the participants in the conservation reserve were apparently more small farmers than under the acreage reserve program. Many participants in the conservation reserve were able to move to nonfarm employment, according to surveys published in *The Conservation Program of the Soil Bank: Effects in Selected Areas,* USDA-ARS Agr. Info. Bull. 185 (1957), esp. p. 2. See also House, *Hearings on Agriculture Appropriations for 1959,* part 1, p. 2004.

grams. It was also in theory an inexpensive method of production control, since per acre costs were to be slightly more than the per acre net profit on the least profitable acreages. However there was little likelihood of immediate income improvement as a result of the conservation reserve program, and production control could be no more than a by-product.

Despite the dwindling support for the conservation reserve in Congress, the administration in 1960 again suggested an expanded program as its main remedy for surplus production. President Eisenhower asked that the conservation reserve program, due to expire December 31, 1960, be extended for three years and doubled in size to 60 million acres.[71] The annual rental payments to farmers would be made from government stocks of wheat and grain rather than in cash. To emphasize production control, the program would be directed into those areas producing wheat and other surplus crops.[72] This expanded conservation reserve program would take the place of wheat acreage allotments, which would be allowed to expire.

As a principal negative incentive to attract wheat acres into the reserve,[73] the administration asked for authority to lower the price supports on wheat to 75 percent of the average market price received by farmers during the past three years.

Neither congressional agriculture committee took action on the administration request for extension and expansion of the conservation reserve. Senator Bourke Hickenlooper (R., Iowa) put forward the administration proposal on the Senate floor as an amendment to the wheat bill (S. 2759). His amendment was defeated 53–28.

Subsequently the Freeman administration, like Congress, showed no enthusiasm for renewing the conservation reserve program. Freeman did introduce his own small voluntary land rental program in 1965, but only after elaborate precautions had been taken to dissociate it from Benson's conservation reserve program. The Freeman program, called the conservation adjustment program, mainly served the purpose of renewing or permitting renewal of existing conservation reserve contracts. Experience indicated that unless these contracts were renewed, the majority of these converted acreages would go back into crops.

Cost-Sharing. Like earlier soil conservation programs, the conservation reserve assumed that there exists a public interest in conserving

71. *Farm Message of the President,* Feb. 9, 1960.
72. U.S. House Committee on Agriculture, *Hearings on Wheat* (1960), p. 177.
73. See testimony of Marvin McLain before U.S. House Committee on Agriculture, *Hearings on Wheat* (1960), esp. pp. 184–87.

privately owned natural resources and that the federal government should therefore share with landowners the costs of conservation measures. As compared with other conservation programs, the government's contribution in this one was among the more generous. Under the existing Agriculture Conservation Payments Program, for instance, the federal government could pay no more than half the cost for a varied list of conservation practices, while under the new conservation reserve programs it could pay up to 80 percent of the total cost for a group of conservation practices the paramount objective of which was to convert land to noncrop uses.

These practices included establishing permanent vegetative cover crops, treating farmland to permit growing of grasses and legumes, establishing trees or shrubs, building dams to protect cover crops or to store irrigation water, and protecting wildlife.[74]

GREAT PLAINS CONSERVATION PROGRAM

Supplementing the conservation reserve cost-sharing practices were other practices authorized under the Great Plains Conservation Program, a special measure spurred by the drought.

As in earlier federal efforts to deal with the Great Plains as a region, preliminary research pointed out that new social measures as well as new soil conservation measures were needed to enable human society to function adequately in the unstable climate. Yet as before, funds were designated mainly for soil conservation.

It was expected that over the long run preventive measures would be far less costly than the drought relief measures which otherwise would inevitably be demanded. During the prolonged drought just preceding the implementation of the Great Plains Conservation Program, federal emergency relief assistance to farmers had totaled $519,322,162.[75] It was the cherished expectation underlying the Great Plains Conservation Program that a $20 million annual expenditure on a long-term basis would better prepare the region to withstand major drought.[76] It was also hoped that this voluntary conservation program would make unnecessary the resort to "alternatives that are neither to our liking nor in the American tradition"—namely enforced land use controls or increased federal ownership.[77]

The USDA estimated that there were 12½ million acres of Great

---

74. *The Soil Bank Program: How It Operates, How It Will Help Farmers*, USDA-Office of Information (November 1956), p. 11.
75. House, *Hearings on Agriculture Appropriations for 1958*, part 4, p. 1552.
76. Ibid., pp. 1708–11.
77. Ibid., p. 1710.

Plains cropland unsuited for continuous crop production, 10 million acres of which could potentially be brought under the Great Plains Conservation Program.[78] In addition, some rangeland needed restoration.

The Great Plains Conservation Program complemented the conservation reserve, in that cost-sharing benefits under both programs were for periods of several years, and some Great Plains Conservation contracts were on acreages rented under conservation reserve. The differences between the cost-sharing provisions of the two programs were as follows:

1. The Great Plains contracts were for treatment of entire farms, under the approach used by the Soil Conservation Service, rather than for treatment of specific acres.

2. The conservation reserve program was administered by the Commodity Program Agency (Commodity Stabilization Service), while the Great Plains Program was administered by the Soil Conservation Service.

3. One objective of the conservation reserve was to reduce the production of surpluses. The Great Plains Program was officially designed simply to shift land use, in accord with its best inherent capability.

SUMMARY

Dust storms in the wheat country were a visible element in the situation during passage of both the Soil Conservation and Domestic Allotment Act of 1936 and the Soil Bank Act of 1956. Although these extended droughts are apparently inevitable, the Great Plains was found in each period to be poorly prepared for them, and it was recognized on each occasion that the society had to be buttressed at many points to withstand this challenge of nature. Yet federal developmental efforts, including those measures applying especially to the Great Plains situation, were devoted mainly to soil conservation.

Soil conservation, as an attractive objective serving the public interest, was featured in the statements of legislative purpose in both laws. However those who implemented the laws were able to use them to channel income subsidies to their commercial farmer constituencies. Also present in both cases was a desire to avoid the market intervention which had characterized much other wheat legislation. In 1936 a

---

78. Undersecretary True D. Morse, in *Report on H.R. 11833, Great Plains Conservation Program*, Senate Rept. 2785 (July 25, 1956).

Supreme Court decision had necessitated new mechanisms through which to channel farm assistance, and in 1956 a conservative USDA administration much preferred to retire unneeded production units rather than to control directly the market price of wheat.

The soil conservation measures that were linked with commodity programs had as one effect the retirement of productive land. Land retirement measures were of two kinds, one of which sought long-term retirement of land. Such a program recognized that marginal cropland, almost by definition, was most likely to be abused; that a long-term rental mechanism would be most likely to attract marginal farmers who needed a way out of farming; and further that marginal acres, the least efficient acres, are appropriately the first to be retired.

However measures for long-term retirement of marginal lands were politically vulnerable. Marginal lands tended to include whole farms, and even whole communities, particularly in the arid Wheat Belt, and the beneficiaries of long-term rentals often moved away from their farm communities. Because of this outmigration this measure met some resistance from the very areas which received most of the funds. Conversely this program served relatively few farmers, in contrast with price supports in which most commercial wheat farmers participated. Finally, the program anticipated that much of the land retired under the program would never be returned to crops, implicitly because commodity price levels were not expected to be high enough to permit a profit on these marginal acreages. This assumption linked the program with the reduction of price supports, which wheat and other commodity spokesmen were opposed to.

This politically vulnerable program also faced technical problems, which the critics made much of. Since no sharp line separated cropland and noncropland, it was difficult to avoid renting some acreage which was not bona fide cropland. In addition, the program's contribution to production control was relatively small.

The other type of land retirement program involved short-term rental of highly productive land, mainly for the purpose of reducing production. Rental payments, rather than price supports or direct production payments as rewards for reducing acreage, were chosen partly on constitutional grounds in 1936 and partly on ideological grounds in 1956. However this method has been used in other commodity legislation as one of several convenient tools to achieve production control.

Efforts to link conservation and acreage control have been only mildly successful in the short run, and over the long run have likely combined to increase rather than decrease production. The Soil Conservation and Domestic Allotment Act of 1936 did not reduce wheat production much, if any, but it did initiate conservation measures, including the present Agricultural Conservation Payments Program, which have likely increased as well as enriched the acreage capable of producing wheat crops. Special programs for the Great Plains have removed some acreage from crops but have mainly improved tillage on arid farmland with the result that national production has not recently been reduced much as a result of droughts in that region. Yet for commercial farmers drought relief was very much in mind during passage of the Soil Bank Act of 1956; and during its short life this act served that purpose. However the soil bank was less a constructive compromise than a residue from election year recriminations and reprisals.

Wheat production was curtailed somewhat by the acreage reserve program, especially in 1957. However the electioneering atmosphere in which the bill was enacted, and its hasty implementation, made obvious some of the facts which most commodity programs take pains to obscure—the fact that the controlled acres are the relatively unproductive ones; that relatively big farmers receive most of the payments; that rules are changed to suit local convenience; that a certain amount of fraud exists, some of which is actually condoned by program rules; that production control payments are payments for agreeing not to produce; that farm programs are likely to encourage farmers to leave the farm rather than to remain on it as the programs intend.

For the acreage reserve program, "the baby turned inwards" very soon, in that the precedent of freewheeling drought relief activities during 1956 discredited the program as a serious production control measure. It came to an end in 1958, when the administration sought to shift production control responsibilities to the conservation reserve, thus subjecting the latter also to political and programmatic burdens beyond its capacity. The conservation reserve came to an end in 1960.

The short-lived Soil Bank Act illustrated that it has been difficult to pass and implement a program which genuinely merges the objectives of soil conservation, income support, and production control, however plausible the relationship between these objectives may seem. In practice, the tendency has been to divert all efforts toward income support, using the other objectives as rationalizations only.

10 / THE FREEMAN PROGRAMS

W<small>HEN</small> the Freeman administration entered office, government stocks of wheat surplus were at an all-time high. In midyear 1961 the carry-over was 1.4 billion bushels, half again as large as the average year's production (Table 10.1). Mountains of surplus wheat had become the symbol of the national "farm problem."

Yields per acre under Benson had increased from an earlier 13-bushel-per-harvested-acre average to 28 bushels per acre in 1959. Yields tended to level off at between 20 to 26 bushels per acre during Freeman's first five years. Exports during Benson's last five years had varied in a range of 400 to 500 million bushels. Increased exports under Freeman were within a range of 500 to 900 million bushels, permitting adjustment of demand to the higher production level which had created the surpluses. The U.S. share of increasing world wheat exports rose from 33.5 percent in 1958 to 42.0 percent in 1960 and then held steady. Over two-thirds of the U.S. wheat exports were shipped under the P.L. 480 surplus disposal program.

Production of wheat continued at about the same levels as during

TABLE 10.1. The situation under Secretary Freeman

Marketing year (July 1– June 30)[a]	Yield per harvested acre	Acres har- vested	Production	Exports		Total	Carryover[a]
				Commercial including barter	Con- cessional		
	(000)			*(million bushels)*			
1957–58 to							
1961–62 (average)	24.2	50.3	1,225.2	173.0	374.6	547.6	1,244.6
1960–61	26.1	51.9	1,357.2	204.2	457.7	661.9	1,321.9
1961–62	23.9	51.6	1,234.7	228.8	491.1	719.9	1,189.4
1962–63	25.0	43.7	1,093.7	153.3	489.0	642.3	1,055.0
1963–64	25.2	45.5	1,142.0	355.3	503.9	859.2	901.2
1964–65	25.8	49.8	1,290.7	170.1	557.9	728.0	817.7
1965–66	26.5	49.6	1,315.6	344.0	523.2	867.2	535.0
1966–67	26.3	49.8	1,311.0	438.8	305.5	744.3	425.0
1967–68[b]	25.8	59.0	1,524.0	373.7	382.4	761.1	537.0
1968–69	28.5	56.0	1,598.0	...	...	...	...

a. June 30, end of year.
b. Oct.—based on Oct. 10, 1968, estimate.

Benson's last three years, although harvested acreage dropped, as a result of farm program controls, from 53 million acres in 1958 to 45 million in 1963.

In 1966 there were no longer any "surpluses," and indeed there was real apprehension as to whether the 535-million-bushel carryover in July 1966 was large enough.

CHARACTER OF FREEMAN ADMINISTRATION

The sources of Freeman administration personnel were in some respects similar to those from which the Truman and Roosevelt administrations had drawn personnel. Some administration officials were program-oriented persons, notably those who had worked their way to the top levels of the farmer committee systems. There were also Democrats representative of regions or crops, or well connected with leading congressional figures. An important source of officials was the National Farmers Union and Farmers Union Grain Terminal Association groups. The Grain Terminal Association was a politically oriented cooperative warehouse federation, headquartered in St. Paul; its principal business was wheat handling, and its territory stretched along the northern tier of Mid-America. The Farmers Union, which controlled local cooperatives, had become a valued member of the national liberal coalition which operated through the Democratic Party, but like the GTA it had a commodity orientation, the main commodity being wheat.

Experience in the state of Minnesota, where GTA and Farmers Union were quite important, gave a common background to many leading persons and groups. Freeman had been a Minnesota governor, and most of his USDA personal staff had served him in Minnesota. Senator (later Vice-President) Hubert Humphrey of Minnesota was the liberal Democratic farm spokesman in Congress and was Majority Whip in the Senate. His Senate office was one of the open ends of this Minnesota complex, having brought into the complex many who had served as members of his senatorial staff or who had associated as supporters of Humphrey for President and then had found a place in the Kennedy government. Other Minnesotans of individual prominence included Senator Eugene McCarthy (D., Minnesota), Professor Walter Heller, Chairman of the Council of Economic Advisors, and Professor Willard Cochrane, who became Freeman's chief economist as USDA Director of Agricultural Economics.

The political creed of the Minnesotans, most of them members of the Minnesota Democratic-Farmer-Labor Party, was probably expressed by the national Democratic Party platforms of recent years. They were on the whole more politically oriented than philosophically minded—in contrast with the Wallace and Benson administrations—and highly partisan.

They were, however, liberals inclined to analyze a major economic problem in terms of what constructive action government could take with respect to it. Freeman saw rapid technological change in agriculture as one of those situations needing the guiding hand of government, all the more so because government had helped to catalyze the technological revolution by means of public research and rapid dissemination of the fruits of that research. Freeman saw the problem of distributing the fruits of this technology as an opportunity for constructive action. The administration accepted responsibility for solving the food distribution problem, and Freeman consoled himself and others with the thought that the U.S. problem of "abundance" was not so difficult as the Russian problem of food shortages. He stated to a congressional committee:

> Might I just say that I refuse to admit the people of our government are not wise enough to learn how to live with abundance. I think we are very fortunate to have it. We ought to have enough brains to learn how to live with it. And if we cannot, we will not do very well at the bar of justice today.[1]

1. Testimony of Freeman before U.S. House Committee on Agriculture, *Hearings on the Agricultural Act of 1961* (1961), p. 47.

The liberal view entered the decision, then, in determining that the farm problem required vigorous government involvement and in influencing a strong commitment to such objectives as food aid and increased farm income.

The Freeman administration appears to have seen no important ideological issues in decisions as to the means available to be employed. Willard Cochrane, chief architect of compulsory controls, regretted that the means chosen were distasteful both to himself and to farmers, but he was unimpressed by arguments that they restricted personal freedom. There was some reluctance to use the processing tax because it would raise bread prices for low-income consumers, but this reluctance was dispelled by the argument that the consumer sacrifice was small in comparison with the benefits to be received by both consumer and producer.

In other cases the choice of mechanisms was made entirely on pragmatic grounds. Secretary Benson had found price supports and production controls to be morally repulsive, and from this judgment had concluded that these mechanisms probably would not work. Freeman began with the question, "Will they work (and will they be accepted)?" With the latter attitude, it is not surprising that a combination of mechanisms picked from the bag of those available were more successful than Benson had predicted they would be.

This preference for technical rather than ideological tests was held also by John A. Schnittker, a Kansas State University economist who as a Freeman appointee became most influential in the determination and passage of wheat policy. Schnittker had served a year on President Eisenhower's Council of Economic Advisors and had led an interuniversity wheat study, completed just before the change of administrations. He had become convinced that a number of technically feasible alternatives were available for stabilizing wheat production, one of which was a framework of tightened compulsory controls with price supports, as advocated in the Democratic platform by Kennedy in the presidential campaign. This framework was strongly preferred by the Minnesota Farmers Union complex and by the Southerners who dominated the congressional agricultural committees. As a member of the Freeman team, Schnittker first served as a staff economist under Willard Cochrane. When Cochrane resigned in 1964 Schnittker took his place, briefly, as Freeman's chief economic advisor; he then was appointed Undersecretary, where he continued to be the central administration figure in the determination of wheat commodity policy.

OBJECTIVES

The Freeman administration began, like that of Wallace, full of plans and hopes for meeting a serious "farm problem." As with the Wallace administration, progress toward objectives was aided both by circumstances and by policy. Just as surpluses under Wallace were reduced by drought, a partly fortuitous expansion of exports greatly aided the Freeman group in warding off the surplus peril. Due partly to the effects of steady reduction of surpluses, the Freeman administration could say, after five years, that it had achieved its major objectives. But also like the Wallace administration, the Freeman administration had by that time become increasingly apprehensive about the long-run capacity to balance production and demand.

Freeman stated his major objectives on many occasions. They are analyzed below.

1. Raising farm income. When Freeman came to office the level of commercial farm income was demonstrably a sensitive nerve-ending of Midwestern Plains and southern politics, regions which had become important constituencies of the USDA. The success of Freeman's administration depended upon improvement of net per capita farm income of commercial farmers. This did not necessarily mean higher prices, if production costs should decline and if the total net income could be divided among fewer farmers.

2. Reducing the cost to government. The surplus was the visible symbol of farm program failure, and it was also extremely costly. Freeman quickly found himself under pressure from the administration to reduce the costs of farm programs. The most obvious way to do this, and yet maintain farm income, was to reduce the surplus.

3. Using abundance constructively. Wallace's great project had been the ever-normal granary; Benson's great desire was to increase cash markets; Brannan wished most to increase family farm income. The challenge to which Freeman responded avidly was the one generated by his Minnesota mentor, Senator Humphrey—that of using our farm productivity as an instrument of international peace, friendship, and development. Freeman was as much an internationalist as he was an agriculturalist, though initially he lacked in both fields the depth possessed by Humphrey and former Secretary Wallace. All three men managed to make farm policy serve international objectives.

Freeman's internationalism was most vigorously expressed in his support for the Food for Peace program. After three years in office, he stated in a letter to Senator Carl Hayden (D., Arizona): "One of the deep satisfactions that come to me as Secretary of Agriculture is the fact that I am able to play a part in carrying forward our nation's highly successful agricultural export program under Public Law 480."[2]

Freeman's enthusiasm for the P.L. 480 program and his impact on it was illustrated in his testimony in 1964 favoring a five-year extension of the law:

> Rarely has any governmental policy and program contributed so much to so many people and to so many diverse interests. It serves all of the people in the United States by promoting greater economic well-being at home and greater security in our relations with the rest of the world. It enables this Nation to advance the interests of its own citizens as they seek to meet their responsibilities to less-favored peoples.[3]

4. Agricultural development. For many years USDA programs have been somewhat incompatible with their presumed major objective: preservation and enhancement of the equalitarian rural community and the family farm. As early as the 1930s Secretary Wallace was aware that most farm program benefits went to the larger producers, thus widening the gulf between the large and small farmers. By the mid-sixties about one-third of the farmers produced most of the commercial product and received most of the commodity program benefits. Little political support has been given for measures to help low-income farmers. The Freeman administration made a hesitant analysis of their needs, suggesting such measures as rural industrialization, training for industrial jobs, better education, and rebuilding of some rural community facilities. Yet financial support for these programs was token compared with expenditures for the commodity programs, and responsibility for them was given to traditional USDA agencies which maintained their first loyalty to commercial farmer constituents.

5. Efficient use of land resources. While this objective covered soil conservation and other existing activities, it included a new interest in developing nonfarm uses for land resulting from retirement of cropland on the one hand and increased use of land for residence, industry, roads, and recreation on the other. But new interests here, like those under agricultural development, were at best only new beginnings, and at worst merely window dressing for the heavy expendi-

---

2. U.S. House Committee on Agriculture and Forestry, *Report on the Extension and Amendment of Public Law 480*, Rept. 1467, 88–2 (1964), p. 31.
3. U.S. House Agriculture Subcommittee on Foreign Agricultural Operations, *Hearings on Extension of Public Law 480, Titles I and II*, Serial LL (1964), pp. 2–4.

tures for commercial farm programs. In short, the major objectives of the Freeman administration remained those associated with the problems of commercial agriculture: raise commercial farm income and reduce costs and surpluses.

STRATEGIES

The Freeman administration was adaptive, flexible, and expedient. In the first five years the Freeman administration did maintain an aggressive stance ("Attack, attack, attack," one critic called it), but this administration prided itself on knowing when to change directions.

Freeman's group had several strategies. Most were complementary and pursued during the same time period, although one major strategy was abandoned and replaced by another. It is useful to categorize these strategies either as those aimed at capitalizing on the situation or those aimed at asserting leadership.

SITUATIONAL

In some ways the farm problem was ripe for resolution, and this was as Secretary Benson had intended. However Freeman put another face on the situation and made it support a different solution than Benson had hoped for.

Focusing on the Surplus. From 1953 to 1961 government commodity stocks had risen to levels beyond any past experience, and with the termination of the soil bank program they were expected to continue to increase very fast. Benson, in the face of the impasse with Congress, had decided during his last few years in office (1957–60) that one way to achieve his objective of ending the price programs was to permit them to be buried under the massive surpluses.

Benson and his political allies had then tried to stimulate a reaction to the surplus—from the public, from business, from consumers, from Congress, even from farmers. While some reaction was forthcoming, and some consternation was felt among program supporters, a chief precedent set by the accumulation of surpluses was the tripling of the amount of federal expenditures for agriculture (Table 10.2).

Thus Freeman began office with a very large budget but with none of Benson's reluctance to institute thoroughgoing production controls. Since it was cheaper per bushel for government to purchase reductions in production than it was to store surpluses, Freeman devoted more

TABLE 10.2.   USDA expenditures, 1950–66 (in millions of dollars)

Year	Expenditures	Year	Expenditures
1950	$2,967	1960	$5,419
1951	650	1961	5,929
1952	1,151	1962	6,669
1953	3,217	1963	7,735
1954	2,917	1964	7,896
1955	4,637	1965	7,298
1956	5,177	1966	5,949
1957	5,006	1967	6,306
1958	4,875	1968	7,851
1959	7,091	. . .	. . .

of his budget, and also made "payments-in-kind" from stocks, to the objective of reducing production. In this way he was able to reduce total costs and even offer farmers slightly more income while reducing the size of the surplus.

Using Food Aid Outlets. Congress had enacted and rallied support for a number of programs using surplus stocks. Secretary Benson had been reluctant to approve them and cautious in implementing them.

Freeman swung open the gates on foreign food aid, school lunch, special milk, and surplus food distribution programs. He also initiated a food stamp program (Table 10.3). Although food programs were charged against Freeman's budget, these expenditures generated support from the agencies and individuals which used or distributed the surpluses. They also had considerable public appeal.

LEADERSHIP

For the Freeman administration the task of leadership involved the pursuit of objectives at several levels—those of the presidential administration, those within the organizational complex of agriculture, and those he would serve as broker among the commodity interests.

The Stern Disciplinarian. The Freeman administration did not underestimate the problem of overproduction. In order to "manage our abundance" they would have to wrangle more funds for that purpose and at the same time compel farmers continually to reduce their production units in order to offset their increasing yields.

In his first comprehensive proposal Freeman chose to pay more attention to these difficult economic and biological realities than to the difficult political facts. He asked Congress to make him a stern

TABLE 10.3. Increasing food aid

Fiscal year	Domestic food aid[a]				Foreign food aid[b]					Grand total
	Domestic donations	Special milk program	School lunch program	Food stamp program	Sales for foreign currency	Sales for dollars on credit terms	Donations P.L. 480 Title II	Donations Section 416[c]	Bartered materials for supplemental stockpile	
					(million dollars)					
1955	168	17.2	81.8	...	129.5	...	86.9	214.5	...	697.9
1956	235	45.8	81.6	...	614.7	...	93.6	271.1	...	1,341.8
1957	236	60.4	98.4	...	1,337.9	...	124.9	234.1	217.3	2,309.0
1958	185	66.3	98.5	...	1,073.2	...	121.5	254.3	83.9	1,882.7
1959	204	74.2	136.5	...	1,022.0	...	97.9	178.7	314.7	2,028.0
1960	146	80.3	154.8	...	1,232.0	...	95.5	130.8	192.4	2,031.8
1961	246	84.0	154.7	.6	1,454.7	...	198.6	173.9	200.5	2,513.0
1962	366	88.7	167.8	13.4	1,454.8	29.0	241.9	235.7	193.3	2,790.6
1963	354	93.3	167.4	19.3	1,483.0	80.2	215.6	260.8	99.7	2,773.3
1964	370	99.2	180.1	29.3	1,415.3	60.5	228.2	345.2	38.1	2,765.9
1965	470	97.2	189.9	33.7	1,293.4	200.2	147.2	211.0	41.9	2,684.5
1966	268	96.0	198.9	67.7	1,137.8	233.5	222.5	190.7	28.4	2,443.5
1967	247	98.8	208.8	111.0	893.8	176.9	335.9	45.5	34.9	2,152.6
1968	368	102.4	218.1	178.9	561.7	298.1	344.6	...	30.6	2,102.4

a. Obligations including administrative expenses.
b. Net expenditures.
c. Sec. 416 of the Agricultural Act of 1949.

disciplinarian of production. He asked Congress to delegate to him—and to farmer committees selected by him—the power to write programs which producers could then accept or reject in a referendum. If producers rejected a workable commodity program, they would be allowed to sell in a free market. In the latter event economists predicted the unsupported prices for commodity might soon fall to disaster levels. If this happened, Freeman was willing to gamble that he could stand the pressure of low prices longer than farmers could, and therefore that farmers would ultimately vote themselves back into a controls program.

As expected, Congress refused to delegate its program-writing power to Freeman. In 1962, however, they did enact a tough compulsory wheat program such as Freeman had hoped to pass under the other procedure. When the program was rejected in a referendum the Freeman administration proved unable to hold the line, even for one year. Decisions following this 1963 wheat referendum suggested again the weakness of democratic planning. Far from having become the dictator his critics maintained he had become, Freeman found he lacked the resources to carry out a referendum decision which would adversely affect prices.

He was then prevailed upon to pass a "voluntary" program which secured compliance by the carrot rather than the stick; he thereby sounded the death knell on future compulsory controls programs and in the future was obliged to resort to the expensive and inadequate subterfuge of penalizing noncompliers by denying them carrots.

The Legislative Package. Objectives at several levels had to be accommodated in a farm program, and Freeman's group served as intermediary among these levels.

At a high level the presidential administration was concerned about the cost, framework, image, and political consequences of farm bills. Freeman himself demanded an attractive and effective program. At another level the farm organizations, the congressional committees, and the other elements of the organizational complex of agricultural politics were concerned primarily with enhancing their role in the decision process. There were also multiple commodity groups, such as the National Association of Wheat Growers, concerned with the technicalities of costs and benefits.

Freeman gained freedom from the fact that the Democratic leadership on both congressional policy committees was dominated by spokesmen for southern crops—cotton, rice, and tobacco; whereas the principal commodities in greatest difficulty during his first two years happened to be wheat and feed grains. The Southerners, most of whom were sympathetic to compulsory controls, provided the needed support to pass compulsory wheat and feed grains controls through both committees.

Negotiation among commodity interests took place at each stage in the legislative process, but it was important for Freeman to gain as much agreement as possible during the framing of the administration programs. Particularly in the case of his major legislative effort, culminating in the Food and Agriculture Act of 1962, extensive negotiations accompanied the framing of the legislative proposal.

In part these early agreements were to allow multiple claims to authorship. They were also to brace the bill against the centrifugal tendencies which it was bound to experience in Congress. Still another advantage of early negotiations was that the costs and benefits of the various provisions could be quantified for use in advocacy.

By finding a realistic outline for compromise beforehand, the burden of defending the legislation, when provisions were challenged, could be shifted to the prospective beneficiaries of those provisions. Moreover the USDA administration believed that a more workable program could be produced within the USDA than through unaided congressional bargaining.

Freeman, like Benson, wished to put commodity programs within a purposive framework attractive to groups other than producers. Freeman's framework would have ideological appeal, but it would include public interest objectives as well as some bread-and-butter provisions for urban groups, even though the agriculture committees would approve only token measures of the latter sort. Freeman's 1962 farm bill was a carefully knit legislative package which included provisions for urban recreation, rural community development, domestic food relief, guarantee of abundant food, and international food assistance. Thus the administration was in a position to seek a majority based on the merits of the legislation rather than depending solely on brokers of rural votes to arrange for trades on unrelated legislation.

The political matrix of the presidency was giving ever more weight to conceptions of national economic and budget policy. The expensive commodity programs were no longer justifiable unless they could be rationalized within a plan for achieving such objectives as high national economic growth, full employment, and stable noninflationary price levels.

Commodity-by-Commodity-Programs. There was certainly a limit to the comprehensive approach, imposed both by the unique problems of each commodity and by the fact that the structure of the congressional subcommittees indicated a continuing desire to treat each commodity separately. Within the package of legislation, programs for each commodity were tailored to its unique problems and the desires of producers.

At the same time the USDA recognized the interdependence of commodity policies and during the five-year period sought to increase this interdependence. This in turn encouraged a greater uniformity among programs, beginning with the proposal for compulsory controls on all commodities in surplus. When these controls proved politically unacceptable, the Freeman administration moved toward income support through federal payments.

Leadership within the Existing Political Framework. Freeman did not really challenge the existing framework for agricultural policy. He respected the curtain of myths and symbols behind which farm policy was made, and in some ways he put policy further into the realm of the occult by adding to program complexities.

Freeman respected the men who dominated policy in Congress. He acknowledged their legislative prerogatives and their claims to special competence—indeed their right to dictate policy with respect to certain commodities.

Although Freeman's initial strategy was to seek to take program-writing authority away from Congress, the congressional policy-makers apparently did not identify him as a serious advocate of procedural change, nor a threat to their status and power. On the whole, Freeman wished to increase political power over the farm economy, in contrast with Benson who wished to reduce it.

Interpreting Costs and Benefits. Another advantage Freeman possessed over previous secretaries in dealing with Congress was his greater willingness to be specific about his income objectives and estimated costs. Cochrane and other able staff economists that Freeman brought into the administration drew heavily upon the USDA's collection of data and experts to "cost everything out," including amendments or changes proposed in committee.

Freeman's group spurred analysis within both the action and staff agencies. Trends were projected with respect to farm size, domestic and foreign yields, markets, agricultural development abroad, production at home, and many other changing factors. Effects of all serious policy proposals were carefully scouted, partly because the Budget Bureau insisted on it after 1960 but also because the ability to state the costs and consequences of complex programs such as that for wheat tended to put the USDA on top in the esoteric but very serious game of numbers.

GENERAL HISTORY

WHEAT CERTIFICATES

It will be recalled that the processing tax in the Agricultural Adjustment Act of 1933 was ruled unconstitutional in 1935 by the Supreme Court. Two years after this decision, the character of the Court having changed, Secretary Wallace suggested that processing taxes should be reimposed as the best way to offset the 1937 downtrend in wheat prices.[4] While this suggestion was not followed, processing taxes were again considered by the USDA in 1940 in a framework surprisingly like that of the program finally enacted in 1964. The plan was suggested at that time as an option to be used in the event that farmers should refuse to approve compulsory wheat controls in the 1941 wheat referendum. This proposal was not enacted.

Such a plan was proposed in 1942 by Secretary of Agriculture Claude Wickard as a way to maintain federal income support despite rising surpluses. In view of the large government wheat stocks, Wickard said, "We just can't keep on getting parity for all the wheat from 55 million acres,"[5] but he felt farmers could gain assurance of parity returns from the 40 million acres on which wheat for domestic food was produced. The study reasoned that during the period of ongoing negotiations toward an international trade organization, a multiple-price program would be less vulnerable to criticism than the existing export subsidy. As another advantage, the federal government was exporting much wheat for food relief, supplies of which might be obtained at the least cost through a two-price plan. The Grange and the Oregon Wheat Growers Association were in active support of a two-price plan for wheat at this time.

In 1954, with government wheat stocks again increasing, congressional and organizational support for a two-price plan grew. The Advisory Committee which served a "Wheat Industry Conference," called by Secretary Benson, unanimously recommended to him a two-price system of wheat marketing "as the most promising alternative to

---

4. Speech to wheat producers, Wichita, Kansas, Nov. 23, 1937.
5. Joseph S. Davis, "World Wheat Survey and Outlook." *Wheat Studies of the Stanford Food Research Institute,* 18(May 1942):343.

the price support programs operated under present legislation."[6]   In 1955 it was accurate to say that the influential wheat legislators, most of them Republicans, favored such a program.

A two-price plan was added as an amendment by Senator Frank Carlson (R., Kansas) to the first 1956 Soil Bank Bill (H.R. 12), which President Eisenhower vetoed. Under Carlson's plan production would be restrained by existing controls and by the proposed soil bank, and many two-price advocates hoped at that time that the two-price mechanism would itself relieve surplus pressures by creating new secondary markets and by reducing production incentives, thereby permitting subsequent relaxation of acreage controls.

Secretary Benson and the Farm Bureau opposed the two-price plans in principle, as they had opposed all new proposals for governmental control of commodity markets and prices.[7]

By 1958 it was clear that the Eisenhower administration would not accept any two-price wheat program. Congressional agricultural committees returned to the search for an acceptable combination of production controls and high price supports for wheat which the administration would accept, a search which proved fruitless.

Freeman decided on the two-price or domestic certificate plan as one among several mechanisms which would permit more flexibility in the use of income and control measures to increase their effectiveness. In the past, various measures had become isolated by identification with a specific person, group, or ideology. This had encouraged a single remedy approach and had increased the likelihood that the best measure for the moment, in a given economic situation, would not have adequate political support. Previously long-sought measures had been enacted only after they were no longer appropriate.

Freeman had mixed success in his efforts to gain use of an adequate variety of mechanisms. He himself ruled out the use of flexible support measures which Benson had sought. He also lost his preferred method for curtailing wheat production—compulsory controls—when his 1963 program was decisively defeated in a producer referendum. However he did gain flexibility in the use of other mechanisms, including voluntary controls and domestic certificates. Freeman's costly innovations in implementing a voluntary wheat program were somewhat more effective in holding production in line than the compulsory

---

6. "The Certificate Allotment Plan for Wheat as Proposed by the Wheat Advisory Committee" (Aug. 28, 1953), mimeo.
7. Helen Farnsworth presents a case against *Multiple Pricing of American Wheat* (Stanford, Calif.: Food Research Institute, 1958). See also Don Paarlberg, *American Farm Policy: A Case Study of Centralized Decision Making* (New York: Wiley, 1964), p. 317.

controls and price supports that they replaced. Extraordinary levels of foreign sales and food aid exports reduced the existing surpluses.

The following is a year-by-year account of Freeman's wheat measures.

THE TEMPORARY PROGRAMS

Freeman made no effort to change the program for 1961, since most of the wheat crop had been seeded when he took office. However a 100-million-bushel surplus reduction occurred in 1961, mainly because China began buying heavily from Canada and Australia, opening additional foreign markets for the United States.

"Emergency" programs were enacted for the 1962 and 1963 crops, as supplements to the continuing compulsory controls and high price supports program. These introduced several changes which ultimately became part of the four-year act passed in 1965.

The 1962 program observed the 55-million-acre minimum allotment but required that farmers divert an additional 10 percent of the allotment for which they received rental payments. In addition, price supports were raised. Harvested acreage dropped sharply in 1962.

In 1963 the additional acreage cuts were no longer compulsory, but about one-quarter of all producers made extra cuts in return for both acreage diversion payments and payments per bushel of expected production. Harvested acreage was again well below earlier levels.

1962 "PERMANENT PROGRAM"

In early 1962 the administration had unveiled its permanent program for wheat, which would have modernized the existing compulsory controls program by tightening loopholes and by further reducing the minimum allotted acreage. It would also have incorporated the two-price or domestic certificate plan as a means of supporting income. The certificates would be issued to farmers on that portion of their crop consumed domestically and would be purchased by processors of wheat for domestic food use. Among the perceived advantages of this tax on domestic processors would be reduction in federal program costs even while farmers' income was increased somewhat. Furthermore certificates would permit juggling of market prices in ways which might expand foreign markets, give grain producers greater flexibility, and facilitate food aid.

The "permanent" wheat program was part of the comprehensive Food and Agriculture Act of 1962, which was opposed in Congress by the Farm Bureau and the Republican congressional parties. The bill was finally passed by small margins in both houses, revised in some respects but with the wheat program intact. However the new program was disapproved in a farmer referendum, because wheat farmers happened to be weary of compulsory acreage controls, which were to be increased even more under the 1962 law; the Farm Bureau and other opponents had convinced many that they could expect a better program if this one were defeated. However the biggest factor in the very decisive referendum defeat was the negative vote of growers with less than 15 acres of wheat, most of them commercial farmers outside the Wheat Belt. For these voters the program controls were a nuisance and the income benefits were small.[8]

When the controls were defeated in 1963 some expected a return to fence-to-fence wheat plantings and chaotic markets. Nothing so extraordinary happened. The 1963 crop, on which harvest was just about to begin, was relatively small. Markets were good abroad due to Communist purchases. Private holders of grain, including farmers, were in no hurry to sell. In the fall planting of 1963 producers abided by acreage limitations almost as if quotas had been in effect, presumably because they expected a new program to be enacted. Since the referendum defeat ruled out the use of compulsory controls, farm legislators and organizations who had supported passage of the 1962 law urged Freeman to put that new program into effect using voluntary controls. In that case, producers who complied with the allotments could enjoy the program benefits.

The administration decided late in the winter that farmers "had voted with their drills." That is, it was assumed that by complying with acreage restrictions despite defeat of the program most farmers had indicated that they wanted a program notwithstanding their rejection of compulsory controls. Accordingly the objective of farmer freedom, earlier advocated by Secretary Benson and championed by program opponents in the referendum, was again allowed to have priority, in 1964, over the objectives of cost reduction, surplus reduction, and higher farm income, all of which were better achieved through compulsory controls. In early 1964 the legislative transition to a voluntary basis was made, and voluntary controls were provided for the 1964 crop.

8. Don F. Hadwiger and Ross B. Talbot, *Pressures and Protests* (San Francisco: Chandler, 1965), ch. 13.

Since the 1964 program was late in being implemented, it had relatively less effect on production, even though the number of farmers participating was higher than in the previous two years. The acres removed from production were more likely to be those on which crop failure was predictable.

The program was revised and extended for 1965. Meanwhile continuing record-breaking exports were eliminating the need to reduce acreage much below levels of the Benson era.

THE FOOD AND AGRICULTURE ACT OF 1965

A four-year program for wheat was passed in 1965 (the Food and Agriculture Act of 1965) which gave new emphasis to exports, particularly food aid. An effort was made to pass on more of the program costs to the consumer by increasing the value of the wheat certificates, but this was frustrated by the opposition of bakers and other allied groups.

PRODUCTION CONTROLS

The Freeman administration had intended to reduce production by means of more effective controls. It moved to reduce acreage in several ways: retaining compulsory controls, reducing the 55-million-acre minimum allotment, firming up the bounds of total crop acreage, providing that those complying under one commodity program must be in compliance under all of them, requiring that part of the non-allotment acreage be completely idled, increasing the penalties to be paid on wheat produced in excess of allotments, offering payments for voluntary acreage diversion beyond that required for compliance, and instituting controls on 15-acre producers. On the other hand, along with tighter controls new liberties were to be provided, including the right to sell wheat from nonallotted acres to make up for low yields on the allotment. Later wheat was permitted to be produced on acreage formerly set aside for feed grains.

1962 PROGRAM

Compulsory quotas were approved by farmers in 1962. Freeman had obtained authority to require diversion of 10 percent of the allotments, in effect reducing the 55-million-acre minimum to 49.5 million acres. The additional 10 percent cut (and any additional allotment acres farmers were willing to divert in return for a per acre payment) was required to be held in "conserving uses." A conserving base, consisting of the acres which had been in conserving uses during 1959 and 1960, was decreed for each farm. Very limited uses could be made of this land. It could be devoted to trees or shrubs, to pasture which could not be grazed, to certain types of crops which were for the purposes of enriching the soil and could not be harvested, or to a few designated crops for which there was no possibility of surplus accumulation. In the last case diversion payments might not be reduced or eliminated.

The outside limit of cropland was to be the total acreage, minus the conserving base, minus the diverted cropland. Despite this intervention, however, numerous adjustments were made in the conserving base, usually in the direction of opening more of it for crops.

The penalty for noncompliance was stiffened. Formerly those not complying with acreage allotments had to pay to the federal government 45 percent of the parity price per bushel of the "normal" yield on excess (nonallotment) acres from which wheat was sold. The "normal" yield, based on the county average yield for recent years, was often far lower than the actual yield. This penalty was raised to 65 percent of parity on *twice* the normal yield (unless the farmer could prove to the local ASC committee that his actual acreage was less than twice the normal yield). In addition, the so-called Anfuso amendment was still in effect, providing for reductions of future allotments as a penalty for noncompliance. Penalties could be voided, as before, by storing the excess or "hot" wheat. Farmers were encouraged to produce and store some excess wheat as insurance against poor crops. This could be sold in poor crop years to make up the deficit between the actual yield and the "normal" yield. ("Normal" yield was based primarily on the reported yield on the farm in prior years with adjustment for abnormal weather during the reporting period. Beginning in 1966, this term was replaced by the term "projected" yield which gave more consideration to upward trends in yield; consequently it was somewhat higher in comparison to the actual average yield on the farm in past years.)

1963 PROGRAM

In 1963 a step was taken toward voluntarism. Compulsory controls were still proclaimed under the 55-million-acre minimum (and approved in a 1962 farmer referendum), but producers were not required to divert additional acreage. Instead they were given strong financial incentives to divert an additional 20 percent of their allotment.

FOOD AND AGRICULTURE ACT OF 1962

Under this program, which was to have gone into effect in 1964, the 55-million-acre minimum was reduced by as much as 10 percent but no less than would be needed to produce a crop of 1 billion bushels. Farmers were required to put the difference between the former allotment and the reduced allotment into conserving uses.

For the first time, those with 15 acres or less were to be subject to allotments. They were not to be penalized for noncompliance but would lose the various income benefits including the results of the previously supported price. One other option open to those harvesting 15 acres or less was to divert their entire acreage in return for a government payment at the rate of 50 percent of the supported price for "normal" production on those acres.

1964 PROGRAM

When producers rejected compulsory quotas in 1963, the emergency 1964 program retained the previous controls, except that there were now no penalties on wheat sold from excess acres. The Anfuso amendment which reduced the allotments of noncompliers was still in effect, however, and noncompliers received no certificates or other program benefits.

One additional requirement for compliers in the 1964 program was "cross-compliance": they must comply with acreage programs on all commodities subject to them. Cross-compliance had been legislated as a companion to a new freedom to substitute (interchange) allotment acreages of wheat and feed grains, but the latter freedom could not be implemented in 1964 because crops had mostly been planted by the time the program had passed.

The official allotment for 1964 was 49.5 million acres, but new program provisions brought about a larger than ordinary departure from this figure by the effective allotment, which was 53.3 million acres. The effective allotment was high because of a provision which increased the amount of wheat in small allotments. But much of this allotment was not expected to be used. The low wheat price support for 1964 was expected to persuade many small farmers east of the Great Plains to switch to feed grains via the substitution clause which permitted interchange of these allotments or to leave wheat allotments idle. Thus the amount the USDA actually expected to be harvested was considerably lower than the official allotment. The USDA estimated that only 44.5 million acres were needed to meet the anticipated needs.

A word should be said about the change in the status of 15-acre growers, instituted under the 1962 act, subsequently included in the temporary 1964 and 1965 programs, and then embodied in the 1965 Food and Agriculture Act. Previously any producer could produce up to 15 acres without being subject to any penalty. Furthermore he could receive an allotment based upon a previous three-year history. Thus if he grew 15 acres during three years, his allotment would subsequently be 15 acres. This privilege of expanding acreage was allowed those producers who accumulated an average history larger than their allotment during the years 1959, 1960, and 1961. In all other respects the special position of the 15-acre grower was terminated. The only provision specifically relating only to small growers now was the one which allowed those with fewer than 25 acres to divert their entire acreage in return for diversion payments.

1965 PROGRAM

The same system of voluntary controls was extended for the 1965 crop, with two major changes. The allotment base, which under the Anfuso amendment had been reduced as a penalty for overplanting, would no longer be affected by a history of overplanting. In effect, the allotment, which had previously been figured as a percentage of a wartime "wheat base," now became an entity in itself, responsive to change only in the sense that it could be terminated if wholly unused for a period of three years.

The other major change was that the substitution clause was implemented. Wheat planted on feed grain allotments was not eligible for certificates, although it was eligible for price support loans. It might be noted that the ordinary feed grain allotment applied only to corn, grain-sorghum, and barley in 1964, but in 1964 wheat producers could also establish an oats-rye base and substitute wheat for these crops as well.

In the subsequent 1965 act, as in the previous three years, compliers could voluntarily divert additional acres in return for a payment.

FOOD AND AGRICULTURE ACT OF 1965

In the four-year act beginning with the crop of 1966, the national allotment was reduced to 47.8 million acres, a 15 percent reduction from the former 55-million-acre minimum. The acreage in the 15 percent reduction had to be placed in conserving uses.

Participants in the program were subject to the rule of cross-compliance and had the freedom to interchange wheat and feed grain acreage. They were still allowed to harvest and store wheat from excess acres, to be sold when yields on allotments were below a "projected" yield level.

For the 1967 crop the wheat allotment was increased 32 percent, or 16.6 million acres more than the 1966 allotment, due to the drain on U.S. stocks occasioned by the shipment of wheat for India famine relief. Due to severe drought in the Southern Plains, however, the acreage harvested in 1967 was 60 million acres, 2 million less than anticipated.

INCOME PROVISIONS

The Freeman programs had several objectives with respect to income provisions. One was to raise the per capita net producer income slightly. This was achieved. No longer was the goal of 100 percent of parity prices considered tenable, and in fact the blend price of wheat (including certificate and noncertificate wheat) dropped from 78 percent of parity in 1959 to 75 percent of parity in 1965. The USDA took the position that the parity price index, a revised formula, was no longer a realistic measure of fairness. Efforts were made to work out an income index, comparing farm income with other income.

Another objective was to make the program attractive enough to gain approval from farm legislators. The third objective was to induce voluntary compliance, particularly after compulsory controls ended with the 1963 crop. Income incentives were placed just high enough to gain the necessary reduction in acreage, using the alternatives on a "typical" or average farm as the main predictor of producer decisions. The overall response invariably proved to be about what had been desired.

1962 PROGRAM

In the first post-Benson program, the support price was raised 21 cents (to $2). Compliers also received diversion payments for the mandatory additional 10 percent reduction. The payment per acre was equal to 45 percent of the county support price for the bushels which would have been produced on this acreage, assuming the 1959–60 adjusted yield; and for additional voluntary diversion, producers received 60 percent of the adjusted yield.

These measures collectively were supposed to—and did—increase

TABLE 10.4.   Gross wheat income

Crop year	Acreage diversion payments[a]	Price support payments	Domestic wheat certificates	Export certificates	Farm value of production	Total
			(million dollars)			
1951	...	...	...	...	2,089	2,089
1952	...	...	...	...	2,729	2,729
1953	...	...	...	...	2,391	2,391
1954	...	...	...	...	2,083	2,083
1955	...	...	...	...	1,859	1,859
1956	45	...	...	...	1,976	2,021
1957	231	...	...	...	1,848	2,079
1958	105	...	...	...	2,544	2,649
1959	...	...	...	...	1,975	1,975
1960	...	...	...	...	2,365	2,365
1961	...	...	...	...	2,258	2,258
1962	285	...	...	...	2,228	2,513
1963	163	79	...	...	2,116	2,358
1964	33	...	305	105	1,765	2,208
1965	38	...	363	120	1,775	2,296
1966	26	...	655	...	2,141	2,822
1967	...	...	727	...	2,120	2,847

Source: USDA.

a. Includes acreage reserve payments under the Soil Bank Act of 1956.

wheat income per farmer by 10 to 20 percent. The higher price support, however, required higher rates for diversion payments, and the program was therefore considerably more costly than in previous years. (See Table 10.4.)

1963 PROGRAM

For 1963 the price support was reduced by 18 cents per bushel. Then instead of requiring cuts beneath the 55-million-acre minimum, producers who diverted an additional 20 percent of their allotment were given a lump sum payment calculated as 18 cents per bushel on the "normal" production on their remaining allotted acres. In addition these producers received acreage diversion payments of 50 percent of the value of normal production on the diverted acres. These incentives for voluntary diversion gained the participation of only one-fourth of the producers, although most of the wheat acreage was in compliance with the quotas.

FOOD AND AGRICULTURE ACT OF 1962

The main income feature of this new program was the wheat certificates, to be given to compliers on 80 percent of their "normal" production on the allotted acres (which would include only about 45 percent of total U.S. wheat production). The value of these certificates was 70 cents per bushel. The wheat price support (and effective price) was to be allowed to fall to about 50 percent of parity ($1.25), which was regarded as the value of wheat as livestock feed if feed grains supports were maintained at existing levels. One of the aims of the act was in fact to allow dryland wheat farmers to grow wheat for animal feed.

Certificates would be forthcoming whether or not the crop was good enough to harvest. The blended price income from the certificated wheat would be about 80 percent of parity.

1964 PROGRAM

When farmers disapproved the quotas under the 1962 act, benefits similar to those provided under it were nevertheless extended to those who voluntarily complied with both the acreage allotments and the provision requiring acreage diversion for the difference in acreage between the allotments based on the 55-million-acre minimum and those based on the lower minimum. Specifically compliers received payments on the diverted acres equal to 20 percent of "normal" production, priced at the county loan rate, and they were free to divert additional acres for the same return. They received domestic wheat certificates valued at 70 cents for 45 percent of the normal production on the allotment, and export certificates valued at 25 cents for an additional 45 percent of normal production on the allotment (for a total of 90 percent of normal production). Compliers could obtain price support loans at $1.30.

1965 PROGRAM

Minor changes were made in the 1965 program, including a reduction in the price support to $1.25, increase in domestic certificates to 75 cents, and increase in export certificates to 30 cents. Export certificates were given on only 35 percent of normal production. No payment was made for the initial diverted acreage, but producers received payment of 50 percent of normal yield for additional diversion.

FOOD AND AGRICULTURE ACT OF 1965

The four-year extension continued to feature wheat certificates as a chief method to raise income and as the chief incentive to obtain compliance. The method for using the certificates was revised, however, in fulfillment of the traditional aspirations of two-price advocates: certificates were to be issued only for that portion of wheat which would be used domestically (calculated as 45 percent of the *projected* yield on allotted acres). Certificates would be valued so as to raise total income from certificated wheat to 100 percent of parity. The value of certificates to the farmers would be the difference between the support rate of $1.25 and full parity, for a total certificate value of about $1.28 per bushel. Since processors paid only 75 cents per bushel for the certificates, about 53 cents per bushel was a disguised direct payment from the federal government.

Again no payment was made for the intial acreage diversion, and for additional diverted acres payment was made at the supported price on 40 percent of "projected" production.

Under the new program, with its lower price supports, export subsidies were not expected to be needed. Quite the other way, exporters might often purchase export certificates for the difference between the lower U.S. market price and the higher world market price. Any net receipts from these certificates were to be prorated among the complying producers.

The provision for storage of excess wheat, the price support loans, and the guaranteed certificates were all intended to stabilize wheat farmers' income. The total income per capita under the 1965 act was expected to be higher than under the programs of the last two years. Government costs were expected to be lower mainly because of the reduction of government stocks and attendant expenses.

RESULTS OF THE PROGRAMS

PRODUCTION CONTROL

In the absence of controls programs, wheat production in 1962–65 would have been far larger than it was. Even assuming a low market price of $1.25 per bushel, it was estimated that U.S. wheat production in 1965 alone would have been 500 million bushels more than the 1.3 billion bushels produced in 1965 in the absence of controls.

As compared with the previous price supports-compulsory controls program, however, the Freeman innovations made less difference. In terms of average production (26 bushels per acre), the additional acres diverted by Freeman (30.2 million cumulative for 1962–65) would have amounted to a reduction of 785.2 million bushels below the previous program. Undoubtedly the actual reduction was less than this due to slippage—such as the tendency of farmers to divert land which was the least productive, on which crops had failed, or which would have been idle in any case.

The objectives with respect to surplus reduction were achieved as much through increased exports as through production controls. Cumulative exports for 1962–65 were more than 750 million bushels above the previous four-year period. Much of this increase was in subsidized food aid shipments, however. Costs for these shipments, in the opinion of the USDA program experts, were definitely more per bushel than the costs of surplus control through diversion of additional acreage. Including expenditures for food aid, annual federal expenditures on the wheat program were over half the total market value of the crop.

Greater reliance on acreage controls, while feasible and less expensive, would assume that food aid was not needed or justifiable on other grounds. It could be assumed that a very large wheat program budget could be justified in the absence of, or even in the face of, needs for food aid. The voluntary controls program may then be said to have become economically viable, conditional upon continued acceptance by farmers of limited income goals, and continued annual federal expenditures sometimes exceeding half the value of the total production.

GOVERNMENT COSTS

Costs of the program were difficult to judge since the reimbursement for stocks sent abroad was based on the book value of the oldest stocks on hand, inflated by years of storage and handling charges.

Acreage diversion payments were a major cost, totaling $374.3 million for the four years. Diversion payments under this program were presumed to be more costly in reducing production or less efficient per government dollar than were land retirement programs such as the conservation reserve of the 1956 Soil Bank Act, because diversion payment rates equaled the profit on the best-producing lands while the Soil Bank Conservation Reserve met the rental value for marginal acres on which profits were very low.[9] Domestic certificate transactions, however, cost nothing in 1964 and 1965, even yielding a small balance, because more certificates were bought by processors than were issued to farmers. This federal balance offset half the $105 million cost of the export certificates in 1964, and a

9. Luther G. Tweeten, "Commodity Programs for Agriculture," in National Advisory Commission on Food and Fiber, *Agricultural Policy: A Review of Programs and Needs* (August 1967), pp. 10–130.

TABLE 10.5. Commodity export payments by Commodity Credit Corporation on wheat and flour (in million dollars).

	Commodity Export Program[a]	P.L. 480 Title I	P.L. 480 Title IV	Wheat Agreement	Total
Fiscal year 1962:					
Wheat	53.0	186.0	4.1	71.7	314.8
Flour	3.8	33.3	.0	18.0	55.1
Total	56.8	219.3	4.1	89.7	369.9
Fiscal year 1963:					
Wheat	19.7	242.3	3.3	62.8	328.1
Flour	6.5	37.0	.3	11.0	54.8
Total	26.2	279.3	3.6	73.8	382.9
Fiscal year 1964:					
Wheat	91.3	169.3	4.9	115.1	380.6
Flour	5.3	30.7	.5	9.9	46.4
Total	96.6	200.0	5.4	125.0	427.0
Fiscal year 1965:					
Wheat	8.5	87.3	13.6	30.1	139.5
Flour	2.6	8.6	.5	4.0	15.7
Total	11.1	95.9	14.1	34.1	155.2
Fiscal year 1966:					
Wheat	149.5	163.9	34.6	9.6	357.6
Flour	10.3	11.2	5.0	.6	27.1
Total	159.8	175.1	39.6	10.2	384.7
Fiscal year 1967:					
Wheat	96.2	28.4	7.9	. . .	132.5
Flour	11.5	5.9	1.0	. . .	18.4
Total	107.7	34.3	8.9	. . .	150.9

Source: USDA, ASCS–BU/CPB (Sept. 28, 1967).

a. Includes costs for shipments under International Wheat Agreement (protocol) from Aug. 1, 1965, to July 31, 1967.

similar situation occurred in 1965. In the future, however, the federal cost of about 50 cents each for 500 million domestic certificates was expected to be about $250 million annually.

With price reductions, the cost of export subsidies on exports for cash was reduced somewhat although it remained substantial (Table 10.5). The cost of the wheat program was still expected to be accrued largely by the acquisition, handling, and distribution of supplies above market needs, rather than in payment of farm subsidies. These costs were great. As a result of them, wheat program costs in fiscal 1964 equaled 66 percent of the value of total wheat production. No longer regarded as surpluses, these supplies were used mainly in food aid programs. The market value of the wheat shipped abroad under the P.L. 480 program for fiscal 1965 alone was $754 million (550 million bushels programmed for fiscal 1965 times the average price, $1.37 per bushel, for that year).

WHEAT FARMER INCOME

Gross income from wheat production during the four-year period 1962–65 was maintained at about the level of the previous four years (Table 10.4). There appears to be no agreed-on formula for measuring adequate income from wheat for those years, since the parity formula probably did not adequately reflect the increasing efficiency of large commercial farms.

It sometimes is maintained that producer income would have been higher under a compulsory controls program, but it is difficult to envision this as true for the years 1962 to 1965, assuming that other objectives were also sought. Assuming mandatory controls, it is difficult to believe that the certificated wheat would have been raised to a value above 100 percent of parity. Furthermore it was not possible to raise the market price of wheat much above feed grain levels and yet enjoy the advantages of sales into the feed grain market as well as free interchange of wheat and feed grain acreages. Conceivably diversion payments could have been terminated, to be replaced by a payment to farmers through some device of direct payments per bushel to complying producers, but this would have amounted to only a different distribution of wheat farmer income rather than a lower income. It appears that producer income was higher under the voluntary programs, because government was obliged to spend more in order to secure the desired reduction in production. The original impetus for a compulsory controls program was indeed to minimize federal costs.

ACTIVITIES OF POLITICAL GROUPS[10]

Groups interested in wheat legislation during the 1960s can be put into three categories: farm organizations, Congress, and processor and service groups.

1. The National Farmers Union, the National Grange, and the National Association of Wheat Growers were active and continuous supporters of administration policy. This support was important in Congress and also in the wheat referendum of 1963. All these groups had substantial memberships in the Wheat Belt. If wheat growers received more federal benefits than other producers, as was sometimes charged, the reason may be that wheat was the dominant commodity interest of all three groups. The administration also received support from the Missouri Farmers' Association and found sympathy and

---

10. For a more extensive coverage of farm group activity in this period see Hadwiger and Talbot, *Pressures and Protests*.

sometimes strong support at all levels within the grain cooperatives, particularly the Farmers' Union Grain Terminal Association (GTA) and the National Federation of Grain Cooperatives.

These groups left their mark on policy. The choice of the two-price wheat certificate mechanism was dictated in part by their enthusiasm for it. Other provisions favoring the commercial wheat areas (such as the tightening up of the 15-acre provision and permission to interchange wheat and feed grain acreages) were included at their urging. When the 1963 referendum failed, the Wheat Growers and GTA joined wheat legislators in overcoming the administration's reluctance to pass an interim program. In 1965 they helped persuade Congress to enact the administration's proposals on a four-year instead of a two-year basis as had been requested.

These groups constantly fought for increases in the proposed amounts of subsidies and price supports and invariably achieved concessions. The administration paid a price for the invaluable aid of these groups in the form of a higher commodity budget.

However these groups received less than they wanted. They constantly took the position that wheat income was too low. For example, they opposed fixing the value of wheat certificates in the hope that the certificates would sell for a higher price in the market. In 1965 President Anson Horning of the National Association of Wheat Growers unsuccessfully sought domestic wheat certificates for an additional 100 million bushels. He also advocated continuance of export certificates and diversion payments on the acreage reduction below the 55-million-acre level. His objective was to raise total farm income to the relatively high 1962 level.

While sharing Freeman's commodity policy views for the most part, these groups tended to resist Freeman's effort to provide retraining and rehabilitation for underemployed farmers.

2. The American Farm Bureau Federation, with frequent assistance from some nonwheat commodity groups, persistently opposed virtually all administration initiatives on wheat commodity policy. Farm Bureau leaders explained their total opposition on the ground that Freeman was going "in the wrong direction"—toward greater government involvement. No doubt it was due also to the fact that Farm Bureau was linked to the Republican Party in the electoral process. Farm Bureau also wished to downgrade the ASCS farmer committee system which in some areas offered the only organizational basis for grass roots opposition to Farm Bureau's claim as farm spokesman. In the Northern plains the ASCS committees were effectively used by Farmers' Union to oppose local Farm Bureau influence.

Farm Bureau opposition took several forms. Farm Bureau mar shalled negative arguments with respect to each Freeman proposal and undertook the burden of exposing the shortcomings of administration policy. It tried to exploit the considerable divergencies of interest among wheat producers and between wheat producers and others. It solicited nonfarm opposition wherever it could be found. It mounted a decisive wheat referendum campaign which led to defeat of the compulsory controls which underlay the Food and Agriculture Act of 1962. It solicited opposition votes in Congress (especially among conservative and urban Democrats), which led to the defeat of the compulsory feed grain program. Farm Bureau also opposed administration Democrats in rural constituencies.

Farm Bureau introduced alternative legislation in the form of a large-scale land retirement proposal unrelated to particular commodities, similar to the soil bank reserve under Secretary Benson. Although Farm Bureau's proposal was regarded as a respectable and viable alternative, it was opposed by the administration and had only a very limited appeal to Republicans.

Freeman apparently accepted as inevitable the opposition of the congressional Republican leaders and the Farm Bureau, and he was able to capitalize on it to a certain degree. Many rural Democrats had suffered from Farm Bureau's election tactics, and many liberal Democrats resented Farm Bureau's hard-line opposition to most of their spending proposals. Farm Bureau was disliked by leaders of the other general farm organizations. Thus Farm Bureau had a considerable negative constituency, which came to the support of Freeman.

3. Farm service and processing groups had growing economic strength and became respectable as farm policy participants during the 1960s. To those who bought, held, exported, and distributed grain, and to managers of grain markets, the wheat certificate plan was preferable to high price supports as a method of maintaining farm income, because it allowed more influence for the marketplace. While these groups supported the wheat certificate plan, they strongly protested against one aspect of the program which the administraion considered to be vital: the sale of government stocks to hold down the market price of wheat. The administration argued that market prices had to be held down in order to assure compliance with the program and to keep the federal costs within defensible limits.

Among wheat-related industries, chief opposition to the wheat certificate program came from the millers and bakers. In 1964, the first year of operation of certificates, the total cost of wheat for milling was not affected much. The price support was reduced from the $2 level of 1962 to $1.25, to which the cost of certificates (75 cents) was added. For 1965, however, the administration proposed to increase the certificate value to a level which would provide full parity—about $2.50—on domestic food wheat. The American Bakers' Association and others formed a wheat users' conference and mounted a campaign against this proposal. They elicited letters from bakers, bakers' unions, and employees, and even generated a "housewife" response by means of fliers enclosed in loaves of bread. As a result of this reaction, the administration agreed to pay the increase in certificate value (50 cents per bushel) rather than pass this added amount on to bakers. This new value enabled farmers to receive full parity on the domestic portion of their crop.

4. Though it is not easy to estimate its influence, Congress was present at each stage of the decision process.

Southern congressional leaders strongly supported the enactment of the compulsory wheat program, which would have reduced costs but which was subsequently defeated by farmers in the wheat referendum. In general the impact of Congress on the costs and benefits of wheat programs was counter to administration efforts at cost reduction. The congressional committees undoubtedly ran interference for or backstopped Freeman in his efforts within the administration to maintain agriculture's share of the federal budget. The administration's effort further to transfer costs to the consumer in 1965 by increasing the tax on processors was stopped by the House Democratic leadership, which feared defeat on the floor. The USDA's desire to retain the compulsory program in 1963 despite the referendum defeat was frustrated in large part by senators from wheat states.

The Wheat Belt was regarded as a Republican region, but some senior wheat legislators such as Senator Clifford Young (R., North Dakota) worked harmoniously with committee Democrats; and wheat legislators did include some senior Democrats, such as Senate Majority Leader Mike Mansfield (D., Montana) and Senator Mike Monroney (D., Oklahoma).

The special attention previously given to the 15-acre provision recalls that some wheat is grown almost everywhere. Indeed, most rural congressmen had some interest in wheat, which is widely grown as a cash crop and which may be purchased for poultry feed. There is a problem in reconciling interests among regions in Congress, surmounted so far through leadership from the administration and from the friendly farm organizations.

SUMMARY

The high levels of production set under the Benson administration, resulting from increased yields of wheat per acre, continued during Secretary Freeman's first five years in office; acreage control measures, however, prevented further increases in total production. With total acreage held at little more than half that of the postwar high, enlarged cash exports and exports for food relief reduced government stocks until by 1966 wheat stocks were below the level considered as an adequate reserve.

The Freeman administration could be considered to be motivated by a liberal ideology in the sense that it viewed government as a constructive institution and it was ready to commit government to fulfilling needs. The Freeman administration was particularly sympathetic to unfulfilled needs with respect to food relief and rural development, to which it sought to commit the federal government more fully.

However the Freeman administration regarded themselves as political realists, who therefore gave first attention to the goals of reducing federal program costs (insisted upon by the presidential administration) and raising incomes of commercial farmers (insisted upon by the rural coalition in Congress and by friendly farm organizations).

Freeman began as an enthusiast of Food for Peace, but he found three reasons for caution with respect to it. One was a fear that farm income goals might be abandoned as the cost and volume of food aid increased. There was also fear that government might be saddled with the adjustment if needs for food were not as great as predicted. The Freeman administration was also realistic about mixed effects of food aid on recipients, and tried to insist that it be used in a constructive fashion. The only legitimate purpose for the aid was to develop self-sufficiency rather than to encourage dependence on a never-failing American cornucopia. America could not feed the world, and to pretend for a few years that it could would ultimately be injurious to others. The better posture for the task of self-development would be a desire to withdraw from food aid rather than a compulsion to give ever more.

The administration's income objective was also pragmatically derived. Giving deference to the respected parity standard, the administration attained not the postwar goal of full parity prices or even 90 percent of parity prices but rather the goal cited in the 1920s of the equivalent of full parity prices on the production used for domestic food. In the 1960s, however, less than half the crop was used for this purpose, the rest being exported at the much lower world price or sold for feed at the low feed grain price. The administration did take pains to see that the blend price would be such as to increase per capita farmer income moderately and that it should be attractive enough to gain congressional approval and farmer participation.

The objective of the acreage controls was to prevent increased production. Yet by permitting storage of hot wheat, interchange of feed grain and wheat allotment acreage, and other freedoms, the administration indicated that another objective of the commodity program was to stabilize incomes of wheat farmers in the Great Plains. In contrast, the 15-acre growers, mostly outside the Plains, were discouraged from growing wheat by being obliged to institute controls on their small acreages in order to receive certificates.

The Freeman administration happened to be wrong, at least over the short run, in its original assumptions about controls. Surplus reduction did not require compulsory controls. Farmers would not accept compulsory controls. Food needs were considerably larger than the Freeman administration had predicted. Fortunately the Freeman administration proved itself quite responsive to these errors and in fact claimed that its greatest achievement was in introducing greater flexibility in the commodity programs of the USDA.

With respect to strategy, the Freeman administration found it possible to capitalize on the circumstances of serious overproduction and surpluses in agriculture. As resources with which to pay for reductions in production, it used both the tremendous federal wheat stocks and the budget which had been required to accumulate and store the stocks. It also used the Food for Peace program as a means of disposing of stocks. Attention having been focused by Benson and others on the enormous size of the stocks, Freeman was able to cite reduced stock levels as a sign of his success.

In seeking leadership, the administration first assumed that achieving production control through the legislative process was impossible; therefore the administration asked Congress to delegate to the Secretary of Agriculture this power to write and implement programs. When Congress refused to delegate this power, the administration used strategies designed to obtain the desired programs from Congress. These included acceptance of the prevailing rationalizations for policy, and responsiveness to the prerogatives and the wishes of those in power within Congress. In recognition of the congressional preferences, policy was presented on a commodity-by-commodity basis. However farm bills were framed in the executive branch, containing commodity programs which anticipated the legislative compromises as well as programs meant to appeal to nonfarm interests, all within a comprehensive framework designed to achieve passage in the form preferred by the administration. In addition, the costs and benefits of programs were calculated in advance, at the request of the Budget Bureau and also as a means of minimizing the concessions necessary to gain congressional approval.

The groups supporting the Freeman administration, with the addition of an active National Association of Wheat Growers, were virtually the same ones which had supported the postwar Brannan administration and which had opposed Secretary Benson. However Freeman was more successful than Brannan in winning support from both southern and liberal Democrats, while being opposed on most commodity issues by the Farm Bureau and a united congressional Republican party.

USDA Photo

11 / MANAGEMENT OF GOVERNMENT STOCKS

Since 1938 U.S. government wheat stocks have been stored and distributed by the Commodity Credit Corporation. Some years the CCC (one of the biggest corporations in the world in terms of its $8 billion capitalization) has held a lien on a considerable portion of the U.S. wheat crop, by virtue of having extended price support loans to farmers. In recent years loans have been taken on only a fraction of the crop.

In addition, CCC has owned virtually all the U.S. carryover stocks in recent years, which amounted to more than a full year's crop in the late 1950s (Table 11.1). Using its stocks and its price support loans, the CCC could and did control the domestic wheat price. It sold its stocks in the market when the price reached 105 percent of the supported price (plus a year's carrying charges on the wheat), and if the price went very far below the support price, farmers cooperating under the price support program would take loans on their wheat and then let the federal government keep the collateral, thus reducing private supplies of wheat and increasing the price. Therefore the market price has generally hovered within a few cents of the supported price.

The Commodity Credit Corporation also furnished all the wheat to be exported or sent abroad as food surpluses during the 1950s; in

TABLE 11.1. CCC loans and inventory

Year	Inventory June 30	Pledged for CCC loan
	(million bushels)	
1938	. . .	85.7
1939	6.0	167.7
1940	1.6	278.4
1941	169.2	366.3
1942	319.7	408.1
1943	259.8	130.2
1944	99.1	180.5
1945	103.7	59.7
1946	. . .	22.0
1947	. . .	31.2
1948	.1	254.0
1949	227.2	335.3
1950	327.7	188.4
1951	196.4	199.5
1952	143.3	398.6
1953	470.0	494.0
1954	774.6	401.2
1955	975.9	277.1
1956	950.7	234.9
1957	823.9	223.6
1958	834.9	564.5
1959	1,146.6	299.1
1960	1,195.4	406.1
1961	1,242.5	262.4
1962	1,096.6	280.7
1963	1,082.5	161.6
1964	828.9	197.9
1965	646.3	170.1
1966	340.3	132.4
1967	123.6	. . .

Source: Commodity Credit Corporation-USDA.

addition it paid a subsidy to exporters (in wheat rather than in cash) as a means of making U.S. wheat competitive on the foreign market. In this capacity, the CCC was responsible for setting the price relationships between the various classes and grades of wheat.

Although the CCC was required to use the services of private enterprise wherever possible rather than to provide its own facilities in acquiring, storing, and distributing stocks, the CCC of course supervised those activities which it contracted from others. However the CCC was not an operating agency, despite the fact that much activity went on under its name. Instead it was simply the financial agent for the large USDA farm program agency, earlier called the Agricultural Adjustment Administration and in recent years called the Agricultural Stabilization Conservation Service (ASCS).[1] (Uuder Truman this agency was called the Production and Marketing Administration, and under Benson it was the Commodity Stabilization Service.) The principal officers of the USDA and the ASCS have constituted the board of directors of the CCC.

Here we will present a short history of the acquisition, management, and disposal of wheat stocks by the USDA. Since these tasks are, in the usual terminology, undertaken by the CCC, we shall for the most part use the designation CCC to refer to the officials and agents of the USDA who carry out the storage program.

STORAGE OPERATIONS

Adequate wheat storage capacity was a *sine qua non* of the wheat commodity program between 1939 and 1963, because loans could not be made, and thus prices could not be supported, unless there was a place to store the wheat furnished as collateral. Provision for adequate storage space was regarded as a solemn duty of every USDA administration regardless how it might feel about the wisdom of price support programs. This was especially true after President Truman made storage problems a significant political issue in the 1948 election. Even if adequate storage had not been demanded by farmer voters, the private and cooperative businesses which constructed and operated storage were present to exert considerable political influence. Since wheat under loan moved through the regular channels, and since it was impractical to reserve space for just the wheat which was under loan or delivered to CCC, in practice it was necessary for CCC to find storage for all the wheat and for all the other price-supported commodities that were produced in the United States.

Most of the storage space which was developed in response to surpluses was built by private corporations, cooperatives, and farmers. This preference for private over governmental facilities was a matter of CCC policy during the Benson administration and was also urged in the CCC Charter Act of 1949 which required the agency to use private channels whenever consistent with "the effective and efficient conduct of the Corporation's business." Private storage, however, was usually developed in the form of permanent facilities even though the surpluses stored in it were presumed to be temporary, and the

---

1. For a discussion of the relationship of CCC to the program agency, see Reed L. Frishknecht, "The Commodity Credit Corporation: A Case Study of a Government Corporation," *Western Political Quarterly* (September 1953), pp. 559–69.

costs of permanent, private storage were much greater than the costs of temporary storage constructed by the CCC.[2]

There were several periods of big surpluses. In 1942 and 1943 all facilities were taxed to the limit, even after modest wartime storage construction had been completed. Between 1949 and 1951 the surpluses of feed grains in turn put pressure on wheat storage facilities, and once again there were hurried efforts to expand storage capacity. Between 1953 and 1955 the wheat surplus stair-stepped to a billion bushels, but due to the strong incentives—mainly in the form of guaranteed high storage rates—given commercial storage construction, construction almost kept pace with needs. And when total stocks in the United States leapt upward again after 1957, to more than a billion and a half bushels, the United States had by then developed a magnificent system of granaries and handling facilities. By 1966 wheat and feed grains stocks had been reduced by more than half, and the United States then had a surplus of storage facilities. The owners of these facilities seemed quite as vocal in describing their hardships as the wheat producers had earlier been in lamenting their surplus.

In the pages which follow we will deal separately with three types of storage which have been used by CCC. These are CCC-constructed storage, commercial storage provided by private or cooperative enterprises, and storage on the farm (Table 11.2).

CCC STORAGE

The least expensive storage for CCC stocks was in facilities owned or leased by the CCC. During 1959, for example, the average cost per bushel for storage by CCC was less than 9 cents, while commercial storage rates averaged 16.5 cents per bushel.[3] Furthermore CCC's temporary storage was easier to cut back when surpluses disappeared. Yet Congress preferred private facilities on the whole, and there were similar preferences within the CCC. Under Democratic administrations, some leading officials of CCC were former representatives from the larger farm co-ops and were more outspoken against "nationalization of grain policy" than were the private concerns. Within Republican administrations the CCC membership included former commercial warehousemen.

As a result, CCC storage has increased sharply in emergencies and

---

2. U.S. House Committee on Government Operations, *Commodity Credit Corporation Grain Storage Activities*, House Rept. 2220 (1960), pp. 6–7.
3. Ibid.

TABLE 11.2. Wheat stored in the United States

Year	On farms	Terminal market, interior mills, elevators, and warehouses	Commodity Credit Corporation[a]	Total
		(000 bushels)		
1933	82,693	295,057	. . .	377,750
1934	61,103	211,790	. . .	272,893
1935	44,051	101,838	. . .	145,889
1936	43,137	97,296	. . .	140,433
1937	21,972	61,195	. . .	83,167[b]
1938	58,857	94,250	. . .	153,107
1939	88,016	161,999	. . .	250,015
1940	79,572	200,149	. . .	279,721
1941	86,675	298,058	. . .	384,733
1942	162,722	463,644	4,409	630,775
1943	189,574	370,333	58,990	618,897
1944	103,622	180,552	32,381	316,555
1945	87,703	167,777	23,700	279,180
1946	41,604	51,131	7,351	100,086
1947	40,501	42,836	500	83,837
1948	94,463	98,950	2,530	195,943
1949	66,505	236,983	3,797	307,285
1950	65,861	353,953	4,900	424,714
1951	76,275	320,594	3,002	399,871
1952	63,387	191,447	1,144	255,978
1953	79,163	518,017	8,364	605,544
1954	103,162	719,640	110,704	933,506
1955	40,644	852,940	142,594	1,036,178
1956	67,318	840,740	125,429	1,033,487
1957	59,920	757,900	91,010	908,830
1958	51,193	751,910	78,270	881,373
1959	114,913	1,099,086	81,067	1,295,066
1960	95,867	1,154,132	63,451	1,313,450
1961	137,098	1,203,682	70,559	1,411,339
1962	102,444	1,160,015	59,547	1,322,006
1963	95,544	1,061,362	38,317	1,195,223
1964	75,669	812,997	12,719	901,385
1965	132,515	673,691	11,049	817,255
1966	130,771	394,878	9,521	535,170
1967	145,479	278,528	997	425,004
1968[c]	228,471	307,941	750	537,162

Source: USDA.

a. Beginning July 1, 1942, wheat owned by CCC and stored in bins or other storage owned or controlled by CCC. Other wheat owned by CCC as well as wheat outstanding under loan is included in other positions.
b. Beginning with 1937, only old-crop wheat shown in all positions. For the years 1934–36 inclusive, some new wheat is included in terminal and merchant mill stock. The figure for July 1, 1937, including the new wheat, is 102,842,000 bushels.
c. Preliminary.

decreased following them. Some wheat was stored in prefabricated granaries and steel bins during a wheat storage crisis in 1942, after which these bins were emptied and disposed of. Having sold a 250-million-bushel steel bin capacity to farmers during the war, the CCC was then without adequate facilities at the onset of a second great storage crisis occurring in 1949.

At that time Secretary Brannan constructed CCC storage with a capacity of about 50 million bushels (only 5 million of which was devoted to wheat). This was intended partly as a yardstick against which to measure commercial storage costs. Secretary Benson was obliged to expand CCC storage in order to handle the unexpectedly large carryovers of 1953 and 1954. In 1953 CCC bought bins with a capacity of 96 million bushels, bringing the total CCC bin capacity to 640 million bushels for all grains.

The height of CCC grain storage of wheat was in 1955 when a total of 56.6 million bushels were stored in bins, and 85.3 million bushels were stored in ships. During the remaining years of the Benson administration this capacity was being phased out. By 1965 Secretary Freeman had ended fleet storage and had emptied most of the CCC wheat storage facilities. Thus CCC wheat storage went from zero in 1941 to 69 million bushels in 1943, from zero in 1947 to 5 million in 1950, and from 1 million in 1952 to a high of 143 million in 1953. By 1965 it was only 11 million bushels.

Given these rapid changes, errors in administration occurred—which Congress was alert to expose. The U.S. Senate Government Operations Committee found that a "substantial number" of the storage bins purchased by Secretary Brannan in 1949 and 1950 were defective, and the loss was calculated at about $1 million.[4] In 1954 the committee charged that the CCC should have profited from Brannan's misfortunes and should have instituted better inspection during the bin construction of 1954.

The U.S. House Appropriations Subcommittee on Agriculture found that inspection of stocks within the bins during the 1950s was inadequate. This committee found that local office managers or farm program committee members whose job it was to inspect the contents of government grain bins in the field in some cases were unqualified or inefficient, and that losses had resulted. By improper sampling, good grain had sometimes been mistakenly judged to be going "out of condition," in which case it had been sold at the bin site, but at prices quoted the day previous. This practice had permitted profiteer-

---

4. U.S. Senate Committee on Government Operations, *Inefficiencies in the Department of Agriculture Grain Bin Program,* Senate Rept. 1443 (1956), pp. 1–2.

ing. The committee also discovered a few thefts of grain from CCC bins. During the 1950s apparently the only large loss (about $1 million) resulted from a late decision (in 1955) to expand bin storage. Urgency had obliged the USDA to spread the work among several contractors rather than using only the low bidders. The committee also found some defective bins at this time.

However the sum of these losses was quite small compared with the amount of grain involved and also compared with the costs of errors in the management of grain held in commercial warehouses. With respect to all charges, CCC and Commodity Stabilization Service officials were accused of negligence or inefficiency rather than of fraud or dishonesty.[5]

Because the CCC had two unpredictable variables to take into account, overconstruction of bin space was also a recurring problem. One of these variables was the crop yield, and the other was the amount of private, commercial storage likely to be provided in a given region at a given time. For example, in 1954 according to the House Appropriations Committee report, the North Dakota State Commodity Stabilization Service surveyed storage needs there in view of the approaching harvest and asked the commercial storage firms to indicate the amount of wheat they wished to store during the coming year. Using these estimates, the CCC then constructed metal bins to store the difference between the expected yield and the commercial storage commitment—about 33 million bushels. At harvest, however, commercial warehouses found that they could handle considerably more than they had requested (Table 11.3). In accord with the policy preference for private storage, most of the CCC bins were left vacant and never subsequently used by CCC.[6]

Storage in "mothball" ships was another paradoxical episode. Secretary Benson's administration decided to use obsolete "victory" ships in 1953. By late 1955, 88 million bushels were stored at harbors in Virginia, New York, and the Pacific Northwest in these old ships with subdecks removed and with aerating equipment installed wherever necessary. The grain in these ships was preserved very well for periods up to nine years at very low cost, and these stocks had a special appeal to buyers because contents were generally of good quality and were not subject to subsequent mixing as might occur in port terminals. But again to conform with the policy of favoring commercial storage, and because there were buyers for this wheat,

5. U.S. House Appropriations Subcommittee on Agriculture, *Hearings on the Department of Agriculture Appropriations for 1957* (1956), part 1, pp. 8–9.
6. Ibid., pp. 17–18.

TABLE 11.3. Commercial warehouse, capacity and utilization

Date	Capacity	Utilization	Percent of utilization
		(bushels)	
Spring 1941	1,500,000ª	. . .	. . .
August 31, 1950	1,124,545ᵇ	. . .	. . .
August 20, 1952	1,240,377	. . .	. . .
December 30, 1953	1,324,007	. . .	. . .
December 1, 1954	1,834,113	. . .	. . .
April 30, 1955	1,930,160	. . .	. . .
March 31, 1957	2,537,189	1,308,006	51.55
March 31, 1958	2,813,583	1,721,411	61.18
March 31, 1959	3,576,435	2,263,881	63.30
March 31, 1960	4,189,921	2,449,791	58.47
March 31, 1961	4,489,150	2,674,684	59.58
March 31, 1962	4,879,632	2,420,496	49.60
March 31, 1963	4,739,759	2,095,704	44.22
March 31, 1964	4,657,960	1,880,046	40.36
March 31, 1965	4,694,912	1,447,157	30.82

Source: USDA.
a. *Wheat Situation,* USDA-BAE (May 1941), p. 15.
b. Numbers since 1950 are for commercial warehouses participating in the Uniform Grain Storage Agreement, including most commercial grain warehouses, and including all those which stored U.S. government stocks.

a decision was made in 1962 to dispose of "fleet stocks." This decision, proposed during the Cuban Crisis, was carried out in 1963.

Akin to this method of storage, for which virtually the only costs were those in loading and unloading, was the proposal by Arctic explorer Admiral Byrd to store all surpluses on Antarctica. At the height of the surplus crush in 1956, the USDA was said to be giving serious consideration to Byrd's proposal.

COMMERCIAL STORAGE

The bulk of the stocks owned by CCC or under loan was stored in commercial warehouses. These included the country elevators where farmers brought their grain, and where CCC preferred to leave it as long as possible to avoid unnecessary transportation and handling expenses. These "line" or "country" elevators and the nearby central storage complexes experienced enormous growth during the Benson era. Other commercial storers were the milling firms which expanded their normal storage facilities to take advantage of CCC storage rates. In addition, private contractors built storage space or renovated abandoned buildings. Finally, the great port or terminal elevators were also expanded considerably during the 1950s. Most of the commercial storage facilities were privately owned, with farmer cooperatives accounting for part of the total.

It is not possible to give a breakdown of the amount of commercial wheat storage capacity, since wheat storage alternated with that of other grains and other storable products. However wheat and corn were the principal surpluses leading to expansion of total grain storage facilities from about 1.5 billion bushels total capacity in 1941 to 2.2 billion in 1951.[7] It was during this period that the producers' cooperatives, from which so much had been expected with so few concrete results during the 1920s, finally became financially strong. A chief means of encouragement to the growth of cooperative grain storage was in the form of very generous loans granted through the USDA's Bank for Cooperatives. Secretary of Agriculture Claude Wickard noted proudly that one of the biggest grain co-ops, the Farmers' Union Grain Terminal Association, grew from a net worth of $30,000 during 1938 to a net worth of $6 billion in 1944. Undoubtedly, easy credit, plus the high storage payments extended by sympathetic administrations (and these included all the USDA administrations during the period from 1938 to 1966), added more substance to the grain-oriented cooperatives than all the official encouragement given them during the 1920s.

While all administrations favored the growth of cooperatives, they were not equally sympathetic toward commercial storage in general. When stocks began to build under Secretary Brannan in 1949, the CCC began a limited program for expanding commercial storage, guaranteeing partial occupancy in future years for new facilities constructed in areas where additional space was needed. However Brannan refused to conduct an all-out commercial storage construction program on the grounds that there would not be adequate time in which to build commercial storage. Brannan relied mainly on farm storage and on CCC facilities and other temporary construction to handle the overflow from 1949 to 1951.

It remained for Secretary Benson to assume that surpluses were a long-term reality, and to provide the incentives needed—high storage rates and guaranteed use—which induced rapid growth of commercial storage. In the eight years Benson served, commercial storage capacity was more than doubled—to 5 billion bushels by 1960. (The warehouse capacity included under CCC's United Grain Storage Agreement, in which CCC stocks could be stored, was 4.5 billion bushels in late 1960, an estimated 85 percent of total commercial storage.

7. *Wheat Situation,* USDA-BAE (May 1941); (January—March 1952), table 7.

The momentum of storage construction continued up to late 1961, for a high of 4.8 billion bushels of approved commercial storage.)

Thus most commercial storage in existence during the 1960s had been constructed after 1951, in response to the very attractive storage rates offered by the Benson administration. Commercial storage rates per bushel, which were 10 cents in 1949, were raised by Benson in 1954 to 16–18 cents, at a time when technical changes had actually lowered the cost of constructing permanent storage. The principal technical economy was the development of huge metal bins, the cost of which was only about 30 cents per bushel of storage. These could be constructed as satellites around a concrete elevator, the cost of which was about 80 cents per bushel of storage at that time. Given the high levels of storage rates, these structures could be paid for in a very few years.

There were still other incentives. Rapid depreciation was allowed for federal income tax purposes, and in 1954 the "use guarantees" such as Brannan had employed, but with more generous terms under Benson, were reinstituted for commercial storage.[8] In addition, the costs of receiving and handling the wheat in storage were paid by the federal government. Added to these income sources, commercial warehouses could also exploit the tolerances allowed for changes in weather, changes in moisture content, and grading errors. The wheat stocks of CCC could sometimes be mixed with lower-quality stocks in the same warehouse to improve the grade of the latter without technically reducing the quality of the former.

The high storage rates inevitably came under congressional criticism and ultimately were reduced. Three USDA rate studies confirmed that rates were much higher than were needed for a reasonable profit. The rates were lowered, under continuing objections from the warehousemen, down to 12–14 cents in 1959. In the meantime, however, the high rates had accomplished the desired objective of expanding permanent commercial storage facilities.

As surplus stocks were reduced after 1961 the percentage of warehouse occupancy decreased also. Whereas in June of 1958 CCC stocks had filled 73 percent of total rated storage capacity, by June of 1965 they used only 27 percent.

Before the age of surpluses it had been customary for commercial bins to be nearly empty toward the end of each year, but it was difficult to readjust to these former circumstances even for those firms which did still rely on the traditional income sources—those

---

8. *Wheat Situation*, USDA-BAE (February 1954).

of buying, processing, and delivering the grain. Under the circumstances, competition for commercial storage became keen—with resort to rate-cutting, bonuses, and gifts and other devices to entice grain into the bins. Meanwhile commercial storage interests sought adjustments in farm legislation.

Administration of Commercial Storage. The supervision or management of CCC wheat surpluses stored by commercial firms was a success story, partly because it was easy enough for the private interests to make an honest dollar and profitable enough that all the facilities needed were provided. Questions were frequently raised in Congress, and most of these questions were answered satisfactorily. There were a few scandals, minor in terms of the volume of business done.[9]

In a much discussed 1949 case, which came at a time when available storage facilities were taxed to the limit, a small firm leased an unused military facility and then contracted to store wheat in it. This venture became a subject of a committee investigation and prompted a wave of indignation based on the use of government facilities to reap a handsome government fee. But as Secretary Brannan's report of this case noted;

> Whether or not [the profit was unreasonable] in the case of this warehouse man or anyone of the other 12,500 warehouse men turns on the per-unit charge specified in the contract. The important point to note is that this warehouse man received the identical amount for storing a bushel of corn that any other warehouse man in the country received.
>
> On the contrary there is reason to believe that this particular warehouse man may have made less than many old-line established firms.[10]

A 1955 investigation by the same committee found no substantial illegal or corrupt activities. Its recommendations were mainly directed to tightening up the standards for grading grain and eliminating a few other loopholes by which legitimate profits had been made at the expense of CCC. The committee's recommenda-

9. There were a number of congressional investigations of CCC operations and surplus management, including the following: U.S. House Appropriations Subcommittee on Agriculture, *Hearings on Warehousing Practices, Commodity Credit Corporation* (1952); House, *Commodity Credit Corporation Grain Storage Activities;* Senate, *Inefficiencies in the Department of Agriculture Grain Bin Program;* House, *Hearings on the Agriculture Appropriations for 1957;* U.S. Senate Committee on Agriculture and Forestry, *Hearings on Investigation of Grain Storage Operations of CCC* (1960); U.S. House Committee on Agriculture, *Hearings on Storage Operations of CCC* (1959).
10. House, *Hearings on Warehousing Practices, Commodity Credit Corporation,* p. 31.

tions were mainly aimed at providing support for proposals already made by the responsible government agency for tightening up the standard agreement with the warehousemen. The committee's staff said that proposals of the Commodity Stabilization Service for improving these contracts, if adopted, would remedy the deficiencies or loopholes found in the existing contract.

Criticisms of commercial storage administration during Secretary Benson's administration were directed more against high rates than against fraud. By the time Benson took office, the responsible USDA agency (the Commodity Stabilization Service) had been given an adequate staff with experienced warehouse inspectors, who inspected commercial warehouses twice annually to determine the amount, the grade, and the condition of the grain, and who also inspected the grain on its arrival at terminal facilities. Prior to 1955 routine inspections of country or line elevators had been conducted by county CSS offices, but regional inspectors took over this task after a few local offices demonstrated a lack of expertise or lack of a strong desire to maintain standards. Firms which violated the rules of the contracts could be suspended from the list approved for CCC storage. As the rules were clarified and the regulators at all levels became expert, CCC was not reluctant to bring violators to court.

Other safeguards against corruption included the attention given to storage administration by the congressional committees, the internal audits and other administrative double-checking, cooperation in prosecution of offenders by the Department of Justice, and the supplementary oversight by local farmer committeemen.

Perhaps the greatest incentive for honesty in the conduct of this vast storage operation was the interest of the commercial grain storage trade in avoiding major scandals. A number of decision makers in the CCC under Secretary Benson were respected members of the established warehouse trade. With CCC paying such extraordinary rates, and with the prospect of more and more surpluses to be stored, the established trade had good reason to avoid a storage scandal. The powers and the agencies of government were therefore effectively used by these experienced men as means of self-discipline but also as a means of eliminating the marginal operators who for one reason or another could not observe the rules of the game under which the established firms made profits.

Still another explanation of CCC success in supervising commercial storage of surpluses was the availability of adequate storage after 1955. It seems most irregularities occurred earlier when space needs were greater than available commercial facilities.

A number of congressional investigations did find irregularities resulting in substantial losses to CCC. These investigations were undertaken as a result of criticisms of policies on the part of opposition political party leaders and also because of the desire of rural legislators to avoid scandals which would embarrass the price-support program. One irregularity between 1949 and 1951 was acceptance of gifts by USDA employees in some regional offices from the enterprises with whom they dealt. Though no large "payoffs" were documented, the manager and his assistant in the Dallas commodity program office were dismissed because of collusion with contractors. In addition, some thefts of grain occurred. The Senate investigation of 1952 concluded that there had been embezzlement or criminal conversion (stealing) of CCC grain by 131 warehousemen (out of 13,000), at a loss to the government of $10 million. One commentator noted with respect to these findings, however, that CCC's record appeared rather good when compared with the total of 400 bank embezzlements reported during 1951.[11]

Nevertheless the committee criticized the CCC for being "slow to recognize danger signals and take corrective action, . . . slow to take adequate measures once shortages . . . occurred, . . . slow in facing up to certain of the problems in grain storage and inventory control, . . . and slow to recognize the necessity of internal controls, . . . failed to bring in specially trained personnel in warehousing . . . and other fields, . . . too tolerant of inefficiency in responsible positions."[12]

Yet some loopholes and errors were discovered in the 1950s. Frost-damaged wheat from Canada, imported on condition that it be used domestically only for livestock feed, was for a brief period mixed with wheat which was owned by CCC and programmed for export. Foreign recipients of this down-graded wheat asked for a reduction in the contract price, and in the future were more likely to distrust the quality of American wheat.

Also criticized were shipments of some surpluses from the Plains states to storage facilities on the West Coast, at a transportation cost of up to 50 cents per bushel. This had been done on the assumption, later shown to be of doubtful validity, that the space previously occupied was needed for the upcoming harvest, and that the commodities were needed on the Pacific Coast to meet export and local demand.[13]

---

11. *Wayne Darrow's Washington Farmletter* (Feb. 2, 1952).
12. U.S. Senate Committee on Agriculture and Forestry, *Study of Storage and Processing Activities of the Commodity Credit Corporation,* Senate Rept. 2048 (1952).
13. House, *Hearings on the Agriculture Appropriations for 1957,* p. 72.

As earlier noted, the CCC profited from this congressional concern, and in the process was allowed more resources with which to supervise the storage program.

FARM STORAGE

Storage of wheat on the farm was not in most cases as efficient as storage in nearby grain elevators, because it was in effect an extra movement of wheat, little of which was actually used on the farm.[14] Yet new storage technology made it possible to store wheat safely in farm granaries, except in humid areas where rot and insect infestation were unsolved problems. It was also possible to move wheat in and out of farm storage with relative ease. Farm handling of wheat nevertheless remained more time-consuming than handling in country elevators, and in practice much farm-stored wheat did deteriorate.

Farm storage has been an important part of the storage system in the United States for several reasons. In the era of the threshing machine, and before the motorized truck, the quickly harvested wheat simply had to be stored on the farm. Farmers spent many winter days hauling wagonloads to a rail junction. Much existing farm storage space was built then, and in fact the total amount of farm storage space has grown relatively little during the era of trucks.

More recently rail transportation has been overloaded during the harvest season, especially during wars and in bumper harvests, so that much of the crop could go no further than the country elevator, which until the 1950s had little room for storage.

During periods when commercial storage space was inadequate, new crops tended to reduce the efficiency of facilities by filling spaces needed for the handling of grain. To prevent this, restrictions were laid down against the movement of newly harvested wheat so that farmers desiring price support loans were obliged to store the wheat on their farms.

Still another reason for farm storage was the desire of CCC and private handlers to move grain as little as possible before its ultimate destination became known. Henry Wallace's reason for farm storage of surpluses might also be recalled: he thought that farmers would be readier to cooperate in production controls if they could see the surpluses out their back door.

14. Thomas E. Hall, "Grain Storage Costs Less in the Elevators," *Co-op Grain Quarterly* (Winter 1953–54), pp. 59–63.

Finally, so long as the CCC was paying costs, it often seemed good politics to pay the storage fees to farmers rather than to the warehouses. Under Democratic administrations, the CCC tended to regard farm storage and commercial storage as equal in value and usually paid the same rates for both. Indeed, CCC sometimes provided greater incentives for the construction of farm storage than it did for commercial storage.

Until the 1950s about half the crop was stored on the farm when harvested. Farm storage space was relatively flexible, since it could be constructed quickly and since existing structures such as vacant theaters, schools, or hotels could be converted to use for "farm" storage. In World War II wheat under loan was even stored in "victory ditches."

Farm storage of wheat under CCC loan was authorized at the beginning of the loan program (in 1938), although a number of problems were always recognized. Regulations were made at the start with respect to the condition of the grain to be placed in farm storage, the condition of the storage facilities, treatment against insect damage, improper removal or use of grain pledged to the federal government, and larceny. These regulations were enforced by county and state farm program offices, under the supervision of the USDA's farmer committeemen, who were to inspect the grain at the time a loan was granted on it and two or three times subsequently during the year.

One problem in farm storage has been the difficulty in enforcing these regulations. The USDA farmer committees were reluctant to press criminal charges against farmers who covertly "borrowed" from bins which had been sealed under government loan, or to penalize farmers severely for allowing the grain to deteriorate. Federal attorneys in the wheat areas have similarly managed to avoid prosecuting farmers for violation of the storage laws.

Dishonesty and carelessness have been the exception rather than the rule. Farm storage has been satisfactory on the whole; the really serious losses occurred when, due to inadequate space, the CCC was obliged to permit commercial storage in inferior facilities.

The amount of wheat under loan stored on the farm has varied considerably. In December 1938 over 25 percent of the wheat under loan was in farm storage.[15] When the farm storage crisis occurred in 1953, a majority of the wheat under loan was farm stored.

The CCC has provided various incentives for farm storage. Initially, from 1938 through the 1950 crop, the CCC made a storage

15. *Wheat Studies of the Stanford Food Research Institute,* 15(December 1938):133.

payment (7 cents and later 10 cents per bushel) to the farmer for farm-stored wheat under loan. This payment amounted to a per bushel subsidy, as evidenced by the fact that the wheat price dropped 10 cents when the payment came to an end in 1951. In addition, producers in those areas where insect damage is not heavy were invited to "reseal" their collateral wheat at the end of the year covered by the loan and for the next year or longer to receive the same attractive storage rate that the CCC paid commercial warehouses. If the grain was ultimately redeemed by the producer, he paid an annual interest charge of 3 to 4 percent on his loan. If it was not redeemed, he paid no interest.

The main purpose of reseal, so long as storage was inadequate, was to encourage the construction and use of farm storage. Other purposes included reducing CCC problems of handling and storage and giving farmers more time in which to decide to repay loans.

The Benson administration tended to discourage reseal by restricting it to a few areas where the natural environment was excellent (mainly the Northern Plains) and restricting it also to areas where there happened to be a local shortage of commercial facilities. This de-emphasis on farm storage was partly from a desire to improve quality of wheat offered in the market and to meet objections raised by the U.S. Food and Drug Administration against certain chemical residues resulting from treatment of farm-stored grain, and other unhealthy materials found in wheat sold for food.

After the surplus had been reduced to a point where adequate commercial facilities were available, the reseal program with its storage payments became mainly a method by which farm legislators and the Democratic administration tried to channel a maximum of the storage fees to farmers. Farm storage through reseal was continued and increased during the period of declining stocks (Table 11.4), mainly because of political pressure favoring it from the Northern Plains states.

Administrators of the USDA have also used the reseal programs as a way to reduce the statistics of surpluses. Technically resealed wheat still belonged to farmers because they could sell it on the market. Therefore this wheat, though carried from year to year, was not counted as part of the CCC stocks. Despite this fiction, resealed wheat in 1964 resulted in losses to the CCC of $79 million, and virtually all of this resealed wheat was destined for delivery to CCC ultimately, since the new wheat program had reduced market prices below the levels of the original loan.

Reseal was provided for the crops of 1938 through 1941, for

TABLE 11.4. CCC reseal loan storage expense for wheat

Fiscal year	Cost
1953	$ 19,085.37
1954	1,936,739.07
1955	2,208,580.68
1956	2,967,804.32
1957	40,656.02
1958	1,898,588.93
1959	3,559,441.31
1960	9,584,925.78
1961	10,552,731.70
1962	10,816,136.77
1963	8,114,376.98
1964	9,253,813.45
1965	8,671,343.31
1966	10,503,825.00
1967	6,938,367.00
1968	12,525,369.00
Total	$99,591,784.69

Source: USDA.

1944, 1948, and 1949, and continuously from 1952. Most resealed wheat was kept for only an extra year or two, although relatively small portions of each crop have been resealed for as long as six years.

DEVELOPMENT OF FARM STORAGE

An indirect incentive for development of farm storage has been the fact that wheat could otherwise not be placed under loan because of the lack of available commercial storage facilities during years when the crop was large and the market price was low. CCC provided various incentives on such occasions for the construction of more farm storage, often to the point of assuring farmers financial profit from building a granary.

When storage space was needed in 1941 the USDA extended financial assistance under the Agricultural Conservation Payments Program (the program whose main objective was soil improvement) for part of the costs of building or repairing farm storage. A storage allowance was paid by CCC to farmers who stored the 1941 wheat crop under loan, and a rate of 7 cents per bushel was paid for the same purpose in 1942. Since the loan rate was well above the market price at that time, farmers could make about 25 cents per bushel profit—more than the total cost of the storage facility—by constructing a granary and storing the wheat under loan rather than selling it on the market. In both 1941 and 1942 farmers were also urged to store wheat produced in excess of the allotment, which could be sold in a future year when yield on alloted acres was below "normal." During the early war years wheat farmers were given a priority in purchasing scarce lumber and nails to be used for granaries. CCC sold farmers prefabricated bins on easy terms and also moved steel bins from the Midwest, later to sell them to wheat farmers at low prices. The first test of steel bins for wheat storage came in 1942, and they proved to be best and least expensive for temporary storage.

In 1949, as stocks again began to accumulate, Secretary Brannan offered a somewhat different but very attractive set of incentives. Farmers were offered loans at 4 percent interest for amounts equal to 85 percent of the initial cost of the farm granary, with the privilege of "working off" the loan through storage of reseal grain, and even of deferring payments on the loan in the event of a poor crop. Some of these incentives established by Brannan were continued into the 1960s, and as a result 222 million dollars were loaned by CCC as of 1966 to finance farm storage structures with an aggregate capacity of 798 million bushels for all storable crops. During the 1950s, however, new construction for farm-stored wheat did little more than balance out the abandonment of obsolete storage. The amount of wheat stored on the farm remained stable while the amount in commercial storage tripled in the 1950s. Under Freeman, who reasserted a preference for farm storage, the amount in farm storage increased while commercial storage was declining by half.

ACQUISITION OF CCC STOCKS

CCC stocks were acquired in three ways—by purchases in the marketplace, by purchase agreements with farmers, and by taking ownership of wheat which had been offered as collateral for price support loans.

Purchases in the marketplace were used during periods of scarcity, in order to obtain commodities needed for relief and aid programs. The other two devices were used to retire market surpluses. Under purchase agreements farmers contracted to sell their wheat to the government at the loan rate. Under the loan procedure farmers pledged their wheat to the government as collateral in return for a loan, the amount of which was based on the support price of the wheat. Under either device farmers were free to sell their wheat on the market during the marketing season lasting up to ten months. Acquisitions through purchase agreements have been only about as large as those through loans.

We may recall that a difference of opinion existed as to whether the loan rate should be used as a device for raising farm prices. Favoring this in 1938 were farm legislators and the Farm Bureau; favoring it in the postwar period were farm legislators, Democratic administrations, and the National Farmers Union. Opposed to this position and preferring to use the loan rate only to discourage wide or seasonal fluctuations while letting the market demand determine the price were Wallace in 1938, and the Republican Party, Secretary Benson, and the Farm Bureau in the postwar period.

In both eras the advocates of using loan rates to raise prices won the battle. The first objective of the CCC loan program in 1940 was "to protect and increase farm prices."[16] Wheat prices were pushed up at that time despite an oversupply, and following the war the "rigid" 90-percent-of-parity supports were established by Congress, oblivious to the supply situation. Benson succeeded in reducing the price support loan rate to 75 percent of a modernized parity standard, but the new, lower price support level nevertheless remained the peg for the market price. As it was for the two-price plan first implemented for the 1964 crop, the original intent was to permit market prices to fall in line with a drastically reduced support price. However the USDA did not continue to hold domestic and world prices down at the loan level, due to a tight supply situation as well as pressure from wheat spokesman.

Except in the recent case, average annual prices have followed very closely the many changes in price support loan levels. While supports were fixed at the 90-percent-of-parity rate, during 1944 to 1955, changes reflected in the parity index resulted in price increases from $1.41 to $2.12. Under Benson's flexible supports, descending ultimately to 75 percent of the modernized parity, prices fell to a 1960 average of $1.74. For 1962 the price support was set at $2.00 and for 1963 it was reduced to $1.82 plus an 18-cents government payment. In 1964, under the domestic certificate or two-price program, the price of wheat followed the loan rate temporarily down to 50 percent of parity.

The other, noncontroversial, function of the loan rate was to prevent seasonal fluctuations disadvantageous to farmers. About half the wheat crop was ordinarily sold by farmers during the first quarter of the season. If the market price at harvest time were much

16. The various functions of loan prices are discussed in Geoffrey Shepherd, "Stabilization Operations of the Commodity Credit Corporation," *J. Farm Econ.*, 24(August 1942):597.

below the loan rate, the local farm program agencies urged farmers to put their wheat under loan—and thus to be guaranteed the loan price—while benefiting from any end-of-season price rises. This diversion of wheat into storage would at the same time raise current prices. The CCC viewed its task as well done when by this device prices were held close to the loan rate throughout the year.

As a rule, the market averaged a few cents below the loan, due to the inconvenience involved in negotiating the loan. Making a loan involved little expense, since the storage had to be paid in any case if the wheat were to be held for end-of-season sale (and until 1951 farmers in most areas received storage payments from CCC for farm-stored wheat under loan). The interest on the loan was payable only if the farmer decided to redeem the wheat and sell it at a higher market price.

In most years the average market price was less than 7 cents below the loan rate, but for several reasons it sometimes dipped further. In 1952 and 1953, prices were 17 cents and 12 cents, respectively, below the loan rate, probably in part because of the uncertainty about the future of farm programs. The main reason for the lower price in these years and in 1954 was the mechanical difficulty in acquiring such a large surplus production. Commodity Credit Corporation took 48 percent of the 1953 wheat crop under loan, little of which was ever redeemed by farmers, but even this amount was not enough to keep the price up. More wheat was not put under loan because a considerable amount of poor-quality wheat did not qualify for a loan, and also, according to some critics, because the USDA was not as alert as it might have been in informing farmers about the surplus situation.

On the other hand, prices went well above the loan rate in periods of real scarcity. These occurred during marketing of the 1946, 1947, and 1948 crops, when CCC had no stocks at all.

Whenever the market price did threaten to rise well above the loan rate in the presence of large CCC stocks, CCC usually sold these stocks on the market to hold the price down. It was authorized though not obliged to sell its stocks at or above 105 percent of the support price (plus carrying charges). Thus, if the loan rate were $2.00, CCC could sell wheat whenever the market price reached or exceeded about $2.10 plus the ordinary carrying charges incurred since the most recent harvest. After 1961 CCC was able to sell substantial amounts in this way, and when the wheat certificate program went into effect, CCC sales at first pushed wheat prices down to near 50 percent of the parity level, which was slightly below world prices. Although this action was protested,[17] the concept was that of Wallace's ever-normal granary, from which CCC stocks had been an outgrowth. Wallace had assumed that the ever-normal granary was to be used for the benefit of the consumer as well as the farmer.

There were other reasons for this "resell" policy during the 1960s which resulted in a storm of farmer protest. One was that "voluntary" control programs of the 1960s presumably could not be effective if noncompliers were adequately rewarded in the marketplace. It seems apparent that some of those wishing to discourage CCC grain sales actually wished to reduce the farm program effectiveness. Harry Graham, testifying at a 1966 hearing in behalf of the Grange, suggested that this was so:

> We [the Grange] do not have any elevators. We have no particular interest at that point. We do have the conviction that a great deal of pressure to change the existing law comes from organizations that have very much of an interest in elevators and elevator storage. . . .
>
> We are convinced that this change (limiting CCC sales) would slow down, stop, and probably reverse the trend toward the reduction of Government stocks and, consequently, elevator space utilization.[18]

The list of witnesses at this hearing, and their views, seemed to bear out Graham's position. The Wheat Growers, like the Grange, opposed legislation which would impede the secretary from selling CCC grain. On the other side were the Farmers' Union Grain Terminal Association, interested in grain storage as well as farm programs, who joined other cooperative and commercial storage spokesmen. The latter group included the grain-marketing exchanges where wheat was bought and sold. The grain-marketing exchanges, like commercial storage interests, wanted free-ranging prices, despite the fact that the volume of sales on the exchanges (within the existing 7- to 10-cent price range permitted by the USDA) was the highest on historical record.

Another supporter of this position, the Farm Bureau, also wanted to keep CCC stocks off the market because Farm Bureau frankly believed that the wheat program was a mistake and should be abolished. Farm Bureau objected particularly to the sales from CCC stocks of the types of high-protein wheat which would otherwise command premium prices on the market.[19]

17. U.S. Senate Committee on Agriculture and Forestry, *Hearings on Minimum Resale Price of CCC Wheat* (1966).
18. Ibid., p. 14.
19. Ibid., pp. 20–28.

Another reason for objecting to a stable price, rarely stated forthrightly, was that such a price limited profits from futures trading. Farmers who were obliged to sell their wheat at harvesttime could be pleased that the price at the end of the year would likely differ only to the extent of reflecting the additional storage costs. Not so the commercial warehousemen and other "middlemen" who were denied profits which they might otherwise have obtained by holding wheat for sale at higher end-of-season prices.

A further criticism of CCC resale policies was that they tended to discourage the private trade from carrying stocks over from year to year. During the 1950s private carryover tended to be less than 50 million bushels, particularly when price supports were expected to be reduced for the next crop. Though CCC could do little about it at that time, the practice of depleting inventories did seem contrary to the spirit of the provision in the 1949 CCC Charter Act, which directed CCC "to establish prices, terms, and conditions that will not discourage or deter manufacturers, processors, and dealers from acquiring and carrying normal inventories of the current crop." There was less basis for this objection under the subsequent certificate program. In both 1964 and 1965 well over 100 million bushels were in private hands at the end of the marketing year.

DISPOSITION OF CCC STOCKS

Almost every year the CCC acquired some commodities through default of loans. The biggest annual acquisitions of the CCC predictably occurred when supply was larger than demand, particularly in the 1953–54 and 1958–59 marketing years when CCC took over more than one third of the total crop.

When it had large stocks, CCC made considerable efforts to get rid of them. It disposed of the stocks in several ways, including cash sales on the domestic market when the price permitted. In 1962, 77 million bushels of CCC wheat were sold on the domestic market; in 1963, 25 million bushels; in 1964, 70 million bushels; and in 1965, 106 million bushels (Table 11.5).

Other outlets for CCC wheat were as follows:

1. Cash exports. A relatively small portion of the total U.S. cash exports came from CCC stocks. Usually these were sent abroad under a special commodity export arrangement to a country which preferred to deal with the CCC rather than with private traders.

TABLE 11.5. CCC sales of wheat, including barter

Fiscal year	Sales for dollars		P.L. 480			Barter export	Payment-in-kind Unrestricted use	Export
	Domestic	Export	Title I	Title II	Title IV			
	(million bushels)							
1962	76.7	4.2	85.6	18.9	...	41.7	...	48.0
1963	24.6	13.0	100.1	24.0	1.5	7.2	...	37.6
1964	70.2	37.4	78.0	22.4	2.4	34.7	9.0	92.0
1965	106.4	14.1	27.7	8.3	3.3	12.8	35.9	75.1
1966	18.6	5.5	74.7	22.4	13.2	45.4	...	151.1
1967	26.3	8.3	a	14.0	a	14.3	...	158.4

Source: USDA-ASCS–BU/CPB (Sept. 11, 1967).

a. Included in export sales for dollars; breakdown not available.

Most of the stocks for export came from the commercial market. However after 1956 the export subsidy paid by CCC to exporters to make up the difference between the commercial price and the export price was in the form of a payment in kind from CCC stocks. Large amounts of CCC wheat entered the export market by this method.

2. On various occasions in 1942, 1943, 1944, and 1945, substantial quantities of wheat were sold for animal feed. In all years relatively small amounts of deteriorated CCC wheat were sold at reduced prices, generally to be used for feed.

3. The domestic food disposal program utilized some wheat, but more often it was in the form of flour, which was in some cases purchased on the commercial market. During surplus years it really did not matter much whether wheat for such purposes was purchased from CCC or on the market, since CCC was destined to own the total carryover.

4. The principal outlet for CCC wheat has been in food aid abroad. This has been the most flexible outlet for CCC stocks.

SUMMARY

Storage operations were essential to the operation of price support programs since 1938. The Commodity Credit Corporation, financial agent of the USDA administration, was judged by its capacity to anticipate burgeoning storage needs and to manage a multibillion-dollar public enterprise without major scandal. These criteria for success were related, in that scandals tended to occur in connection with last-minute storage construction or on the occasion of a shortage of adequate facilities.

Among three types of storage, farmer spokesmen preferred farm storage, while cooperative and business interests preferred commercial storage. The third type of storage was that owned by the CCC, often least expensive and most flexible. Storage preferences differed somewhat by administration, with Republicans favoring commercial storage while Democrats encouraged on-the-farm storage. Democrats were also more likely than Republicans to rely on government-owned facilities.

The big surplus bulge occurred during the Benson administration, which foresaw its development, despite hopes to the contrary, and generously subsidized the massive expansion of commercial grain storage and handling facilities. When surpluses came to an end under Freeman, most commercial storage firms presumably managed to shift to other income sources without major hardship, although they did so reluctantly.

12 / DISTRIBUTION OF PRODUCER BENEFITS

FOLLOWING the common strategy for enacting wheat legislation in Congress, as we have seen, representatives of the affected producers develop a program on which affected producers can agree; then, assuming that few other interested parties are unsatisfied by the program, they rely upon the united support of producers to achieve passage.

Thus the actual process of developing legislation, both within the executive branch and in the congressional committees, seems to be one of hard bargaining between groups of producers. Provisions are designed with a view to the interests of specific producers; therefore each group agrees to support provisions favorable to others in return for support for provisions favorable to itself. The process of enacting commodity programs is essentially an exercise in political logrolling. The purpose in this chapter is to describe the distribution of benefits which results from this policy process.

Important differences among producers give rise to the bargaining strategy. These include differences between commodities, among

292

wheat regions, as to the size of farm, and between owners and tenants. Regional and commodity differences, substantial issues in the logrolling process, are much reflected in the law. Until recently less attention has been given to differences as to ownership and size of farm, although distribution of benefits is greatly affected by these differences.

WHEAT VERSUS FEED GRAINS

Wheat policy is related to policy for other commodities, particularly policies for crops used as animal feed (feed grains), because wheat and other feed grains can be produced on the same acreage and can be put to the same uses. On much cropland wheat may be an alternative to corn, barley, sorghum (maize), rye, or oats, depending on the relative returns.

Wheat is itself an excellent feed grain, although wheat policy until 1962 assumed that the amount of grain used for that purpose would be insignificant. With diets in advanced countries including more of animal products and less of cereals, wheat and feed grains programs since 1962 have been designed to facilitate a shift of acreage from wheat to other grains and also to expedite the use of wheat for animal food. This new flexibility, gained by relating wheat and other feed grains in government programs based on their comparability as sources of animal feed, also permitted a shift toward using more wheat for food in response to food needs in the underdeveloped countries.

Regional lines help define the relationship of feed grain and wheat producers. The dominant feed grain is corn, raised in a belt of rich land in the humid Central Midwest. Other grains have lower yields per acre and can be produced on the less-valuable acreages. Barley is found throughout the Midwest, mainly on its fringes, and is a strong competitor to wheat in North Dakota and Minnesota. Grain sorghum is a strong competitor to wheat in sorghum's homeland, the Southern Plains. The other major feed grain is oats, which tends to be a weak contender in all the areas where other grains are grown (Fig. 12.1).

Wheat usually does not yield as much animal feed per acre as corn, barley, sorghum, oats, and other feed grains. Yet in some arid areas when side benefits of wheat are counted in, such as pasturage during the wheat incubation period, wheat can indeed be raised and fed more efficiently per nutritive unit in those areas than any feed grain. Also in favor of wheat feeding are the habits of cash wheat growers, who may continue to raise wheat even after statistical projections of

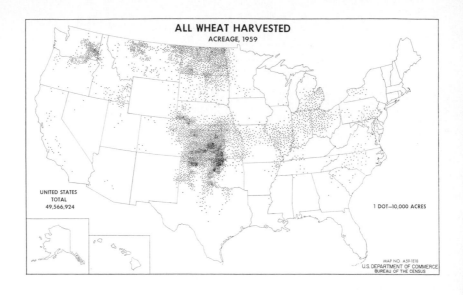

FIG. 12.1. Where commodities are grown. These maps reveal that corn, cotton, and wheat are regional commodities with overlapping areas. Sorghum is a feed crop alternating with wheat in the Southern Plains.

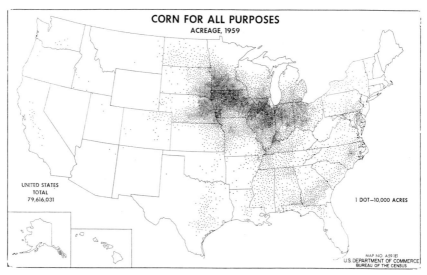

SORGHUMS FOR ALL PURPOSES
ACREAGE, 1959

UNITED STATES
TOTAL
17,927,257

1 DOT—5,000 ACRES

MAP NO. A59-1EIU
U.S DEPARTMENT OF COMMERCE
BUREAU OF THE CENSUS

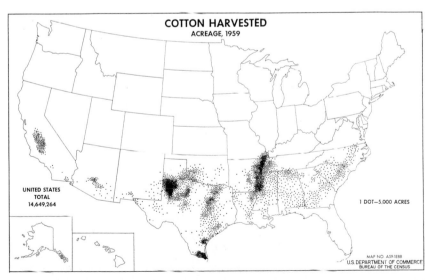

COTTON HARVESTED
ACREAGE, 1959

UNITED STATES
TOTAL
14,649,264

1 DOT—5,000 ACRES

MAP NO. A59-1EB8
U.S. DEPARTMENT OF COMMERCE
BUREAU OF THE CENSUS

prices and yields indicate that they should have switched to another feed grain.

Wheat prices become related to other feed grain prices when the supply of wheat is larger than the demands for it in the food market, as has been the case in recent years. Every bushel of wheat not used for food is a potential addition to feed grain supply. Therefore programs for reducing wheat production and for increasing food outlets for wheat have been of direct concern to feed grains producers. In the absence of government control programs, wheat production would perhaps have been 40 percent larger than could be marketed or exported as food.[1]

Assuming a surplus of wheat on the cash food market, wheat growers have had even more reason than feed grains producers to be concerned about the relationship of feed grains and wheat, because the price of the entire production of wheat in a free market would in that event be its feed value. Even if government programs preserved the higher status of the wheat food market, the feed grain price would continue to be important to wheat producers, because the price of other feed grains relative to wheat would tend to determine how much wheat would be produced.[2]

FEED GRAIN SITUATION

Combined production of the main feed grains—corn, grain sorghum, barley, and oats—is much larger than that of wheat. In 1965 the ratio was 6,208 million bushels of feed grains to 1,327 million bushels of wheat, almost 5 to 1. The value of feed grain exports for fiscal 1965 ($956.3 million) approached that for wheat ($1,239 million),[3] although well over half the 1964 wheat crop was exported, compared with only one-sixth of the 1964 feed grain crop.

Uses for feed grains have been increasing. Use for livestock and poultry feeding has increased somewhat between 1950 and 1965. De-

1. C. W. Nauheim, W. R. Bailey, D. E. Merrick, *Wheat Production—Trends, Problems, Programs, Opportunities for Adjustment*, USDA Agr. Info. Bull. 179 (March 1958), p. 52; and Luther Tweeten, Earl Heady, and Leo Mayer, "Farm Program Alternatives," CAED Rept. 18, Iowa State University, Ames (May 1963). The Iowa study suggested that 64–66 million acres of wheat would be harvested in the absence of controls. The USDA estimated in 1965 that about 1,800 million bushels would have been produced without controls, about 600 million above average 1958–62 wheat production.
2. Laurel D. Loftsgard and Norbert A. Dorow, "Market Situations and Policy Alternatives for Wheat," *Supplement to Farm Policy in the Years Ahead*, National Agriculture Advisory Commission (November 1964).
3. *Foreign Trade in Agricultural Products*, ERS-USDA (December 1965), table 7, p. 25. Other statistics used in this section are from the *Wheat Situation* and the *Feed Situation*, ERS-USDA (February 1966).

mands from rising meat production have fully offset the decline in the use of feed for draft animals, which had created much pessimism in the surplus-ridden 1930s.

Use of corn in food products, though still minor, has increased sharply. Cash exports of the four feed grains doubled between 1960 and 1965, leading to widely varying optimism about future foreign markets. The United States was furnishing increasing amounts of feed grains to the wealthier countries as meat consumption increased. Questions remained as to how far foreign tastes would develop toward American meat products and whether other exporters would continue to underbid America in the sale of meat.

On the production side hybrid seed corn, fertilizer, and many other production improvements (plus favorable weather) literally doubled feed grain yields between 1954 and 1965. Although planted acreage was sharply reduced, production increased by half. During the latter 1950s government stocks of feed grains jumped to 2 billion bushels. By 1966 controls and food aid had depleted wheat surpluses to levels considered necessary for reserves, but feed grain stocks hung at a billion bushels, much larger than needed. However the prospects for future market growth in feed grains were promising.

Most predictors have indicated a need for a long-run increase in feed grains, in contrast to a long-run decrease in food grains. However these projections have not assumed enlarged food exports and food aid programs. One estimate of projected needs, made in 1960 by H. L. Stewart, predicted the need for 4 million fewer acres of food grains and 15 million acres more of feed grains by 1975.[4]

In addition the production and the price of wheat affect the production and the prices of other commodities, and vice versa. These relationships complicate the task of measuring and negotiating program benefits. Each commodity and regional interest, using its preferred measuring scale, has continually found evidence that it is being discriminated against. Nevertheless until 1948 the commercial producers of wheat, cotton, feed grains, and some other commodities had found it possible to agree upon an omnibus program. After 1948 the commodity programs became an election issue—and the subject of bitter party conflict within Congress. In this party dispute regional lines were reflected. The initiatives of Republican Secretary of Agri-

4. H. L. Stewart, "The Organization and Structure of Some Representative Farms in 1975," *J. Farm Econ.* 42(December 1960):1367–79. *See also Supplement to Farm Econ.* 42(December 1960):1367–79. See also *Supplement to Farm Policy in the Years Ahead*, p. 19; the testimony of Theodore Schultz before U.S. House Committee of Agriculture on *Hearings on World War on Hunger* (1966), pp. 156–72.

culture Ezra Benson proved most acceptable to much of the Corn Belt heartland including Ohio, Illinois, and Indiana, while they generated much opposition from the cotton, wheat, and marginal feed grains areas. Republican farm legislators in the latter areas were under considerable stress.

Another apparent regional division was between the productive and the marginal areas, irrespective of commodity. Representatives of the most productive cotton and wheat areas were more likely to vote with the Corn Belt and to support Secretary Benson than were representatives of the marginal lands producing these commodities.

In contrast, Democratic Secretary of Agriculture Orville Freeman's support came originally from the areas which had opposed Secretary Benson's programs. In general the leadership of the congressional committees and the congressional Democratic party spoke in behalf of the wheat-cotton-commercial feed grain producers, while the Benson administration, the Farm Bureau, and some Corn Belt Republicans spoke for those who fed grain to animals, as well as for other types of farmers.

POLICY ISSUES

The following policy issues are some of those raised in relating commodity programs for feed grains, wheat, and cotton. Note that spokesmen for still other commodities were interested and active in policy decisions. However no effort is made to state the relationship between the supported crops and other commodities.

Location of Feed Grains. Feed grains are raised everywhere, but in the Midwest they are the dominant crop. Corn is the principal feed grain in the Midwest, where humid climate and good soil have supported a new corn technology with yields far greater than those for feed grains anywhere else.

A relatively small portion of the corn is sold on the market. Farmers who do sell most of the crop rather than feeding it to animals on the farm live in the "commercial" corn areas such as northern Iowa and are interested in a high market price. The majority of corn growers who feed most of their production, as in the eastern Corn Belt states of Ohio and Indiana, are not so concerned about prices.

While not in agreement on some issues, Corn Belt producers have shared a concern that federal programs might be spurring their competitors in other regions to increase production of feed grains. Under cotton, wheat, and other commodity programs, for example, acres removed from those crops could be planted to feed grains. In the Northern Plains barley was planted on acres removed from wheat production, and sorghum was planted on the nonallotment acres in the Southern Plains. It seemed clear in 1956 that three-fourths of the acreage diverted from wheat under the control program was planted to feed grains.[5] Secretary Benson estimated in 1956 that acreage removed from wheat and cotton under federal programs had produced barley, oats, and sorghum equivalent to 800 million bushels of corn.[6] Benson concluded that increased feed grain production had in turn caused depressed prices for milk, meat, and eggs during the 1956 marketing year.

Indeed, it seemed that the chief effect of production controls was not to reduce production but to shift it from one crop to another. Benson's economic advisor, Martin Sorkin, reported that a 25 percent decline in wheat and cotton acreage in the Southern Plains between 1953 and 1959 had been accompanied by 12 percent increase in feed grain acreages there.[7] During this time the Benson administration clearly desired to make a large overall reduction in cropland acres. The intent was to permanently retire marginal acreages located mostly in the South and in the arid parts of the Wheat Belt, mainly in the Southern Plains. As we have seen, the Benson soil bank program passed in 1956 contained one measure, the conservation reserve, that authorized long-term rental contracts featuring low per acre payments.

In these various acreage shifts the Corn Belt had held its own. It was chiefly responsible for increases in feed grain production, by virtue of increased corn yields. High-yielding corn hybrids saturated the Corn Belt, while corn acreage elsewhere was in decline.[8]

So many factors other than farm programs were at work in influencing production areas that it was not easy to predict how the patterns of acreage and production would have been different in the absence of these programs.

5. C. W. Nauheim, et al., *Wheat Production.*
6. U.S. House Committee on Agriculture, *Hearings on General Farm Legislation* (1956), p. 5.
7. Martin Sorkin, "Feed Grains, Soybeans, Livestock: A Situation Paper," *Proceedings of the First Annual Farm Policy Review Conference*, CAEA Rept. 7, Iowa State University, Ames (1960).
8. Geoffrey Shepherd and Allen Richards, *Effects of the Federal Programs, for Corn and Other Grains on Corn Prices, Feed Grains, Production and Livestock Production*, Iowa Agr. Exp. Sta. Res. Bull. 459, North Central Reg. Publ. 89 (August 1958).

Program Benefits. More basic than the dispute over location of production was the question of relative benefits for the programs. Before 1956 only a minority of corn growers had participated in the federal feed grains program. This program was designed to complement the federal wheat programs. However the program was voluntary, unlike those for wheat and some other commodities under which producers who did not comply with acreage controls were penalized. The feed grains program did encourage some corn growers to shift acreage to lower-yielding feed grains in return for subsidized prices on the remaining production.

The Midwest gave more support than did other regions to Secretary Benson's soil bank program, enacted in 1956. One soil bank measure (acreage reserve) authorized substantial rental payments on productive acres. This short-lived measure was hastily implemented in 1956, proving popular because payments were authorized for plowing up crops already heavily affected by drought. Most of the 1956 funds were spent in a few Corn Belt states. (See Table 9.3, page 218.)

In contrast, the wheat certificate program passed under Secretary of Agriculture Orville Freeman benefited the Wheat Belt. Through the certificates the federal government subsidized wheat to be used for food at a price level higher than its value as a feed grain; at the same time they facilitated production of additional wheat which was expected to enter the feed grain market at the lower price. Although participating farmers were obliged to idle a small portion of their cropland, much land remained on which feed grains could be grown.

The certificate program, while attractive to the Wheat Belt, discouraged the "15-acre plots" of wheat formerly raised in the Corn Belt (Table 12.1). Complementing the wheat program, however, was a feed grains program featuring a direct government payment to the feed grains farmer. This feed grains program presumably retired up to 30 million acres annually, though at six times the annual cost of Secretary Benson's short-lived soil bank (acreage reserve program).

Thus while the impetus for programs seemed to come more from the cotton and wheat areas than from the very productive Corn Belt, the Corn Belt seemed always to be treated favorably, regardless of administration. Senator Allen Ellender, Chairman of the Senate Agriculture Committee, continually made this point by referring to corn as "the blue-eyed girl" among the supported commodities.

The relative costs and benefits of the various price supports programs were difficult to compare. Professor Walter Wilcox of the Congressional Reference Service estimated that for every $100 of federal

TABLE 12.1. Migration of commodities during the Freeman programs

Commodity	Harvested acres			Percentage increase 1963–65
	1963	1964	1965	
		(000)		
Kansas				
Wheat	8,627	9,576	10,151	17.7
Feed grains:				
Corn	1,350	1,053	1,053	...
Barley	29	19	18	...
Oats	426	405	259	...
Sorghum	3,789	3,069	3,038	...
Soybeans	832	691	912	...
Total feed grains	6,426	5,237	5,280	−17.8
Ohio				
Wheat	1,415	1,373	1,195	− 15.5
Feed grains:				
Corn	2,903	2,961	2,931	...
Barley	276	406	138	...
Oats	893	722	693	...
Soybeans	1,755	1,862	2,083	...
Total feed grains	5,827	5,951	5,845	.3

Source: USDA.

expenditure on the 1964 and 1965 wheat program, wheat producers' returns increased by $225, while for feed grains producers the increase per $100 was $186.

As a result of the world food crisis in 1966, the administration momentarily became far more concerned to obtain adequate wheat production than to assure that program benefits would be equitably proportioned among commodities.

DIFFERENCES AMONG WHEAT REGIONS

The divisions among wheat regions are based upon differences in type of wheat and in the use of each, in location of markets, in cost of production, and in the results or feedback from federal commodity programs.

USE

Wheat varieties are in four major classes, defined by appearance and inherent qualities.

Soft red winter wheat is grown from Missouri to the eastern seaboard. Most acreage is spotted on the poorer crop acres of Illinois, Indiana, Ohio, and Michigan, although some soft wheat is raised in the Piedmont of the Southeast. Production of soft red wheat has been evenly downward since 1900, as has its use since the advent of mechanical baking. Soft wheat is used for pastries—biscuits, hot cakes, pie dough, cakes, cookies—and for the all-purpose flour purchased for home baking.

Soft white wheat is grown mainly in the Palouse and Big Bend districts of southeastern Washington and the adjoining areas in Idaho and Oregon. In the areas in the Orient where it is exported, white wheat is used for pastries, bread, and animal feed.

Hard red winter, the major class of wheat, is grown in the Southern Plains Wheat Belt centering around western Kansas. Used for bread, it has been the chief U.S. wheat export. Production of hard red wheat was increased substantially at the end of World War II by virtue of yield increases, expansion onto newly broken sod in the arid plains, and migration into areas where other classes of wheat formerly had been grown. Production of hard red winter wheat as a percentage of all wheat has remained at that postwar high (Table 12.2).

Hard red spring wheat, also used for bread, is grown in the Northern Plains where severe cold prevents winter incubation. Formerly grown north and east of a long line from Montana to Iowa, spring wheat in recent years has retreated before the challenge of a better-adapted winter wheat, so that it is now found mainly in the Dakotas. The North Plains also produces a minor wheat with a specific use—durum, used for macaroni and similar pastas.

TABLE 12.2.   Percentage of all wheat produced; averages 1920–64, annual 1960–65

Year of harvest	Hard red winter	Hard red spring	Soft red winter	White	Durum
1920–24	37.8	19.0	26.9	9.1	7.2
1925–29	40.5	20.5	20.4	10.3	8.3
1930–34	43.2	15.8	26.0	10.9	4.1
1935–39	41.3	14.0	28.4	12.7	3.5
1940–44	44.1	22.1	19.2	10.7	3.9
1945–49	50.5	17.5	16.9	11.8	3.3
1950–54	46.8	18.4	16.8	15.9	2.1
1955–59	50.1	16.7	16.0	14.7	2.5
1960–64	53.5	13.2	16.4	13.0	3.9
1960	58.5	13.9	14.0	11.1	2.5
1961	61.0	9.4	16.4	11.5	1.7
1962	49.0	16.0	14.4	14.2	6.4
1963	47.7	14.1	19.2	14.5	4.5
1964	49.8	13.3	17.8	14.0	5.1
1965	53.0	14.7	14.1	13.7	4.5

Source: *Wheat Situation,* ERS-USDA, no. 193 (July 1965), table 23.

Except perhaps for durum, all these classes of wheat can be interchanged in use, in some substantial portion, in modern milling operations. The actual amount of interchange is to a considerable degree a function of the relative prices.

LOCATION

Price, not unique quality, is usually the most important consideration in purchase of wheat, and the consistent element of price difference is the cost of transportation. Northwestern wheat has usually not been competitive for the major U.S. markets because transportation costs were as much as half the value of the wheat. Within recent years the Northwest has become less disadvantaged because of the opening of large Oriental markets.

Increased exports have also been a boon to the Southern Plains, which were relatively distant from the great mills and domestic population centers, and which have benefited from their proximity to the busy gulf ports.

Soft red winter wheat profits from the fact that its major markets—a few large biscuit and flour companies—are located in or near the area of production. The North Plains spring wheat growers have prospered from the development of the Great Lakes–St. Lawrence waterway and from proximity to Minneapolis and Chicago milling centers.

YIELD

Much of the change in the proportion of varieties produced and in location has been in response to changes in yields. Improved varieties have sharply altered the geographic lines between classes of wheat without much regard for the small price differentials that reflected millers' preferences. Until recently the faster-improving hard red winter yields have moved this class of wheat north, west, and east. Even when yields of winter and spring wheat were comparable, farmers preferred the early-maturing winter wheat, because an unpromising winter wheat crop could be plowed up in the spring and reseeded to a spring variety or replaced by a feed crop. Recent improvements in soft red winter wheat have pushed hard red winter out of the more humid areas where its quality was very low, and back into its appropriate climatic setting.

The miracle crop has been soft white wheat, whose yields have multiplied with the dissemination of a new variety during the 1960s. It has become master of the area west of the Rockies but has not been adapted elsewhere.

The adaptation of wheat to the arid plains has been most remarkable. A number of earlier efforts to farm the western parts of North Dakota, Kansas, and Nebraska and the eastern sections of Colorado and New Mexico were periodically terminated by prolonged drought. Wheat cultivation in this dry area expanded in the late 1920s as a result of mechanization,[9] and contracted as a result of abandonment, and federal conservation programs, during the dust bowl era.

In a USDA report on "Agricultural Conservation in 1937,"[10] the hard red winter wheat region was divided into three parts for purposes of making recommendations. The USDA report prescribed that the eastern and central portions were to continue raising wheat. In the western dust bowl, erosion control was to get high priority. It was recommended that "considerable acreages should be permanently shifted from arable farming into permanent grass, and many farm units need to be enlarged in order to be operated economically." However many thousands of acres which were abandoned or were returned to grass have subsequently reverted to wheat in response to good weather and good prices. The increase in wheat acreage between 1942 and 1949 was almost 50 percent in North Dakota, Kansas, and New Mexico, but more than 80 percent in Oklahoma and Texas and over 150 percent in Colorado.[11]

In one Colorado county, acreage increased fiftyfold. The USDA still argued in 1949 in favor of a major reduction in acreage in these marginal areas, but much of the "new" lands stayed in wheat production despite sustained drought during the 1950s. On these arid fringes of both the Northwest and the Great Plains wheat areas, tremendous improvements in seeds and tillage practices and mechanization of farming have apparently checked wind erosion and other ravages of drought, although poor crop cycles must still be endured. Much of the "new" area is probably still marginal, however, in terms of comparative net returns over the long run.[12]

---

9. "The Contractility of Wheat Acreage in the U.S.," *Wheat Studies of the Stanford Food Research Institute*, 6(February 1930):171–76.
10. USDA, 1938.
11. *Wheat Situation*, ERS-USDA, no. 113 (August 1949), p. 9.
12. One effort to capture some of the major variables which determine regional relative advantages of production areas is Alvin C. Egbert and Earl O. Heady, *Regional Analysis of Production Adjustments in the Major Field Crops: Historical*

Linked to yield, as a determinant of where wheat will be grown, has been relative income from wheat versus other products. Where wheat and corn grow equally well, for example, corn is usually chosen because of its higher yields. In fact, wheat has a considerable history as a marginal crop, produced on the geographical and biophysical out-skirts of the cropland complex.

Wheat is again migrating toward the Plains, for several reasons. Wheat had been planted earlier in the Midwest as part of a crop rotation process which is being abandoned. In addition, specialization on farms is proceeding very rapidly in areas where wheat was once a secondary source of income. Farm program changes had something to do with the migration, as shall be discussed. In the absence of gov-ernment support for both wheat and feed grain prices it is probable that some areas would have produced a larger proportion of both grains, while marginal producing areas would have gone back to grassland.

PROGRAM BENEFITS

Many program provisions benefit or burden one region more than another. Some were designed to do so, and others are explained as rules which could not be modified for each region without making the program too complicated to be understood and administered. It has been assumed that the program should be fair and beneficial to all producers, and certain equity norms have been used to judge the final product.

One oft-stated norm is that every producer should have a chance to make an adequate income. Put differently, the interests of wheat producers who have the opportunity to produce other commodities, such as the farmer who can raise either feed grains or wheat, should give way to the interests of the producer who can raise only wheat. So if wheat production must be reduced, it would be considered prefer-able to eliminate the producers who have options to produce another crop, even though they might be the most efficient wheat producers. This norm tends to benefit the marginal crop areas (Table 12.3).

Related to this is a tendency to conceptualize wheat farmers as those who specialize in production of wheat. This concept neglects

and Prospective," USDA Tech. Bull. 1294 (1963). Neither this study nor any other is regarded as conclusive. In general, the study indicates that marginal or the un-needed crop acres are mostly in the southeastern United States and in most arid sec-tions of the Plains. Another test of marginality has been the conservation reserve program, under which the federal government offered to rent acreages at fixed low rates. The above areas were major participants in the program.

TABLE 12.3.   1965 wheat program signup (average)

Class of wheat; State	Allotment on enrolled farms as a percentage of allotments on all farms
Hard winter (few 15-acre allotments)	
Colorado	90
Kansas	94
Nebraska	93
New Mexico	71
Oklahoma	91
Texas	88
Utah	73
Wyoming	85
Total	91
Soft red winter (many 15-acre allotments)	
Arkansas	28
Illinois	54
Indiana	51
Iowa	58
Kentucky	52
Michigan	55
Missouri	66
Ohio	58
Tennessee	50
Wisconsin	40
Total	56

Source: *Wheat Situation,* ERS-USDA, no. 192 (May 1965), table 14.

the diversified farmers for whom wheat may be an important minor crop, and is probably due to the commodity specialization of the decision makers themselves. In both Congress and the executive branch responsibility for writing wheat programs is parceled out to interested legislators from areas where wheat dominates.

Favoritism for the specialized producer is reinforced by the desire for a simple and comprehensible program. Programs tend to be built around "model" farms—that is, constructed from among "typical" operations in which wheat is a major product rather than from a variety of farms where just a little wheat is raised. Diversified farms with small wheat acreages have sometimes been permitted to operate outside program requirements, but this attempt to prevent hardship does not take away the fact that producers who can most conveniently comply with the requirements are likely to get the most benefits from the program. Norms favoring the specialized producers appear to be reflected in the program provisions.

The specific effects of major program provisions follow.

Transportation and Export Subsidies. The wheat areas of today were settled by means of subsidized transportation systems. The transportation systems serving the wheat areas have developed with the aid of financial assistance, at critical moments, from the federal government. A chief goal of farmer protest movements during the last century was government regulation of rail rates. In addition to transportation development and regulation in behalf of the remote producers, the federal government has subsidized some rates, sometimes directly, as in starting the movement of Plains wheat into Japanese markets.

Government subsidies enabling export of wheat have complemented price supports as a means of maintaining wheat prices throughout the country. At the onset of the Great Depression, for example, the wheat surplus in the Northwest was eased by subsidized exports, while prices elsewhere were being influenced by government purchases. In general, federal export programs have concentrated on the commodities in surplus in recent years, principally the white wheat of the Northwest and the hard red winter of the Southern Plains.

Market development efforts were greater with respect to hard winter wheat and white wheat than for other types. This was partly because producers of these classes took the initiative in seeking foreign markets. But it was due also to the large stocks of each of these classes, which influenced the goals set by USDA policy makers for sales abroad. In addition CCC sales personnel, viewing themselves as good businessmen, were anxious to sell from the larger inventories. Another consideration was the desire to see that adequate supplies of each class were available for domestic use. The greater emphasis on hard red winter wheat and white wheat exports is particularly reflected in programming for P.L. 480 (Table 12.4).

The P.L. 480 (Food for Peace) program is especialy important for western white wheat producers. Because they are remote from domestic processing centers, exports are the major outlet for the recently increased production of this class of wheat. New Oriental markets for white wheat have been growing, partly as a result of federal market

TABLE 12.4. Export movement under P.L. 480, July–June 1964–65

Class of wheat	P.L. 480
	(mil. bu.)
Hard winter	388.6
Red winter	37.5
Hard spring	13.1
Durum	.2
Western white	65.2
Mixed	.8
Total	495.4

Source: *Wheat Situation*, ERS-USDA, no. 193 (July 1965), table 3.

TABLE 12.5 Percentage of each class of
wheat used domestically

Class of wheat	Percent used domestically in 1964–65
Hard red winter	43.5
Soft red winter	63.3
Hard red spring	78.5
Durum	50.0
White	34.3
All wheat	49.9

Source: *Wheat Situation,* ERS-USDA, no.
193 (July 1965), table 2.

promotional activities, but a crucial three-fifths of the white wheat exports moved under P.L. 480 in 1964–65.[13] White wheat is strongly preferred by India and some other large recipients under P.L. 480.

Domestic Certificates. In 1964 a long-advocated measure went into effect which provided for additional income to producers for that portion of the crop (about 45 percent of the national wheat crop) sold domestically for food. However each producer's share of the additional income was based on the *national* percentage, although the amount actually used for domestic food varied substantially among classes (Table 12.5). For example, most of the soft red winter and hard spring wheat produced in 1964 was used domestically, compared with less than half of the white and hard red winter wheat. This suggests why Oregon and Washington white wheat producers have long been ardent champions both of export subsidies and of the wheat certificate mechanism.

Defenders of the wheat certificate have usually said that it is administratively necessary to use the national percentage for all producers, and in any case subsidies are distributed under this rule in the same way as under previous price support programs. This is only to admit that these same producers, particularly the remote northwest white wheat area, were favored both by the certificate program and by the high price supports and excess subsidies in the previous program. The distribution of benefits under price support programs of 1938 to 1963 is illustrated in the next three sections, reflecting the size of the surplus, relation of price support, and amounts of subsidies.

Size of Stocks. Favoritism is suggested in the fact that certain classes of wheat have piled up in government stocks while others seemed to be

13. *Wheat Situation,* USDA-ERS, no. 193 (July 1965), tables 2 and 3.

TABLE 12.6.   CCC-owned stocks, by classes, July 1, 1959

Class of wheat	000 bushels
Hard winter	867,097
Hard spring	187,563
Soft winter	7,831
Durum and red durum	11,250
White	57,212
Mixed	1,921

Source: *Wheat Situation*, ERS-USDA, no. 165 (August 1959), table 4.

in short supply. In 1959 U.S. supplies of eastern soft red wheat were low, and some mills shut down to await the harvest rather than pay end-of-season prices. Meanwhile the CCC owned surpluses of hard wheat equal to a year's production and owned a half year's production of white wheat (Table 12.6). One reason for this situation was that the USDA had tended to minimize price differences between wheats which would have reflected differing demand; another was that too few soft wheat producers participated in the price supports program.

With reference to the first reason, price support loan rates have taken account of the differing market values of varieties and grades of wheat. This has been done by applying a schedule of discounts and premiums, but this schedule has been based upon the leveling average of previous prices rather than being based on current demand. Since 1961 current prices have been further influenced by the policy of selling desired wheats from government stocks whenever the premium prices edged above the support price.

Premium prices were thus discouraged. In practice grain handlers would have benefited most from these premiums since facilities for discovering premium wheat are often inadequate at the crossroads elevators where farmers sell their wheat. As a means of enabling farmers to derive the benefits from market premiums the USDA tried to implement a simplified test of wheat quality which could be administered at the crossroads elevator. This test (protein test) did not prove wholly reliable, and processors ultimately declined to use it.

Greater price differences would have presented some discouragement to production of hard wheat or would have increased the effective demand for it. In the absence of large discounts based on quality, a low-quality mongrel wheat came to be produced, resulting from the use of high-yielding hard wheats in areas best suited for soft wheat. Subsequently the USDA was able to discourage this and other undesirable wheats by discounting them severely (20 cents per bushel) in setting price support rates. However it was the introduction of new

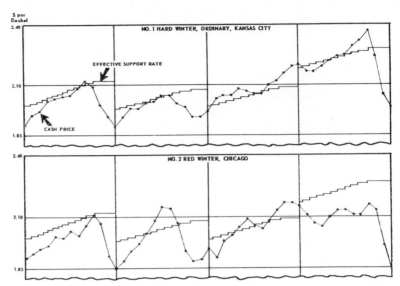

FIG. 12.2. Wheat prices by classes. Soft red winter wheat prices fell lower than others because the price supports mechanism was not working well. Too few producers participated in the program; therefore the amount of wheat under price support loans was not large enough to clear away market surpluses.

Source: *Wheat Situation,* USDA-ERS, no. 185 (August 1963), p. 34. Prepared by USDA-AMS.

high-yielding soft wheat varieties in the 1960s which finally restored a traditional pattern of soft wheat production.

Another reason for the meager U.S. stocks of soft red wheat was the fact that much soft wheat was not eligible for wheat price supports. Most soft red winter wheat producers harvested more acres than they were allotted, by virtue of a provision exempting small acreage from controls. Since such producers were not eligible to receive price support loans, soft red wheat was dumped into the marketplace at a price lower than that of other classes (Fig. 12.2). Indeed because of its low price, millers may have purchased more soft red wheat than was necessary to achieve the desired blends of flour. Only the price, not the acreage ratio, of soft red winter wheat declined relatively while control programs were in effect during the 1950s.[14]

Allotments for "New" Lands. The rules for apportioning acreage allotments have apparently tended to capture acreage for the marginal,

14. *Wheat Situation,* USDA-ERS, no. 165 (August 1959), table 5.

arid areas, at the expense of the more humid areas within the heart of the Wheat Belt. Until 1966 allotments were apportioned on the basis of the history of plantings over the previous ten years, but large allotments could be locked into the marginal areas by virtue of a provision allowing dryland farmers to count their previous allotments as history even when weather conditions actually prevented planting the acreage. An even more important shift took place when allotments were assigned to those acreages which had been broken out from grassland following World War II and during the Korean War. The USDA had discouraged this plow-up of the Plains, even though additional production was urgently needed. Once these new lands were in production, however, Congress insisted that beginning in 1950 they be put on equal footing in the farm programs. As a result the postwar "wheat base" (harvested basis)—among which the 55-million acre allotment was divided—was increased to 79 million acres, about 10 million more than the prewar base. In the process the established wheat areas had to contribute a larger share to the state of Colorado, for example, whose allotment base had more than doubled since 1943 (Fig. 12.3).

Insurance Features. In the Plains generally, particularly on their arid western fringes, and also in the arid parts of the Pacific Northwest wheat area, uncertain climatic conditions result in extremely variable yields. A good yield is a pleasant surprise, and crop failure is frequent.

A number of program provisions are in the nature of free insurance against crop failure, and these thus enhance the competitive position of the high-risk areas on the dry fringes of the Northwest and Plains wheat belts.

1. Wheat certificates. The certificates, granted as a percentage of projected yields, were distributed whether or not the crop was good enough to harvest. In some areas crop failures may be predicted at planting time by virtue of low levels of moisture in the soil. When failure was a near certainty producers were likely to comply with the program in order to receive the negotiable certificates.

2. Voluntary diversion. Similarly acreage which lacked adequate moisture to raise a crop could be rented in part to the federal government. From the time of Benson's soil bank, acreage diversion provisions have been a method of subsidizing drought-stricken farmers.

3. Excess wheat provisions. In those states where crop failure is frequent farmers could frustrate Providence by overplanting during good years and storing the wheat then harvested from the excess acre-

FIG. 12.3 Increase and decrease in total cropland, 1949–54. Much of the cropland increase following World War II took place in the marginal cropland areas in the Wheat Belt. These areas were then brought into the wheat base, requiring the established areas to share with the new areas the existing 55-million-acre national allotment.

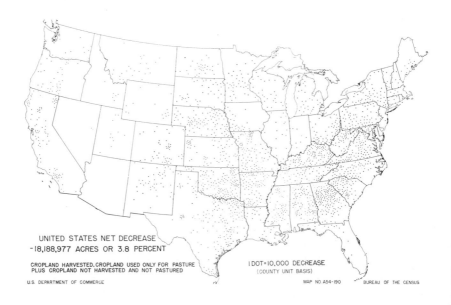

UNITED STATES NET DECREASE
-18,188,977 ACRES OR 3.8 PERCENT

TABLE 12.7. Excess wheat, farm, and warehouse
stored as of December 31, 1959

Selected states[a]	Percentage of total 1959 production
Wyoming	18
Colorado	13
Nebraska	13
Montana	11
Kansas	3
South Dakota	2
Utah	2
Oklahoma	1
North Dakota	1
Washington	1

Source: *Wheat Situation,* ERS-USDA, no. 169
(June 1960), table 7.

a. All other states had less than 1 percent.

age, to be sold in years when yields were not up to the projected average (Table 12.7).

4. Disaster aid. The federal government has reacted to drought and other acts of God by providing millions of dollars in various forms of disaster relief, as in the severe Plains drought of the 1950s. The cost of drought relief, however, was apparently less than the cost of subsidies during the years of crop production.

5. Agriculture Conservation Payments. Cost-sharing payments have been made to farmers by the ASCS to promote conservation of soil. In practice the bulk of the payments has been for the purpose of making marginal lands usable (see Chapter 9). The same has been true of federal water projects which permitted irrigation of formerly worthless land. Under irrigation, however, most of this land became too valuable to devote to wheat production.

6. Substitution clause. A provision for interchange of wheat and feed grain allotment acres, in effect since 1965, has been used primarily by wheat farmers in the dry areas where feed grains do not grow well, rather than by farmers who wished to plant feed grains on wheat allotments. In addition, the substitution clause has given high-risk wheat areas a valuable second chance: if the wheat crop should be killed during the winter, that acreage could be shifted to feed grain.

7. Acreage controls. The acreage controls were a boon to the marginal crop areas, to the extent that they prompted farmers to resist the temptation toward annual plantings. Whenever acreage controls were instituted, larger acreages were summer fallowed, and

yields in the arid areas tended to climb rapidly. By 1966 dryland farmers proved they had been persuaded of the value of summer fallow: when given a chance to plant a very large acreage, they generally refused to do so if this meant a return to annual plantings. Under present technology the only benefit from fallowing land is restoration of moisture, so areas with ample rain have not gained any yield windfalls from idling land.

Also, after 1954, compliance with compulsory controls was on a harvested acre basis. Farmers could begin the growing season as noncompliers, and after surveying the crop on the excess acreage in the spring, they could make a judgment as to whether it would be worthwhile to pay the penalties and then harvest and sell the wheat.

8. Price supports. The above are advantages tending to stabilize and increase production in high-risk areas. The component of gross income other than production is price. The farmer for whom wheat is the principal or only source of income probably benefits most from stable prices, which enable him to plan his operations and to obtain the credit he needs for expansion. Furthermore, to the extent that wheat prices are supported at higher levels than other commodities (if they are), the producer with the greatest proportion of wheat is the biggest beneficiary.

Benefits outside the Wheat Belt. These provisions included the 15-acre exemption and the exemption of some wheat grown for feed.

1. 15-acre exemption. The provision exempting small wheat acreages from controls has been heralded as a concession to the small farmers, although most farmers who produced no more than 15 acres of wheat were likely to be rather "large" farmers for whom wheat was a minor product. Most of these farmers lived outside the Wheat Belt. Indeed the 15-acre exemption was added as a result of the "revolt of the Ohio farmers" at the time that compulsory quotas were first applied on wheat in 1941 (Act of May 26, 1941). These midwestern producers protested the inconvenience of acreage controls on a minor crop.

Opinions differed and sometimes changed on the question as to whether this 15-acre exemption was a loophole permitting wheat acreage to drift into the Midwest, East, and South, and away from the specialized producing areas. In 1953 the Benson administration held that this was not a major loophole and tentatively suggested that the exemption be raised to 25 acres. This would exempt 64 percent of the producers of wheat, but it was pointed out that these small acreages would be responsible for only 20 percent of the product.[15] The Senate managed to resist this invitation to modify the controls.

In 1959, however, the USDA noted that the 15-acre provision had permitted "an enormous increase" in the number of farms producing wheat on 15 acres and less. From 1955 to 1959, the USDA estimated, 385 million bushels had been produced on the small noncompliance acreages.[16] At that time the USDA asked that the 15-acre exemption be abolished.[17]

Several considerations have guided choices on the question of ending the 15-acre exemption. Plains State congressmen were concerned about its effect on regional acreage. While there had been no significant change in the regional distribution of wheat acreage during the operation of the 15-acre provision from 1954 to 1961, some Plains spokesmen felt that it had interrupted the migration of acreage onto the Plains which previously had seemed to be in process.

The 15-acre exemption was a problem also with respect to its impact on farmer opinion. Farmer opinion about programs was important because compulsory controls such as were featured in the wheat programs had to be approved by a majority of two-thirds of those voting in farmer referendums. Because of the 15-acre exemption, many Plains farmers were inclined to vote against the program. On the other hand, if the exemption were ended, its former beneficiaries would be subject to the controls and presumably eligible to vote against them. In 1956 Senators Milton Young (R., North Dakota) and Frank Carlson (R., Kansas) supported a new wheat certificate program, ultimately passed by Congress, which would have allowed 15-acre growers to comply with the program (and receive subsidies) or to stay out of it; but in either case, under the program prepared by these wheat senators the very numerous 15-acre growers would not have been allowed to vote in the referendum.[18] Many observers did not regard this as fair play for the 15-acre farmers.

15. Testimony of Howard Gordon (PMA Administrator) before U.S. House Committee on Agriculture, *Hearings on Wheat Marketing Quotas* (1953).
16. U.S. House Committee on Agriculture, *Hearings on the Wheat Situation in Review* (1959), pp. 5–6.
17. During the same time period, noncompliance acreages on the larger wheat farms had produced only 90 million additional bushels. In 1958, when overplanting on large farms was at its maximum, the large farms overplanted by only 2 million acres, as compared with 4.5 million acres overplanted via the 15-acre exemption. See *Wheat Situation in Review*, p. 13.
18. *Congressional Record* (bound), March 13, 1956, p. 4071.

TABLE 12.8.   Wheat and feed grain substitution under the 1966
wheat and feed grain programs

Class of wheat	Net change in wheat acreage
	(acres)
White (western)	423,877
Hard spring and durum	591,176
Hard winter	2,052,868
Soft red winter (major area)	—79,528
Soft red winter (other)	808

Source: *Wheat Situation,* ERS-USDA, no. 201 (August 1967),
table 24.

In the 1962 Food and Agriculture Act 15-acre producers were given the right to vote if they intended to comply with the new certificate program. As had been feared, the great majority of them voted against the program, and their votes proved to be a decisive element in its defeat.

In the voluntary certificate program begun in 1964, the 15-acre program provision was ended, in the sense that producers of any size who did not wish to receive program subsidies were free to plant as much as they wished. The only remnant was a provision offering producers with fewer than 25 acres an opportunity to divert their acreage in return for a diversion payment. The effect of the new voluntary program was immediate. In 1964 and 1965 the wheat acreage east of the Mississippi (soft red winter) dropped sharply (Table 12.8).

2. Wheat for feed. Another exemption for noncommercial wheat producers was permission to grow up to 30 acres of noncompliance wheat without penalty, on the condition that the entire production be used on the farm for feeding animals or for food. This was an early Benson proposal which wheat state legislators resisted until its enactment in 1957. This—and a provision for exemption of "noncommercial" states with fewer than 25,000 wheat acres—proved to have little effect on total or regional production of wheat.

To summarize the situation of the midwestern, eastern, and southeastern producers, the wheat program of the 1950s did encourage the production of soft red wheat by allowing producers to claim most of the price benefits without accepting controls. The voluntary wheat certificate program beginning in 1964 discouraged production on the small acreages because the certificates were often not worth the inconvenience of complying with the program. However this disincentive to wheat production in the Corn Belt was complemented by increased incentives for corn production, in the form of increased yield and increased program benefits for feed grain producers.

Soft wheat supplies, however, remained adequate. The soft wheat milling and baking companies had opposed the price support programs even when they were the beneficiaries of bargain prices on soft red wheat. Since the dissemination of high-yielding soft wheat varieties happened to coincide with the enactment of the certificate program, the production of soft red wheat, rather than declining, has simply moved further west.

Durum Program. The 15-acre provision was not a special program for soft red wheat, although eastern producers were the principal beneficiaries of it. One program explicitly applying to a particular class of wheat has been that for the durum wheat. The macaroni market has been rather constant, but durum supplies have varied (based on yield relationships with hard spring wheat in areas where both are grown) as a result of poor crops in the United States and elsewhere due to weather or disease. Acreage quotas were increased for durum in the mid-fifties and again in 1962. With the additional stimulation of premium prices in the marketplace, North Dakota and Minnesota farmers more than filled a temporary deficit. Durum was returned to the regular allotment basis in 1963. With the development of disease-resistant seeds, the government then acquired a larger supply of surplus durum (relative to the amount produced) than of any other variety of wheat.

BENEFITS BY SIZE OF FARM

In practice the medium- and large-sized farms have received most of the direct benefits from wheat commodity programs. Program rules have been framed for the convenience of the larger farmer. The acreage cuts have been inherently unacceptable to the farmer whose total farm size was already inadequate. For these and other reasons fewer small farmers have participated in the programs and in the benefits flowing from them.

This has been true since the beginning of the programs. A study of 1933–35 pork programs indicated that only 32 percent of the smaller farms participated, compared with 93 percent of the commercial farms.[19] It was true for wheat in 1958 (Table 12.9).

---

19. *Participation Under AAA Programs, 1933–1935*, AAA-USDA (October 1938).

TABLE 12.9. Frequency distribution by size of wheat acreage planted, 1958

	0	.1–10.9	11.0–15.9	16.0 and over	Total
			(acres)		
Complying farms	48.5	7.9	5.3	38.3	100.0
Noncomplying farms	0	38.4	56.2	5.4	100.0
All farms	30.2	19.4	24.5	25.9	100.0

Source: USDA-CSS, Grain Division, in U.S. House Committee on Agriculture, *Hearings on Wheat Situation in Review* (1959).

Not only have the rules for participation been more favorable to the large farmers, the benefits have also gone mainly to the large farmers, since they were apportioned based on volume of production. In fact volume of total sales (or gross receipts) has been accepted as a good measure of the distribution of program benefits. Applying this measure of gross cash receipts in North Dakota for 1959, for example, 8,417 cash grain farmers produced 55 percent of the total sales in that state. These were the larger farmers, who earned more than $10,000 each in gross sales (Classes I, II, and III in the *1959 U.S. Census of Agriculture*).[20] They constituted only 30 percent of all cash grain farmers in North Dakota.

Why have wheat programs distributed so sizable a share of benefits to medium- and large-sized farms? Several reasons may be suggested. Larger commercial farmers have more political influence because they are more aware of the results of farm programs, are more articulate, and are participants in program decisions as members of farm organizations and as members of the farmer committees which administer the farm programs. The large-farmer bias is also due to the fact that the goal of income support must share a place with the effort to achieve production control. If subsidies are to be an adequate incentive for production control, then they must be commensurate with the income capacity of the units retired, regardless of size of farm.

Federal price support programs have been blamed both for speeding and retarding the growth in farm size. It appears that effects of farm programs on farm size have been mixed and are not of major importance.

One hypothesis is that if prices were allowed to fall, some farmers would expand volume (acreage) in order to maintain existing levels

20. Vol. 1, part 18, state table 18. In Kansas 37 percent (14,846) of the cash grain growers received 68 percent of all the benefits, by this same measure (vol. 1, part 21, state table 18.)

TABLE 12.10. Size of ownership and size of farms in the Great Plains

Acres	Percentage of Distribution		
	Farms 1954[a]	Owners of farm and ranchland, 1958[b]	Cropland acres owned, by size of ownership unit, 1958[c]
	(percent)		
Under 260	36	56	16
260–499	27	20	20
500–999	20	13	22
1,000–1,999	17[d]	11	17
2,000–4,999	...	...	13
5,000–9,999	...	...	5
10,000 and over	...	...	7
Total	100	100	100

Sources:
a. *Farming in the Great Plains: A Survey of the Financial and Tenure Situation in 1957,* USDA-ARS Prod. Res. Rept. 50 (May 1961), table 3.
b. *Land Ownership in the Great Plains,* USDA-ARS Stat. Bull. 261 (April 1960), table 35.
c. Ibid., table 36.
d. This amount is for all farms of 1,000 acres and over.

of income.[21] Farmers unable to expand would sell to those who could then and would move to other employment. Much of farm policy decision making has used the theory that high prices will keep farmers on the farm (preserve the family farm) and low prices will result in off-migration and farm consolidation.

In contrast, it is noted that high prices have been converted into capital for greater mechanization, thus permitting an increase in the ideal size of efficient one-operator units. Off-migration was faster without any doubt when prices were very high, as in both wars, than when they were very low, as in the depression period of 1929 to 1935. However off-farm movement during war and prosperity is better explained by the pull of employment elsewhere than by the level of farm prices.[22]

LANDOWNERS AND TENANTS

While the operating units in agriculture are farms, another economic unit is that of landownership. Landownership units vary

21. For example, see *Dryland Grain Farms in Montana,* Montana Agr. Exp. Sta. Tech. Bull. 579 (July 1963), p. 18; Fred D. Sobering and Luther G. Tweeten, "A Simplified Approach to Adjustment Analysis Applied to Wheat Producing Areas in the Western States," *J. Farm Econ.* 46(November 1964):820–34; and Harold E. Barnhill, *Resource Requirements on Farms for Specified Operator Incomes,* ERS-USDA Agr. Econ. Rept. 5 (1964), p iv.
22. See the following in *Labor Mobility and Population in Agriculture* (Ames: Iowa State Univ. Press, 1961): Larry Sjaastad, "Occupational Structure and Migration Patterns"; Varden Fuller, "Factors Influencing Farm Labor Mobility"; and C. E. Bishop, "Economic Aspects of Changes in Farm Labor Force."

TABLE 12.11. Farm operators: Percentage distribution by tenure of operator, areas of the Great Plains, 1957

Tenure of operator	Spring wheat	Northern range	Wheat-corn	Cotton-wheat	Winter wheat
			(percent)		
Full owners	31	32	26	36	29
Part owners	51	54	36	34	42
Managers	...	1	1	...	...
Tenants	18	13	37	30	29
Total	100	100	100	100	100

Source: *Farming in the Great Plains: A Survey of the Financial and Tenure Situation in 1957*, USDA-ARS Prod. Res. Rept. 50 (May 1961), table 15.

greatly in size. Table 12.10 shows that over half the owners have less than 260 acres. Yet the third column reveals that 42 percent of the cropland acreage is in units exceeding 1,000 acres. Many units presumably embrace more than one farm.

According to a 1958 study of landownership in the Great Plains, 23 percent of the landowners owned more than one farm.[23] Ownership of half the land was highly concentrated: 10 percent of the owners with the largest holdings owned 63.8 percent of the land, and 48.7 percent of the total value of land. At the other end of the spectrum the 50 percent with the smallest holdings owned in aggregate only 11 percent of the total land value.[24]

The trends in size of ownership between 1945 and 1958 indicated little or no tendency toward greater concentration.[25] As large holdings accumulated, many were divided by the process of inheritance or were sold. It would appear that the number of owners will likely not decline as quickly as the number of farms.

CHARACTER OF OWNERS

According to all studies, one-third of the farmland is owned by someone other than farmers or retired farmers. The USDA survey of the Great Plains in 1958 indicated that 65 percent of all farms and ranchland was owned by farmers (56.2 percent) or retired farmers (9.0 percent).[26] Most farm operators owned part of the land they farmed (Table 12.11). "Tenant only" status was viewed as temporary,

23. Robert W. Strohbehn and Gene Wunderlich, *Land Ownership in the Great Plains*, ARS-USDA Stat. Bull. 261 (April 1960), table 37. The states included in the study were North Dakota, South Dakota, Nebraska, Kansas, Montana, Wyoming, Colorado, Oklahoma, Texas, and New Mexico.
24. Ibid., table 38.
25. Ibid., table 39.
26. Ibid., table 7.

and farm tenants have been in the process of beginning or increasing farm ownership. The goal of tenants was presumably to acquire adequate land to enable them to retire in later years to the status of nonoperating landlord.

As farms are enlarged both by land purchase and land rental, an increasing percentage of total acreage of cropland has been owned by operators who are part owners and part renters.[27] Some of the land not owned by farmers or former farmers was in the possession of widows or business and professional persons living in the area in which the land was located.[28] Very little of the land was held by corporations.[29]

Answers to one survey question in the 1958 USDA study of the Great Plains indicated a tremendous amount of absentee landownership. One-fourth of the nonoperator landlords visited their farms less than twice per year. Another fourth visited their farms less than ten times per year. Only 17 percent visited the farm 25 times or more each year.[30] Many of the absentees were retired farmers, but others were suitcase farmers. In 1958 Great Plains farmers owned 53,689,800 acres of land outside their home states, most of it in other Great Plains states.[31]

OWNERSHIP AND PROGRAM BENEFITS

There has been controversy as to how much of federal program benefits have gone to the landowner (either for rental or from appreciation in value) in comparison with the proportion going to the farm operator for his labor and management. For those farmers or retired farmers who owned 65 percent of all the land, this may seem merely a bookkeeping question. Yet the benefits they have received as owners have come later in life, and the income benefits they have received as operators helped them to become owners in the first place.

As we also noted, size of holdings varied more widely than size of farms. There were more small owners than small farmers. Conversely the very large economic units in the Wheat Belt were land-

---

27. A projection of future cropland ownership was done for the Texas Black Land Prairie area, in *Projections to 1970 of Selected Characteristics of Farms in the Blackland Prairies,* Texas Agr. Exp. Sta. Tech. Monograph 2 (June 1965), table 7. The conclusion in this projection agrees with the earlier trend for the period 1945 to 1958 as revealed in *Farming in the Great Plains: A Survey of the Financial and Tenure Situation in 1957,* ARS-USDA Prod. Res. Rept. 50 (May 1961), table 15.
28. Strohbehn and Wunderlich, table 6.
29. Ibid., table 3.
30. Ibid., table 31.
31. Ibid., table 41.

holdings rather than farms. There is little question that the land barons with a dozen or more square miles within one county, and the suitcase farmers with extensive holdings scattered over a thousand miles, have been principal beneficiaries of the farm programs.

Some authorities have said—or have almost said—that virtually all farm program benefits have been channeled into increased land values rather than into increased net income. Varden Fuller stated:

> The inflationary spiral in farm real estate has in effect miscarried what is broadly assumed to be the purpose of the price support programs because their effects have been realized in higher land values rather than in better returns on labor. At the present stage of affairs, price or income programs designed to give effect to a policy goal of comparable returns to labor and investment are not likely to overcome this miscarriage; rather, they would add further to fueling the fires of inflation.[32]

Thus each round of increases in operator income payments had been cancelled out by increased land costs.

This assumes, incorrectly, that land costs exactly reflected land values. It supposes, as in one study, that if the price of wheat sorghum acreages in northwestern Kansas were increased by 10 percent, an increase of 8 or 9 percent in gross sales would be required in order to maintain previous operator earnings.[33] In practice, however, the division of income between the owner and the operator is often fixed by local custom or by long-term arrangements rather than in proportion to current land values.

Certainly farmland values have climbed steadily in recent decades while programs were in effect (Table 12.12). The following calculation suggests that this return to land has at least equaled the total cost of federal wheat programs.

In 1958 the value of all farmland and ranchland in the Great Plains was $29 billion dollars.[34] In the subsequent period ending November 1965, farmland and ranchland values in North Dakota increased by 44 percent and in Kansas by 39 percent. Using a conservative 40 percent as the average increase for the Great Plains, the total increase in land values over this seven-year period would have

32. Statement prepared for the U.S. Senate Committee on Agriculture and Forestry (January 1965), printed in *Congressional Record* (daily), Apr. 1, 1965, p. A1581. See also Mason Gaffney, "The Benefits of Farm Programs: Incidence, Shifting, and Dissipation," *J. Farm Econ.*, 47(December 1965):1252–63; and Don Paarlberg, *American Farm Policy: A Case Study of Centralized Decision-Making* (New York: John Wiley, 1964).
33. Barnhill, table 13.
34. Robert W. Strohbehn and Gene Wunderlich, table 35.

TABLE 12.12. Land value and cash returns per acre on 5 types of commercial farms

Type of farm	1937–41	1947–49	1957–61	Percent of 1947–49 1937–41	1957–61
		($)		*(%)*	
		Land value per acre			
Cash grain	120.80	219.70	376.00	55	171
Wheat-small-grain-livestock, Northern Plains	16.60	27.30	46.20	61	169
Winter wheat, Southern Plains	28.00	64.00	95.00	44	148
Wheat-pea, Washington and Oregon	66.04	174.70	267.62	38	153
Wheat-fallow	19.51	43.56	82.92	45	190
		Cash returns per acre			
Cash grain	8.33	28.92	14.65	29.0	51.0
Wheat-small-grain-livestock, Northern Plains	.25	5.88	.79	4.3	13.4
Winter wheat, Southern Plains	1.17	11.48	8.32	10.2	72.5
Wheat-pea, Washington and Oregon	5.31	20.01	13.89	26.5	69.4
Wheat-fallow	.73	7.90	6.19	9.2	78.4

Source: *Agr. Econ. Res.*, 16 (April 1964):45. Computations made from data supplied by the Cost, Income, and Efficiency Branch of the Farm Production Economics Division, USDA.

been $11.6 billion dollars. This amount is comparable to the cost of the federal wheat program which, expressed in terms of realized losses and commodity credit corporation costs from fiscal 1958 through fiscal 1965, was $11.3 billion dollars.[35] However this parallel becomes less impressive when it is realized that farm values have risen comparably in other areas which have not benefited from federal programs.

Still other statements can give perspective to the coincidence between government costs and increased land values. First, returns to Plains farmland have been comparatively quite low in recent years despite farm programs (Table 12.13). Returns both in income and in appreciation of values have been less than (as little as half as much as) the appreciation and income from the same amount invested in a representative cross section of major common stocks.[36] Increased values therefore have explanations other than increased returns. One explanation is that many persons who generate capital in the Plains area, and in other farming areas, prefer to invest this capital

35. Commodity Credit Corporation, *Report of Financial Condition and Operations*, ASCS-USDA, Annual Schedule 8, 1958 through 1965.
36. *Summary of Current Developments in Farm Real Estate Market*, ARS-USDA, series 43, no. 74 (May 1958), p. 27.

TABLE 12.13. Annual percentage return on current value of land, 20 types of commercial farms

Type of farm	1937–41	1947–49	1957–61
		(percent)	
Wheat-small-grain-livestock, Northern Plains	1.5	21.5	1.7
Winter wheat, Southern Plains	4.2	17.9	8.8
Wheat-pea, Washington and Oregon	8.0	11.4	5.2
Wheat-fallow	3.7	18.1	7.5
Cash grain	6.9	13.2	3.9
Cotton, Black Prairie, Texas	7.4	12.0	3.6
Cotton (large scale), Mississippi Delta	a	16.3	11.0
Cotton-general (irrigated), San Joaquin Valley, California	a	16.3	7.3
Cotton, Southern Piedmont	5.7	6.6	4.7
Northeast dairy	5.3	16.1	4.6
Eastern Wisconsin dairy (Grade B)	—2.7	—4.4	—6.0
Hog-beef fattening, Corn Belt	9.3	22.6	4.5
Cotton, High Plains	9.6	20.7	14.7
Dairy-hog, Southeastern Minnesota	.7	3.9	—.9
Sheep ranches, Southwest	4.9	2.9	3.8
Cattle ranches, Northern Plains	1.1	8.4	1.9
Cattle ranches, Southwest	2.9	4.6	3.6
Tobacco (small), Coastal Plains, North Carolina	a	11.6	7.6
Tobacco-cotton (large), Coastal Plains, North Carolina	a	9.4	6.7
Cotton (small), Mississippi Delta	a	22.3	5.7

Source: *Agr. Econ. Res.*, 16 (April 1964):45.

a. Not computed.

in their locality. Often the only principal local outlet for capital has been land purchase. Assuming this behavior, the price of land might well have gone up whenever farmers in the area were able to accumulate savings. Therefore the immediate determinant of land values would be accumulated earnings rather than returns from land, although these are indirectly related.

SUMMARY

It is apparent that the relationships among commodities have been reflected in a variety of policies. Earlier arrangements were the product of careful negotiations which had the support of a coalition of different supported commodities. In the Benson and Freeman administrations, they were instead the product of party and regional conflicts. In both eras, however, the legislative product extended specific protection to many different producer interests.

Earlier programs tended to increase the overlap of wheat and feed grains acreages by providing that acreages removed from wheat or cotton could be planted to feed grains, and by permitting the 15-acre exemption from the feed grain program in the feed grain areas. This tendency was reversed by the Freeman programs which permitted farmers to interchange wheat and feed grain allotments, depending on which crop grew better in a particular area.

Federal commodity policy has helped to shape the price pyramid which relates to production and use of the food and feed grains. One feature of federal intervention has been to set the price of food wheat at levels higher than this commodity would be valued in a free market, for its value would be determined by its secondary use as a feed grain. Federal policy has also recognized nonmarket demands by acquiring a national reserve of wheat and by acquiring wheat for food aid.

Federal farm programs nevertheless seem for the most part to have responded to historic relationships between wheat and other grains. The main effect of the program apparently has been to lift the old price pyramid rather than to shape or distort it. In responding to policy initiatives by wheat, cotton, high-risk and marginal areas, federal policy has provided, in the end, equally generous assistance to the highly productive areas. The highly productive areas may have benefited relatively more than the areas farm policy was prompted to assist, because the relatively higher returns to productive land had permitted fast adoption of new techniques and a more intensive cultivation of this land. Whether or not programs were a contributing factor, it does appear that the Corn Belt has improved its economic position, relative to wheat and cotton, during the postwar years of farm commodity programs.

There are differences among wheat grower operations with respect to use, distance from markets, yields, and the impact of government programs. Differences are recognized by permitting flexibility in administering the general program provisions and by including some provisions which are of importance mainly to particular regions or groups of producers.

Wheat provisions are presumed to afford to all groups a balance of benefits over sacrifices, although important and costly measures are of most assistance in the form of guaranteed income for the arid, high-risk areas. Likewise the export programs have provided outlets for the areas remote from the domestic mills. Approximately these same areas benefited most from the use of a national formula for distributing wheat certificates. In addition these white and hard red winter wheat farmers produced most of the wheat which accumulated in government stockpiles during the 1950s.

It thus appears that producers in the commercial wheat areas, and particularly on the arid fringe, were the chief beneficiaries of the wheat programs. They achieved their favored position because of the tendency in Congress to delegate program writing to the single-minded legislators from the specialized areas, and also because both program norms and program mechanics favored the "typical" specialized producer.

The attractiveness of programs has depended in part upon the way they were administered. Producers everywhere rushed to participate whenever program rules were loose or unenforced.

Although it is safe to say that no producer interest is ever wholly satisfied with the benefits received from an existing program, it is difficult to measure the relative benefits deriving to each group. There are, however, several bases for dividing benefits:

1. Relative demands for unique products, both in the commercial markets and as a result of food aid commitments.

2. Equity norms for commodity policy. These in fact have tended to favor the high-risk commercial producers in the one-crop areas, particularly in the arid fringe of the Wheat Belt.

3. Relative productivity. Competing with the equity norms have been standards of relative productivity. Rather than assuming that each farmer had a right to an adequate income, the soil bank program sought to remove the least-productive farms from crop production, while offering generous rental payments as an incentive for temporarily idling a portion of the most-productive farms.

Wheat farms have increasingly trended toward efficient-sized units. Most were still too small. Many small farmers were semi-retired, employed part-time elsewhere, or were expecting to expand the farm size. The range of size which permits maximum efficiency has been increasing slowly. Relatively few farms have grown much beyond 2,000 harvested acres, which seems to be the high side of the efficiency range.

It is unlikely that federal policies or the level of market prices will stimulate the organization of massive "factories in the field" or "corporation farms." The type of federal farm programs chosen might, however, influence the rate of decline in small farms.

The 10 percent of the landholders who owned 64 percent of all land in the Plains were mainly retired farmers or farm operators past middle age. These persons had gained the accouterments of upper-middle-class living. They had considerably more time for leisure or secondary employment than most Americans, time available both through long off-seasons and early retirement. This concentrated wealth has served mainly to increase land values. It has resulted in no significant export of capital and no distinctive contribution to America's social and cultural deposit.

While the large landowners have had no passion to dominate local political affairs, federal farm policy has been made to serve this group well. Large landowners continued to have a large stake in federal programs, because if wheat income should decline emphatically, they would possibly suffer a depreciation of capital as well as a loss of current income. The landowners were generally in good position to bear such losses, because most of their capital was free and clear.

Although landowners and larger farm operators have made good incomes, the periods of bonanza have been leveled, in a long-run average, into a lower rate of return than would have been forthcoming from investment of comparable resources in industrial enterprise. Because returns have been moderate, little investment has entered from outside the region. Since the land is owned by local individuals and is periodically redivided through the process of inheritance, the average size of landholding is growing at a slower pace than the average size of farm. Apparently an increasing proportion of cropland is owned by operators or by retired farmers.

Since the wheat-producing work force has already become quite small, there is no reason to expect that further reduction would much affect the political position of wheat producers. Rather the prosperity of the Wheat Belt will depend, it appears, on political and economic decisions with respect to the future use of wheat (such as those discussed in the next chapter) and on the ability of wheat spokesmen to make their interest coincide with national food policy and with the interests of other producers.

USDA *Photo*

13 / FOOD AID

WHEAT has been the chief vehicle of food aid to those people or areas which lack supplies or the capability to purchase their own food. Wheat made up well over half the bulk of all commodities exported in the food programs of both world wars[1] and also under the large-scale Food for Peace (P.L. 480) program operated since 1953.[2] Wheat was the instrument of food aid because it was the abundant food in the food surplus nations, inexpensive and yet nutritious, and it was a food to which hungry peoples were accustomed or could adapt. Wheat was also one of the few storable foods, and the least likely of these to deteriorate in the uncertain conditions of transit.

Another reason wheat was the principal item of food aid during the past century is that the United States has been both the chief exporter of wheat and the chief donor of food. The United States has responded often to extraordinary needs, such as those caused by war's aftermath or by such an act of God as drought.

1. Frank M. Surface and Raymond L. Bland, *American Food in the World War and the Reconstruction Period* (Stanford, Calif.: Stanford Univ. Press, 1931), p. 8.
2. *Food for Peace, 1964 Annual Report on P.L. 480* (1964), table 14.

TABLE 13.1. Major famines since 1800

Date	Area	Notes
1803–4	Western India	Due to drought, locusts, and war. Thousands died.
1837–38	Northwest India	800,000 deaths.
1846–47	Ireland	Due to potato blight. 2–3 million deaths.
1866	India Bengal and Orissa	1 million deaths.
1869	India Rajputana	1½ million deaths.
1874–75	Asia Minor	150,000 deaths.
1876–78	India	5 million deaths.
1876–79	China	Almost no rain for 3 years. Deaths estimated at 9–13 million.
1891–92	Russia	Widespread distress, mortality relatively small.
1899–1900	India	1 million deaths.
1918–19	Uganda	4,400 deaths.
1920–21	N. China	500,000 deaths.
1920–21	Russia	Due to drought. Millions died.
1929	China Hunan	2 million deaths.
1932–33	Russia	Due to collectivization. Excess mortality estimated at 3–10 million.
1943	Ruanda-Urundi	35,000–50,000 deaths.
1943–44	India Bengal	Excessive rain and wartime difficulties of supply. 2 million deaths.
1960–61	Congo Kasai	Due to civil disturbance.

Source: G. B. Masefield, *Famine: Its Prevention and Relief* (London: Oxford Univ. Press, 1963), pp. 13–14.

More than other nations, perhaps, America has been responsive to appeals to prevent mass starvation. Recently the United States has turned attention also to chronic health problems such as malnutrition, both in the United States and abroad.

Until World War I, and in some cases thereafter, the amounts of U.S. food aid were not a reflection of the need, or even of the resources available for meeting the need. This is suggested by the compilation of major famines[3] since 1800 (Table 13.1), most of which elicited little or no response from the United States. Since 1914, however, U.S. food aid has greatly moderated European famines after each world war and has averted a number of famines since 1953.

Congress was responsible for the first recorded U.S. food aid by means of an appropriation in 1841 to purchase food for earthquake victims in Venezuela. In 1902 Congress appropriated $200,000 for relief to those made destitute by a volcanic eruption on Marti-

3. According to G. B. Masefield, "Any satisfactory definition of famine must provide that the food shortage is either widespread or extreme if not both, and that the degree of extremity is best measured by human mortality from starvation. A time element should probably also be included. The minimum acceptable definition would then imply a wide and prolonged shortage of food resulting in an increased human death rate." In his book *Famine: Its Prevention and Relief* (London: Oxford Univ. Press, 1963), pp. 3–4.

nique, French West Indies. In 1908 President Theodore Roosevelt diverted two supply ships to relieve victims of a Sicilian earthquake.

Most food aid before World War I was from donations taken at the initiative of private groups or local governmental officials. In response to news of the Russian famine of 1891–92, a group of flour millers began to assemble aid, and then a group of distinguished Americans formed a committee which ultimately contributed more than $700,000 in foodstuffs and cash. State officials and local governments in the Midwest played an important part in raising supplies for this famine relief project. Similar groups raised funds for Russian food relief in 1907 and for Armenia in 1893–94, and food was sent to China and India on numerous occasions after 1890.

These token food shipments by governmental and private groups apparently proceeded from a variety of motives. These shipments were often no more than flamboyant acts by elected officials or the popular philanthropy of a magazine or newspaper and its readers. In 1921, for example, *Country Gentleman* detailed the conditions of life in the China famine and accepted contributions to be used for purchase of U.S. grain for famine relief. One writer in the series on famine in *Country Gentleman* stated, "For myself, I need a new hat—should have bought it weeks ago—but that new hat is going to China. It makes a man feel good, doesn't it, to think his hat can line an entire Chinese inside and out?"[4] At that time wheat was in oversupply, "dammed up from the ocean port all the way back to the farm." *Country Gentleman* did not expect that food shipments would reduce the surplus much. Reporting that 40 million Chinese were confronted with death, *Country Gentleman* nevertheless seemed confident that America's token donations would "nurse China back to health."[5]

Some aid had political or nationalistic overtones. The offer of aid publicized the existence of a food shortage—and perhaps of the inadequacy of a recipient political system. The government of Czarist Russia was usually uncooperative with the frequent U.S. efforts to distribute food in Russia, because the Czar was quite reluctant to admit to food shortages and because indigenous relief agents would likely be reformers who would carry on revolutionary propaganda while feeding the hungry.[6]

---

4. William T. Ellis, "A Farmer's Famine," *Country Gentleman*, 86(March 26, 1921): 31.
5. *Country Gentleman*, 86(Jan. 22, 1921):12.
6. H. H. Fisher, *The Famine in Soviet Russia, 1919–1923* (New York: Macmillan, 1927), p. 479.

FOOD AID IN WORLD WAR I

At the beginning of World War I the United States and governments of the allied nations provided funds for an organization headed by Herbert Hoover, called the Commission for the Relief of Belgium, which distributed food to civilians in the areas of North France and Belgium occupied by the Germans. The CRB was granted immunity under its own flag.

After the United States entered World War I, a U.S. government corporation assumed control over many U.S. food resources, including all wheat. By restraining domestic use and by exhorting farmers to grow more wheat and deliver it quickly, the United States was able to channel more than 600 million bushels of grain to allied countries (Table 13.2).

The wartime shipments of wheat to Europe were viewed as an important part of the war effort. "Food will win the war" was an often-repeated slogan, presumably referring to the good effect of food shipments upon allied strength and morale. Humanitarian considerations were also prominent at that time. In counseling farmers to select their corn seed carefully for the 1918 crop, *Wallaces Farmer* magazine reminded farmers that "starving people on the other side of the water are looking to the United States for something to eat. The longer the war continues, the more serious this problem will become. It is little short of a crime, therefore, not to make dead sure of an ample amount of good seed for next year's crop."[7]

The relief effort in the year following that war was directed by Herbert Hoover. The United States established the American Relief Administration, which together with the U.S. War Department furnished about three-fourths of the $1 billion spent in postwar relief.[8] The remainder was contributed by the Allied governments and private agencies.

The large amounts of U.S. food aid during and after the war were regarded as a precedent in humanitarianism, and for purposes of measuring human progress were thought to balance the destructive power of firearms. Hoover stressed that food aid would "maintain an ideal and faith which must be the foundation of the world's hope in civilization."[9] Presumably the United States was interested in saving a civilization as well as in setting an example in civilized conduct, although this effect of U.S. aid was emphasized more by foreign ob-

---

7. *Wallaces Farmer*, 42(Oct. 5, 1917):4.
8. Surface and Bland, pp. 35–72.
9. *Wallaces Farmer*, 42(Sept. 7, 1917):16–17.

TABLE 13.2. U.S. wheat exports under concessional programs

Fiscal year	Total	World War II Military UNRRA	Foreign economic aid	P.L. 480 (Food for Peace) I	II	III Barter	III Donation	IV
				(000 bushels)				
November 1914–August 1919[a]	136,758	...	...	...	...	...	...	...
April 1917–June 1919[b]	407,943	...	...	...	...	...	...	...
November 1918–June 1919[c]	60,902	...	...	...	...	...	...	...
1919–1924[d]	31,469	...	...	...	...	...	...	...
1945	169,754	169,754	...	...	...	...	...	...
1946	160,022	160,022	...	...	...	...	...	...
1947	325,838	277,906	47,932	...	...	...	...	...
1948	376,011	167,508	208,503	...	...	...	...	...
1949	256,790	118,845	137,945	...	...	...	...	...
1950	172,968	31,493	138,856	...	...	2,619	...	..
1951	159,341	5,254	137,163	...	...	16,924	...	..
1952	29,605	2,702	22,965	...	...	3,938	...	..
1953	100,544	1,517	89,063	...	...	9,964	...	..
1954	158,025	963	70,811	23,802	15,991	46,459	...	..
1955	240,693	...	64,978	94,347	11,864	66,716	2,788	..
1956	375,119	...	63,574	200,536	12,188	87,086	11,735	..
1957	246,826	...	25,713	179,023	14,290	9,807	17,993	..
1958	303,002	...	23,946	227,914	10,861	20,062	20,219	..
1959	374,552	...	13,264	300,648	10,722	25,662	24,256	..
1960	457,720	...	35,568	327,214	30,490	34,090	30,358	..
1961	491,072	...	2,539	379,110	25,702	41,337	35,098	7,28
1962	488,980	...	1,433	407,381	30,589	6,493	37,400	5,68
1963	503,414	...	584	387,925	30,167	35,167	37,394	12,17
1964	565,885	...	133	438,883	19,399	12,443	35,248	59,77

Sources: Information on World War I food programs was obtained from Frank M. Surface and Raymond L. Bland, *American Food in the World War and Reconstruction Period* (Stanford, Calif.: Stanford Univ. Press, 1931), table 101. This table does not include substantial nongovernmental contribution in work, funds, and grains commodities by private U.S. groups. The amounts are for food grain or equivalent, almost all of which is apparently wheat and flour, except for shipment to the Soviet Union after 1921, which were all in corn.

Information for programs since 1945 was obtained from files of the Economic Research Service (USDA) and from *Wheat Situation,* USDA-ERS (February 1961), table 3, and (October 1965), table 17.

a. The Commission for Relief in Belgium. The U.S. government contributed 47.5 percent of the funds for this group, and it is assumed that this percentage of the wheat or wheat equivalent used by the CRB was furnished by the United States.
b. Shipments to the Allied powers by the U.S. Food Administration.
c. Relief shipments to European countries during the armistice period.
d. Reconstruction period, including the feeding of European children, and furnishing seed wheat as part of the famine relief to the Soviet Union in 1921–22.

servers than by Americans. Thus in 1920 John Maynard Keynes congratulated the U.S. aid administrators for this achievement:

> Europe, too, should never forget the extraordinary assistance afforded her during the first six months of 1919 through the agency of Mr. Hoover and the American Commission of Relief. Never was a nobler work of disinterested goodwill carried through with more tenacity and sincerity and skill, and with less thanks either asked or given. The ungrateful Governments of Europe owe much more to the statesmanship and insight of Mr. Hoover and his band of American workers than they have yet appreciated or will ever acknowledge. The American Relief Commission, and they only, saw the European position during those months in its true perspective and felt towards it as men should. It was their efforts, their energy, and the American resources placed by the President at their disposal, often acting in the teeth of European obstruction, which not only saved an immense amount of human suffering, but averted a widespread breakdown of the European system.[10]

While wishing to be a good neighbor, U.S. policy makers were constrained by the desire to avoid being made a sucker. The allies were expected to repay the loans under which wartime food had been shipped, and Hoover was careful to see that the U.S. government controlled the postwar relief funds and that due credit was received for U.S. relief activities.

With the signing of a draft of a peace treaty in mid-1919, the remaining U.S. relief supplies on hand were donated to a private relief agency headed by Hoover, which utilized them to conduct a feeding program for war orphans and other children in Europe and in the Balkans, and which was still on the scene when famine occurred in the Soviet Union in 1921. In response to the Soviet famine, the U.S. government donated $20 million to be spent mainly for the purchase of and transport of U.S. corn. At that time an outlet was needed for the market surplus of U.S. corn, which was selling as low as 11 cents per bushel. When purchases for Soviet relief were made, the corn price quickly advanced to 60 cents per bushel.[11]

In addition to food surplus disposal and humanitarian objectives, political considerations surrounded the Russian famine aid program. A Communist (Bolshevik) regime had come to power in the uncertain conditions of postwar Russia. Some observers (mostly in Europe) maintained that food aid would help the Communists maintain their tenuous hold on that country. France, England, and the United States had recently supplied troops and other assistance to the anti-

---

10. Roy Walker, *Famine Over Europe* (London: Andrew Dakers, 1941), pp. 17–18.
11. Surface and Bland, pp. 114–15.

Communist counterrevolutionary forces within Russia. Hoover, in pressing for the famine relief, suggested that famine had contributed to the severity of change in Russia, from the "tyranny of the extreme right to the tyranny of the extreme left." Hoover said, "The poor were starved and driven mad in the presence of extravagance and waste."[12]

Some had suggested food be made available to Russia only in the context of military intervention to achieve political objectives. Hoover, although an outspoken anti-Communist, opposed this course. As a result of military intervention, he said:

> We should probably be involved in years of police duty and our first act would probably, in the nature of things, make us a party to re-establishing the reactionary classes in their economic domination over the lower classes. This is against our fundamental national spirit, and I doubt whether our soldiers under these circumstances could resist infection with Bolshevik ideas. It also requires consideration as to whether or not our people at home, on gradual enlightenment as to the social wrongs of the lower classes in these countries, would stand for our providing power by which such reactionaries held their position, and we would perchance be thrown into an attempt as governors to work out social reorganization of these countries. We thus become a mandatory with a vengeance.[13]

Hoover did not suggest that food aid was an adequate antidote to Bolshevism, although he made the point that Bolshevik propaganda was most successful where the people were most troubled.[14] Hoover was confident that in due time the pendulum of the Russian revolution would swing, as in other revolutions, to a more moderate position. "No greater fortune can come to the world than that these foolish ideas should have an opportunity somewhere of bankrupting themselves."[15]

Famine relief efforts in the Soviet Union were further embarrassed by the decision of the Soviet government to export wheat despite the food shortage, and by its refusal to sell the crown jewels, which were widely known to be in the Communist government's possession. Despite this resistance, the relief group persisted in distributing food until it was apparent that the famine threat had been relieved.

In 1932 feeding the hungry again served as a way to dispose of unwanted surpluses. At that time the chairman of the Federal Farm Board proposed to donate 45 million bushels of wheat—approximately

---

12. Fisher, p. 11.
13. Ibid., p. 13.
14. Ibid., p. 12.
15. Ibid.

half the board's remaining holdings—to the Red Cross for purposes of relieving distress. However Senator Reed Smoot (R., Utah) suggested instead that the entire stock be donated:

> I want to be perfectly frank about my position. As long as you hold that wheat here in bulk, the price of wheat to farmers all over the United States is going to be the same. I do not know how you feel about it, but I think it would be better for the government, the farmers, and everybody else—better for the whole country—if the whole thing were absolutely closed out. . . . This is hanging over the wheat market, . . . it hangs like a pall.[16]

In agreement with Senator Smoot's view, the full amount of wheat was donated for domestic relief.

FOOD AID IN WORLD WAR II

Immediate postwar relief (1945–46) from the United States was distributed in several war-torn countries by the United Nations Relief and Rehabilitation Agency, which began operations as an agency in the U.S. Department of State. The UNRRA received its international charter in September 1944. It was intended as a cooperative effort of the Allies and their associates, ultimately 48 governments in all, with private groups also contributing.

The U.S. government contributed about 70 percent ($2,700 million) of total UNRRA resources.[17] Most contributions were given in commodity credits rather than in dollars. In addition the funds first designated for rehabilitation were spent for food, due to the great need for food at that time, so that about half of total UNRRA expenditures were for food aid.[18] The bulk of the food was bread grains obtained from the grain-exporting countries and from army stocks in various countries.[19] During its brief existence the UNRRA handled over 25 million long tons of goods, more than three times the total of post-World War I relief.

Most assistance went to seven war-torn countries in southern Europe and the Balkans, plus the Ukraine and Belorussia. China was also a major recipient, and lesser amounts of aid went to Ethiopia, Finland, Hungary, Korea, the Philippines, and the Dodecanese

16. U.S. Senate Appropriation Subcommittee on Agriculture, *Hearings on Distribution of Government-owned Wheat and Cotton* (1932), p. 7.
17. United Nations Relief and Rehabilitation Agency, *The Story of UNRRA* (February 1948), p. 10.
18. Ibid., p. 18.
19. Ibid, pp. 19–20.

Islands. Western European countries were not assisted because they possessed adequate foreign exchange to pay for their own relief supplies.

Food assistance was channeled through governments wherever these existed, but the UNRRA under a succession of U.S. directors exercised a firm review over requests and checked on administration of the aid. Relief was to be given free to all who could not pay, but for the most part people were able to pay in local currency for the supplies they received. Governments sold relief supplies as a means of fighting inflation.

Despite charges such as one that the Yugoslav (Communist) government was diverting relief supplies to its army, UNRRA administration concluded that the great preponderance of its supplies were distributed "without discrimination," that is, to those who needed them most. The major exception was China, where administration was poor due to civil war.[20] (Secretary Anderson said later that of 200,000 tons of wheat sent to China under the UNRRA, less than 20,000 tons arrived at the famine area.)[21]

In addition to the problem of overseeing distribution, the UNRRA faced temporary shortages of ships and docking facilities. However the "headache" word was "nonavailability" of food which could be purchased for relief. Scarce food was often rerouted in mid-ocean as one desperate need became greater than another. Grain which was to be used for seed often had to be used instead to sustain life.

In evaluating results, the UNRRA staff noted that "nutritionists of wide reputation say that three specific famines which seemed almost inevitable were averted by UNRRA: one in urban Austria and one each in rural Yugoslavia and rural Greece."[22] These nutritionists concluded that postwar relief had failed to prevent acute hunger throughout Europe. "Great pools of human beings have had barely enough food to live on for years. Underfeeding, and the diseases that mushroom with it, spreads out across Europe and the Far East like a mantle."[23]

The UNRRA operation was closed down beginning in August 1946. The United States and the United Kingdom took the position that the governments which had resumed operation in most liberated countries could better procure and ship supplies through loans from

20. Ibid., p. 17.
21. Testimony before U.S. Senate Committee on Agriculture and Forestry, *Hearings on Wheat for Pakistan* (1953), p. 11.
22. UNRRA, p. 18.
23. Ibid.

the International Bank for Reconstruction and Development or with unilateral assistance from a friendly country.[24] The long-range plans of UNRRA for rehabilitation were to be unrealized except as some of these plans were implemented by other international agencies.

THE EUROPEAN RECOVERY PROGRAM

The limited geographic scope of the UNRRA, as well as its demise, were due in large part to conflict between great power interests which produced the Cold War beginning in 1947. The humanitarian sentiments which had prompted the UNRRA became less important than the political aim of containing the Soviet Union. The U.S. government, which had become alarmed at Communist successes in European domestic politics, concluded that the best defense against European communism was economic aid. In the words of the State Department staff study memorandum which influenced the decision to aid Europe, the proper action under the circumstances was "not to combat communism, but the economic maladjustment which makes European society vulnerable to exploitation by any and all totalitarian movements and which Russian communism is now exploiting."[25]

This new objective of containing communism prompted a new bilateral U.S. aid program, called the Marshall Plan and later named the European Recovery Program. An effort was made to avoid the Cold War stance by inviting the Soviet Union to participate—but with the intention of stating conditions which the Soviet Union would very likely decline to accept.[26]

One significant cause of the European economic crisis was undernourishment.[27] Per capita food consumption was only two-thirds of the average for the United States. As a means of preventing inflation in France, the bread ration had been reduced in 1947 to previous low wartime levels.[28] With another poor crop due in 1947, resulting from drought, Europe was critically short of food and lacked the financial means at that time to import it.

Food thus became an important component of Marshall Plan aid. President Truman's Committee on Foreign Aid (the Harriman Committee) said in an interim report in November 1957 that "the urgency

24. Ibid., pp. 44–45.
25. Harry Bayard Price, *The Marshall Plan and Its Meaning* (Ithaca: Cornell Univ, Press, 1955), pp. 21–28. © Governmental Affairs Institute.
26. Ibid.
27. Ibid., p. 30.
28. Ibid., p. 31.

of the current food crisis in Europe cannot be overemphasized."[29] It asserted the responsibility of the United States to maximize exports from domestic supplies of grains and other foods. Truman persuaded Congress, in special session during the fall of 1947, to furnish food and fuel to help Italy and France "survive this critical winter as free and independent nations."[30] This emergency aid was in advance of the longer-range European Recovery Program, which also financed huge shipments of U.S. grain to Europe.

Wheat supplies for ERP had to be obtained at first in a tight world market. Farmers were no doubt as happy about the resulting inflation as the executive branch was anxious to contain it. The President's committee urged that more ERP food be purchased from countries other than the United States "to avoid adding to inflationary pressures that are pushing prices upward here, and to enable the needy countries to buy in the lowest markets."[31]

In an effort to avoid strain on the U.S. economy, the executive branch pressured European countries to reduce their expectations with respect to bread grain imports and other agricultural imports for 1948–49 and 1949–50.[32] The world grain shortage was short-lived, however, and ERP was soon appreciated as an outlet for U.S. grain surpluses. Secretary Anderson stated that the ERP was needed to provide adequate postwar markets for wheat and some other products.[33] His successor, Secretary Brannan, suggested in 1949 that the great advances in U.S. productive capacity during the war had left a serious problem of "balance," although this was temporarily concealed by the large agricultural exports.[34]

United States aid dollars permitted Europe, during the time that its agriculture was in disrepair, to purchase considerably more U.S. wheat than in prewar years. Aid shipments in fiscal 1948 and 1949 were larger than total average U.S. wheat exports in past decades. During 1945–49 the U.S. share of the world wheat market rose from a long-term average of about one-quarter to almost one-half of the total world wheat exports.

Whether and how U.S. farm surpluses should be used as an instrument of foreign aid was the chief point of controversy in constructing the aid programs. European recipients preferred dollar aid

---

29. *European Recovery and American Aid, A Report by the President's Committee on Foreign Aid* (Nov. 7, 1947), p. 39.
30. Price, p. 47.
31. Ibid., p. 29.
32. Seymour E. Harris, *The European Recovery Program* (Cambridge, Mass.: Harvard Univ. Press, 1948), pp. 221–22.
33. Ibid., p. 149.
34. *New York Times,* July 29, 1949, p. 24.

which could be spent for goods needed to rebuild their industry. They preferred to buy most agricultural products in nondollar markets or to rely on their own agriculture.[35] The government of France, for example, apparently wished to return to wartime food rationing in 1949, meanwhile stimulating its own agriculture, in order to devote its dollar purchasing power to meeting a high target of industrial imports.

United States farm legislators, in contrast, wanted to be certain that U.S. farmers got their share of the foreign aid market. In addition Secretaries Anderson and Brannan both hoped that through food aid U.S. products could maintain access to European food markets and perhaps even increase their share. This was one reason why the major farm organizations strongly supported the European Recovery Program.[36]

There were continual efforts to earmark aid funds specifically for purchases of surplus farm products, supported by some legislators but usually opposed by the major farm organizations. In April 1949 Representative Eugene Worley (D., Texas) proposed that no ECA funds should be used to purchase U.S. farm products until CCC surpluses were liquidated. Presumably the effect of the amendment would have been to pressure the U.S. administration to ship government stocks directly to Europe rather than permitting cash loans to be used for the purchase of both surplus and nonsurplus U.S. commodities. His amendment failed two-to-one in a vote in the House of Representatives.[37]

The foreign aid appropriations bill of 1949 was the subject of a parliamentary hassle due to Senate approval of an amendment by Senator John L. McClellan (D., Arkansas) which would have "frozen" about $1.8 billion in ECA funds in order to divert them to disposal of surplus farm products into the countries receiving aid.[38]

In March of 1950, by which time wheat stocks were large, the U.S. House Foreign Affairs Committee voted to cut $1 billion from the $3.1 billion fund for the third year of the Marshall Plan and to replace this appropriation with an equivalent value in American agriculture surpluses (Vorys amendment). This proposal was opposed by Paul Hoffman, director of the U.S. agency administering the aid. Hoffman

35. "Summary of the Report of the Committee of European Economic Cooperation (CEEC)," *European Recovery Program: Basic Documents and Background Information*, U.S. Senate Doc. 1111 (1947), pp. 82–83.
36. Don F. Hadwiger, "Farm Organizations and U.S. Foreign Trade Policy, 1946–1955" (Ph.D. diss., University of Iowa, 1956), pp. 217–21.
37. *New York Times*, Apr. 12, 1949, p. 3.
38. *New York Times*, July 15, 1949, p. 6; July 30, 1949, p. 2.

said that considerable study would be needed to determine to what extent farm surpluses could meet European needs. Like the earlier efforts to earmark funds, the Vorys amendment was opposed by the major farm organizations and by the USDA. Vorys gave this explanation for farm group opposition: "The farm bloc wants another billion in the bill in tax money to buy more farm products for Europe. They offer no suggestion as to how we can use the surplus the taxpayers already own and have paid for. They assume that we are to go on and on buying surpluses and doing nothing with them, that we don't dare sell them or give them away any place in the world."[39] It appeared, therefore, that the various earmarking amendments were designed primarily as economy measures, although they were no doubt part of the effective pressure upon U.S. aid administrators as well as foreign recipients to make maximum use of surplus farm products. As economist Seymour Harris remarked at the time, "No competent observer of the ERP will gainsay the fact that it is in part an organization for dumping surpluses."[40]

Surpluses were disposed of in other ways as well. In 1949 Secretary Brannan put the "full approbation" of the U.S. government in support of a committee of fourteen nations to act as an international commodity clearinghouse for surplus commodities.[41] In August of 1950 the USDA offered surpluses (mostly of perishable products) to all 62 members of the U.N. Food and Agriculture Organization. These could be purchased at a nominal price, on the conditions that the food should supplement rather than replace normal imports and that it could not be purchased with U.S. aid funds.[42] President Truman asked for authority to pay the costs of inland transportation of these commodities to the port at which they were loaded for export, since costs were paid in full on the food shipment to Israel for relief of refugees at about that time.[43]

Alternatives to surplus disposal were suggested particularly by those who opposed it or by those who looked ahead to when Europe would again depend on its own resources. As an alternative the CCC, in the Commodity Credit Corporation Charter Act of 1949, was permitted to barter surpluses for strategic materials to the extent that these were needed by the U.S. military agencies. A committee of a private research group, the National Planning Association, gave its

39. *New York Times,* Mar. 26, 1950, p. 3.
40. Harris, p. 12.
41. *New York Times,* Dec. 6, 1949, p. 22.
42. *New York Times,* Aug. 5, 1950, p. 13.
43. *New York Times,* Aug. 5, 1950, p. 13; Sept. 15, 1950, p. 20.

approval to a proposal by Senator George Aiken (R., Vermont) that the United States "eat its surpluses" rather than dump them overseas or curtail crops. Aiken's plan was to raise both the quantity and nutritive value of food consumption, mainly through a domestic food stamp program.[44]

Foreign observers too were concerned about the growing U.S. surplus productive capacity. The Deputy Director General of the Food and Agriculture Organization, Sir Herbert Broadley, noted that the United States could continue exporting heavily at the end of the aid program if it were able to take produce in exchange for its own exports; but since the United States already produced "almost all the other goods used by mankind," he felt that the best solution would be "a long-term investment policy on the part of the United States and the planning of its own production program in such a way as to enable interest and repayment of its loans under conditions which it deliberately leaves to the debtor countries."[45] In other words, the United States could go on sending food abroad in the form of capital or food, under long-term loan arrangements. Another observer, Dr. H. H. Hannam of Canada, expressed fear that surpluses would prompt an orgy of competitive dumping.[46]

One constructive expression of international concern over increasing surpluses was the negotiation and signing of the International Wheat Agreement in 1949. Then the Korean War provided temporary relief. In 1950, the first year of the war, U.S. farmers were asked to step up their production rather than to restrain it. In 1952, however, U.S. exports slumped as both European aid and the war came to an end.

POST-KOREAN SURPLUSES

In 1953, at the end of the Korean War, U.S. stocks of wheat and some other commodities were growing rapidly. New moves were clearly needed to reduce production or increase use if surpluses were not to become unmanageable.

Most decision makers looked forward to reduced production as a main long-run remedy, yet they could not agree on how to bring this about. Secretary Benson would have accomplished it by means of reduced price supports, while the dominant opinion in Congress favored federal production controls. This deadlock over means lasted throughout the Benson administration. In retrospect, both groups

44. *New York Times,* Mar. 8, 1949, p. 15.
45. *New York Times,* June 14, 1949, p. 23.
46. *New York Times,* May 30, 1950, p. 20.

may have been right in suggesting that the other's remedy would have proved inadequate.

While policy makers were deadlocked over how to reduce production, most were concerned with the growing stocks of surpluses. However there was reluctance to dispose of surplus wheat by donation or on concessional terms, or to transfer wheat in any other manner than through the cash market.

There were several grounds for this reluctance. The costs of any such surplus disposal program would likely be regarded as part of the costs of a farm program and be charged against the agricultural budget in a manner not subject to direct congressional control (disposal from existing Commodity Credit Corporation stocks). Farm congressmen would bear the burden of political support for these expenditures even though agriculture was not the only beneficiary. In addition many conservative Republicans and southern Democrats had been philosophically opposed to foreign aid programs. Many of them had voted against the bill which gave the President discretionary power to donate CCC commodities to people threatened by famine.[47] In the words of Representative Pat Sutton (D., Tennessee), this measure was a "continuation of the Santa Claus program."[48] Wheat and cotton congressmen were worried that U.S. food donations would tempt some recipient countries to shift acreages away from food grains and into profitable cotton and other export crops.

The dilemma was exasperating for those farm congressmen who wanted to prevent surplus buildup and yet who were not enthusiastic for domestic or foreign food aid programs. Not only was food aid the only major outlet for surpluses (other than outright destruction of commodities), there was an impelling need for food to remedy serious dietary deficiencies throughout the world and to prevent actual starvation in famine areas. The chairman of the House Agriculture Committee, Clifford Hope (R., Kansas), warned legislators that the price support program would fall into disrepute if CCC commodities should spoil while there were starving people elsewhere in the world.[49]

Some few rural liberals professed to be happy about U.S. agricultural "abundance." Surpluses could serve humanitarian purposes. These liberals were inclined to emphasize the actual growth of world hunger which Secretary Henry A. Wallace had predicted and worked to prevent in the late 1930s. They envisioned "permanent" food pro-

47. *Congressional Quarterly Almanac*, 9(1953):232–33, 254.
48. Ibid., p. 222. See also U.S. House Committee on Agriculture, *Hearings on Famine Relief* (1953), pp. 18–19.
49. *Congressional Record* (bound), June 22, 1953, p. 7024.

grams such as the food stamp program of the late thirties rather than temporary disposal programs, and they posed humanitarian or foreign policy goals.

This view was espoused by the National Farmers Union and its president, James Patton. Its chief expositor, however, was Senator Hubert Humphrey (D., Minnesota) whose viewpoint expressed in 1953 came to be incorporated, subsequently, in official policy. Testifying for the famine relief bill in 1953, Humphrey stressed that the farm problem was one of distribution not of production: "The farmers have done their work well. The fault, if there is any, is with the rest of us—we have not kept pace in making wise use of all that our farmers can produce. . . . We have not yet learned to live with the abundance with which we are blessed."[50]

Humphrey believed that food aid would strengthen America's world position. It would insert "a new positive, humanitarian force into the world's ideological struggle." It was also a good means to secure world cooperation as compared with the means of military aid and containment. He noted that 300 million pounds of dried skim milk in CCC stocks could prevent childhood deaths due to lack of protein. "Aren't we as ready to make use of our resources to save the world's children as we are to pour vast resources into destructive channels?"[51]

Also optimistic that food aid would find adequate popular support, Humphrey felt that the people of the United States "can and will understand and approve making use of American food and fiber to feed and clothe hungry and suffering people throughout the world. They will not only understand such efforts—they will welcome them. . . . It's a simple, Christian, humanitarian approach to better world understanding that makes sense to every American family."[52]

Humphrey suggested a comprehensive program, initially relying primarily on a combination of existing mechanisms to use food for humanitarian and other purposes. In 1953 Humphrey was an early advocate of famine relief for Pakistan, and he suggested a number of longer-range food uses which had been or were subsequently adopted. These included donations, sales at concessional prices, sales under very long term loans, sales for foreign currencies, distribution through voluntary organizations, and barter of surplus food for strategic materials to be stockpiled in the United States. Humphrey also was an

---

50. U.S. Senate Committee on Agriculture and Forestry, *Hearings on S. 2249 Emergency Famine Assistance Authority* (1953), pp. 23–27.
51. Ibid.
52. Ibid.

instigator of a huge food grant to Pakistan to prevent famine in 1953. This was an important first step toward making food a major instrument of U.S. policy and toward a U.S. commitment to fill any serious world food deficit.

AID TO PAKISTAN

In this environment of growing surpluses and mixed feelings about food aid, President Eisenhower asked Congress for authority to grant one million long tons of U.S. wheat to the government of Pakistan. In his statement to Congress, the President said that Pakistan was normally self-sufficent in food but faced famine due to an extraordinary two-year drought and could not afford to buy food abroad.

This substantial grant was a precedent in the use of food as a major instrument of postwar foreign policy. In testimony supporting the gift, Secretary of State John Foster Dulles reminded Congress that Pakistan occupied a strategic position on the border of the Soviet Union, since it contained the Khyber Pass, the historic invasion route from the north into the subcontinent of India. He said, "I can think of no spot in the world where it is more to our advantage to try to be helpful at this particular moment than in Pakistan."[53]

Dulles recalled that Pakistan had given the United States crucial support during the negotiation of the Japanese Peace Treaty. He was certain that the Pakistanis were anti-Communist and "strong in their faith." He was also impressed by the "martial spirit of the people."[54] An explicit purpose of the aid, according to aid director Harold Stassen, was to enable Pakistan "to keep a strong defensive force" in that strategic area.[55] Secretary Dulles suggested that political strength and food were related. "No country or government can remain strong if its people are starving, and I am convinced that Pakistan's need for wheat to avert starvation is great and urgent. Failure on our part to help Pakistan promptly and in some measure needed would permit disaster."[56]

The Farm Bureau Federation opposed the financing arrangement in the bill, under which the wheat would be sold in Pakistan, with proceeds to be used jointly by the United States and Pakistan for

---

53. Senate, *Hearings on Wheat for Pakistan*, p. 5.
54. Ibid., pp. 4–5.
55. Ibid., p. 34.
56. U.S. House Committee on Agriculture, *Hearings on Wheat to Pakistan*, (1953), p. 6.

technical assistance and economic development.[57] The Farm Bureau preferred payment in foreign currencies equal to the value of the wheat, to be used by the United States for its own purposes within Pakistan. On the other hand there were some legislators, including former Secretary of Agriculture Clinton Anderson (D., New Mexico), who would have preferred free distribution. Anderson believed the purpose of the surplus disposal should be to relieve suffering and to create popular goodwill for the United States rather than to strengthen the Pakistan government or the economy.[58]

This was also an appropriate time to raise the question as to why U.S. aid was not in the form of dollar loans rather than in wheat. Dulles explained that since Pakistan lacked the capacity to repay such a loan, a financial obligation would have served only to embitter relations between the countries.[59]

Finally a number of conservative legislators wondered whether they were setting a precedent which would lead to extensive food aid shipments in the future. Secretary Dulles indicated that grants of wheat would be made only in grave natural disasters; and in subsequent hearings on the famine relief bill enacted shortly thereafter, Assistant Secretary of State Samuel C. Waugh affirmed that the President intended to use commodities for relief of "famine or other urgent relief requirements but not for a general matter of just decreasing the dietary deficiencies in certain countries."[60]

At the House hearings for Pakistan, Secretary Dulles said that he saw no emergency or relief need in the world at that time comparable to that of Pakistan, nor did he feel that the situation in Pakistan would recur. Neither did he feel that the United States would be under pressure in the future to make grants of wheat rather than loans for relief as in the past. Nevertheless this new policy alternative became available as a result of the Pakistan precedent, and was shortly tied in with a number of other devices for distribution of surpluses in noncommercial channels.

The Pakistan act authorized the shipment of 1 million tons of grain, of which 608,000 were shipped for immediate relief. The United States decided against shipping the remainder, which was to have been used to create a food reserve in Pakistan.[61]

57. Senate, *Hearings on Wheat for Pakistan*, p. 31.
58. Ibid., pp. 11–13.
59. Ibid., p. 7.
60. House, *Hearings on Famine Relief*, p. 7.
61. The U.S. House Committee on Agriculture, *Hearings on the Long Range Farm Program* (1954), p. 4159.

PUBLIC LAW 480

In 1954 Congress passed P.L. 480, which elevated food surplus distribution to a major role in farm policy and ultimately in foreign policy as well.[62] This law renewed existing provisions for relieving famine and natural catastrophes abroad, for barter of farm surpluses for strategic materials, for distribution of surpluses domestically, and also for distribution abroad through private charitable agencies. Humanitarian as well as foreign policy aims were in the minds of several sponsors, including Senator Hubert Humphrey and officials in the Farmers Union. But these were not the major purposes of P.L. 480 as passed in 1954. Most liberal legislators supported the measure even though humanitarian and foreign policy objectives were subordinated, in the expectation that the thrust of the program might change, as indeed it did.

Initially the main purpose of P.L. 480, aside from the immediate purpose of reducing surpluses, was to increase U.S. commodity sales abroad. The original proposal, adopted at the 1952 convention of the American Farm Bureau Association, assumed that countries which preferred to use their scarce U.S. dollars for capital purchases would be willing to buy U.S. farm commodities also if they could pay with their own currency.[63] The architects of the law were the Farm Bureau and conservative rural legislators. The main feature of their legislative product was Title I, which authorized the sale of $700 million of surplus commodities in exchange for currencies of the recipient country.

These foreign currency proceeds could not be traded for dollars, but the foreign currency could be spent abroad for things of value to the United States. Since something worthwhile was gained from the exchange, foreign currency sales were seen as "new markets." These sales could also serve as a wedge opening new cash markets in which the United States would have an advantage over other competitors. Thus it was hoped that P.L. 480 would eliminate sur-

---

62. Statements here relative to the source of P.L. 480, the purposes of its original sponsors and supporters, and the role of Farm Bureau in gaining administration support for it are generally supported in the following research: David S. McClellan and Donald Clare, *Public Law 480: The Metamorphosis of a Law* (New York: McGraw-Hill, Eagleton Institute Cases in Practical Politics, 1965); Elmer L. Menzie and Robert G. Crouch, *Political Interests in Agricultural Export Surplus Disposal Through Public Law 480*, Arizona Exp. Sta. Tech. Bull. 161 (September 1964); Hadwiger; and Peter A. Toma, *The Politics of Food for Peace* (Tucson: Univ. of Arizona Press, 1967).

pluses and in the process find cash markets adequate for future production.

Farm Bureau can be credited not only with putting the emphasis on trade expansion rather than political goals but with selling the measure to a reluctant Eisenhower administration. The administration's reluctance to accept the program was attributed to the State Department, which began to be attacked by influential rural legislators early in 1954.[64] Senator James Eastland (D., Mississippi) said the State Department was not an American agency of government.[65] Senator Hubert Humphrey said, in reference to the State Department: "Once in a while political appointees have to be taken to the woodshed and taught a lesson. I think that time has come when the shilelagh should be wielded in order to get some action on the part of those departments in the area we have been discussing.[66]

P.L. 480, besides strengthening U.S. agriculture's economic position, was effected to give farm groups influence in decisions on international trade, vis-à-vis the State Department, since P.L. 480 was to be administered mainly by the USDA. Partly as a means to reduce the State Department's influence over agricultural trade and aid, U.S. agriculture attachés had already been transferred from State Department jurisdiction to the USDA, where they were expected to become aggressive in arranging for market and nonmarket dispositions of U.S. surpluses.

SALES FOR FOREIGN CURRENCY

Foreign currency sales were first provided for in an amendment by Senator John McClelland (D., Arkansas) which was added to the Mutual Security Act in 1953 (section 550, P.L. 118). The amendment authorized as much as $250 million to be spent for purchase of U.S. surpluses by the Economic Cooperation Administration (the foreign aid agency). These surpluses would be sold abroad for foreign currencies. The Economic Cooperation Administration did spend the bulk of these authorized funds, at the insistence of farm interests.

A bill authorizing sales of surpluses for foreign currency which later became Title I of P.L. 480 was introduced in 1953 by Senator Andrew Schoeppel (R., Kansas) and in the House of Representatives

63. McClellan and Clare, p. 2.
64. Hadwiger, p. 234.
65. *Congressional Record* (bound), Feb. 25, 1954, p. 2235.
66. Ibid.

by Representative Walter Judd (R., Minnesota) and other representatives. Schoeppel's bill passed the Senate by a unanimous voice vote, despite the administration's expressed desire to await the results of the section 550 experiment. In 1954 the administration gave the proposal a mild endorsement. Secretary Benson said, "We are inclined to look with favor on it."[67]

The USDA subsequently suggested an authorization of $1 billion dollars to be spent for foreign currency sales over a three-year period. This was more than the $700 million finally authorized by Congress. However the State Department apparently continued efforts sub rosa to undermine the legislation,[68] and in subsequent years was blamed for a "go slow" approach to the administration of surplus disposal. The State Department was represented on an interdepartmental committee established to make decisions on Title I sales, and it apparently vetoed a number of proposed Title I contracts submitted by the USDA. In doing so the State Department was taking heed of continual and fairly serious complaints from friendly competitors, including Canada, Argentina, New Zealand, Denmark, Mexico, Uruguay, Australia, Burma, Italy, and Peru.[69] United States surplus wheat disposal was a nettle threatening a breakdown of U.S.-Canadian political and military cooperation during 1957 and 1958.[70]

RATIONALE FOR TITLE I

The rationale for establishing a major program of foreign currencies sales was presented by John C. Lynn, the legislative director of the American Farm Bureau Federation.[71] Lynn pointed out that an adequate farm export market was traditionally important for farm prosperity. This was even more so in recent years during which the increased U.S. production had been exported as a result of the European Recovery and the Korean War aid programs. These having ended by 1954, production of wheat and some other commodities exceeded demand. Rather than reduce production at this time, via government controls, Farm Bureau preferred to increase foreign sales "as a sound basis to assist in solving this problem."[72]

---

67. House, *Hearings on Long Range Farm Policy*, p. 2625.
68. Hadwiger, p. 236.
69. *New York Times*, May 25, 1957.
70. Statement of Thorsten Kalijarvi (Assistant Secretary of State for Economic Affairs), in July 1957, printed in the *Congressional Record* (daily), June 24, 1958, pp. 10974–76.
71. House, *Hearings on the Long Range Farm Program*, pp. 4177–213.
72. Lynn, p. 4190.

Lynn implied that the proposed new measures were also needed in order to compensate for the unfair bargaining position in which farmers found themselves. That is, foreign countries were inclined to use their scarce dollars to purchase unique U.S. industrial goods, while purchasing farm commodities from nondollar markets. In addition other agricultural exporters had first access to the existing markets simply because most were unable to hold their products off the market. Since it was inevitable that "weak" exporters sold first and at the lowest prices, the United States was obliged to act as a residual supplier, absorbing most of the reductions in international markets. Through sales for foreign currency, the United States might become more competitive. Although in section 550 the ICA had been instructed to safeguard the usual marketings of friendly countries as well as the dollar markets of the United States, Lynn said this protection should be dropped from the 1954 act, as "too inflexible."[73]

Farm Bureau did want guarantees against displacement of normal U.S. dollar markets. Indeed they intended to merge the Title I sales with cash marketings as an inducement for food importers to increase the total size of cash purchases from the United States. Farm Bureau wanted insurance against the subterfuge of transshipment of Title I goods from nondollar to dollar markets. They also suggested that foreign currency sales should be at prices somewhat above (or on the "high side" of) world prices.

It was assumed that sales for foreign currencies would usually be made in underdeveloped or developing market areas (such as in Spain, Italy, Iran, Egypt, Pakistan, India, Burma, Ceylon, Indochina, Brazil, Bolivia, Chile, Peru, and many others)[74] which had both a food deficit and a dollar shortage.

Foreign currency sales were regarded as a preferred method for making surpluses available to these countries. The alternatives included free distribution by private groups or through recipient governments. Free distribution by recipient governments had rarely seemed appropriate or useful. As another alternative, recipient governments preferred to sell the commodities and deposit the proceeds in a "counterpart" fund, as in the case of the Marshall Plan aid, or in a "blocked account," as in the case of the Pakistan food aid of 1953. In either case the funds would be used in developmental projects as agreed to by the United States and recipient countries.

---

73. Ibid., p. 4192.
74. Ibid., p. 4193.

Foreign currency sales, in contrast, were presumed by Farm Bureau to be real sales. They were an exchange for something of value to the United States rather than a gift. Title I, as enacted, provided that the United States could use the currencies received to pay for its market promotion programs, to purchase strategic materials, to procure military equipment, materials, and services, to purchase goods and services for other friendly countries, and to pay U.S. obligations in the recipient country (such as the cost of running the U.S. embassy).

Congressional agriculture leaders also preferred to believe that transactions for foreign currency could be considered sales rather than gifts. In Senate debate on the bill, its sponsor, Senator Schoeppel, said, "This bill does not involve a give-away program. The program under the bill is a dollars-and-cents program, involving exchange with the currencies of other countries."[75]

To further assure this interpretation the legislators informally insisted that each Title I sales contract contain a "maintenance-of-value" clause, which would prevent the depreciation of U.S.-owned currencies as a result of the currency inflation which was common in some recipient countries. Farm congressmen also spent much effort while the law was in effect to devise new uses for U.S. balances of foreign currency. With the support of Chairman Harold Cooley (D., North Carolina) of the House Agriculture Committee, a provision was added in 1957 setting aside 25 percent of the foreign currencies for loan to private businesses (to U.S. companies in virtually all cases). Funds were also allocated for translation of books; for American-sponsored schools and centers; for scientific, medical, cultural, and educational activities; for buildings to be used by the U.S. government; for trade fairs; for acquiring, indexing, and dissemination of foreign publications; for overseas expenses of American educational institutions; for workshops and chairs in American studies; for purchase of nonfood items for emergency uses; for audiovisual materials; and even for sales of dollars to U.S. tourists. As a result, most of the major departments and public agencies of government gained access to P.L. 480 currencies. At first the agencies were fearful that by relying on foreign currency they might jeopardize their regular appropriations budget. On the other hand, foreign currencies were more generously distributed, and with less supervision, than were the funds distributed from the regular budget.

75. *Congressional Record* (bound), July 28, 1953, p. 10084. See also the following case studies of the objectives of P.L. 480: McClellan and Clare; and Menzie and Crouch.

Thus the program ultimately gained much support from these many agencies, as well as from private groups who received substantial amounts of foreign currency.

While emphasizing the direct return to the United States from foreign currency sales, Farm Bureau also supported the use of foreign currencies for economic development on the ground that this was a way to expand markets. Farm Bureau's John Lynn said that this use was in fact the most important one.[76] With development came increased purchasing power. This could be oriented toward U.S. farm markets by creating a taste for U.S. surplus products and by using some development funds for construction of bakeries and other processing facilities.

The more liberal farm spokesmen also stressed the cause-and-effect relationship between development and increased markets, but they placed more emphasis on the immediate welfare benefits of aid than upon emergence of future markets. Farmers Union president James Patton said in 1956:

> There are two markets in the world. There is a commercial market, and it is taking just about all it can take at the present time of any commodity. Sure, we can probably, if we have an aggressive policy, put more cotton into it. We might even put a little more wheat into it. But the effective demand commercial market is pretty well filled. . . . The reason it is filled is because there isn't any more income to buy any more, in many countries.
>
> The second market is the larger market, and, that is, for lack of a better term—social market, a market where people can be helped a great deal to get their economic airplane off the ground. . . .[77]

Well over half of the Title I funds were used as grants or loans for development. However some of the farm legislators were dubious that economic development would increase U.S. markets. More obvious to them were instances where technical assistance programs improved the yields of foreign competitors or where food aid shipments had permitted a recipient country to increase its acreage of export crops. They acted on this fear of foreign competitors in 1957 by prohibiting loans of foreign currencies to private businesses when they would be used to increase competition with exports.

Furthermore recipient governments proved reluctant to become indebted to the United States for developmental funds when they could gain much the same end simply by printing more of their

76. House, *Hearings on Long Range Farm Policy,* p. 4195.
77. U.S. House Committee on Agriculture, *Hearings on General Farm Legislation* (1956), p. 525.

own currency.[78] Meanwhile U.S. balances of local currency became larger in some countries, much larger than prospective use. When the U.S. holdings and loans came to be a sizable portion of a country's total currency, they became a source of irritation in political relations. In view of the difficulty in using these foreign currency or "funny money" funds, many rural congressmen shifted their interest to other means of exchanging surpluses for things of value. One such means was the provision for bartering farm surpluses for strategic materials.

BARTERING SURPLUSES

The barter provision had originated in an earlier law (Agricultural Act of 1949). As included in P.L. 480, it established a "policy of encouraging the barter of surpluses."[79] However since barter was to be "in addition to other authorized methods" of disposal, it was not expected to be used much. The provision did not include safeguards of U.S. cash markets, much less the markets of competitor countries.

The bartering of surpluses proved profitable to the contractors. Barter became attractive to those leading rural legislators who wanted surpluses to be exchanged for things of value, and who also appreciated the fact that bartered commodities were not charged against the farm program budget.[80] Barter became a major surplus disposal program during 1955 and 1956.

In 1957 the USDA suspended barter deals, explaining that there were "increasing indications" that the program was cutting into U.S. cash sales. Then responding to strong congressional pressures, the USDA reopened barter, but only after administratively reducing the profit incentive for private traders engaging in it; the department also provided for protection of U.S. cash markets, and finally sharply reduced the list of strategic materials eligible for importation through barter. As a result of these changes, the barter traffic was considerably reduced.

Influential farm legislators who favored a return to open-ended barter enacted a provision in 1958 virtually countermanding the new USDA rules. They charged that the USDA had never demonstrated that any substantial incursion on U.S. cash markets had occurred, and that the State Department was using this reason as a means of protecting the interests of some U.S. firms which were

78. McClellan and Clare, p. 12.
79. U.S. House, *First Semi-annual Report on Activities under P.L. 480*, H. Doc. 62 (1955).
80. Menzie and Crouch, pp. 24–25.

producing cotton abroad. The legislators felt the State Department was mistaken in responding to a flood of sharp protests from Canada and other competitors with respect to the barter program. One analysis stated the congressional position as follows: "By implication, the State Department had no business trying to protect the normal markets of America's friends and allies; business is business and the disposal of surpluses for barter should take precedence over the other goals of U.S. foreign policy."[81]

In 1958 Congress enacted a minimum requirement of $500 million yearly in barter, omitting any reference to protection of competitor markets. Congress put the burden of proving incursions on U.S. markets upon those who would restrict barter transactions on that ground, and the conference report on this bill (H. Rept. 2694) noted the dissatisfaction of Congress with the way the program had been administered. Thus those who had favored barter won the legislative battle. Again, however, barter business was restricted administratively by permitting open-ended barter only in soft-currency countries. The barter advocates in Congress tried again in 1959 to enact another provision designed to require increased barter of surpluses, but this time without success.[82] The effort to make barter a major problem had not succeeded.

In 1963 the purpose of the limited barter program was shifted away from the goal of adding to the large stockpiles of strategic materials. Instead the program became one among several measures to reduce the outflow of U.S. gold. In the future the barter program was to be used to obtain materials abroad which the U.S. would otherwise have to purchase with dollars.[83] However the amount of barter remained at levels which congressional critics had formerly regarded as far too modest.

DONATIONS THROUGH VOLUNTARY AGENCIES

As previously noted, earlier food aid from the United States was often extended through churches, through nonsectarian charities such as the Red Cross, or through ad hoc private groups responding to some natural disaster abroad. During and after World War I aid was given by numerous private agencies, as well as by several governments, under the coordination of Herbert Hoover.

In World War II many private relief committees were hastily

---

81. McClellan and Clare, p. 23.
82. Ibid., pp. 17–26.
83. U.S. House, *18th Semi-annual Report on Activities Carried on under P.L. 480*, Message from the President (1963), p. 56.

organized to aid those overrun by Nazi troops. To maintain the neutral status of the United States at that time, the State Department found it necessary to regulate these war relief endeavors. A committee was formed at that time to examine the relief problem, and in July 1942 a regulatory board was created. This was succeeded in 1946 by the Advisory Committee on Voluntary Foreign Aid, composed of private citizens serving without pay. The function of this committee, still in existence, has been to coordinate the work of the relief agencies with the programs of U.S. foreign aid.[84]

Private relief agencies have usually registered with this committee, though not obliged to, because registration entitled them to receive free food supplies from the government, as well as freight subsidies covering most transportation costs of all supplies that these agencies sent abroad. In 1943 the private agencies formed the American Council of Voluntary Agencies for Foreign Service, through which they have achieved remarkable harmony in their policy requests.

These groups have received large amounts from U.S. surplus stocks, supplementing supplies they raised from private sources. Faced with deteriorating stocks of perishable commodities in the late 1940s, Congress provided in section 416 of the Agricultural Act of 1949 that the Commodity Credit Corporation could barter these stocks for commodities produced abroad, or they could donate them for domestic school lunch programs, other federal welfare programs, private welfare activities in the United States, and in last priority, for relief abroad through voluntary organizations. Under section 416 moderate amounts of some butter, cheese, dried milk, and other commodities were made available for foreign donation (Table 13.3).

The provision permitting private agencies to donate CCC stocks abroad was made part of P.L. 480. Under the new provision, stocks needed only to be available, not necessarily perishable; therefore the largest surpluses—wheat and other grains—were the ones most often used. Foreign donations had the lowest priority of all claims upon the surplus stocks; fats and oils therefore were frequently unavailable even though needed as a diet supplement for the recipients of food. Even dry milk was once unavailable, due to "rapid and unexpected depletion of CCC uncommitted stocks."[85]

After 1956 the CCC at its own expense converted wheat for donation into flour, bulgur, rolled wheat, or some other food product.

84. *A.I.D. and U.S. Voluntary Agencies, The Growing Partnership* (Agency for International Development, May 1963).
85. U.S. House, *Eleventh Semi-annual Report on Activities Carried on under P.L. 480,* p. 31.

TABLE 13.3. Quantities and cost of section 416 donations, domestic and foreign, July 1, 1954 through December 31, 1965

Commodity	Domestic donations		Foreign donations		Total	
	Quantity	Cost[a]	Quantity	Cost[a]	Quantity	Cost[a]
	(000 pounds)	(000 dollars)	(000 pounds)	(000 dollars)	(000 pounds)	(000 dollars)
Beans, dry	576,331	46,197	263,208	20,856	839,539	67,053
Bulgur	12,251	863	1,018,578	155,364	1,030,829	156,227
Butter	878,137	540,560	227,344	152,641	1,105,481	693,201
Butter oil	...	...	299,168	243,114	299,168	243,114
Cheese	720,928	284,140	616,549	266,979	1,337,477	551,119
Corn	6,946	261	492,392	18,407	499,338	18,668
Cornmeal	1,443,081	59,785	3,237,699	282,833	4,680,780	342,618
Flour	3,934,396	227,555	9,339,513	562,674	13,273,909	790,229
Ghee	...	...	9,402	7,771	9,402	7,771
Grain sorghums	...	...	6,147	110	6,147	110
Grits, corn	10,780	407	...	...	10,780	407
Milk, nonfat dry	1,239,301	213,604	5,213,910	903,266	6,453,211	1,116,870
Rice	1,078,746	119,139	736,062	90,156	1,814,808	209,295
Shortening	52,562	10,097	260,330	49,967	312,892	60,064
Vegetable oils	...	...	483,668	88,766	483,668	88,766
Wheat	22,240	1,101	1,235,806	55,230	1,258,046	56,331
Wheat, rolled	269,072	18,956	170,939	9,383	440,011	28,339
Total	10,244,771	1,522,665	23,610,715	2,907,517	33,855,486	4,430,182

Source: *Annual Report on Food for Peace* (1966), p. 103.

a. Estimated CCC cost.

With ample supplies on hand over the entire period through 1965 wheat flour became the most important commodity donated as measured by bulk, and the second largest (dry milk was largest) in terms of CCC cost (Table 13.3).

Meanwhile the total federal contribution to voluntary aid grew to $355 million in 1955, and donations of U.S. surpluses in 1963 were $340 million. Transportation costs paid by the federal government were additional to this amount. Added to the federal commodities in 1963 were 65 million in supplies purchased by the voluntary agencies.[86]

RECIPIENTS

Need was not the only or always the primary consideration in determining where donated surpluses would be sent and who would receive them, although presumably the food went to needy and destitute people in most cases. To receive food the voluntary agencies requested such quantities as could be distributed by their own organization. These distribution proposals were reviewed by the Advisory Committee and the Council of Voluntary Agencies. When requests were larger than available food, they were pared down by the USDA and by the U.S. Foreign Aid Agency. The criterion for cutting the proposals was not apparently made explicit, and the voluntary agencies were often unable to surmise the reasons.[87]

In the first years of the program (1955–60) about half the surplus commodities were distributed in Europe, where they went to the many refugees and to poverty or drought areas in eastern and southern Europe and in the Iberian peninsula. As the European shipments declined, Latin America received the largest amounts (1963–65).

AGENCIES

In 1965, 21 agencies were listed as distributors abroad of CCC-donated surpluses. These included the Cooperative for American Remittances Everywhere (CARE), which had begun operations in 1945 as a service agency through which individuals or groups in the United States could mail food packages to individuals or groups in Europe. CARE, adapting the food package idea to the P.L. 480 program, selected the recipients and with the benefit of free surpluses and freight subsidies was able to assemble and deliver an impressive

---

86.   *A.I.D. and U.S. Voluntary Agencies,* p. 7.
87.   Monsignor Edward E. Swanstrom, before U.S. House Agriculture Committee (1959), *Hearings on Extension of P.L. 480,* p. 713.

package for each dollar of charitable contributions. In addition to this activity, CARE, under contract with foreign governments, also managed "country programs" in which U.S. surpluses were rationed to needy families or more often used in institutional feeding, such as in school lunches. By 1957 the "country programs" were CARE's biggest activity.[88] Later CARE also supervised self-help programs financed in part by U.S. surpluses. CARE was the biggest user of U.S. surpluses among the voluntary agencies.

One reason for large shipments to Latin America and to other areas with large Catholic populations was the ability of another distributor, the Catholic Relief Service, to use surpluses effectively in these areas. By 1965 CARE and the Catholic Relief Service were feeding 95 percent of all persons benefiting from surplus food donations.

Most other voluntary agencies were either Protestant or Jewish groups, the most notable being the Church World Service, a foreign relief organization supported by Protestant and Eastern Orthodox churches affiliated under the National Council of Christian Churches. Nonsectarian groups included the United Nations International Childrens' Emergency Fund (UNICEF) and the American National Red Cross.

OBJECTIVES

Officials in Congress and the executive branch made it clear in statements, legislation, and administration that the donation programs were clearly intended as a last resort for surpluses which had no other outlet. The only commodities available at first were those in danger of deteriorating, and later were only those surpluses for which CCC was bearing the burden of storage costs.

Other objectives of less importance were sought or suggested. Rural congressmen often pointed out that the donated foods changed tastes and thus created new markets. The distributing agencies never reacted to this new evidence supporting the old suspicion that the missionary is the leading edge of national or economic imperialism.

Some distributing agencies, especially the church groups, received sectarian benefits from food distribution, whether or not they sought these benefits. Although the source of the food (Americans) was printed on food packages whenever possible, food did serve as a point of contact between missionaries and local residents, and the prospect of a good meal admittedly encouraged attendance at school and at medical

88. U.S. Senate Committee on Agriculture and Forestry, *Hearings on Policy and Operations under P.L. 480* (1957), pp. 255–56.

clinics. All distributing groups gained a better image within the United States by virtue of their ability to turn a small private contribution into a relatively large shipment of food.

Yet from the beginning some private groups tried to express a larger purpose for foreign distribution. In 1954 Dr. N. E. Dodd, representing CARE, advocated a continuing nutritional program as an American objective and as a means to dispose of the permanent U.S. surplus. Dodd, who had been involved in the McNary-Haugen movement of the 1920s, suggested that U.S. farms under good land practices produced 10 to 15 percent more than was needed and that it would be well for the national economy as well as for the world to devote this surplus production to improving nutrition in less fortunate countries.[89] The voluntary agencies invariably asked that commodities be made available based upon program needs rather than based upon supplies in CCC stocks.

Several spokesmen for voluntary groups suggested that the United States had a moral imperative to use the surplus to improve nutrition throughout the world. Dr. R. Norris Wilson, Executive Director of Church World Service, said in 1959:

> Supposing, for example, we were to take our membership in the United Nations seriously and to ask other surplus producing countries to take their membership seriously, and supposing we were to take what we all know, that two-thirds of the world's people are undernourished, as the basis for consultation on the problem of the use of surplus. And supposing we were to take the money, or even a part of the money, a small fraction of the money we are now using to store these surpluses, and to buy them, pour our money into our food and start a school feeding program in every country of the world. Take a child from the age of 4 to the age of 12 or 14 at this time, when nourishment and malnutrition, and so on, permanently distort.[90]

Congressman Thomas Abernathy (D., Arkansas) queried Wilson as to whether he meant "that the production of the American agriculture or any other American industry should be geared to this highest potential production and the surplus distributed to the needs of other peoples of the world." Wilson answered that the need was there, and in response to another question he stated that the main objective of the U.S. government should be to fulfill this need rather than to dispose of surpluses.[91]

---

89. House, *Hearings on the Long Range Farm Program,* p. 4316.
90. House, *Hearings on Extension of Public Law 480,* p. 721.
91. Ibid.

This moral imperative was further expanded in 1964 by C. Edward Behre, representing the Friends Committee on National Legislation. Behre suggested that the obligation to feed the needy extended also to feeding Communist nations. He therefore urged elimination of the provision for aid only to the people of friendly nations. "When Christians pray, 'Give us our daily bread' is it not clear that 'us' must refer to all the children of God? As a nation do we choose to flout the New Testament injunction, 'If thine enemy hunger, feed him'?"[92]

Expanded food distribution was seen by the voluntary agencies as a way to fulfill nonfood needs in the underdeveloped world as well. For example, school lunches greatly increased school enrollment and gave students strength to study. Food donations were used successfully as a device to encourage periodic medical examination and treatment. A 1964 survey of Church World Service food distribution activities revealed a belief that institutional feeding programs had a very high value, as compared with family feeding programs. By 1965 most of the donated food surpluses were used in school lunches, summer camps, maternal and child health centers, and in other institutional feeding programs.

The voluntary agencies were inclined to conclude that their own food distribution activities were not in any sense a solution to the long-range food deficit. Monsignor Swanstrom said, speaking for the entire Council of Voluntary Agencies in 1959, "In most of the countries we are working in, we are trying to get the authorities and the people we work with to realize that some day they will have to get this food themselves from their own resources."[93] Some groups, such as CARE, asked for a share of foreign currencies generated under Title I, which would permit them to undertake liberal developmental projects, including the improvement of local agriculture. CARE had long been financing developmental efforts from private contributions.

The Eisenhower administration was reluctant to permit voluntary agencies to enter into developmental activities, even though the objective was to make recipients self-sufficient. During the extensive survey of P.L. 480 operations in 1957 Senate Agriculture Committee hearings, Senator Hubert Humphrey queried John B. Hollister, Director of the International Cooperation Administration about the possibility of permitting voluntary agencies to use foreign currencies accumulated under Title I to carry on "rehabilitation and self-help

92. U.S. Senate Committee on Agriculture and Forestry, *Hearings on Extension of P.L. 480* (1964), p. 103.
93. House, *Hearings on the Extension of Public Law 480*, p. 711.

projects where feeding programs are now being carried on, so that when the programs are reduced or cut off, people will not be left helpless."[94]

Hollister replied that this was not the current policy. He added, "And there is the danger, Senator, if we carry it too far; perhaps we are getting beyond the place where a charitable organization should be working and getting into a more real general support of the economy of the country. . . . When you once start to give funds so that voluntary agencies can build up an organization that is supported by Government funds, you raise some interesting social problems, which I am not fully qualified to pass on, except to indicate that this problem is there." Humphrey agreed that "you raise some very serious problems. And I think we have to face up to that fact."[95]

The Congress did face up to that question in 1960 at the instigation of the voluntary agencies.

FOOD FOR WORK PROJECTS

In 1960 Representative George McGovern (D., South Dakota) introduced a bill amending P.L. 480, at the request of the Council of Voluntary Agencies, which would permit these agencies to use donated commodities as compensation to persons employed in work projects and which would also permit payments-in-kind for services of the local food processors, such as bakers.[96] The administration opposed this bill on grounds that development should remain on a government-to-government basis. The bill passed, nevertheless, authorizing both voluntary agencies and friendly governments (including U.N. agencies) to carry out food-for-work projects, but the Eisenhower administration did not implement it.

It was finally permitted after the authority was extended for three years in 1961.[97] At that time the U.S. government went further, permitting the sale of surplus commodities in recipient countries as a means of generating funds needed for expenses additional to those covered by the payments-in-food. Presumably care was to be taken to avoid disruption of the ordinary markets. With this encouragement, food-for-work projects proliferated, until by 1965 more than one-third

---

94. Senate, *Hearings on Policies and Operations under P.L. 480,* pp. 165–66.
95. Ibid.
96. McGovern, before U.S. House Committee on Agriculture, *Hearings on P.L. 480 Amendments* (1960), pp. 45–46.
97. U.S. House, *15th Semi-annual Report on Public Law 480* (April 9, 1962), p. 46.

of the donated commodities was being used in food-for work projects.[98]
Most of these commodities were in the form of bread grains and flour.[99]

DISASTER RELIEF

Each year during the operation of P.L. 480 the voluntary agencies
as well as the United States and recipient governments responded to
emergency food needs caused by earthquakes, droughts, political revolutions, and other disasters. By December of 1965 almost $1 billion
in commodities and transportation expenses had been contributed for
disaster relief, out of a total value of almost $5 billion for all pro-
grams using donated commodities (under Titles II and III, P.L. 480).[100]

HISTORY OF DOMESTIC DISTRIBUTION

Wheat has been a major item among commodities distributed under various domestic food programs since 1931. On several occasions
the existence of farm surpluses alongside extraordinary domestic need
provided a powerful argument for food programs, outweighing the
dilemmas involved in the administration of the programs.

During the Great Depression, need and surpluses coexisted for
some time before it was decided in 1932 to donate government-owned
wheat and other commodities to the American Red Cross for direct
distribution to needy persons.[101] In 1933 the Federal Surplus Relief
Corporation was chartered and given the responsibility of distributing
food made available by the Agricultural Adjustment Administration.
The AAA purchased surplus foods with funds from processing taxes
and from appropriations for drought relief and other purposes.[102]

Initially the operating expenses of the corporation were paid by
state and local government which received the food for distribution.[103]
During the remainder of the Depression food was the largest item in
the relief budgets, especially in the programs emphasizing direct distribution of commodities.[104]

---

98. U.S. Congress, *Food-for Peace, 1965, Annual Report on P.L. 480* (June 1, 1966),
tables 22 and 24.
99. Ibid., table 20.
100. Ibid., tables 16 and 24.
101. Josephine Chapin Brown, *Public Relief 1929–1939* (New York: Holt, 1940),
pp. 68–120.
102. *Report of the Federal Surplus Relief Corporation for the Period Oct. 4, 1933,
to Dec. 31, 1934* (Washington: GPO, 1935), p. 1.
103. Ibid.
104. *Final Statistical Report of the Federal Emergency Relief Administration*
(Washington: GPO, 1942), pp. 17–18.

TABLE 13.4. Domestic food distribution: Millions of bushels of wheat distributed by the USDA to schools, institutions, and needy persons

Fiscal year	Million bushels	Fiscal year	Million bushels
1932–33ᵃ	95.0	1949–50	. . .
1933–34ᵇ	8.2	1950–51	. . .
1935–36	5.6	1951–52	. . .
1936–37	ᶜ	1952–53	. . .
1937–38	9.7	1953–54	. . .
1938–39	14.7	1954–55	. . .
1939–40	9.9	1955–56	2.0
1940–41	10.7	1956–57	5.7
1941–42	5.6	1957–58	6.4
1942–43	2.0	1958–59	9.3
1943–44	.2	1959–60	8.4
1944–45	.02	1960–61	10.0
1945–46	.04	1961–62	13.3
1946–47	. . .	1962–63	13.1
1947–48	. . .	1963–64	12.4
1948–49	. . .	1964–65	12.4
		1965–66	. . .

Source: Records of the USDA.
a. Includes period from March 1932 to December 1933.
b. Includes both calendar years.
c. The 1937 amount was not available in the series records. However the USDA provided and donated 14.2 million bushels of wheat in fiscal 1937, according to the *Report of Federal Surplus Commodities Corporation for the Fiscal Year 1937*, p. 6.

The Federal Surplus Relief Corporation was made part of the USDA in 1935, because "it became apparent that the corporation's greatest value was not as a relief organization but rather as an agency to assist the Department of Agriculture in the execution of surplus removal programs conducted by the Agricultural Adjustment Administration."[105]

Also in 1935 Congress enacted P.L. 74-320 containing the versatile section 32, which earmarked U.S. customs receipts for attaining certain broad farm policy goals. Section 32 funds were used to purchase market surpluses, which were in turn made divertable for distribution to the needy. Rather large amounts of wheat (processed into flour) were distributed annually in the decade before World War II (Table 13.4).

Section 32 was also the basis for a food stamp program conducted by the USDA for 1939–43 and also on a pilot basis in 1961–63. Food stamp plans gained many critics among congressional farm interests, and the Benson administration also resisted congressional pressure favoring a food stamp plan during the 1950s. The first plan had proved difficult to administer, but of more concern to farm interests

105. *Report of the Federal Surplus Commodity Corporation for the Calendar Year 1936* (Washington: GPO, 1936), p. 1.

was the fact that the program did not boost farm prices or reduce U.S. stocks as directly as did the direct distribution of surplus commodities. Nevertheless the Johnson administration enacted a permanent food stamp program in 1964 (P.L. 85-525), authorizing over $100 million in appropriations during each of the first three years of operation.

Meanwhile Congress had enacted some direct distribution programs, including the national school lunch program in 1946 (P.L. 79-396) and section 416 of the Agricultural Act of 1949 (P.L. 81-439), which became the major authority under which wheat surpluses were donated to needy persons at home and abroad. Under section 416 sizable amounts of wheat were processed into flour and distributed to the needy through private agencies and through local governments after 1954 (Table 13.4). Chief shortcomings of a direct distribution program were that recipients had to travel to a warehouse where the commodities were stored and distributed. Another shortcoming was that the package of available surpluses was usually not appetizing nor was it nutritionally adequate; also distribution was haphazard and dependent upon the initiative of local governments or agencies; standards of need varied and often were inequitable.[106]

The inadequacies of food programs became a partisan issue in 1959 because of Secretary Benson's reluctance to expand the distribution program and his refusal to implement a food stamp program even after a congressional enactment encouraged him to do so. In 1960 candidates Nixon and Kennedy, in one of their debates, disputed whether many Americans went to bed hungry. President Kennedy's first executive order expanded the commodity distribution program. Despite his and Secretary Freeman's enthusiasm for the domestic food programs, by 1967 they remained unavailable in large areas of the United States and were in any case out of reach of some of the very poorest citizens. School lunch programs, for example, were in effect in middle-class suburbs and generally not in effect in the ghettos. These facts were given emphasis in citizen investigations[107] and congressional hearings,[108] which also pointed to reasons why programs so highly heralded had fallen so short. The reasons included executive branch budget ceilings, administrative difficulties, apathy or opposi-

106. U.S. Senate Subcommittee on Agriculture and Forestry, *Hearings on Food Distribution Programs* (1959).
107. In particular, *Hunger, U.S.A., A Report by the Citizens' Board of Inquiry into Hunger and Malnutrition in the United States* (Washington: New Community, 1968); and *Their Daily Bread, A Study of the National School Lunch Program* (Atlanta: McNelley-Rudd, 1968).
108. In particular, Subcommittee on Employment, Manpower, and Poverty of the U.S. Senate Committee on Labor and Public Welfare, *Hearings on the Examination of the War on Poverty* (1967).

tion by local governments, and resistance to programs within the congressional agriculture committees. "Food for the Hungry" became the cause célèbre of the Poor People's March in Washington and a chief policy issue in 1968. Efforts were taken then to make the decision process more amenable to demands from the poor, including the establishment of a select committee in the U.S. Senate which would presumably compete with the Senate Agriculture Committee as the forum for consideration of the food issue.

FOOD FOR PEACE

By 1959 it was clear that P.L. 480 had not achieved its initial objectives. It had not expanded cash markets as much as had been hoped for, if at all. Some of its sponsors, including Farm Bureau leaders and the Benson administration, were concerned that P.L. 480, having been enacted as a remedy for temporary surpluses, had become a temporary palliative forestalling basic remedies for overproduction. In that case P.L. 480 was adding to rather than subtracting from the growing surpluses of wheat and other price-supported commodities. Secretary Benson and Farm Bureau leaders began to talk of phasing out the program, but instead the P.L. 480 program was given a more permanent footing, with new emphasis on using U.S. agricultural abundance for economic development and other foreign policy goals. The new concept assumed that U.S. production would continue to exceed market demand, and that this dependable surplus could be put to constructive use.

The extensive 1957 Senate hearings conducted by Senator Hubert Humphrey were a search for new ways to make surpluses serve humanitarian and foreign policy goals. Meanwhile surpluses grew, and dissatisfied farm constituencies swelled the number of rural Democratic congressmen. Many of these joined with Humphrey and other legislators in insisting that surpluses be viewed as an asset rather than as a burden on the U.S. Treasury. In harmony with this view, President Eisenhower in 1959 renamed the P.L. 480 program "Food for Peace."[109] However major administrative policy changes awaited the arrival of the Freeman administration.

Under the new administration the State Department for the first time strongly endorsed P.L. 480 as a foreign policy tool.[110] In 1961

109. "Food for Peace" was first attached to proposed resolutions circulated in Democratic congressional offices and introduced in 1959. It then appeared in Eisenhower's farm message of January 1959.
110. Toma, p. 63.

President Kennedy asked that the law be extended for a five-year period, to permit its more effective use in foreign economic development (Congress allowed only three years).

In 1962 the administration unsuccessfully sought authority to purchase surpluses in addition to those in federal stockpiles and to donate food surpluses through international programs. It successfully expanded a provision for long-term loans (Title IV) which had been enacted by Congress in 1959. Congress in 1963 began to take a more critical view of P.L. 480. In 1961 and 1962 the program—as a part of controversial omnibus farm bills— had received relatively little congressional attention; then in 1963 several congressional statements and reports criticized aspects of Food for Peace policy and administration.[111]

In the 1964 extension of P.L. 480, Congress rejected several administration initiatives, including a five-year extension period (changed by Congress to two years) and sale of Title I currencies to voluntary agencies. Congress furthermore added restrictions on Title I sales to certain unfriendly countries; the extension increased some recipient country expenses and provided for closer congressional scrutiny of Food for Peace administration.

New objectives were given verbal priority in the administration's Food for Freedom bill of 1966. In 1966 the administration accepted the conclusion that some recipients of U.S. surpluses faced increasing food deficits which could not be filled by U.S. aid shipments. Therefore future U.S. aid would be made conditional upon a number of steps taken by recipient countries toward development of food self-sufficiency. Development of self-sufficiency would be the most important objective. A five-year extension was requested (Congress allowed a two-year extension), although recipients were no longer to be given long assurances of supplies. Instead food aid was to be subject to continuous review and revision based upon the recipients' performance.

The administration sought to eliminate the "surplus" concept of food aid, emphasizing instead the nutritional needs of recipients and proposing (with the end of surpluses) a reserve of wheat and other foods to assure "adequate" supplies to be used for food aid and other purposes.

However other objectives were still prominent. The "old guard" farm legislators still valued the program because it disposed of potential wheat surpluses and buoyed markets.[112] The 1966 law specified that

111. Ibid., pp. 73–74.
112. Ibid., p. 130.

the program should be conducted so as to insure a progressive transition (by 1971) from foreign currency sales to cash or hard-credit sales. Congressional leaders also insisted that the programs serve Cold War foreign policy objectives. Finally numerous private and public institutions benefiting from the program insisted that it continue to serve their various interests. The program will be discussed below in terms of its service to these various objectives.

ECONOMIC DEVELOPMENT

Food assumed a prominent position in U.S. foreign assistance policy under the Kennedy administration, due partly to two considerations. One was a new appreciation by aid agencies of the role of agriculture in economic development. As late as 1960 P.L. 480 had been justified officially as a way to permit poor nations to divert scarce resources from agriculture to industry.[113] The Kennedy administration accepted the view, however, that an efficient agriculture must be developed as a precondition of industrialization.

In this concept food imports including food aid could be sufficient to permit adequate levels of nutrition, but much greater care would have to be taken so that offers of food aid should not be a means of aiding or avoiding local agricultural development. Indeed food aid should serve as a resource and an incentive for improving local agriculture in the recipient country. The Johnson administration's 1966 Food for Freedom plan went further to make food aid conditional upon developmental performance. Senator Allen Ellender, Chairman of the Agriculture Committee, who previously had opposed the foreign aid objectives of food aid, expressed satisfaction with the new emphasis: "In this new concept of Food for Peace, we are attaching strings to it to the recipient country. If they do not do what is best for them, aid can be chopped off over night.[114]

Legislators who had helped win the new emphasis on agricultural development and nutrition obviously favored laying down conditions to assure local development.[115] However they did not want restrictions so severe as to reduce the size of the food aid program in the future.

Others in Congress questioned whether food was as good a developmental tool as was dollar aid. They doubted whether as a

113. U.S. House, *12th Semi-annual Report on Activities Carried on Under Public Law 480* (August 20, 1960), p. 37.
114. *Congressional Record* (daily), Aug. 29, 1966, p. 20219.
115. Ibid., pp. 20233–41.

practical matter food could be used as an incentive to local development, since congressional decision makers (and perhaps some within
the administration) remained more interested in increasing farm
exports than in developing agriculture to the point where it might be
competitive,[116] and since recipients were still resisting agricultural
development in favor of more prestigious industrialization. Also
pointed out was that the value of food aid to recipients was only about
half the original value of the commodities shipped, after subtracting
costs of transportation and storage.[117] Once U.S. supply and demand
were in balance, dollars rather than food would become a more efficient vehicle of aid, assuming that dollars would be used efficiently and
with few overhead costs. The chief answer to this criticism was that
the public was not prepared to increase dollar aid by a magnitude
comparable to that of the food aid program.

MEETING THE FOOD GAP

Famine prevention rather than economic growth as such became
the focus of the 1960s, as it became clear that some of the developing
areas, including some of the largest nations, were losing the race between food and population.

There was an immediate need for massive food aid in 1966 and
1967 to stave off famines in India. This need had been met, more or
less, but only by drawing down U.S. supplies which had accumulated
during several years of surplus production. With reserves gone, should
the United States tap its reserve acreage in the future for the purpose
of warding off starvation abroad? Or would the U.S. government
maintain production controls in the presence of famine?

Chairman Harold Cooley of the House Agriculture Committee
had expressed himself on this point in 1954. Cooley said the United
States did not have the responsibility to feed the whole world:

> We should let them know that while the products of the earth are
> God-given, man has to dig it out of the earth. I am just as charitable
> as anybody and I voted for all of these foreign aid programs, but I
> can't agree with the philosophies set forth in the attached statements
> to the effect that we have no right to put restrictions on our produc-
> tion. . . . If we should embark on this sort of a program, giving to
> the needy people of the world all the wheat and all the cotton and food
> and fibers we can produce, we would completely disrupt our foreign

---

116. Theodore W. Schultz, "Value of U.S. Farm Surpluses to Underdeveloped
Countries," *J. Farm Econ.* 45(December 1963):1019–30.
117. Ibid., p. 1022.

trade channels and we wouldn't have any foreign markets in which we could trade profitably. . . .[118]

A decade later the chairman of the Senate Agriculture Committee, Allen Ellender (D., Louisiana) took the same position when it seemed the United States would no longer need to produce a market surplus. Senator Ellender's main concern was to find a program which would maintain farm income at a low cost to government: "The time will soon come when our farm program will cost very little unless our planners expand our food production in order to do more than our share to feed hungry people the world over."[119]

Some Food for Peace supporters, while finding appropriate uses for production controls, believed that there would be occasion to tap the U.S. acreage reserves to provide food aid. Senator George McGovern, former Food for Peace Director under President Kennedy and a principal innovator of food aid and policy administration, suggested that the United States would have to assume major responsibility for filling and ultimately closing the world food gap. McGovern noted the facts that population was accelerating faster than food production, that prospects for increasing food adequately in areas of greatest need were not encouraging, and that U.S. food reserves and those elsewhere were being rapidly depleted. McGovern said:

> In spite of the magnitude of the problem, however, there is no escaping the challenge of world hunger. Neither our national security nor our moral and political position in the world will permit us to turn our backs on this No. 1 problem of the last third of the 20th century. Furthermore, in spite of difficulties, a nation that can send a man to the moon can unlock the doors to food production and distribution.
>
> I believe that we ought to declare an all-out war against hunger for the balance of this century. We should call on our farmers and our agricultural technicians to enlist for the duration in the war against want. We should announce to the world now that we have an unused food producing capacity which we are willing and anxious to use to its fullest potential. Our Government should leave no doubt that we will bend every effort to see that no nation—friend or foe—starves while we permit land and surpluses to remain idle.[120]

The war McGovern had asked for was subsequently declared in a 1966 Food for Freedom program sponsored by the Johnson administration. In a message to Congress accompanying his proposed legisla-

---

118. House, *Hearings on the Long Range Farm Program*, pp. 4118–19.
119. *Congressional Record* (daily), Aug. 29, 1966, p. 20217.
120. *Congressional Record* (daily), Sept. 23, 1965, pp. 23918–19.

tion, President Johnson said, "I propose that the United States lead the world in a war against hunger."[121] Secretary Freeman explained to the House Agriculture Committee, "Victory in this war will save more lives than have been lost in all the wars of history."[122]

Remaining was the question as to the long-run impact of U.S. aid upon world food production. It was generally agreed that the food gap would ultimately have to be filled mainly through increased production (and controlled population) within the developing nations.

Some congressmen seemed to feel that substantial U.S. assistance, especially if given in the form of food aid, would have a negative effect upon supplies of recipient countries over the long run. The administration, however, was optimistic that U.S. aid could be programmed so as to have positive results. AID was planning to increase its agricultural assistance by one-third, "to a total of nearly $500 million,"[123] and the administration was hopeful, based on its experience with Indian drought relief, that food aid could be used as an incentive rather than a disincentive to self-development.[124]

Still further along the spectrum in the direction of greater food aid were McGovern and other Food for Peace supporters who emphasized that the developed world possessed an abundance of developmental resources, and recipient countries relatively few, and who argued that self-help requirements must not be so severe as to prevent a massive transfer of resources, or at worst, to serve as an excuse for continuing assistance at existing token levels. This view favoring much-increased aid, which would as a practical matter include increased food aid, put these "easy-givers" or "doves" at odds with the "hawks" in the administration who insisted upon an ounce of development for an ounce of food, and who viewed food aid, over the long run, as a way to manipulate governments to seek long-range food sufficiency by driving hard bargains with countries threatened by famine.

WEAPON IN THE COLD WAR

The conservative farm spokesmen generally insisted that farm policy objectives should have first priority in the P.L. 480 program;

121. *Message to Congress from the President of the United States Relative to a War on Hunger,* Feb. 10, 1966.
122. U.S. House Committee on Agriculture, *World War on Hunger Hearings* (1966), p. 188.
123. Ibid., p. 194.
124. See testimony of AID administrator David F. Bell and Undersecretary Thomas C. Mann. ibid., pp. 269, 280.

they decried State Department influence in program administration, but they were nevertheless keen to use food aid as a weapon in the Cold War. They agreed with the State Department that P.L. 480 should be used to bolster "friendly" governments (though they were relatively much less worried over the fact that the program on occasions jeopardized political friendships with competitors such as Canada). In testimony before Congress the State Department invariably stressed the contribution of P.L. 480 (or Food for Freedom) in the Cold War.

Yet there were differences over Cold War tactics. The conservative farm legislators who handled Food for Peace in Congress took an uncomplicated view of the Cold War struggle, believing that food should be given to non-Communist nations in order to maintain or increase their powers of resistance to communism and it should strengthen their friendship with the United States. These farm legislators were ready, when the State Department was not, to deny food aid to countries having intercourse with the Communist enemy, and they were more reluctant to give food aid to Communist-oriented countries.

Public Law 480 had originally been fashioned as a Cold War tool. Concessional sales were to be made only to friendly nations—unfriendly nations being the Soviet Union and any other "nation or area dominated or controlled by the foreign government or foreign organization controlling the world Communist movement."[125] Emergency relief donations could be given to friendly nations, or to friendly but needy populations without regard to the friendliness of their government. The barter provisions encouraged the stockpiling of strategic materials needed by the military services. Foreign currencies received as a result of concessional sales could be used for military assistance and for support of U.S. forces stationed abroad. An amendment in 1964 permitted use of these currencies for "internal security" purposes.

Continually in controversy was the issue of aid to Communist satellites.[126] In 1964 a congressional conference committee excluded Yugoslavia and Poland from Title I sales. President Johnson had termed this decision unwise on the ground that food aid to these countries had helped free them from Soviet influence.[127]

At that time Congress also prohibited aid to countries (such as Egypt) which used U.S. funds for any purpose inimical to U.S. foreign

125. P.L. 480, sect. 107, 1954.
126. Toma, p. 64.
127. *Congress and the Nation, 1945–1964* (Washington: Congressional Quarterly Service, 1965), p. 744.

policy. Congressional decision makers often urged a priority system for classifying needy nations, under which more food aid would go to those whose governments cooperated with the United States both in self-development plans and also in Cold War activities.

In 1966 a majority on the House Agriculture Committee consisting of Republicans and southern Democrats insisted on a provision, vigorously opposed by the administration, that would deny any food aid to nations exporting goods to North Vietnam and Cuba. Despite threats by the administration that wheat allotments would have to be reduced by 15 percent if the provision were passed, and despite criticism from Senator J. William Fulbright (D., Arkansas), Chairman of the Senate Foreign Relations Committee, that such legislation dictating the trade policy of the other nations belonged in his committee,[128] the final act did apply the provision with respect to trade with North Vietnam but not with respect to Cuba.

INSTITUTIONAL INTERESTS

Several federal agencies and congressional committees have been vitally interested in the food disposal program, and so have some private groups and overseas governments.

The many different objectives of the program have invited conflict as to which agency would supervise it. Beginning as an agricultural disposal act, P.L. 480 has been referred to the congressional agriculture committees, except in 1959, when the first Senate bill was referred to the Senate Foreign Relations Committee. However on that occasion the Senate instead acted upon a bill from the Senate Agriculture and Forestry Committee, at the behest of its chairman. Even though Chairman Ellender had sought to maintain USDA control within the executive branch, the agriculture committees have retained control because they have felt that they are best able to protect farmers' interest in the program, and that USDA is best able to administer it.[129]

In the early years the USDA and the agriculture committees of Congress were inclined to emphasize the market development and surplus disposal objectives of the program. Farm interests pushed the USDA to dispose of the surpluses, restrained only by the desire not to diminish the usual U.S. cash markets abroad. But among farm interests in Congress and the USDA was a desire to use surplus food for humanitarian or other welfare purposes. Rural liberals

---

128. *Congressional Record* (daily), Aug. 29, 1966, p. 20218.
129. Toma, pp. 77–89.

who developed the concept of using food for foreign aid viewed the surpluses as a way to add to existing dollar aid; they felt that food shipments might be more beneficial to the developing countries than the military assistance which Congress had been persuaded to pass.[130] Beyond stressing food aid, some rural liberals also urged that agricultural development be given first priority in foreign aid.

The champions of bilateral agricultural technical assistance beginning under President Truman's Point Four Plan had usually been leaders within the agricultural complex. In contrast the State Department had assumed that industrial development should come first, and official policy had assumed that food aid would sometimes permit developing nations to bypass agricultural development.

Major administrative decisions under P.L. 480 have been undertaken by an interagency committee which included several executive agencies.[131] Since 1959 continuous supervision and coordination of the program has been exercised by a Food for Peace Director, first located within the White House and after 1965 within the State Department. The director has functioned as a vigorous promoter of the program, although only as an observer rather than as a member of the interagency committee; in practice he has exercised little power. In addition to the director, the other two major administrators of P.L. 480 have been the USDA and the State Department, "which has delegated the bulk of its authority and responsibility to the Agency for International Development."[132] Title I foreign currency sales, barter, and some other provisions have been administered by the USDA, while developmental and relief activities have been carried out largely by AID.[133]

The USDA should be considered as a group of agencies rather than a single entity. In addition to the office of the secretary, which has vigorously promoted food aid in recent years, the department contains other agencies with interest in this program. Such agencies have been built on a developmental function (such as soil conservation, rural electricity, and farm credit)[134] and have staffed developmental missions.

As manager of U.S. production, the ASCS has, as earlier indicated, been more comfortable with a condition of scarcity than with

130. Lawrence Witt, commenting on Theodore W. Schultz, "Value of U.S. Farm Surpluses to Underdeveloped Countries," *J. Farm Econ.*, 42(December 1960): 1046–51.
131. Toma, p. 45.
132. Ibid.
133. Ibid., pp. 47–48.
134. The Farm Credit Administration has been an independent agency since 1953.

one of surpluses, and in a sense it has been a competitor to food programs in its functions as a production control agency. The Foreign Agricultural Service, a substantial agency under Secretary Benson, has been the agency through which the USDA acted on Title I sales and some other programs, but FAS has been more interested in expanding commercial sales than in its work under the Food for Peace program.

In the Executive Office of the President, the Council of Economic Advisers and the Budget Bureau have continually been skeptical of large food aid expenditures and of the price support programs from which they originated.

The State Department had opposed the enactment of P.L. 480, as already noted, and had subsequently restrained the USDA administration in making Title I agreements. In the 1960s, however, the State Department became a genuine supporter of Food for Peace. The change was due partly to the increase in food needs abroad and partly to approval of the changed emphasis of the P.L. 480 program. Undoubtedly the foreign policy agencies had become reconciled to the inevitability of such a program and the probability of its increased size. As one official noted in 1960, there was a "moving tide of intent" to use U.S. surplus production abroad, and a desire on the other side to receive them. Indeed, support for food aid was a bright exception to the declining congressional support for U.S. foreign aid. Public Law 480 was extended regularly by large majorities, while Congress typically balked before passing the dollar aid programs of about equal cost.

Public Law 480 provided foreign aid in the sense that it expanded the amount of goods in recipient countries relative to the amount of money, thus preventing inflation. However this anti-inflationary benefit could be sacrified for other ends if foreign currencies obtained from the concessional sales were spent by the United States or the recipient government. The congressional agriculture committees insisted that they should be spent. Congress authorized use of the funds for most ordinary expenses of U.S. agencies abroad and generated many new U.S. activities as well. Although federal agencies were first reluctant to use these funds for normal activities, from fear that they might lose their ordinary appropriations, they came to appreciate the fact that Congress was readier to appropriate foreign currencies and was less concerned with supervising expenditures than in the case of regular appropriations. (In fact congressmen themselves received generous allotments of the foreign currencies while on official visits in countries where the United States had accumulated them.) Congressional decision makers seemed far more concerned to find ways to spend the amassing currencies, which had accumulated to embarrassing levels in a few large recipient countries, than they were about the appropriateness of the expenditures. Therefore the allotment of currencies, often in huge amounts, became a matter for quite serious interagency negotiations. United States foreign aid agencies and military agencies often invited foreign governments to apply for Title I, P.L. 480 contracts as a means for the agencies to gain funds to undertake activities in those countries. Congress presumably might not have covered these activities in regular appropriations.

Foreign currencies were also used for developmental loans to private businesses (usually U.S. businesses). Without doubt, the distribution of currencies to agencies and businessmen won much new support for the food aid program.

Still another source of support for Food for Peace was the requirement that 50 percent of all food shipments must travel in U.S. Merchant Marine ships. This "50-50 requirement" (included in all postwar aid legislation) was the major subsidy to the U.S. shipping industry and the major reason why the industry was able to continue operation at noncompetitive rates. Therefore the entire shipping industry was in support of Food for Peace.

These various institutional interests were reconciled in the Food for Peace program. In practice, the USDA administration had to accept the toughest burden of maintaining the support of rural legislators for a surplus foreign aid program. Secretary Freeman argued that the 1966 Food for Freedom (Food for Peace) program gave increased prestige to the agriculture establishment by making food the critical element in the contest between freedom and totalitarianism. "We now have top billing. We are sitting right up there to the table. We are not just getting the crumbs from the table."[135] However some influential farm legislators still preferred to consider Food for Peace as a surplus disposal program, in which case it would be terminated with the availability of adequate markets or adequate production controls.

Among the institutions not accommodated in the new scheme was the Senate Foreign Relations Committee. Senator Fulbright, Chairman of the Senate Foreign Relations Committee, and some other decision makers began to question the results of a wedding

135. House, *Hearings on World War on Hunger,* p. 230.

between agricultural legislators and foreign policy. They began to wonder whether unilateral aid programs really served the long-range interests of recipient countries, based as they tended to be upon short-range donor interests. Fulbright's doubts about earlier unilateral programs seemed to be verified by the Food for Peace program. Fulbright pointed out that it permitted decisions to be made effectively by the agriculture committees and by the USDA, whose main interest was surplus disposal, who were not presumed to be experts on foreign affairs, who were often quite at odds with official U.S. policy, and who were not in any case institutions officially responsible for foreign policy. Fulbright suggested that as a surplus disposal program, Food for Peace had not served the interests of foreign policy: "Very responsible people feel that this surplus disposal program has tended to remove the incentive for India to grow her own food."[136] Fulbright noted that the dollar aid program, of about equal size, was administered by AID, and supervised by his committee.

> It seems to me an odd development for the Committee on Agriculture and Forestry to continue this program in this guise. I should think the sensible thing to do would be to merge this program with the existing economic aid program, so that we would not have two full-fledged aid organizations to administer this program.[137]

Fulbright suggested that if the surpluses were indeed gone, and if Food for Peace has indeed become a developmental program, that it should no longer be administered by the USDA. Chairman Ellender of the Senate Agricultural Committee responded that "there is no doubt in my mind that the Department of Agriculture is much better equipped to handle the program for the production of more food abroad than is the Department of State or AID."[138]

The original sponsor of the Food for Peace legislation, Senator McGovern, preferred a middle ground—direction by a person in the White House. He supported control by the USDA and the agriculture committees, as did the administration, mainly because the farm interests were still considered to be the main sources of support for the program. Without that support there might be less aid.[139]

Senator Fulbright seemed to agree that there would be less aid if the farm bloc were alienated. It seemed to be his position

136. *Congressional Record* (daily), Aug. 29, 1966, p. 20236.
137. Ibid., p. 20218.
138. Ibid., p. 20219.
139. Ibid., pp. 20230–41.

that developing nations were hurt more than they were helped by aid designed primarily to serve the domestic interests of the donors.[140] There was no doubt—despite the occasional disclaimers—that the food aid program was still very much a farm program.

SURPLUS DISPOSAL

In a sense, Food for Peace was regarded as one of two viable farm programs. In an era of increasing cash markets, it could be assumed that U.S. production could be reduced to market needs, through the payment of farmer subsidies. Or instead of idling land the federal government could at somewhat greater expenditure purchase the surplus from that "surplus" acreage for use as food aid. McGovern described the choice as follows: "The Government is now paying farmers $1.6 billion annually to idle 60 million acres of land. If this land were returned to production, the Government could buy the entire output at current market prices for $2.5 billion for use in the war on hunger."[141]

It was obvious which program would be most popular with farmers (who disliked acreage controls) or with agricultural service businesses and industries (whose profits increased with volume). While Food for Peace was a boon for all agriculture, it would be particularly beneficial to the wheat industry. Senator McGovern noted:

> . . . the heart of the Food for Peace program—the basic commodity—has been wheat. We have taken a good many million acres of wheatland, as well as some feed grains acreage, out of production. The total now idled is approximately 60 million acres. Now with our surpluses gone we have had two announcements of increases in wheat acreage that have met with general approval by producers all over the country.[142]

Thus wheat farmers had found a relationship with foreign aid perhaps more direct and more pleasing than in any previous foreign aid program. So long as U.S. production exceeded cash markets, wheat farmers could be expected to support food aid enthusiastically.

SUMMARY

For more than a century the U.S. government and various groups within the United States have frequently made gifts of food

140. Ibid.
141. Ibid., p. 20232.
142. Ibid., p. 20233.

in recognition of extraordinary needs abroad. In most cases this food aid consisted of grain shipments—token in terms of the need. An expression of humanitarian sentiments, they also served to exhibit U.S. generosity, to demonstrate superior U.S. production, and to censure the governments of recipient countries for their inability to insure local food supplies.

Substantial aid was given during and immediately following the two world wars. Humanitarian impulses were again evident on these occasions when the main purposes of the aid were to sustain allies during the conflict and to prevent radicalism, particularly to prevent the success of communism during the recovery period.

Substantial food aid otherwise has been a spillover during periods of overproduction of certain U.S. commodities. Wheat surpluses following World War II found outlets first in the European Recovery Program, then in the Korean War, then in aid during a drought in Pakistan, and since 1954 in a legislatively authorized surplus disposal program. This program was first called P.L. 480 and in 1959 was renamed Food for Peace.

Public Law 480, although passed in response to the pressure of surpluses, was originally supported by free-market advocates as a promotional device to develop adequate commercial markets. These groups regretfully concluded, after several years of experience, that the program did not expand foreign markets much but rather that it did perpetuate overproduction and as a result led to more rather than less governmental intervention.

Meanwhile coming to the fore were other purposes for food aid, which were adequate so long as surpluses existed. These purposes included maintenance of friendly governments (in India as earlier in Pakistan) and use of surpluses to obtain strategic materials or to meet government expenses abroad. Humanitarian and goodwill purposes were also served through very substantial emergency food relief, including donations which were made through private voluntary agencies. In addition the State Department under the Kennedy administration became less skeptical about the usefulness of U.S. surpluses as a tool of foreign policy. The Food for Peace program took cognizance of food deficits in developing areas that in the short run would require very large subsidized shipments from wheat-exporting countries, but the program emphasized the need for agricultural development in the deficit areas as the long-run solution to an overall world food deficit. Food relief shipments were to serve as an incentive for agricultural development.

Questions were continually raised, however, as to whether food

aid was as efficient as other forms of aid, whether it did in fact
promote long-run solutions, and whether the United States should
in any case assume a major responsibility for world food sufficiency.
Some conservatives on the congressional agriculture committees,
given the decision that surpluses were to be used as an instrument
of foreign policy, insisted that they be used as a Cold War tool. In
contrast some congressional liberals advocated creation of a bridge
of international cooperative endeavor to achieve a better food-
population ratio, using resources which were otherwise committed
to Cold War armaments. The Kennedy administration moved tentatively in the latter direction, and the Johnson administration's Food
for Freedom program increased the symbolic commitment to the
end of international cooperation for world sufficiency. However,
with U.S. surplus stocks at an end, the administration was reluctant
to encourage wheat production in excess of anticipated cash markets,
at least adequately enough to permit food aid at levels authorized
by the 1966 Food for Freedom program. Therefore it remained to
be seen whether food aid, which had come into being as a farm
policy measure, could remain a substantial program, let alone be
expanded to meet world needs, once it was no longer a necessary
part of domestic farm policy.

USDA Photo

14 / CONCLUSIONS

IN THIS FINAL CHAPTER, these questions are again addressed: What was the situation? What was intended to be done about it? What was the policy and its results? Significant findings are reiterated, and the policies of different periods are compared in order to notice differences and also to make statements which may be applied to more than one period.

The United States has regularly had more wheat than was needed for domestic food. What to do about the surplus has been the main concern of federal policy. Wheat prices, which in theory should have produced a balance between supply and demand, were, in practice, only one of several factors influencing production and consumption. Expansion of wheat acreage came with the release of the frontier onto the Great Plains. This semiarid region proved to be well suited to raise wheat, but production per acre was governed by the erratic weather rather than by prices. Subsequent technology further augmented wheat acreage, and yields per acre were dramatically boosted during the past twenty years by improved seeds.

On the demand side, domestic per capita demand for wheat as food was inelastic—and declining. Although additional wheat markets were available through exports or through sale of wheat for feed, producers felt that these secondary markets tended to establish the price of all wheat, and at low levels which did not adequately cover the costs of production.

For the world as well as for the United States, wheat production increased faster than world demand during the present century. Wheat exporters at first could muster little bargaining power against the principal importing countries, which erected tariff barriers in an effort to rely as nearly as possible on home production. With the passage of time, the world's surplus capacity grew; despite this, U.S. policies were finally successful in stabilizing world prices at fairly high levels.

Wheat has become a substantial political interest in the United States even while its economic significance has been declining. This happened because producers were able to find a basic harmony of political interest among producers of different wheats, among the different wheat-farming operations, and among the different wheat-growing regions. At the same time they were able to differentiate wheat from other grains and to establish wheat in a relationship of superiority to other grains. The expression "wheat is wheat" proved to be a sound rule on which to base policy as wheat farming became regionalized and specialized. Despite the general rule, however, some differences among wheats were recognized and could be catered to on a *quid pro quo* basis.

Wheat was not really significant in the total economy, and wheat growers constituted but a miniscule fraction of the total U.S. population. However wheat was important in the regions where it was produced, and political leaders there gave first priority to wheat commodity policy as the means to improve regional income. Through this strategy the regions achieved large per capita federal subsidies.

RELATIONSHIP OF POLICY TO THE SITUATION

Wheat policy was almost always designed to prevent surpluses, yet its timing and its substance were not always an accurate response to the surplus situation. Reasons for the deficiencies in planning include:

1. At times the situation was misperceived. Surpluses were viewed as temporary maladjustments during the 1920s and again during the 1950s. The resulting policies were inadequate when balanced against a basic trend toward overproduction, and this resulted in huge surpluses at the end of each decade. In the Korean War the Truman administration, on the other hand, was apparently worried about possible food shortages, although what developed was an avalanche of surpluses. Wartime governments more typically underestimated their food requirements or failed to take timely steps to meet them. The ensuing shortages caused much human suffering and unsettled the wheat economy thereafter.

Misperceptions of the situation were due to many things: to the reluctance especially on the part of Congress to admit a need for unpopular production control measures; to ideological biases, especially on the part of USDA administrations; and above all, to difficulties in predicting the upcoming supply and demand. Equally as surprising as the effects of erratic weather were changes due to size of acreage, technology, and trends in demand. Given so many variables, both the successful and the unsuccessful predictions owed much to accident. Supplies were generally underestimated, so the "successful" programs turned out to be those blessed with unanticipated outlets.

2. Policy was not always a timely response to the situation because of the inability of decision makers to resolve conflicts. Remedies for depressed prices during the 1920s and for the market collapse in 1929 were stalled by conflict between Congress and the Executive. This was true also in the 1950s when all parties saw a need for innovation but could not agree on a new program.

3. Vigorous, persistent, and ultimately conciliatory leadership was usually required in the enactment of major commodity legislation, and such leadership was lacking during some crisis situations. In the farm depression of 1923 the Secretary of Agriculture was unable to lead because he did not have the President's confidence. In the depression of 1929 the President could not command the confidence of Congress, nor could Secretary of Agriculture Benson command it during the 1950s. In 1949 Secretary of Agriculture Charles Bran-

nan was unable to secure support from farm legislators for his post-war farm program.

4. Viewed on the other side of the coin, the political system was not fully responsive to pressures from a depressed farm economy. Action was on occasion prevented or much delayed by a branch of government or by private groups.

5. Until recently government lacked comprehensive remedies for the more serious farm depressions. In 1923 a most responsive Congress was unable to suggest a comprehensive measure, and subsequently when Coolidge vetoed the McNary-Haugen plan he was aware that most economists did not think it workable. As for subsequent measures, the 1929 act was intended only as a catalyst; the 1933 act was a temporary relief measure whose sponsors seized the opportunity to experiment with various price and production measures; and the 1936 act was admittedly a stopgap measure even though it provided additional building blocks for a permanent program. In 1938 the USDA was still unready to stabilize the wheat economy, but Congress gave the department that responsibility; subsequently, until 1961, the USDA sought both to increase its resources and authority and to moderate stated legislative objectives in an effort to achieve a more realistic relationship between its responsibilities and its competence. It was not until the 1960s that the USDA seemed capable of doing what farm interests had asked for since the 1920s. Even then it successfully resisted efforts to set supports at the level of parity.

These reasons may help explain why policy was not, on balance, a response to the severity of the times. Farm recessions and surplus situations definitely spurred activity but did not guarantee policy, and the really comprehensive programs, as in 1938 and in 1965, were products of optimism and not of deep crisis.

OBJECTIVES OF WHEAT COMMODITY PROGRAMS

Viewing the whole history of wheat commodity programs, one program objective stands above all others: achieving higher returns or income for commercial farmers. Under every major program the income objective has invariably become preeminent even when not featured in the law. Around the income objective other goals have clustered, some emerging as approved by-products of income programs, some as instruments for the achievement of income objectives, some serving as justifications or "window dressing," some as reactions against the overachievement of income goals, and some with independent origins which were nevertheless found to be compatible with the income objective.

These various pursuits are discussed below, beginning with the income objective.

Income objectives have varied over time. Until the mid-thirties, for example, it was presumed that commodity policies could be a vehicle to raise the incomes of all farmers; since then it has become clear that the smallest farmers have received little or no help, while the large commercial farms have been the principal beneficiaries. Therefore efforts have been made to evolve other programs for small farmers.

There have been changes in the level of income specified as the objective, despite the continued use of a statistical parity standard. Programs shaped by Congress and by the farm organizations have tended to specify high income levels, while the influence of the executive branch has been in the direction of moderate or low price levels.

High-Income Programs. A high-income objective specifying full "equality" for the farmer was featured in the McNary-Haugen plan of the 1920s. In the 1938 act Congress and the Farm Bureau raised the possibility of achieving full "parity." In the early war years Congress succeeded in pushing up wheat price levels to near parity and then fought to hold them there during the Benson administration.

Moderate and Low-Income Programs. In contrast, moderate levels— or simply income stabilization—were sought under Hoover's Farm Marketing Act, and under relief measures passed by the Roosevelt administration in 1933 and 1936. Wallace favored seeking moderate levels under the 1938 act. During World War II, as during World War I, the administration's antiinflation policy worked actively to hold farm prices as low as possible, even below parity. Subsequently Secretary Benson also favored moderate price levels in his flexible price supports proposals beginning in 1954 and in his acreage reserve program of 1956. Moderate rather than high prices and income were the apparent goal of the Freeman wheat certificate programs of the 1960s.

There were at least two "low-price" proposals. Both would have made income goals secondary to other goals. Republican administrations during the 1920s appeared to believe that low prices must be tolerated as an occasional occurrence as a mechanism for discouraging overproduction. Secretary Benson's conservation reserve program of 1956 was expected to work well under the assumption of low prices. The program offered to rent marginal acreages, but at rental rates which farmers would find attractive only if they were no longer making a profit from production on the land.

AIDING THE FREE MARKET

Federal programs suggested during the 1920s were defended as efforts to make the marketplace work better rather than as efforts to replace it. At that period policies were justified as instruments of the free-market economy. Tariff protection and development of cooperative bargaining power would permit farmers to obtain higher income in the market.

The Benson administration also gave first emphasis to the free-market objective and called for eventual repeal of the price support and production control programs then in existence. Under Benson the free-market objective also had a political dimension. He advocated reversal of the trend toward "big government" in order to gain more individual freedom.

RELIEF

Whenever the farm economy happened to be depressed it became an objective of the existing program to serve as a vehicle for distributing relief money sufficient for farmers to meet current expenses. The precedent for using commodity programs in this way was set under the 1929 act, after the market collapse, when funds spent for price stabilization were expected to serve no real purpose except farmer relief. Payments under the 1933 and 1936 acts, and under the 1956 soil bank, also served primarily to relieve distress.

The relief objective, after becoming paramount in a program, tended to spoil the program for use in achieving other goals. Once farmers had received program benefits primarily as a gift to tide them over, these benefits were no longer very usable for other intended objectives, such as production control.

PRODUCTION CONTROL

Program proposals up to 1933 usually did not include production controls, which were regarded as improper, unpopular, and unnecessary. But the announced lesson to be learned from the failure of the 1929 program was that an income program must incorporate production controls.

Controls were experimented with in the 1933 and 1936 acts. In 1938 firm controls were implanted at Farm Bureau's urging, designed to reduce market supplies and in turn to raise wheat prices. In contrast to Farm Bureau's view of controls as income measures, subsequent administrations viewed controls primarily as a device to reduce government burdens. Thus controls were proposed by Benson as a means of clearing away surpluses in preparation for a return to a free market. The Freeman administration sought mandatory controls as the least expensive remedy for surpluses, and when farmers rejected these controls the congressional and farm organization coalition adopted a more expensive "voluntary" controls program.

AGRICULTURAL DEVELOPMENT

Farming as a vocation and the family farm as a production unit have been considered to be vital in the firmament of U.S. society and important as a branch of the U.S. economy. Commodity programs gained status from the fact that one of their objectives was to aid the family farm.

Program results, however, led to redefining this objective. It turned out that commodity programs did not preserve the rural community or guarantee a satisfactory income for the mass of family farmers. However they did assure that the large commercial units which developed were for the most part family enterprises. Hence the recent program objective has been to provide a satisfactory income for the relatively few "adequate-sized" family farms.

CONSERVATION

The wheat dust bowl of the 1930s spurred attention more than anything else to the problem of soil erosion. Soil conservation, following its inclusion in the 1933 act, became an objective of all wheat commodity programs. In the 1936 law conservation was listed in first place in order to impress the Supreme Court which had just invalidated the income-oriented 1933 law. Since that time, however, conservation has been achievable within the commodity programs only as a by-product in the achievement of income objectives. The one recent effort to reverse these priorities—the conservation reserve program of 1956—was terminated in 1960 due to lack of congressional

support. Several conservation programs have been authorized in-
dependently of commodity programs but with relatively small budgets.

Any benefits seeming to accrue to the whole nation or to groups
other than commercial farmers were added to the list of objectives
of the commodity programs. The following such goals have been
associated with commodity programs.

Serving the Consumer. A program which assured a fair return on
production was assumed to serve the interests of consumers as well
as producers. Although consumer interests were not uppermost in
mind, reinvestment of high farm income did create a more efficient
industry, one result of which was relatively lower consumer prices.
In addition the programs were adapted to antiinflation objectives
when the economy required these. In 1967 many farmers became
suspicious that the wheat commodity program passed in 1965 was
being used by the administration in pursuit of a "low-price policy."

Adequate Supplies. Farm policies reflected some concern, however
realistic, that planning was needed in order to assure adequate food
for the future. For example soil conservation initiatives of the 1930s
reflected the fear that continued abuse of land could result in food
shortages.

Farm interests—often suspicious that policy makers wanted adequate food at low prices—accused industrialists supporting the Republican administration of the 1920s of wanting plentiful and "cheap"
food as a means of reducing labor costs and thus improving the competitive position of U.S. industrial exports. More recently Cold War
comparisons between U.S. and Russian food production have produced statements that the United States was "lucky" to possess abundant food. Food aid to other nations has become an important
commodity program objective and a major justification for the large
federal budget for commercial agriculture.

Export Earnings. Foreign sales of wheat and other agricultural products have earned the exchange currencies needed to purchase the
goods and services desired by the U.S. government and society.

CHARACTER OF LEADERSHIP

Not the needs of the situation so much as the existence of well-positioned and determined leadership was the prerequisite for passage of general commodity policy. On occasion this leadership arose from Congress or from farm organizations; some private individuals—including some economists—also have been important in generating new policy. Most policy in recent years has developed in the executive branch, as a negotiated product which could receive support during the legislative process from farm organization leaders and senior members of the agriculture committees. Vigorous leadership by the Secretary of Agriculture was needed in order to mold a welter of demands into a workable program; administration opposition, on the other hand, ordinarily doomed a proposal. The administration found it difficult to terminate existing programs which had gained strong support among Congress, the bureaucracy, and commercial farm interests.

Leadership in various periods is characterized below.

1. Farm policy leadership during the 1920s was exercised by bipartisan coalitions of rural legislators in the houses of Congress receiving outside help from farm groups and individuals. The original Senate farm bloc was brought together with the help of American Farm Bureau officials, and the farm bloc's income proposals were developed and refined by sympathetic USDA employees and by private individuals.

This leadership complex presumed to speak for all farmers and positioned itself against the business-industrial America which controlled the executive branch during this decade. This group articulated a desire to preserve and enrich rural life, but the test that it applied to all proposals was whether they would increase returns in the marketplace for specific cash crops, particularly wheat. Thus these were spokesmen not for a way of life but for the economic interests of commercial agriculture, and these spokesmen were served by economists who lacked a comprehensive view of the internal structure of American agriculture. Farm economists, accepting the credentials of commercial farm interests as political spokesmen for rural America, helped them carry over to the New Deal the concept that the federal government's proper role was to strengthen agriculture's position in the marketplace.

2. Business groups, business interests, and an ideology favoring business guided Republican administrations during the 1920s. These administrations were intent on delaying or minimizing government's response to farmer pressures favoring market intervention. This strategy culminated in the enactment of the Farm Marketing Act of 1929, passed by President Herbert Hoover after his 1928 election victory. The act seemed to stop short of the market intervention which wheat spokesmen were demanding.

3. The Wallace administration of the 1930s—by enacting temporary and then permanent programs and by instituting large bureaucracies to administer these programs—gave the USDA its enduring character. Wallace's initial associates were a mixed group, including a left wing of urban intellectuals whose attention was fixed on social remedies for a deprived rural America, and a right wing held over from the McNary-Haugen era which looked askance at any governmental activities not directed at providing high domestic farm prices. Wallace was one of a middle group of progressives drawn from commercial farm backgrounds. These progressives had social concerns, including an abiding interest in conserving and developing the soil, but they were aware that social reform measures were not supported by farmer electorates, and they knew that organized commercial farm interests strongly preferred that benefits be distributed through the marketplace. The organized groups included farm organizations, congressional agriculture committees, and public bureaucracies, all of which were allowed to gain a dominant position under the New Deal administration.

4. Interests in Congress representing wheat and several other commercial crops were mobilized by the Farm Bureau, and these passed the 1938 permanent program with income goals higher than the administration recommended. In World War II this group again raised price supports despite objections from the administration.

Following the war this coalition lost its Farm Bureau leadership. Farm Bureau abandoned the price-maximization objective partly out of concern that the price program agency was becoming a competitor for Farm Bureau's political role. Yet this commodity coalition continued to have adequate leadership, provided in the last analysis by the Department of Agriculture under Secretaries Brannan and Freeman. Leadership was also forthcoming from senior figures on the congressional agriculture committees and from officials in other farm organizations. These interests managed a successful holding action against the unfriendly Benson administration.

5. Secretary Benson's personal beliefs and style set the tone of the

Benson administration. Religion and economics were the most important dimensions for Secretary Benson, and in both areas he found fundamental principles which were actionable and not subject to being compromised. Most significant were his belief that humans should trust in God rather than in government and his belief that the law of supply and demand operating in the marketplace was more likely to be beneficial and just than were any public policies which contravened these laws. Even though these beliefs were in harmony with one side of rural America, Secretary Benson was not able to identify closely with his rural constituency. He was cast as an outsider by farmers and also by the political establishment of commercial agriculture. Benson in turn lacked respect for the motives and methods of leading farm politicians whose cooperation he needed.

Secretary Benson was a practitioner of the politics of commodity logrolling. For himself, however, he set a strict rule that every policy to which he was a party should represent at least a small step toward his objectives. He preferred to be stymied or defeated rather than to accept tactical retreats, and his rigidity was exploited effectively by his opposition.

6. In contrast, leadership in the Freeman administration was in some measure an earlier product of the commodity programs that it administered. Freeman and his immediate staff had emerged through the Minnesota Democratic-Farmer-Labor Party, which had used the commodity programs both for garnering farmer votes and as a means of recruiting cadre. Other Freeman leaders, whether from universities, farm organizations, or up through the ranks of the ASCS farmer committees, tended to have had careers associated with the program as a whole or its application to a specific commodity such as wheat. Thus Freeman's vigorous and successful leadership was directed toward making the existing commodity program politically and economically viable. Moralistic and humane aspirations within the "liberal" Freeman administration were manifested mainly in the expansion and development of food aid for foreign countries. Freeman was taken to task late in his administration because he had allowed commodity interests to take precedence over humane goals in the administration of domestic food distribution and food stamp programs.

STRATEGIES OF LEADERSHIP

Leadership strategies (defined as planned sequences for achieving objectives) have been differentiated in three ways. Some strategies were characterized by their intent to exploit a situation that was presumably

receptive to innovation, such as economic depression. To secure passage of policy, another category embraced lobbying strategies, which
were complemented by program or legislative strategies in which
policy itself was a tactic to attain group objectives. Strategies could
also be differentiated on the basis of which agent employed them and
against whom they were employed.

These sets of categories tend to overlap: some strategies are simultaneously administration, lobbying, and situational strategies. In this
summary, therefore, it seems practical to discuss major clusters rather
than exclusive categories of strategies. Two clusters will be discussed:
(1) lobbying strategies used by the administration, along with strategies countering these, and (2) legislative strategies generally.

ADMINISTRATION LOBBYING STRATEGIES

The USDA had the burden of achieving passage of its programs
in Congress, and it had the lesser burden of defeating programs it
opposed. One question which it had to answer in deciding on the
proper lobbying strategy was how many participants—and which ones—
were to have influence in the decision process. This was a matter over
which the USDA could exercise some control, although some groups
with developed means of access were virtually certain to become influential participants. Still the influence and even the identity of these
"certain" participants varied over time.

The certain participants included the official decision makers in
Congress: the chairmen and members of the congressional committees
dealing with agriculture. Also certain to play a role in the decision
were the commodity interests mainly represented by farm organizations, and also the affected bureaucracies. These groups expected the
administration to acknowledge them as the legitimate farm policy
decision makers, even while also expecting that the administration
would secure support from outside groups.

The USDA could and did bring in other interests. To the extent
that the USDA was able to decide upon the number of effective participants and the scope of the conflict, it could weight the influence
of both the certain and the "outside" participants.

The administration had several options in dealing with certain
participants. It could unify them around a program of their own
choice, and then depend heavily upon this core of support in passing
the program through Congress. Permitting the farm coalition to write
its own ticket sometimes seemed the easiest as well as the wisest course,

as in 1933 when the Roosevelt administration adopted the domestic allotment scheme that most farm spokesmen had earlier considered and approved. Under the Roosevelt administration, farm interests were permitted to develop procedures as well as policies which would assure their control so long as they maintained unity. Major participants institutionalized their power and also enacted "permanent" legislative provisions which bolstered their peculiar interests. By 1949 the failure of the Brannan Plan revealed that these participants would likely veto any programs which were not regarded as a product of the farm coalition. Also subsequently rejected were procedural changes which would reduce congressional power, as in the Freeman administration's 1961 farm bill.

Yet it was by no means easy to unify farm interests. Typically each commodity interest negotiated its own program, and then measures satisfactory to the affected groups were put together in a bill. However some commodity programs elicited interest and support from groups other than the producers. Several wheat measures, including the McNary-Haugen scheme, the domestic allotment scheme, and the two-price scheme, were supported by nonwheat interests because these wheat measures were regarded as experimental prototypes which might subsequently be applied to other commodities.

This commodity-by-commodity approach was complicated by the existence of interrelationships among commodities, as for example the interchangeability of wheat with other grains. Increasingly wheat and feed grain programs have merged. The 1965 act, in which measures for wheat and feed grains were highly interrelated, was an achievement in effective programming and was the successful result of years of negotiation with corn and wheat representatives.

The USDA administration has never exercised simply a broker's role in developing coalition unity. Instead it has usually preserved the initiative, granting concessions to commodity interests, but getting in return some concessions from them. As minimum terms, the USDA has insisted on workable programs—that is, programs with mechanisms sufficient to fulfill both income and production objectives. The USDA has also wanted to limit program costs, to make programs serve general economic goals, and to make them politically attractive to persons other than farmers.

Thus the USDA has actively bargained with the farm bloc. Compromise on both sides and then cooperation by all parties usually has been a necessary condition for passage of legislation. Unfortunately both sides have not always felt an equal sense of urgency. The admin-

istration has usually felt pressure for action during situations of surplus, since large government stocks and large budgets were regarded
as a responsibility of the executive branch. In contrast, temporary reductions in farm income due to low prices or drought were likely to
be first reflected in the results of biennial congressional elections. For
example, the Roosevelt administration, clearly out of concern over
approaching surpluses, was keen to enact production controls for
wheat and other commodities during 1937. At the time Congress was
relatively unworried by the threat of surpluses. Not until after the
cotton price had fallen late in that session did members of the congressional agriculture committees begin to plead for relief measures.
President Roosevelt granted relief, in the form of higher price supports, after exacting a promise from committee leaders that they would
enact effective production controls during the next session. In retrospect, exchanging relief in one year for permanent legislation in the
next year proved to be good timing in comparison with agreements in
which both needs were to be satisfied in the same year, as in 1933 and
again in 1956. These efforts to remedy both low income and surpluses
in the same enactment were not equally successful on both counts.

Efforts often misfired also when urgent pressures were felt by only
one side. During the 1920s farm legislators clamoring for relief were
ignored by an administration which as yet had felt no burden of production control. In contrast, during most of the 1950s farm legislators
were able to enjoy the income benefits of existing programs without
having to remedy the production imbalance, and the Benson administration mistakenly assumed it also could ignore demands for surplus
reduction. Thus it remained for the Freeman administration to make
the necessary concessions to congressional commodity interests in order
to obtain a workable program.

Wartime has been another situation in which the administration
has had to make concessions to the regular or certain participants.
Farm groups were able to achieve important price concessions from
the administration during the crisis of World War II.

Thus the main elements in the bargaining equation have been
the desire by commodity interests for near-term or short-range income
benefits, versus the administration's desire for longer-term stability.
The bargain had to be struck in such a way as to contribute to satisfaction of both desires, sometimes to the neglect of other considerations.

Equity considerations were one instance of neglect. Concern was
continually expressed that the basic commodities should receive equal
treatment, but the administration did not employ an across-the-board

measurement of equity among all commodities. Instead the basis for distribution among commodities was usually relative strength within the coalition of participants. Meanwhile the distribution of benefits among producers of the same commodity was worked out by the producers themselves, again based on political strength. Among wheat grower leadership, large growers in marginal areas were apparently overrepresented, so that smaller growers as well as growers located in the wheat heartlands received fewer benefits. Inequities in the wheat program were not expected to be noticed by producers of other commodities, and wheat growers were not expected to be concerned about inequities in the cotton program and in the other programs they helped to pass.

Their exclusive interest in one commodity made the inside participants dependent upon those who could conciliate their interests and form the participants into a working coalition. Individuals and leadership groups on the congressional agriculture committees and within the general farm organizations have played this conciliatory role at times, as have congressional party leaders. However commodity interests depended mainly on the USDA administration to lead and unite them.

Indeed they were at pains to establish and maintain the norm that Secretaries of Agriculture must play a unifying rather than a divisive role with respect to commodity interests. Secretary Benson, by choosing to play a divisive role, demonstrated that commodity interests could not easily coalesce without leadership from the secretary. It is therefore understandable that his violation of the unity norm earned him the hostility of principal participants within the congressional committees and within the USDA bureaucracy.

Logically complementing the norm that the secretary should unify the inside participants was the norm that a Secretary of Agriculture should secure for these commodity coalitions the necessary support from the executive branch and from nonfarm groups. Thus Secretary Freeman fought within the executive branch to maintain agriculture's fair share of the federal budget; he embellished programs so as to make them attractive to urban legislators. He stressed to nonfarm audiences that farm programs were equitable and that they provided good and inexpensive food for consumers. Secretary Benson, using the divisive strategy, mustered outside support with the argument that farm programs were costly and inequitable.

Thus the bidding in of outside participants can be viewed as an administration strategy for achieving a relationship with the certain participants whether as a supporter or opponent of existing commodity programs. But it is also useful to emphasize that this is basically a strategy for increasing the leverage or influence of the Secretary of Agriculture. Secretary Freeman chose to bid in outside support for commodity programs, but conditional on acceptance of workable controls by commodity interests.

LEGISLATIVE STRATEGIES

A number of strategies relied upon substantive policies for achievement of their objectives. A tactic to reduce government involvement, used by Secretary Benson, emphasized reductions in federal income guarantees, price support levels, and a relaxation of acreage controls. Administratively Benson's policy strategy encouraged casual and even careless administration of controls and subsidy programs, while tightening up and improving administration of marketing programs and grain storage programs.

Policy changes could also be aimed at the development of friendly bureaucracies. On occasion various groups felt threatened by existing or potential bureaucratic power; these groups included business interests in the 1920s, Farmers Union in the early 1930s, and Farm Bureau after 1940. The Benson administration feared bureaucratic power in general, and the rejection of the program in the wheat referendum in 1963 was due in part to farmers' resentment against the local and national bureaucracy. Policy strategies to reduce bureaucracy included governmental reorganization, reductions in appropriations, and changes in authorized functions.

Usually the policy strategy of the USDA administration was the enactment of workable commodity programs. Practicable programs would maximize prices or commercial farm income and yet not stimulate production of surpluses. The word "adjustment" was frequently used by USDA administrations to suggest that policies should help farmers make the most of their markets but should not seek to attain impractical goals. Generally the USDA resisted efforts by Congress to specify income goals, seeking instead discretion to keep the goals in line with available opportunities. However administrative discretion, as a strategy, often did not have the expected success. Congressional counterpressure could be applied in ways other than through the provisions of law, and constituency counterpressures felt in national elections were in response to existing price and income levels without any reference to specific program performance.

WHEAT POLICY HISTORY

Quite clearly there have been evolutionary trends in the political support for wheat commodity policy; the effort is made here to conceptualize them. Then the policy itself will be discussed, also as a product of an evolutionary process.

TRENDS IN THE POLITICAL BASES OF COMMODITY POLICY

Specification of Benefits. The relatively uncomplicated program proposals advocated in the 1920s were usually presumed to be for the benefit of all farmers. Even the two-price measures were expected to provide "equality for agriculture," though they were to be applied only to wheat and to a few other commodities. With experience, it became well understood that a given measure could benefit some producers more than others, and farm decision makers became competent in assessing the distribution of benefits from a given mix of income provisions.

Subsequent farm programs contained varied measures, each tailored for a particular group, a complex mosaic of benefits reflecting superimposed interests formed by region, by commodity, by variations in the production and use of a given commodity, by size of farm, by amount of landownership, by rainfall, soil, atmosphere, marginality of production, and many other factors.

Farm decision makers became particularly good at calculating the immediate income benefits from program provisions, and this became their basis for evaluating programs. Yet other program results often proved more significant over the long run, as for example the contribution of commodity programs to the revolution in productive capacity and to the demise of the rural community. These longer-range effects were not so easy to anticipate and were in any case usually of low political relevance. An exception was the negative response to Secretary Benson's conservation reserve program of 1956, after it had become clear to representatives from some marginal farming areas that this program enabled a virtual majority of their constituents to migrate elsewhere. More often, however, longer-range projections were used simply to justify measures which produced immediate income improvement. Examples of such rationalizations of commodity programs were presumptions about the contribution of price supports to preservation of the "family farm" system of agriculture, and the use made of projections by economists that farm income would enter a period of consistent decline under a policy of reducing price supports.

As it became the pattern for each influential group to specify measures beneficial to itself, the next step required the USDA to assert the need for harmony among these varied measures. The Secretary of Agriculture made a virtue out of necessity in acceding to a variety of special measures, on the condition that these should not be counterproductive. It became the secretary's role to create unity among diversity, harmony, and efficiency among the different programs. This role was best exemplified by Secretary Freeman's success in establishing a certificate program for wheat only, while at the same time permitting an interchange of wheat and feed grains acreage allotment.

Over time a measure of harmony was achieved within both the economic and the political spheres. Political harmony, however, consisted of forming supportive majorities in the congressional committees and in the two houses of Congress. A further difficult step of securing approval by producers was abandoned on a formal basis after defeat of the Freeman program in the wheat referendum of 1963.

Institutionalization of Inside Participants. Decision making on farm policy came to be institutionalized in the hands of the inside or certain participants. Large bureaucracies grew up, taking pains to build support for farm programs in Congress and in the constituencies. Ever larger expenditures for agriculture, even though due mainly to farm program inadequacies and administrative mistakes, tended to set budget precedents favoring future large expenditures. Laws once on the books were continually amended to suit the interests of the regular supplicants, and care was taken to fortify them against repeal. The congressional agriculture committees came to be dominated by representatives from commercial areas (such as the arid Wheat Belt), which were most dependent upon federal relief, federal production research and development, and federal price-supporting operations.

The success in institutionalizing policy making was proven when Secretary Benson, violating institutional norms himself, found it impossible to achieve substantial policy change over the opposition of the congressional committees and of the program agencies of the USDA.

Additional access to decisions was provided through recognition of commodity programs in the major party platforms and through campaign promises of support for farm programs by candidates for national office.

Experience in Administration of Programs. Many problems were solved to permit the evolution of workable programs. Ways had to be found to raise market prices, to reduce actual production, to store surpluses, and to secure producer participation. Finally, world wheat markets had to be stabilized, a task largely performed by the U.S. government.

Policies based on successful experience had to be modified as times changed. Unfortunately policy did not always keep pace with change, partly because future projections based upon past trends usually underestimated current trends, but mainly because the policy process was often quite unresponsive to new information.

EVOLUTION OF POLICY

During a period of scarcity in World War I, wheat prices were effectively pegged by government. Following the war, during a peacetime decade of abundance, representatives of commercial farmers wanted government to place a floor under domestic prices. However some assumptions underlying this particular proposal proved to be dubious or false: It was not true that wheat could be dumped abroad, that domestic consumption of wheat for food was increasing, or that the suggested administrative mechanisms were workable. These schemes for price improvement were beaten or vetoed by the Republican administrations in the 1920s, so that the policy process during this decade served chiefly as a steam vent for rural discontent.

In 1929 an ill-fated measure was passed which was not intended as very serious legislation either by Congress or by the Hoover administration. Its ambiguous wording, however, permitted considerable policy experimentation during the economic depression that befell the nation. This experience revealed mainly that production controls should accompany income measures.

During the Wallace administrations, a number of other farm program characteristics took shape either in practice or as stated goals. The first Wallace administration introduced measures which avoided government storage and government price fixing; instead it stressed income insurance, noninterference with existing marketing systems, and self-financing of programs. Unrealized at that time was the intent to assure that domestic price programs contributed to the stability of the world wheat market.

The second Wallace administration was marked by a spirit of moderation in price and production objectives—and marked by indecision as to how to achieve stability in the wheat economy. This posture was changed by passage of the Agricultural Adjustment Act of 1938, urged by commodity interests. This act reached for the goal of parity prices, and it included compulsory controls. Nevertheless surpluses accumulated even before World War II; so the decade of the 1940s, experiencing high prices, was dominated by the fear of postwar surpluses. The Brannan administration briefly exuded confidence that the farm economy would not suffer from abundance, but Brannan left his successors a burden of rising wheat stocks.

Benson reintroduced the Wallace theme of moderation in both supports and controls, and adjustment to market supply and demand. In conflict with him were commodity interests who preferred continued high prices with more effective production controls. Benson's moderation policy, like Wallace's, failed the tests of both politics and economics. However his soil bank program introduced in 1956 was an economically viable alternative, which proved to be politically unviable. Its acreage reserve measure was sacrificed for use as drought relief, and the conservation reserve feature proved unpalatable.

Much experimentation occurred during the Benson administration. In addition to the use of the soil bank programs, huge storage facilities were erected, surplus food disposal programs were put in effect at home and abroad, and great efforts were made to increase foreign markets for wheat and other products. Benson enhanced the bureaucratic strength of marketing agencies, while dealing blows to the price-production control agency. He also sought unsuccessfully to bring other groups, particularly business and consumer interests, back into the policy process.

The Freeman administration proved to be a vehicle for reconciling the branches of government and for re-forming a majority coalition of commodity interests behind a workable program. Farm policy had become intensely partisan under Benson, with the Democratic Party being the main beneficiary of the farm policy election issues. The Freeman reconciliation of commodity interests was accomplished within the framework of the Democratic Party.

Freeman initially suffered two major political failures, and the successful program finally passed under his administration in 1964 was to a considerable degree the product of initiatives from Congress. Freeman had first tried to achieve change in the procedure for passage of farm policy, and then his administration had achieved passage of a program which strengthened the compulsory controls system for wheat. These controls were vetoed in a producer referendum, causing Freeman to reexamine the workability of voluntary incentives for reducing surpluses.

The new voluntary program of 1964 was a product of the surpluses of the 1950s and of the surplus productive capacity of the 1960s.

Budget outlays for the voluntary program were obtained in part from the sell-off of surplus stocks. High current-program costs could be justified only by comparing them with the costs of carrying large government stocks. Yet there were good reasons for continuing to carry large stocks, in which case the program budget was still not large enough to finance a workable program.

COMMODITY PROGRAM RESULTS

Results, as earlier discussed, have referred mainly to the degree of immediate success in raising wheat prices and in reducing or controlling wheat production. Certainly prices and production were the chief concerns of those who framed the programs, but obviously there were longer-run results, many of them not economic and not easily measurable, but these can at least be referred to here.

Indeed the early programs failed entirely to achieve the economic goals. The 1929 Farm Board made a brave, brief struggle to hold up the price, before succumbing to surpluses. Production controls under the 1933 act became an exercise rather than a policy when prolonged drought served as a more effective balancer of supplies. Rather than impacting on the wheat economy, the 1933 act served as a social vehicle for channeling federal subsidies to destitute farmers. It did spur development of grass roots political strength in the form of the county and township farmer committees. Furthermore the first New Deal also delivered the Department of Agriculture into the hands of the commercial farm interests which had already gained control of Congress and the general farm organizations, thereafter assuring the dominance of major commodity interests in all future commodity legislation.

The political strength of wheat and certain other commodities was well revealed by passage of the 1938 act, with its mandatory controls and ambitious income goals. This program substantially increased income from wheat and also increased food supplies in a time of great postwar food need by accumulating large federal stocks and improving fertility of wheat cropland.

Wheat price-production programs which encouraged greater investments in capital and in land must, in some degree, have been a spur to the technological revolution which increased the efficiency of wheat production—and which drastically reduced manpower requirements. After World War II productive capacity increased well beyond the control of existing programs, to an extent not evident to most farm policy makers. This tended to frustrate policy efforts. Secretary Benson's attempt to reduce production by reducing prices would have been inadequate on economic grounds, even if it had found full political acceptance. His conservation reserve program was too small, and his soil bank measure was made a vehicle for relief rather than for control, so that the Benson programs were ineffective in controlling production.

However the resulting surpluses proved useful, as they had in the 1940s. Benson first sought to use them as a lever for increasing cash exports, but they came instead to be used as an instrument of U.S. policy—partly in exchange for political concessions, but mainly to prevent the occurrence of famine in a number of developing countries. Food aid became a most significant outlet for domestic wheat production.

Under Freeman the place of food aid became the key question. On the one hand, food aid had become the great national product of the commodity programs. On the other hand, as Freeman apparently mastered production control, food aid was no longer needed for the success of commodity programs. Henceforth food aid would have to stand on its own merits, as a foreign policy tool. On that ground, was it a good product or a bad one? Obviously it is in the light of this judgment as to the value of food aid, and the value of commodity programs in assuring adequate domestic supplies, that most Americans would reach a judgment on the wheat commodity programs.

INDEX

Abernethy, Rep. Thomas (D., Miss.), 358
Acreage allotments. *See* Production controls
Acreage controls. *See* Production controls
Advisory Committee on Foreign Aid, 354, 356
Agency for International Development, 369, 372
Agribusiness groups, 263, 374, 394
Agricultural Act of 1949, 352, 354
Agricultural Act of 1954, 188
Agricultural Adjustment Act of 1933, 27, 383–85, 392, 397, 399: implementation, 120–31; objectives, 116–17; passage, 113–20; provisions, 124–26, 391
Agricultural Adjustment Act of 1938, 31, 138, 383, 397, 399: costs, 161–63; implementation, 152–61; objectives, 140–41, 144–46; passage, 141–52
Agricultural Adjustment Administration, 361. *See also* Farmer committees
Agricultural Marketing Act of 1929, 25–26, 109–12, 383–84, 388, 397
Agricultural Stabilization and Conservation Service, 269–70
Agricultural Trade Development and Assistance Act of 1954. *See* Food aid
Aiken, Sen. George D. (R., Vt.), 341
American Council of Voluntary Agencies for Foreign Service, 351, 356
American Farm Bureau Federation, 105, 121–22, 124, 146, 383, 394: AAA of 1933, 133–34; AAA of 1938, 31, 38–143, 149–52, 164–66; Benson administration, 199–200; CCC resell, 288; Food and Agriculture Act of 1962, 250; food aid, 344–47, 364; Freeman administration, 262; geographical strength, 298; leadership roles, 387–89; 1920s, 89–90, 99; price supports, 286; P.L. 480, 348–51, 480–82; Soil Bank Act, 189, 210–12, 218;

trade expansion, 347; wheat certificates, 248
American Red Cross, 353, 361
Anderson, Sec. Clinton P., 35, 38, 39: flexible price supports, 183–84; food aid, 338–39
Andresen, Rep. H. Carl (R., Minn.), 210
Anfuso amendment, 252–53
Argentina, 22, 52, 60, 64, 71
Armenia, 330
Australia, 22, 42, 71, 64

Bailey, Warren R., 15 n, 16, 296 n
Baking industry, 132, 263
Balassa, Bela, 52 n
Baldwin, Sidney, 115 n
Barnhill, Harold E., 318 n, 322 n
Beals, Gordon P., 72 n
Bean, Louis H., 120 n
Behre, C. Edward, 359
Belgium, 331
Bell, David F., 369 n
Bennett, Merrill K., 60 n, 71 n
Benson administration, 270, 384: character, 169–72; effects, 192–98; flexible price supports, 187; grain storage policies, 273, 275–81, 283; objectives, 172–74; policy leadership, 393, 394; programs, 186–92; results, 201–3; Soil Bank Act, 210–12; strategies, 174–82; surpluses, 341; Wheat Industry Conference, 247
Benson, Sec. Ezra Taft: acreage reserves, 212, 216; beliefs, 169–72; conservation reserves, 224, 229 n, 395, 400; food aid, 42, 364; geographic support, 298; market development, 75; 1954 farm program, 175 n, 187; price supports, 168, 169, 173 n, 175 n, 286; production controls, 299; role of executive, 180–81; wheat certificates, 248

401